Jus Internationale et Europaeum

herausgegeben von

Thilo Marauhn und Christian Walter

206

Sustainable Finance in the EU

Edited by

Jens Ekkenga and Martin Winner

Mohr Siebeck

Jens Ekkenga holds the Chair of Civil Law, Commercial and Business Law, Comparative Law at the University of Giessen.
orcid.org/0000-0001-8485-6217

Martin Winner holds the Chair of Commercial Law at Vienna University of Economics and Business Administration.

ISBN 978-3-16-163722-3 / eISBN 978-3-16-163723-0
DOI 10.1628/978-3-16-163723-0

ISSN 1861-1893 / eISSN 2568-8464 (Jus Internationale et Europaeum)

The Deutsche Nationalbibliothek lists this publication in the Deutsche Nationalbibliographie; detailed bibliographic data are available at *https://dnb.dnb.de.*

The book was typeset by Martin Fischer in Tübingen using Minion typeface, printed on non-aging paper by Laupp & Göbel in Gomaringen, and bound by Nädele in Nehren.

Printed in Germany.

Preface

It is with great pleasure and enthusiasm that we present this conference volume, the culmination of an ambitious and collaborative endeavor about the regulation of sustainable finance in the EU. Bringing together academic expertise from universities across 14 different European Union countries, this project sought to explore the multifaceted dimensions of sustainable finance within the regulatory framework of the European Union.

The motivation behind this project was to delve into critical aspects of sustainable finance that are reshaping the financial landscape in the EU. Our focus extended across diverse domains, encompassing the integration of sustainability into corporate governance structures (Sustainable Corporate Governance), the role of shareholders in promoting sustainability (Sustainable Shareholder Governance), and the incorporation of sustainability considerations into the decision-making processes of investment funds (Sustainable Fund Governance). Furthermore, the project delved into the development, marketing, and management of financial products with sustainability at their core (Sustainable Product Governance), as well as the interface between financial institutions and their customers in delivering sustainable financial services (Sustainable Financial Services in Customer Business).

Each participating university contributed a comprehensive country report, offering unique insights into the distinct challenges and opportunities faced in their respective regions. A key aspect of our exploration involved a thorough legal comparison, shedding light on the intricacies and implications of relevant EU legislation. Specifically, we delved into the Sustainable Finance Disclosure Regulation (SFDR), the Markets in Financial Instruments Directive II (MiFID II), and the Shareholder Rights Directive II (SRD II). Through this legal lens, we aimed to unravel the complexities and highlight the evolving landscape of sustainable finance within the member states of the EU. As the global community grapples with the imperative of addressing environmental, social, and governance (ESG) considerations in financial decision-making, the insights generated by this project hold significant relevance. Sustainable finance is not merely a trend but a paradigm shift, and understanding its nuances is crucial for academics, practitioners, policymakers, and stakeholders alike.

We express our deepest gratitude to all the participating universities, researchers, and contributors who dedicated their time and expertise to this collaborative effort. The diversity of perspectives and experiences reflected in the country reports enriches the discourse on sustainable finance and provides a comprehensive panorama of its implementation across the EU. May this conference volume serve as a valuable resource, fostering ongoing dialogue, research, and action towards a more sustainable and resilient financial future in the European Union.

Inhaltsverzeichnis

Sustainable Finance in the EU – An Introduction

Jens Ekkenga

A. Sustainable Finance According to the Action Plan of the EU Commission from 8/3/2018

The acronym "ESG" (Environment, Social, Governance) is associated with current legal policy objectives which the EU Commission formulated in its "*Action Plan: Financing Sustainable Growth*" of 8/3/2018.[1] The plan is divided into 10 sections including announcements of measures, some of which have already been implemented.[2] Among the key regulations is Taxonomy Regulation (EU) 2020/852, which establishes criteria for qualifying an economic activity as environmentally sustainable "to which an investment is environmentally sustainable" (Art. 1 para. 1). As of November 2019, corporate finance issues have been regulated by the Sustainable Finance Disclosure Regulation (SFDR) 2019/2088. It refers to Measure 10 of the Action Plan, which is entitled "Fostering sustainable corporate governance and attenuating short-termism in capital markets".

B. The Optimization Target: ESG

The sustainability postulate goes back to a report by the UN World Commission on Environment and Development in 1987 (the so-called Brundtland Report). It was originally based on the idea of *intergenerational justice*, thus aiming to create, develop and secure the legal framework for ecologically, socially and economically stable conditions.[3] The ESG acronym reflects these three elements. Clear ideas about mutual functionalities within this "triple bottom line" do not yet exist. The legal idea as such is apparently supported by the basic conviction that the optimization of one sub-goal simultaneously increases the degree of goal achievement of another sub-goal. In other words, what serves to improve environmental sustainability is at the same time social progress, and whatconstitutes social progress serves at the same time to promote economic consolidation.[4] Less

[1] COM(2018)97 final.
[2] Good overview at *Glander/Lühmann* RdF 2020, 12, 13 f.
[3] *Bruns/Meyer-Bullerdiek,* Professionelles Portfoliomanagement, 6th edition 2020, p. 320 f.
[4] *Bruns/Meyer-Bullerdiek,* Professionelles Portfoliomanagement, 6th edition 2020, p. 321.

emphasis is placed on the fact that, conversely, the creation and preservation of ecologically and socially sustainable framework conditions of an economic community are inconceivable without micro and macroeconomic stability. A certain asymmetry of values becomes visible here, which is also indicated by the order of enumeration – the economic element of corporate governance is only mentioned in the third place.[5]

The existence of ESG-immanent *conflicting goals*, moreover, is not denied from the outset, but is largely ignored in terms of legal policy. In the field of fund management, this is achieved by the declared *renunciation of regulatory target optimization*. The goal is not an environmental, social or economic welfare maximum, but an "optimal balance" based on the lowest common denominator.[6] As a consequence of this consensus-oriented strategy, developments in empirical research have been regressive recently as far as the search for meaningful *target definitions* is concerned. There is uncertainty everywhere about the core question of what "sustainability" in the sense of the Sustainable Finance Doctrine actually is and what exactly it is measured by.[7] Regulation under minimalist auspices entails likewise the risk that the regulatory yield will be too low in relation to the regulatory burden. That is, those who aim to please everyone will not achieve anything significant in the end.

In the broader frame of reference of the EU Taxonomy Regulation, the environmental concept dominates, behind which social and economic concerns take a back seat when necessary, i.e. in case of doubt. In contrast to the traditional ESG strategy and probably also against the principles of sustainable risk management, this is a clear decision on the direction to be taken, which at the same time reveals the EU Commission's commitment to using sustainability rules as a political steering tool. The imbalance in the weighing of objectives implies a consistent enforcement of the agenda, while the legal impulse of balancing interests to smooth out conflicting objectives recedes into the background. Admittedly, the Commission certainly ties its action plan to the expectation that allocative advantages in the financial markets are ultimately achieved by the freely chosen decisions of investors.[8] Whether the framework conditions set for this are limited to promoting the market functions of supply and demand or are centrally prescribed by the administrative power of the state, however, remains an open question for the time being. In the literature, there is already talk of an "inefficient planning economy".[9]

---

[5] *Bruns/Meyer-Bullerdiek*, Professionelles Portfoliomanagement, 6th edition 2020, p. 819 f.
[6] *Bruns/Meyer-Bullerdiek*, Professionelles Portfoliomanagement, 6th edition 2020, p. 321.
[7] *Bueren* ZGR 2019, 813, 859.
[8] *Commission*, Action plan p. 4.
[9] *Möslein/Sorensen* Europ. Comp. L. J. 15 (2018), 221, 224; *Ekkenga* ZHR 187 (2023), 228, 243.

C. The Object of Optimization: Sustainable Finance

I. The scope of the study: financing or investing or both?

The term "sustainable finance" does not quite capture the essence of what the action plan primarily aims to do. In order to – as the Commission puts it – "reorient[...] private capital to more sustainable investments" (Commission, Action Plan p. 1), it would be necessary above all to influence the *use of funds in companies*, i. e. the investment of existing capital. In contrast, influence on the *supply of funds* ("financing") can, as far as the circular economy on the performance markets is concerned, at best be exerted via the tried and tested steering and channeling mechanisms on the free capital markets. Legal systems may use publicity regulations to ensure that investors are made more aware than before of the ESG ambitions and successes of companies seeking capital, and couple this with the expectation that this will favor capital offers for ESG-affine companies. In this way, it may also be possible in the medium term to enhance the value of sustainability aspects as a parameter for action in competition and to give them more weight than conventional return targets. However, the Commission leaves this legal idea of function-protecting market promotion far behind by claiming for itself in its action plan the task of classifying economic activities in a binary way as sustainable or non-sustainable.[10] Whether this plan is realistic is open to interpretation. After all, the profit-oriented companies in the performance markets for services, production or trade goods have so far evaded the desired classification in case of a certain degree of diversification or when the use of their resources does not permit a clear classification according to ESG criteria.[11] The situation may be different in certain market niches for non-governmental organizations (NGOs) whose capital is earmarked for one or more ESG sub-goals.

The frequently encountered labeling of reform efforts with the more or less synonymously used abbreviation *SRI (Socially Responsible Investment)*, however, suggests that the Commission's plans do not stop at the mere reflection of conditions and processes through classification, but rather, aim to further influence those conditions and processes through the legalization of asset management in the sense of sustainability in planning and design. Professional financial investors such as investment funds are expected to play a key role here, seeing as they are primarily expected to review the business plans and measures of the companies seeking capital within the association for their reasonableness and to judge them competently accordingly.[12] As a further consequence, they are expected to use the voting power of their membership in an activist manner in the

---

[10] *Bueren,* ZGR 2019, 813, 861; *Ekkenga/Posch* WM 2021, 205, 206 f.
[11] *Stump* ZBB 2019, 71, 76 f.; *Möslein/Sorensen* Europ. Comp. L. J. 15 (2018), 221, 224 f.
[12] *Bueren* ZGR 2019, 813, 858; *Ekkenga* WM 2020, 1668 ff..

spirit of the SRI doctrine and thus assume the role of a social control authority within the portfolio companies.

II. Open questions

The completely novel legal figure of the *activist investor as an ESG/SRI agent on a governmental mission*, which is thus launched, raises a multitude of unresolved conceptual and implementation issues. In detail, these include:

Still in the development stage and arguably still far from consolidated concepts are those legislative approaches that aim to directly promote "*sustainable corporate governance*" by imposing binding standards on board behavior. They touch on the subject of "investment business" insofar as the inclusion of funds as control activists only promises success where the structure of the shareholder base leaves room for the influence of individual shareholders including voting and communicatory impact. Less attention has so far been paid to the fundamental question of whether and under what conditions investment funds are in any way institutionally suitable for the task of ESG/SRI-compliant management control – a framing issue that can be referred to as "*shareholder governance*" in line with the proliferating terminological practices (see D., E.).

Within the given institutional design framework, the question arises as to the existence and (further) development of sufficiently efficient regulations in the sense of the ESG/SRI doctrine which relate to fund management as such and are widely discussed under the collective term "*fund governance*". The issue is characterized by an area of tension in which funds, as *financial intermediaries*, have a dual function of both product demand (shares) and product supply (fund units). That is, while they are supposed to guard the interests of the common good vis-à-vis the portfolio companies, they also have to represent the interests of investors in relation to their customers, the purchasers of fund shares (see F. below).

Comparatively new and hitherto scarcely discussed is a third level of consideration for this whole equation, which is currently only a contemplation in the Commission's 10-point agenda. This matter is the question of whether and to what extent the legal system is in any way equipped to facilitate progress in sustainable corporate governance at the downstream market level for the placement of fund shares with the investing public. This requires the orderly distribution of fund shares within the goal of promoting the marketing of ESG-compliant fund shares in a regulatory manner. The matter has been discussed for some time under the heading of "*product governance*" (see G. below).

The final link between fund share sales and fund share purchasers, insofar as the shares are not sold directly to the customer by the fund sponsor or, more frequently, by a sales intermediary, is formed by securities services companies such as, in particular, banks, savings banks and financial services institutions, which act as intermediaries or service providers on behalf of the ultimate beneficiary end customers. Art. 2 No. 11 SFDR refers to securities service companies in the customer business with fund shares as "*financial advisors*". As client representatives in the financial service, they are strictly and uncompromisingly bound to the individual interests of their clients. For the development of "sustainable" financial service governance, the question of how to reconcile the protection of these individual interests with the service of general public interests is therefore particularly urgent (see H. below).

D. Discussion Level 1: Sustainable Corporate Governance

I. Initial situation in the portfolio companies

The institutional framework for the 10-point agenda is partly predetermined by competition on capital markets. Whether and to what extent sustainability goals can be implemented through the use of membership voting rights and the access to communication channels is determined by the *degree of independence of the portfolio company*, which, in turn, depends on trading activity on the stock markets. Paradigmatic for the ideal type of a portfolio company controlled by grassroots democracy, as apparently envisaged by the EU Commission, is the listed stock corporation in free float, whose shares are managed according to the "voice or exit" strategy, i. e. are either continuously restructured in daily stock market trading or are held for the longer term by "*anchor shareholders*" with the contribution of their own shareholder interests. The opposite type is the listed but group-dependent AG, whose shares are majority-owned by an unlisted company and whose business policy cannot be decisively influenced via voting rights without cooperation with the parent company. In between, there is a whole range of possible condensation and blocking maneuvers, which may also be flanked by contractually generated rights of influence on the part of members or third parties.

II. Possibilities of influence at the membership level

The problems raised here concern, on the one hand, the level of influence and design of the members of a target company. Here, the main question is what structural fitness conditions the *shareholder base of a portfolio company* must meet in order to become receptive to membership influence for promoting "sustainable" corporate governance. From a comparative law perspective, the focus shifts to what conclusions can be drawn in this context about the legally ascertainable distribution of membership in listed companies in the individual EU member states. On the other hand, questions arise from the perspective of the management of a portfolio company. They concern, for example, strategies aimed at taking defensive measures against activist ESG/SRI controllers, e.g., by equipping the articles of association with transferability clauses that prevent outside investors from being able to enter the membership circle. Furthermore, *contractual obligations of the portfolio companies* vis-à-vis shareholders or third parties (company agreements, voluntary commitments vis-à-vis lenders or mezzanine capital providers via covenants) deserve attention, which could serve to hinder the implementation of ESG/SRI objectives via voting rights in whole or in part. Further options for exerting influence arise in the relationship between the shareholders. The focus of interest here is the practice of *voting rights agreements* including relaxed cooperation schemes in the manner of "acting in concert".

E. Discussion Level 2: Sustainable Shareholder Governance

I. The actors: investment funds as financial intermediaries

Institutional limits are imposed on the Commission's sustainability program not only in the capital markets, but also by the regulatory *function of investment funds* as financial intermediaries. Their singular influence potential in the general meetings and internal decision-making bodies of the portfolio companies is initially similar to that of small activist shareholders, since the funds' distribution task calls for a balanced diversification of their assets in order to avoid cluster risks. However, the more comprehensive and detailed the ESG/SRI standards for funds become, the more holistic measurement data becomes meaningful in the future. In any case, the behavior of funds in their capacity as shareholders can be expected to provide information on the maximum frame of reference for ESG/SRI-driven shareholder governance, especially in an international context. In terms of legal statistics, this raises the question of what proportion of the total volume of membership stakes in listed companies is attributable to institutional investors, and what differences can be identified in a cross-country comparison. In this context, we are also interested in the ratio of such holdings to the free float of private households on the one hand, and to the group holdings of unlisted companies, on the other.

The *suitability of investment funds* for carrying out the management and control tasks assigned to them is determined not only by their high level of expertise in exercising shareholder rights, but also, above all, by the scope of action institutionally assigned to them. This is subject to an *a priori* inviolable limit, since the funds can only fulfill their function as financial intermediaries in any way if – unlike the "anchor shareholders" – they do not pursue any entrepreneurial goals. Seen in this light, the almost proverbial passivity of the exercise of voting rights by professional investors is not a systemic or developmental flaw[13] but, on the contrary, a system-supporting element of market-mediating organisms with a capital accumulation function. On the other hand, it is not only in line with the system, but likewise required of the fund companies by supervisory law that the voting rights of shares held be handled appropriately in the interest of the final beneficiary fund investors (cf. Art. 37 of Delegated Regulation 231/2013/EU). However, it is hardly possible to speak of shareholder governance in the sense of the ESG doctrine in this respect; rather, under previous EU law, it was essentially a matter of the third-party management of individual positions to maximize shareholder value (rather than stakeholder interests at association level), such as in case of the use of pre-emptive rights in the event of capital increases or dividend prospects. Where the boundary lines run in this context between return-oriented management of individual memberships and (no longer permissible) corporate influence on management is one of the key questions requiring clarification.

II. The instruments: "ESG-Oriented Participation Policy"

In clear contrast to the "best practice" principles of investment law according to the previous model, the obligation of professional investors *as representatives of a publicly accountable "engagement policy"* according to Art. 3 g of EU Directive 2007/36 on the exercise of certain rights of shareholders in listed companies as amended by EU Directive 2017/828, requires the addressees to explain their shareholder governance according to the tried and tested regulatory pattern of a "comply-or-explain" policy. Meanwhile, "engagement policy" refers to influencing internal association processes in portfolio companies through certain channels of influence, including the exercise of shareholder rights, in particular, voting rights. The non-corporate location of the funds in the regulatory structure of financial service providers may give rise to the idea that institutional investors should be obliged in future to look after "soft" public interests to the point of interference of "hard" return targets, and thus to a certain extent be assigned the role of an opposition in the associations that are concerned with ESG issues. Apart from the fact that this target weighting is hardly likely to be compatible with the likewise institutionally anchored commitment of the funds to the investor interests of their customers,[14] however, the broadly conceived and quite strikingly formulated regulations in the new version of EU Directive 2007/36 do not permit a safe conclusion, but nevertheless expressly include "hard" factors as well.[15] The relationship between the two sets of regulations thus remains in need

[13] But this way *Tröger* ZGR 2019, 126, 136: "Marktversagen".
[14] *Volhard/Jang*, in: Weitnauer/Boxberger/Anders, KAGB, 2nd edition 2017, § 1 mn. 25.
[15] *Tröger* ZGR 2019, 126, 151 f.

of clarification. In particular, a closer look is needed to determine whether the content of the "comply-or-explain approach" overlaps with fund management under the regulatory provisions, which would result in a less desirable and hardly intended mixing of mandatory and permissive norm content.[16]

III. Possible sources of error

Less encouraging experiences with the "comply-or-explain" rules in Anglo-Saxon countries have led to the realization quite early on that, in order to maintain a control-effective voting management system, professional investors need the support of *professional proxy advisors*, who act as information intermediaries in corporate governance matters (proxies) linking the management and membership levels. Regardless of the still unmet empirical backlog,[17] the EU has adopted this concept in Art. 3 j of the amended EU Directive 2007/36. The matter as such has long been an integral part of Anglo-Saxon association constitutions. In view of the widespread reception of codes of conduct and their formability in the spirit of the ESG/SRI doctrine, it deserves updated consideration.[18]

The key question thus raised is generalizable; it also relates to other activists who influence the voting behavior of professional investors. What is meant is the danger of misdirection of shareholder governance through such means as deliberate misinformation or signals of all kinds generated by actors with goals or motives that are alien to or hostile to sustainability. The issue boils down to the theoretical and legal-practical *demarcation of cooperation and collaboration*. Two aspects are worth emphasizing on that note. First, as far as voting advisors are concerned, there is a risk of neglecting action parameters that serve the common good by being too close to the management level. According to Anglo-Saxon experience, the latter results from the dual function that proxy advisers hold as operators of professional *corporate governance ratings*. Many of them are prompters of both investors and advisors in the service of the issuing company. The conflicts of interest rooted here are numerous and varied; they fundamentally call into question the enforceability of ESG/SRI objectives by way of shareholder governance.[19]

The second aspect relates to activist investors without a long-term equity interest whose influence on corporate governance sends out pre-determining signals to fellow shareholders with a free-rider attitude. *Hedge funds* in particular are reported to frequently act as a guide for mutual funds, which align their voting and communicatory behavior more or less synchronously for cost-saving

[16] *Baums* ZHR 183 (2019), 605, 609.
[17] *Tröger* ZHR 2019, 126, 152.
[18] In detail *Zetzsche*, in: KölnKommAkt, 3rd edition 2016, Nach § 135 mn. 1 f.
[19] *Tröger* ZGR 2019, 126, 151 f.

reasons.[20] So far, the question is open as to whether this trend will continue or be allowed to continue under the new regulations. The answer depends on whether the proper perception of ESG/SRI-affine voting management entails a minimum level of autonomy. In any case, the obvious thesis that the whole system could falter unless the current trend is reversed is unlikely to be based on the orientation of hedge funds alone. Finally, it is also conceivable that the M&A business of the future will trigger positive sustainability effects because ESG/SRI-affine companies will prevail in competition as attractive acquisition targets. In No. 10 of the Action Plan, however, the Commission indicates that it does not intend *a priori* to consider this possibility in further initiatives in exploring the legal environment.

F. Discussion Level 3: Sustainable Fund Governance for Asset Managers

I. The subject of regulation: investment strategies of investment funds

With the "Regulation (EU) 2019/2088 of the European Parliament and of the Council of 27 November 2019 on sustainability-related disclosures in the financial services sector" (OJEU of 9.12.2019, L 317/1), the Commission had item 7 of its 10-point action plan transposed into applicable law. Article 3(1) of the Regulation requires investment funds in addition to other financial market participants, to publish information on their "policies on the integration of sustainability risks in their investment decision-making process." There is no provision for curtailing the scope for decision-making by means of prohibitions or restrictions on conduct; instead, the legislator uses the indirectly effective means of exerting pressure – as it did previously in the context of the CSR regulations – by imposing an obligation to make a negative declaration whether and to what the extent "sustainability factors" are taken into account in investment decisions (Art. 4 (1) a) of the Regulation). The regulation supplements and modifies the provisions introduced on the basis of Art. 3 lit. i ff. of the amended EU Directive 2007/36 on the obligation of professional investors to *disclose their investment strategies.*

In terms of content, the aim is to consolidate the concept of a *sustainable engagement policy* in voting and dialog management, which was also implemented with the Shareholder Rights Directive, or at minimum, introduce it into practice in the first place. This is because continuously circulating shares are hardly associated with incentives to participate constructively in the issuer's decision-making processes. Actionist ("predatory") small shareholders are known to have a tendency to put pressure on management by bringing actions for defective

[20] *Tröger* ZGR 2019, 126, 139.

resolutions. However, this is always done with the intention of blocking action and for self-interested purposes; the interests of the common good are unlikely to play a role here. "Sustainability" within the meaning of the new Disclosure Regulation consequently encompasses the *long-term holding of shares* while accepting real price losses and opportunity losses resulting from the omission of profit-taking through short-term selling. Going further, it can be inferred from the EU's overall regulations that shares and other trading objects circulating on organized capital markets, as so-called "short term" securities, are classified as more environmentally and socially damaging than unlisted "long-term" securities. Recital 49 to EU Regulation 2019/1238 of 20 June 2019 on a Pan-European Private Pension Product (PEPP) literally states:

"In the context of deepening the CMU, the understanding of what constitutes instruments with a long-term economic profile is broad. Such instruments are non-transferable securities and therefore do not have access to the liquidity of secondary markets. They often require fixed term commitments which restrict their marketability and should be understood to include participation and debt instruments in, and loans provided to, non-listed undertakings. Non-listed undertakings include infrastructure projects, unlisted companies seeking growth, real estate or other assets that could be suitable for long-term investment purposes. Low-carbon and climate-resilient infrastructure projects are often non-listed assets and rely on long-term credits for project financing. Considering the long-term nature of their liabilities, PEPP providers are encouraged to allocate a sufficient part of their asset portfolio to sustainable investments in the real economy with long-term economic benefits, in particular to infrastructure projects and corporates."

II. Possible sources of error

In view of the undisputed importance of professional investors as functionaries and guarantors of smooth securities trading, this regulation – with its intention directed against the capital market – has the potential of a break with economic-historical implications. A first, obvious assumption is that the systematic prevention or obstruction of short-term buying and selling decisions could noticeably weaken the *liquidity of secondary trading* – with the foreseeable consequence that the supply quantity gradually freezes and the increasing market tightness leads to notoriously excessive price formation. The allocation mechanism for individual stocks in the organized markets could thus be undermined across a broad front, which would be reflected above all in equally excessive subscription bids for new issues. Since the parameters of action in the struggle for a more environmentally or socially friendly financial product are not determined in free quality competition but by the authorities in accordance with the Taxonomy Regulation, well known research questions ultimately arise in a new guise, revolving around the alternative of "*decentralized market control through competition versus centralized market control through planned economic influences*". Within the market segment for collective capital investments, the forced concentration on long-term financial products – according to the second assumption – could result in the *end of actively managed investment funds*. After all, their business thrives precisely on the fact that they're trying to beat the index through continuous "stock picking" and frequent rebalancing, thereby gaining a competitive advantage over passively managed index funds.[21]

III. Institutional barriers

Mutual funds stand as the ideal type of capital accumulation institutions that transfer funds raised from households into collective investments for the purpose of risk transformation. They can only fulfill their fiduciary intermediation function if they pursue an investment strategy based on the principle of risk diversification and spread. The *principle of quantitative risk diversification* requires a sufficient diversification of the investment objects with the consequence that the investment is spread over as many portfolio companies as possible. However, the more widely the investment is spread, the less profitable it is for the fund to invest in the constructive use of voting rights or in accompanying initiatives; the costs incurred for this increase with the number of portfolio companies, irrespective of whether and to what extent the fund is tailored to ESG/SRI-affine companies from the outset. Simultaneous fund management and shareholder governance are therefore not compatible objectives; rather, optimizing necessarily comes at the expense of the other. The EU's regulatory approach confronts mutual funds with a dilemma from which there seems to be no way out without breaking with the foundations of the fund system altogether.

The conflict of objectives is further exacerbated by the equally elementary and compelling principle of *qualitative risk diversification*. This means that the portfolio must consist of investment securities with different, sometimes even opposing risk/reward profiles, so that no cluster risks can form. So if the calculation is that investments in sustainably managed companies will yield a higher return in the long term than their competitors on the capital markets, a certain balance must be achieved by adding stocks of ESG/SRI-averse companies (so-called negative correlation) accordingly.[22] In this context, it is unclear not least to what extent an ESG/SRI-affine investment strategy may be restricted by the systemic relevance of ESG/SRI-averse or neutral companies, for example, in the case of the preferential acquisition of shares in a major bank threatened with collapse as part of a state-sponsored restructuring program.[23]

---

[21] *Köndgen/Schmies*, in: Ellenberger/Bunte, Bankrechts-Handbuch, 6th edition 2022, § 93 mn. 22.

[22] *Ekkenga*, in: Festschrift E. Vetter, 2019, p. 115, 134.

[23] *Bueren* ZGR 2019, 813, 819.

IV. Movable barriers

Openings for an ESG/SRI-affine investment strategy present themselves where the investment conditions explicitly provide for this, i.e. where specialization tendencies emerge in the quality competition for the more attractive investment offer. This is because the fund management will hardly be able to ignore the fiduciary commitment of the funds to the interests of their fund customers, which are agreed in the *investment contract*. Sufficient indications of a systematic departure from this elementary principle are not yet discernible at present – notwithstanding many differences of opinion on the legal details[24] – but further developments remain to be seen. At the international level, however, there are increasing signs of efforts at developing binding standards for sustainable investment strategies in the investment business or even to derive them from existing law. The latter is happening at the UN level, for example, in that it is claimed that, based on practical experience to date, the return interests of fund clients are theoretically neither impaired nor even promoted by the preferential alignment of the portfolio with ESG criteria; they therefore stand as an integral part of fiduciary asset management as such.[25] Point 10 of the EU Action Plan, as already mentioned, points in the same direction, with the declared aim of requiring the management of all companies to adhere to binding "sustainability strategies". An interesting but currently unanswered question in this context is whether there are already signs of a *lex mercatoria* for fund managers manifesting from soft law in the cross-border context.[26]

In case of SRI-averse fund types such as *hedge funds* – whose business model stands and falls with short-term investments in target companies –, legitimization by means of adjustment of the investment conditions is naturally out of the question. Whether and to what extent they are affected *de lege lata* and *de lege ferenda* by the legal concept of sustainable finance at all and whether they can be included as addressees of corresponding restrictions in the sense of the ESG doctrine by means that conform to the constitution are questions that have not yet been conclusively clarified. Conversely, there are alternative mutual funds with clearly defined ESG agendas for which the EU has created special legal bases, including Regulation 2015/760 for European long-term investment funds (ELTIF) and Regulation 2013/346 for European social entrepreneurship funds (EuSEF). Investments are either required to be predominantly non-listed financials, or else they derive their qualification from an upstream sustainability labeling process. So far, their broad impact is considered to be low; there is talk of funds with

[24] In detail *Bueren* ZGR 2019, 813, 847 f.
[25] *Bruns/Meyer-Bullerdiek*, Professionelles Portfoliomanagement, 6th edition 2020, p. 326.
[26] In general *Schwarze* EuR 2011, 3 f.

"rarity value"[27] or of "niche offering(s)"[28]. As long as the demand level does not improve, the sustainability concept in retail trading with fund units is unlikely to lead to satisfactory results without government intervention, namely without maintaining remotely controlled "product governance" by the authorities (for more details, see G. below).

V. Inconsistencies at the intersection of shareholder governance and fund governance

Unit-linked pension insurances have another special regulation in EU Reg. 2019/1238 for so-called Pan-European Private Pension Products (PEPP Regulation). It explicitly obliges fund managers to pursue an investment strategy that takes ESG criteria into account in accordance with the Paris Agreement on Climate Change and the UN pronouncements on sustainable development and business and human rights (see recital 51). In addition to insurance companies, the addressees of the standard also include banks, company pension funds and asset managers of all kinds, along with investment firms. There is probably no overlap with the shareholder governance regime, as the latter is limited to shares in organized trading,[29] whereas the PEPP Regulation only provides for investments in over-the-counter securities including shares (recital 49). In contrast, Art. 2 of the SFDR 2019/2088 draws the scope of addressees much more broadly and explicitly includes PEPP providers in No. 1 lit. f.

In this context, the problem discussed above under B. takes on an additional layer of explosiveness. That is, if it is true that the institutional consolidation and maintenance of stable pension systems is one of the core social concerns of the community of states, then the *return interests of future pensioners* cannot be reduced to the macroeconomic aspect of a public welfare promotion. The social benefit of an investment strategy manifests itself not only at the level of the target companies, but also, or even less directly, in the "output" of the investment; the social and microeconomic components of the ESG triad flow inseparably into one another. Thus, if a socially or environmentally beneficial long-term investment proves to be suboptimal or even useless in real economic terms,[30] fund managers have only the short-term alternative of an "exit" at their disposal where the "voice" option does not promise immediate success. Against this background, the fundamental or even tendential disavowal of short-term portfolio shifts by a primarily profit-oriented asset management as "unsustainable" appears to be contradictory to the overall system.

[27] *Niedner/Städter* EuZW 2019, 68, 73.
[28] *Bueren* ZGR 2019, 813, 847.
[29] Cf. *Koch*, in: Koch, AktG, 18th edition 2024, § 134b mn. 5.
[30] On the econometric research initiatives in this regard *Bueren* ZGR 2019, 813, 823.

The aforementioned concerns do not apply to *private equity funds*, however, whose business model includes obtaining control over an unlisted company. Their instrumentalization for global sustainable financing could nevertheless provoke a fundamental debate on whether and to what extent the new rules disproportionately hamper the constitutionally guaranteed regulatory principles of a free exercise of trade. This applies, in particular, to *special AIFs* (alternative investment funds), in which only professional and "semi-professional" investors frequently with their own entrepreneurial agenda may participate. Similar questions arise in case of special AIFs in the variant of *venture capital funds*. Investment standards for them have existed since 2013, but they do not yet have a direct ESG reference (Art. 7 of EuVECA Regulation 345/2013). The situation is once again different with private equity funds in the guise of *closed public AIFs*[31]. They could offer themselves as a substitute solution for mutual funds in the UCITS category (Undertakings for Collective Investment in Transferable Securities, Art. 1(1) KAGB) that wish to avoid a direct or indirect constraint on voting activism, which would be tantamount to an escape movement from ESG regulations at the membership level. Evasion tactics of similar intentions can be easily suspected in other respects as well. It is worth recalling, in particular, the recent increase in the tendency to provide "passively" managed index funds (ETFs) with *synthetically replicating fund contents* (cf. Art. 9 VO 2019/2088). It follows then, that if shares are not held in real terms in the portfolio, no voting rights can be exercised from them either.

G. Discussion Level 4: Sustainable Product Governance in the Distribution of Fund Shares

I. Distribution and trading restrictions upstream of the customer transaction

The label "product governance" goes back to the Second EU Markets in Financial Instruments Directive (MiFiD II) of the year 2019. Its key elements include the regulatory obligation of financial service providers to formally approve newly issued financial products and to continuously monitor product distribution, including distribution chains in the business with fund shares.[32] The goal is to create a comprehensive protection regime that focuses on private investors as "consumers" and aims to prevent "dangerous" financial products with an excessively high risk potential from entering into circulation in the first place. According to the original legal idea, *this market and behavior control mechanism – which*

[31] In detail *Eckhold/Balzer*, in: Assmann/Schütze/Buck-Heeb, Handbuch des Kapitalanlagerechts, 5th edition 2020, § 22 mn. 61.

[32] Overview by *Ekkenga*, Münchener Kommentar HGB, 6th volume: Bankvertragsrecht, 4th edition 2019, Effektengeschäft mn. 86 ff.

is supervised by the authorities – aims less at effectuating public welfare concerns, and more at rather improving the protection of individual investors.[33] However, the accompanying text to Action Announcement 4 in the Action Plan indicates that the Commission intends to include retail customer business in financial products in its ESG agenda.

In addition to the portfolio companies (D. above) and the financial intermediaries, in particular the mutual funds (E. and F. above), the third group of addressees of a comprehensive ESG governance concept to be considered under the new regulatory concept are the *public investors*, or more precisely: their decision-making behavior as *potential purchasers of fund shares*. However, the latter are neither steered in certain directions nor controlled in any other way through, for example, the disclosure provisions of capital market law, insofar as the creation of market transparency as its regulatory core is concerned. "Influencing" here merely means the communication of information relevant to decision-making in order to protect investors from faulty decision-making (individual protection). The disclosure of significant features inherent in the various financial products is also only intended to support market forces in the sense of a utility function (market function protection). Under such conditions, "sustainable" financial securities will only be able to establish themselves on the market in the long term if "sustainability" is ultimately rewarded with higher returns.

II. Steering effects of product advertising and labeling

Additional incentive potential naturally unfolds vis-à-vis investors where more or less *sophisticated advertising techniques* are used above and beyond the pure information transfer. A distinction must be made here in the approach, in that mandatory publications that inform the public about the substance of privately developed and competitively tested ESG labels for fund units do not yet constitute a means of (re)directing financial flows, but nevertheless serve to combat manipulative communication content (green washing) and thus to protect market functions. On the other hand, the relevant information program goes beyond the limits of value-neutral reproduction in that sustainability aspects are selectively emphasized and upgraded to special quality features alongside return aspects. These positively connoted product descriptions alone – as now prescribed by the SFDR – are tantamount to an advertising-effective (legal) "label"[34], whereby a further distinction can be made between the "advertising" of financial products for the financing of practiced sustainability in Art. 8 (1) SFDR and the "solicitation" of financing for intended investments in accordance with Art. 9 (1) SFDR. Negative advertising effects triggered by mandatory statements

[33] Critical to the whole *Ekkenga*, in: Festschrift 25 Jahre WpHG, 2019, p. 975 ff.
[34] *Ekkenga* WM 2020, 1664, 1667.

on the neglect of "sustainability impacts" at the portfolio company level (Art. 4 para. 1 lit. b SFDR, see above under B., I. serve to both complement and complete this sophisticated signaling system as such.

Meanwhile, with the increasing proliferation of sovereign, semi-sovereign or private labels which are awarded to ESG-compliant investment funds by accredited certification bodies as a seal of quality, advertising with "sustainability" is also becoming more and more of an institutional phenomenon. Government reference values, such as those enshrined in the ESG Benchmark Regulation 2019/2089 for index funds, are doing the rest, as is the still relatively new *sustainability rating*, which has so far primarily surfaced in the context of the business doing the issuing with individual securities.[35] However, all of this is not just about product marketing, but also about improving market transparency and opening and closing movable barriers to market entry. Rating agencies, for example, are not only seen as advertising media, but also as information intermediaries between market supply and demand.[36] In addition, they are seen as gatekeepers at the margins of the market, evaluating product quality and keeping "inferior" products out of the market or favoring "superior" products in competition.[37] How these subfunctions find congruity with each other and what incentive and steering effects result from "gatekeeping" were issues that already needed clarification for conventional (credit) rating. In the future, the problem area will expand to include the question of whether and to what extent special procedures such as sustainability rating will lead to a gradual reorientation of the market environment or its influence through "gatekeeping" – away from serving monetary protection and return interests and toward emphasizing ecologically and socially beneficial impact financing even at the price of lower personal benefit. Disruptions in the operation of rule-based product marketing are likely to result, among other things, from the fact that the various functionaries obtain their information material not necessarily from the mandatory publications monitored by the authorities, but from informal sources,[38] not infrequently acting on behalf of those parties that are supposed to be providing information about.[39]

---

[35] *Stumpp*, Nachhaltigkeitsratingagenturen, 2022, p. 28, 37 f., 51.
[36] *Stumpp*, loc. cit. p. 35 ff.
[37] *Stumpp*, loc. cit. p. 46 ff.
[38] *Kühnberger/Wohlgemuth* DStR 2022, 668, 672 ("with its own set of sustainability criteria")
[39] *Stumpp*, loc. cit. p. 59.

H. Discussion Level 5: Sustainable Financial Service in the Customer Business

I. The players: financial advisors in the customer business

Financial advisors involved in individual client business are subject to the same rules of conduct as other investment advisors. That is, as contractors are obliged to perform their services in the best interests of the client (Art. 64 et seq. DelVO 2017/565/EU). A key element of financial advice is to provide the best possible information to the client so that the client is able to make an informed purchasing decision. Since the financial advisor must act in accordance with the concrete preferences expressed by his/her client (know your customer), he/she acts in the market-supporting and steering-neutral role of an *information intermediary*, who directs the publicly available data to a specific application and thus contributes to *individual publicity* that promotes transparency.[40] According to Art. 6 (2) SFDR, the provision of information must relate, among other things, to the consideration or relevance of *sustainability risks* as defined in Art. 2 No. 22 SFDR. In addition, there is information on the consideration and relevance of *sustainability factors* within the meaning of Art. 2 No. 24 SFDR, wherein the financial advisor must disclose to the public via the internet, i.e. by means of general publicity (see Art. 4 (5) SFDR as well as already above under B., I.). In both cases, the disclaimer option is open to the financial advisor. However, the associated incentive effect is not aimed at public investors, but at the financial advisors as information intermediaries.

A second key element of financial advice consists of making selection decisions with the aim of providing the client with a *purchase recommendation*. By their very nature, recommendations have a controlling effect. They generate market-opening effects, for example, when they are directed toward the purchasing of ESG-compatible financial products that would not otherwise be a resounding market success from a return perspective. The counterpart to the market-opening recommendation is the market-closing *issuance of warnings*. Such warnings have always been an integral part of the advisor's duties under the general conduct of business rules as defined by MiFiD II and the supplementary provisions in DelVO 2017/565/EU. They have a market-constricting effect, for example, when they force profitable financial instruments out of trading on account of being insufficiently "sustainable". Financial advice thus becomes a mixture of functions consisting of elements of information provision and gatekeeping.

---

[40] Undisputed; cf. instead of other *Zahrte*, in: MünchKommHGB volume 6: Bankvertragsrecht, 4th edition, Chapter M.

II. "Green" impact investing in the customer business

Since August 2, 2022, Art. 54 (2) lit. a) DelVO 2017/565/EU in the version of Art. 1 No. 6 a) of DelVO 2021/1253/EU additionally applies. According to this, the positive or negative *sustainability preferences* of the investor belong – in addition to his/her risk tolerance – to the essential selection criteria for a recommendation and thus also to the core objectives of the upstream customer exploration. The customer should apparently decide for him/herself what is decisive when sustainability preferences and risk tolerance cannot be served equally by a financial product; in any case, the explanatory text in the recitals does not necessarily give the impression that the new version of the service governance rules was intended to anchor "green" impact investing in an institutional way with the order business.[41]

However, a closer look reveals a varied, differentiated picture. In the meantime, it has been recognized that simply confronting the customer with the alternative of "yield optimization" versus "ESG optimization" carries with it a certain level of noticeable nudging potential that can definitively contribute to a broad-based and lasting redirection of capital flows into projects worthy of ecological and/or social support.[42] Art. 54 (10) DelRL 2017/565/EU n.v. is apparently intended to considerably strengthen this effect by extending the exploration procedure by a second course stage. For the first time, the service provider is obligated here to proactively influence the purchasing motives of the clientele – and thus the demand behavior *in toto* – by refraining from making a recommendation based on the initial survey for the time being and by working towards a subsequent adjustment of the sustainability preference to the existing offer through supplementary explanations. Although the text of the standard does not go into detail on whether this can also mean "downward corrections" in case of fund securities with a low sustainability factor and with high yield prospects in danger of being left behind, the drafters probably had the reverse case primarily in mind. That is, rather low-yielding but very sustainable investment funds are to be placed after all with a little "help".[43] Recommendations enter into precarious proximity to the territory which vernacular refers to as the "persuading"" – in a negative sense ("Aufschwätzen" in German) – of undesirable products. This neglects the protection of the customer from situational risks and thus a core concern of consumer protection, as it has found its way into the law of investment services most recently since MiFiD II.[44] As a standard practiced on a mass scale in financial services, steering-oriented customer influence also increases the

[41] Recital 8 by DelReg 2021/1253/EU.

[42] *Waschbusch/Kiszka/Runco* BKR 2021, 609, 614; *Kruse/Winter* ZBB/JBB 2020, 178, 183; *Bueren* ZGR 2019, 869.

[43] Cf. Again recital 8 by DelReg 2021/1253/EU.

[44] *Ekkenga*, loc. cit. chapter P, 81.

risk of market failure if the investor's hastily made decision is followed by subsequent regret and dissatisfaction with the financial instrument purchased. The same applies to frustration due to lost profits if the customer has refrained from acquiring lucrative fund securities with a low sustainability factor in compliance with corresponding warnings from the advisor.

In the customer business with *active investment* funds as well as with *real-backed index funds*, additional dysfunctions are to be expected, caused by the clamping down on various financial and information intermediaries for product governance purposes. Against investment advisors or securities banks which, under the impression of official impulses, carry out preferential marketing for "green" or "socially friendly" financial securities, the end-beneficiary or end-burdened private investor will hardly be able to take up his/her own position for lack of professional competence. It is therefore feared that the imbalance of product governance in current trading will lead to politically motivated misdirection of capital flows – for example, by persistently steering customers toward particularly expensive and low-return SRI funds.[45]

[45] Very clear and to the point by *Bueren* ZGR 2019, 813, 870.

The European Union and the Sustainable Finance agenda

Between ambition and reality

Pierre-Henri Conac

A. Introduction

Since 2018 the European Union (EU) has taken the lead globally in the field of sustainable finance. It has introduced or already adopted very ambitious initiatives and introduced legislative proposals at an incredible pace.

These legislative developments have already had a strong impact on the Member States because EU financial legislation is very precise and granular. By acting so quickly, the EU has positioned itself at the forefront of international developments. It should be noted that the United States (US) lagged behind because of former President Donald Trump's scepticism regarding climate change. However, since the election of Joe Biden in 2020, the US has begun to catch up but differences remain. For instance, on 21 March 2022, the US Securities and Exchange Commission (SEC) published a proposal on "The Enhancement and Standardization of Climate-Related Disclosures for Investors".[1] However, the SEC only focuses on the financial impact on issuers of climate change rather than on sustainable finance. This is due to the fact that its mandate is limited to investor protection. The promotion of sustainable finance is a political decision that the SEC cannot take on its own, unlike the European Commission (EC), which is a political body.

There is a legal basis for sustainable finance in the European Treaties. Article 3(5) of the Treaty of the European Union (TEU) states that

> "(The EU) shall contribute to peace, security, the sustainable development of the Earth, solidarity and mutual respect among peoples, free and fair trade, eradication of poverty and the protection of human rights, in particular the rights of the child, as well as to the strict observance and the development of international law, including respect for the principles of the United Nations Charter".

---

[1] Securities and Exchange Commission 17 CFR 210, 229, 232, 239, and 249 [Release Nos. 33–11042; 34–94478; File No. S7-10-22] RIN 3235-AM87, The Enhancement and Standardization of Climate-Related Disclosures for Investors, 21 March 2021.

This provision was originally introduced when the Treaty of Lisbon came into force in 2007. In addition, Article 11 of the Treaty of the Functioning of the European Union (TFEU) holds that

> "Environmental protection requirements must be integrated into the definition and implementation of the Union policies and activities, in particular with a view to promoting sustainable development".

This provision was originally introduced by the Treaty of Amsterdam of 1997.

The EC adopted the first capital markets union (CMU) plan in 2015. In 2018, a High-Level Expert Group on Sustainable Finance published a report on this issue. It aimed at improving the contribution of finance to sustainable and inclusive growth by funding society's long-term needs. In order to achieve this goal, the report advised incorporating environmental, social and governance (ESG) factors into investment decision-making. Sustainability and ESG are two different concepts since sustainability is a wider concept.

As a follow-up, in 2018, the EC published a Sustainable Finance Action Plan (SFAP) to establish a sustainable finance policy.[2] It referred to the Paris Climate Agreement of 2015 and the United Nations (UN) "2030 Agenda for Sustainable Development", also adopted in 2015. The UN Sustainable Development Goals must cover the three pillars of sustainability: (1) environmental, (2) social and (3) economic/governance. They aim at improving the contribution of finance to sustainable and inclusive growth by incorporating ESG factors into investment decision-making.

The EC set out the "European Green Deal" on 11 December 2019 which underlined the need to better direct financial and capital flows towards "green" investments.[3] The Commission adopted the goal for the EU to reduce net greenhouse gas emissions by 55 % by 2030 compared with 1990 levels. It also aimed to achieve a climate neutral economy by 2050 and to be the first climate-neutral continent. The adoption of the European Green Deal in 2019 led to rapid policy changes. For instance, the EU adopted in 2020 a European Green Deal Investment Plan (EGDIP) designed to support sustainable investments over the next decade through the EU budget and associated instruments (eg InvestEU), to create an enabling framework for private investors and the public sector to facilitate sustainable investments and to provide support to public administrations and project promoters in identifying, structuring and executing sustainable projects. Following on from its 2018 Action Plan, the Commission published a

---

[2] Communication from the Commission 'Action Plan: Financing Sustainable Growth', COM(2018) 97 final, 8 March 2018.

[3] Communication from Commission to the European Parliament, the European Council, the Council, the European Economic and Social Committee and the Committee of the Regions, The European Green Deal, COM/2019/640 final, 11 December 2019.

Communication on its "Strategy for Financing the Transition to a Sustainable Economy" in 2021.[4]

The sustainable finance agenda was introduced in the mandates of the European Supervisory Authorities (ESAs). As part of the 2019 reform of the European Securities and Markets Authority (ESMA), its mandate was changed to include sustainability and "taking into account sustainable business models and the integration of environmental, social and governance related factors".[5] The political changes incorporated in the ESMA mandate led to the adoption of a "Strategy on Sustainable Finance" in 2020,[6] and a "Sustainable Finance Roadmap 2022–2024" in 2022.[7] In May 2022, the EC asked ESMA and the other ESAs to look into "greenwashing" risks in relation to sustainability claims, especially by asset managers. The ESAs have two years to deliver on this mandate and are expected to issue recommendations, including, potentially, level 1 legislation.

The European banking sector has embraced sustainable finance. The Capital Requirements Directive (CRD V) of 2019 required the European Banking Authority (EBA) to assess potential dedicated prudential treatment of exposures related to assets or activities associated substantially with environmental and/or social objectives with results to be delivered by 28 June 2025.[8] The Capital Requirements Regulation (CRR II) of 2019 tasked EBA with assessing the potential inclusion of ESG risks in Supervisory Review and Evaluation Process (SREP) with results to be delivered by 28 June 2021.[9] In 2020, EBA issued guidelines on loan origination and monitoring which provide that financial institutions should incorporate ESG factors and associated risks in their credit risk appetite and risk management policies, credit risk policies and procedures.[10] As part of the implementation of Basel III, in 2021, the EC introduced the proposal of CRD VI

[4] Communication from the Commission 'Strategy for Financing the Transition to a Sustainable Economy, COM(2021) 390 final, 6 June 2021.

[5] Art. 1(3) of Regulation (EU) No 1095/of 24 November 2010 establishing a European Supervisory Authority (European Securities and Markets Authority).

[6] ESMA, Strategy on Sustainable Finance, 6 February 2020, ESMA22-105-1052.

[7] ESMA, Sustainable Finance Roadmap 2022–2024, ESMA30-379-1051, 10 February 2022, ESMA30-379-1051.

[8] See Article 501c added of Regulation (EU) 2019/876 of the European Parliament and of the Council of 20 May 2019 amending Regulation (EU) No 575/2013 as regards the leverage ratio, the net stable funding ratio, requirements for own funds and eligible liabilities, counterparty credit risk, market risk, exposures to central counterparties, exposures to collective investment undertakings, large exposures, reporting and disclosure requirements, and Regulation (EU) No 648/2012, OJ L 150/1, 7 June 2019.

[9] Article 98 paragraph 8 added of Directive (EU) 2019/878 of the European Parliament and of the Council of 20 May 2019 amending Directive 2013/36/EU as regards exempted entities, financial holding companies, mixed financial holding companies, remuneration, supervisory measures and powers and capital conservation measures, OJ L 150/253, 7 June 2019.

[10] EBA, Final Report, Guidelines on loan origination and monitoring, EBA/GL/2020/06 29 May 2020.

and CRR III.[11] This legislative package requires bank strategies and processes to assess internal capital needs to cover for short, medium and long term ESG risks as part of their risk management. All banks will also have to disclose the degree to which they are exposed to ESG risks. It also establishes clear responsibilities of the management body as regards ESG risks.

The European Central Bank (ECB) has also been very active. Following the lead of Mark Carney in 2015,[12] the ECB considers that the fight against climate change is part of its monetary policy mandate[13] although such interpretation is debated.[14] The Single Supervisory Mechanism (SSM) also requires banks to take action and raise capital in order to reflect climate risk.[15] In 2020 the ECB adopted a Guide on climate-related and environmental risks[16] and recently expressed its dissatisfaction with the level of disclosure by the banking sector.[17] A climate risk stress test on systemic financial institutions, which it held in 2022, proved to be a useful exercise for the future.[18] The ECB considers that the failure to disclose the exposure to climate-related and environmental risks constitutes a breach of the CRR. This is also a clear difference with the US. The chair of the Federal Reserve declared in January 2023 that

[11] Proposal for a Directive of the European Parliament and of the Council amending Directive 2013/36/EU as regards supervisory powers, sanctions, third-country branches, and environmental, social and governance risks, and amending Directive 2014/59/EU, Brussels, 27 October 2021 COM(2021) 663 final, 2021/0341 (COD); Proposal for a Regulation of the European Parliament and of the Council amending Regulation (EU) No 575/2013 as regards requirements for credit risk, credit valuation adjustment risk, operational risk, market risk and the output floor, Brussels, 27 October 2021, COM(2021) 664 final, 2021/0342 (COD).

[12] "Breaking the tragedy of the horizon – climate change and financial stability", speech by Mr Mark Carney, Governor of the Bank of England and Chairman of the Financial Stability Board, at Lloyd's of London, London, available at: https://www.bis.org/review/r151009a.pdf (21 May 2024).

[13] See Press release, ECB presents action plan to include climate change considerations in its monetary policy strategy, 8 July 2021. The Press release is available at: https://www.ecb.europa.eu/press/pr/date/2021/html/ecb.pr210708_1~f104919225.en.html (21 May 2024).

[14] For an intermediate view, see: C. Zilioli and M. Ioannidis, "Climate Change and the Mandate of the ECB: Potential and Limits of Monetary Contribution to European Green Policies", *Common Market Law Review*, Vol 59, 2022, p. 363–394.

[15] When you need change to preserve continuity: climate emergency and the role of law, speech by Frank Elderson, ECB Legal Conference 2021, Frankfurt am Main, 25 November 2021, at: https://www.ecb.europa.eu/press/key/date/2021/html/ecb.sp211125~2da387f2ce.en.html (21 May 2024).

[16] ECB, Guide on climate-related and environmental risks. Supervisory expectations relating to risk management and disclosure, November 2020.

[17] ECB, Supervisory assessment of institutions' climate-related and environmental risks disclosures. ECB report on banks' progress towards transparent disclosure of their climate-related and environmental risk profiles, March 2022.

[18] ECB, 2022 climate risk stress test, July 2022.

"Without explicit congressional legislation, it would be inappropriate for us to use our monetary policy or supervisory tools to promote a greener economy or to achieve other climate-based goals," and that "We are not, and will not be, a 'climate policymaker'."[19]

Within just a few years, major changes have occurred in the relationship between EU legislation and finance. Before the great financial crisis of 2008, finance would only be regulated if and when it were considered necessary. Protecting investors was the ultimate goal and was achieved through disclosure. Financial stability should be achieved by regulating the invisible hand of the market. This was a liberal approach. After 2008, especially through the impulse of the G 20, finance became subject to extensive regulations and was essentially reined in. Instead of relying exclusively on self-regulation and disclosure, the EU legislator introduced rules on product governance on behavioural finance assuming that investors need to be protected. Therefore, investors should be protected through product control. Since 2018 and the SFAP, finance has been enrolled in the fight against climate change and in support of environmental and social issues. The invisible hand of the market has been replaced by the visible hand of the government steering public and where possible, also private funding towards mostly or exclusively sustainable investments.

The EU framework in the field of sustainable finance is quite developed. It includes disclosure (B.) and substantive requirements (C.). However, it also raises challenges (D.).

B. Disclosure regulation in the field of sustainable finance

The EU legislative sustainable finance agenda is designed to increase disclosure by issuers (I.) in order, among other things, to help investors choose sustainable investments II.).

I. Issuers

Disclosure on sustainability is to be imposed on issuers by the Corporate sustainability reporting directive (CSRD). The proposal of CSRD was introduced in April 2021[20] and published in December 2022.[21] In 2014, the EU legislator had

[19] Available at: https://www.riksbank.se/en-gb/press-and-published/conferences/2023/international-symposium-on-central-bank-independence/ (21 May 2024).

[20] Proposal for a Directive of the European Parliament and of the Council amending Directive 2013/34/EU, Directive 2004/109/EC, Directive 2006/43/EC and Regulation (EU) No 537/2014, as regards corporate sustainability reporting, Brussels, 21 April 2021 COM(2021) 189 final, 2021/0104 (COD).

[21] Directive (EU) 2022/2464 of the European Parliament and of the Council of 14 December 2022 amending Regulation (EU) No 537/2014, Directive 2004/109/EC, Directive 2006/43/EC

adopted requirements for large companies to disclose non-financial and diversity information (NFRD).[22] The NFRD also applied to banks (credit institutions) since they are "public interest entities" even if they have no transferable securities listed. Therefore, the banking sector was already subject to these types of disclosures. However, the NFRD was criticised because of complaints by investors on issues of quality and comparability of information.

The CSRD covers all large companies, whether they are listed or not and without the previous 500-employee threshold. It includes listed small and medium enterprises (SMEs), with the exception of listed micro-enterprises. There is a special regime for SMEs. They will be allowed to report according to standards that are simpler than those applicable to large companies. The ESG reporting will be included in the management report and not in a separate statement. This means that they will be subject to civil liability. The CSRD provides for an audit requirement on sustainability information. However, this audit will only provide a "limited" assurance requirement. It is a significant advance on the current situation but it does not go as far as imposing a "reasonable" assurance requirement, which would have been more costly and difficult.

The European Financial Reporting Advisory Group (EFRAG) was requested by the EC to develop European Sustainability Reporting Standards (ESRS). EFRAG was set up in 2001 to assist the European Commission in the endorsement of International Financial Reporting Standards (IFRS) by providing advice on the technical quality of IFRS. Those ESRS will be applicable to companies subject to the CSRD. In April 2022, EFRAG submitted to a public consultation exposure drafts of ESRS. Some ESRS are "transverses" while others are specific to "Environment", "Social" and "Governance". After taking into account the results of the consultation, draft standards were published in November 2022. Compared to the April version, the draft ESRS are less numerous. They have been sent to the EC, which is also planning to consult on them. They are planned to be adopted in June 2023 in order to respect the deadline for the implementation of the CSRD. In the meantime, EFRAG will be working on additional sector specific standards.

In June 2020, the EU legislator adopted a Taxonomy Regulation, which provides clarity on what is environmentally sustainable ("green") and under which circumstances.[23] The "Green Taxonomy" is designed to be an alphabet applicable to issuers and investors.

---

and Directive 2013/34/EU, as regards corporate sustainability reporting, JOEU L 322/15, 16 December 2022.

[22] Directive 2014/95/EU of the European Parliament and of the Council of 22 October 2014 amending Directive 2013/34/EU as regards disclosure of non-financial and diversity information by certain large undertakings and groups, OJ L 330/1, 15 November 2014.

[23] Regulation (EU) 2020/852 of the European Parliament and of the Council of 18 June 2020

The Taxonomy Regulation includes three categories of activities which are to be considered (ecologically) sustainable or not. The first category is low carbon and is considered to be truly green (Article 10(1)). Another category is considered to be "transitional" (Article 10(2)). Finally, some activities are labelled as "enabling" as they simply enable a transition by reducing greenhouse gas emission (Article 16). The Regulation also includes a list of 67 activities that help mitigate climate change and other criteria for determining whether a financial asset can be considered green. It must make a substantive contribution to at least one of six environmental objectives. These goals are climate change mitigation to climate change adaptation, sustainable protection of water and marine resources, circular transition, pollution prevention and control and the protection and restoration of biodiversity and ecosystems. In addition, the issuer of the financial asset, while pursuing one of those goals, must do no significant harm (DNSH) to any of the other five goals wherever relevant. Finally, the issuer must meet minimum safeguards regarding ESG such as the OECD Guidelines on Multinational Enterprises, the UN Guiding Principles on Business and Human Rights (MS).

The delegated Act on Article 8 of the Taxonomy Regulation was adopted in July 2021 and requires companies falling within the scope of the existing Non-Financial Reporting Directive and the additional companies brought under the scope of the proposed CSRD to report on the extent to which their activities are Taxonomy-aligned.[24] The Delegated Act specifies content, methodology and presentation of information to be disclosed by large financial and non-financial companies on the share of their business, investments or lending activities that are aligned with the Taxonomy Regulation. Non-financial companies are required to disclose the share of their turnover, capital and operational expenditure associated with environmentally sustainable economic activities. For financial undertakings (investment firms, asset managers, insurers, credit institutions), Key Performance Indicators (KPIs) relate to the proportion of environmentally sustainable economic activities in their financing activities, such as lending, investment and insurance.

The Taxonomy also applies to financial market participants, for instance investment firms and banks, offering financial products in the EU (Article 5 to Article 7). It requires them to determine how and to what extent the Taxonomy was used in determining the sustainability of the underlying investments, to what environmental objective(s) the investments contribute and the proportion of

on the establishment of a framework to facilitate sustainable investment, and amending Regulation (EU) 2019/2088, OJ UE L 198/13, 22 June 2020.

[24] Commission Delegated Regulation (EU) 2021/2178 of 6 July 2021 supplementing Regulation (EU) 2020/852 of the European Parliament and of the Council by specifying the content and presentation of information to be disclosed by undertakings subject to Articles 19a or 29a of Directive 2013/34/EU concerning environmentally sustainable economic activities, and specifying the methodology to comply with that disclosure obligation, OJ L 443/9, 10 December 2021.

underlying investments that are Taxonomy-aligned, as a percentage of the investment, fund or portfolio. The "Green Taxonomy" will allow the future labelling of funds as green. There will be also Key Performance Indicators (KPIs).

In addition to the "Green Taxonomy", the Commission is also preparing a regulation on Social Taxonomy. It aims to set out a list of socially sustainable activities. A report was published in February 2022 and the structure of the regulation will probably be similar to that of the "Green Taxonomy".[25] This implies the development of social objectives, types of substantial contributions, the "do no significant harm" (DNSH) criteria and minimum safeguards. The list of stakeholders affected by business is likely to be the same as that selected in the EFRAG draft approach which is based on three stakeholder groups: own workforce (including value-chain workers), end-users/consumers and affected communities (directly or through the value chain).

II. Investors

The EU legislative framework is also designed to help investors to choose funds which are aligned with the sustainable finance agenda.

The Sustainable finance disclosure regulation (SFDR) of 2019 strengthens the protection of end-investors by standardising and enhancing ESG-related disclosures.[26] Its objective is to help mobilise private capital to finance the transition towards a sustainable economy through disclosure by funds. It is the first and most important piece of legislation of the SFAP. It applies to investment firms and credit institutions since they operate as large asset managers. Art. 2(17) of the SFDR covers both environmental and socially sustainable investments and the DNSH refers to both.[27] It is designed to bring accountability and discipline to sustainability claims made by manufacturers of financial products. The SFDR distinguishes three types of funds according to their degree of Taxonomy-alignment. Some funds ("dark green") are those that have sustainability goals as

[25] Final Report on Social Taxonomy, Platform on Sustainable Finance, February 2022.

[26] Regulation (EU) 2019/2088 of the European Parliament and of the Council of 27 November 2019 on sustainability-related disclosures in the financial services sector, OJ L 317, 9 December 2019.

[27] Art. 2 (17) of SFDR: " 'sustainable investment' means an investment in an economic activity that contributes to an environmental objective, as measured, for example, by key resource efficiency indicators on the use of energy, renewable energy, raw materials, water and land, on the production of waste, and greenhouse gas emissions, or on its impact on biodiversity and the circular economy, or an investment in an economic activity that contributes to a social objective, in particular an investment that contributes to tackling inequality or that fosters social cohesion, social integration and labour relations, or an investment in human capital or economically or socially disadvantaged communities, provided that such investments do not significantly harm any of those objectives and that the investee companies follow good governance practices, in particular with respect to sound management structures, employee relations, remuneration of staff and tax compliance;"

their explicit aim (Article 9). Other funds ("light green") have environmental or social characteristics among other goals (Article 8). Article 8 funds can promote environmental or social characteristics for instance by taking into account principal adverse impacts. They have to take into account the DNSH principle only where they make sustainable investments. The remaining category are those funds without a specific sustainability agenda (Article 6). Fund managers must state how their funds align to one of these three levels of sustainability. The EC adopted a Level 2 Act in order to flesh out the requirements of the SFDR and to align it better with the EU Taxonomy. The Commission Delegated Regulation (EU) 2022/1288 of 6 April 2022, which came into force in January 2023, requires funds to report pre-contractual documents and through periodic disclosure principal adverse impacts (PAI) of their Article 8 and 9 funds.[28]

The EU legislator has also adopted substantive regulation designed to promote sustainable finance.

C. Substantive regulation in the field of sustainable finance

The EU legislator has adopted or is developing substantive regulation addressed not only to issuers (I.), but also financial market participants, including retail investors (II.).

I. Issuers

In 2019, the EU legislator adopted a regulation on EU Climate Transition Benchmarks, EU Paris-aligned Benchmarks and sustainability-related disclosures for benchmarks ("Green benchmarks").[29] It includes two new categories of low-carbon benchmarks: a climate-transition benchmark and a specialised benchmark which brings investment portfolios in line with the 2015 Paris Agreement goal to limit the global temperature increase to 1.5° above pre-industrial levels.

---

[28] Commission Delegated Regulation (EU) 2022/1288 of 6 April 2022 supplementing Regulation (EU) 2019/2088 of the European Parliament and of the Council with regard to regulatory technical standards specifying the details of the content and presentation of the information in relation to the principle of 'do no significant harm', specifying the content, methodologies and presentation of information in relation to sustainability indicators and adverse sustainability impacts, and the content and presentation of the information in relation to the promotion of environmental or social characteristics and sustainable investment objectives in pre-contractual documents, on websites and in periodic reports, OJ L 332/2, 27 December 2022.

[29] Regulation (EU) 2019/2089 of the European Parliament and of the Council of 27 November 2019, amending Regulation (EU) 2016/1011 as regards EU Climate Transition Benchmarks, EU Paris-aligned Benchmarks and sustainability-related disclosures for benchmarks, OJ EU L 317/17, 9 December 2019.

In 2021, the EC introduced a proposal for a Regulation on bonds that pursue environmentally sustainable objectives within the meaning of the Taxonomy Regulation ("Green bonds" or "EuGB").[30] The proposal has not yet been adopted. EuGB would be available for all types of bond issuers such as corporate or sovereign and also non-EU issuers. Issuers must allocate 100 % of the proceeds of the bond to finance Taxonomy-aligned economic activities. The use of the EuGB standard would be voluntary, which would give issuers the possibility to continue to use existing industry. However, it would establish a benchmark and allow investors to purchase bonds with environmental credentials. Those bonds would be subject to a pre- and post- issuance review by external reviewers who would be required to register with ESMA.

Finally, the EC is considering introducing a regulation on ESG ratings. The goal is to establish minimum standards for ESG ratings and possibly supervise ESG rating agencies. The Commission asked ESMA to provide advice on the issue. ESMA published a call for evidence in February 2022[31] and sent its advice to the Commission in June 2022. ESMA concluded that a small number of large non-EU headquartered providers and smaller more specialised EU entities co-existing who provide a more comprehensive suite of services have emerged.[32]

II. Investors

The EU legislator is also trying to promote sustainable finance with financial market participants, including retail investors. This is done through product governance and the inclusion of sustainability preferences in the suitability assessment.

As far as product governance is concerned, the Commission adopted a Level 2 regulation 2021/1269 of 21 April 2021 under Directive 2014/65/EU of 15 May 2014 on markets in financial instruments (MiFID II) which requests investment firms to take into account sustainability preferences of investors.[33] Recital (2) holds

> "(...) that objective requires that clear signals are given to investors with regard to their investments to avoid stranded assets and to raise sustainable finance".

[30] Proposal for a Regulation of the European Parliament and of the Council on European green bonds, Strasbourg, 6 July 2021 COM(2021) 391 final, 2021/0191 (COD).

[31] ESMA, Call for evidence, On Market Characteristics for ESG Rating Providers in the EU, 3 February 2022, ESMA80-416-25.

[32] ESMA, The Chair, Ref: Outcome of ESMA Call for Evidence on Market Characteristics of ESG Rating and Data Providers in the EU, 24 June 2022 ESMA22-328-603.

[33] Commission Delegated Regulation (EU) 2021/1269 of 21 April 2021 amending Delegated Directive (EU) 2017/593 as regards the integration of sustainability factors into the product governance obligations, OJ EU L 277/137, 2 August 2021.

Article 9 (9) provides that

"Member States shall require investment firms to identify at a sufficiently granular level the potential target market for each financial instrument and specify the type(s) of client with whose needs, characteristics and objectives, including any sustainability related objectives, the financial instrument is compatible. As part of this process, the firm shall identify any group(s) of clients with whose needs, characteristics and objectives the financial instrument is not compatible, except where financial instruments consider sustainability factors. Where investment firms collaborate to manufacture a financial instrument, only one target market needs to be identified."

Investors are also allowed to include sustainability preferences in their suitability assessment. These preferences can be expressed within the scope of the provision of investment advice and portfolio management. A Commission Delegated Regulation (EU) 2021/1253 of 21 April 2021 provides explicitly for investors to be allowed to include sustainability preferences.[34] As a follow-up, in September 2022, ESMA adopted Guidelines on sustainability aspects of the MiFID II suitability requirements.[35] They clarify that the suitability of the product must be assessed first in accordance with the criteria of knowledge and experience, financial situation and other investment objectives and the client‘s sustainability preferences are assessed as a second step. They are predisposed towards promoting sustainable investments. For instance, if the client has expressed specific sustainability preferences but there are no such financial products, an investment firm may recommend other investments but only once the client has adapted his sustainability preferences.[36] The investment firm cannot propose non-sustainable investments before the profile has been changed. In addition, ESMA considers that

"Where a client adapts his sustainability preferences, this change should only refer to the investment advice in question and not to the client's profile in general."[37]

These rules seem designed to keep the investor who has expressed sustainability preferences within the scope of sustainable investments.

---

[34] Commission Delegated Regulation (EU) 2021/1253 of 21 April 2021 amending Delegated Regulation (EU) 2017/565 as regards the integration of sustainability factors, risks and preferences into certain organisational requirements and operating conditions for investment firms, OJ L 277/1, 2 August 2021.

[35] ESMA, Final Report, Guidelines on certain aspects of the MiFID II suitability requirements, 23 September 2022, ESMA35-43-3172.

[36] Article 54 (10 of Commission Delegated Regulation (EU) 2017/565.

[37] Point 83, ESMA, Final Report, Guidelines on certain aspects of the MiFID II suitability requirements, 23 September 2022, ESMA35-43-3172.

D. Challenges

The speed at which those developments have taken place have left little room for reflection about the possible problems associated with sustainable finance. There are challenges associated with sustainable finance probably due to the speed of the adoption of this agenda. Some of them concern governments and public institutions (I.) while others concern investors themselves (II.).

I. Challenges for public institutions

Public institutions might face problems with the sustainable finance agenda. Those are political institutions such as the European Commission and the Member States as well as securities supervisors.

The ultimate goal of the sustainable finance is to reduce, sooner or later, the financing of companies and activities which are not aligned with this agenda. However, the social acceptability of sustainable finance raises issues if the speed of change is not well calibrated to the growth of alternative. This could lead for instance to an increase in the price of oil due to insufficient investment in fossil fuels, which is necessary to avoid sudden decreases in production. In such a case, the production of fossil fuels might be faster than the development of decarbonised alternatives, leading to an increase in the price of oil. Larry Fink, the CEO of Blackrock, raised this issue in his 2022 "Letter to CEOs" when he noted that

> "Any plan that focuses solely on limiting supply and fails to address demand for hydrocarbons will drive up energy prices for those who can least afford it, resulting in greater polarization around climate change and eroding progress."

The EC has also been very hostile to nuclear power and did not want it to be considered "green" under the Taxonomy Regulation. Since nuclear energy is decarbonised, this approach is rather surprising. Recent geopolitical events have created an energy scarcity in the EU. This led France and some other Member States to ask the EC that nuclear energy be considered "green" under certain conditions.[38] Their request was successful. Certain gas-related activities were also included and considered as "substantially contributing to" the EU climate and environmental objectives. This sudden change by the Commission shows that the reflection behind the Green agenda might not always have been deep enough and should take into account all elements such as industry, economic challenges, or geopolitical developments.

---

[38] Commission Delegated Regulation (EU) 2022/1214 of 9 March 2022 amending Delegated Regulation (EU) 2021/2139 as regards economic activities in certain energy sectors and Delegated Regulation (EU) 2021/2178 as regards specific public disclosures for those economic activities, OJ L 188/1, 15 July 2022.

The EU sustainable finance agenda also raises issues as to the competitiveness of European companies. As a consequence of the risk that companies incorporated in the EU and subject to the CSRD would lose competitiveness, the EU legislator decided to apply the CSRD extra-territorially. The criteria is that a third-country company has a net turnover of more than EUR 40 million and a branch in the EU. This is an implicit admission that the CSRD poses a risk to the competitiveness of EU-based companies. As to the effective enforcement of this requirement, it seems doubtful especially considering that it implies that a branch request it from a parent company. Finally, as to the ESRS, they are more granular and demanding than those prepared by the ISSB so that they could also put the competitiveness of European companies at risk.

The sustainable finance agenda also raises problems for supervisors and especially for ESMA with regard to supervisory convergence. The SFDR lacks "minimum standards backing up asset managers'sustainable disclosures". This has created a patchwork of national regulations with many divergences, which will be eliminated over time, but they have created significant risks including for the promoters of the fund.

The EU sustainable finance agenda is also not without risks for investors.

II. Challenges for investors

The regulatory framework put in place by the European legislator is extremely complex. It is full of new concepts and definitions. The provisions are not always easy to interpret and Level 2 texts are often quite long which adds to the complexity. It is made even more complex by the silo and the phased-in approach to their adoption. Each regulation is adopted separately, at different times, so that there are issues of coordination. The result is a complex regulatory jungle in an already overly complex field.

The SFDR and Taxonomy Regulation have been developed separately, which has led to inconsistencies. For instance, as noted by the ESMA Securities and Markets Stakeholders Group (SMSG),

> "The Taxonomy Regulation defines that the percentage of Taxonomy aligned investments in investee companies should be calculated based on turnover, Opex or Capex. No such definition is available for environmental or social objectives under SFDR. Should a similar calculation methodology be used or can both follow a different calculation methodology? Given that many companies have some degree of diversification, the range of companies that have 100% Taxonomy aligned activities in terms of turnover, Opex or Capex is restricted to niche companies. If a similar calculation methodology is to be followed, this would make it very difficult to have 100% sustainable investments in an investment product, which in turn impacts the scope of Article 9 products."[39]

[39] SMSG, Advice to ESMA, SMSG advice to the ESMA Consultation Paper on Guidelines on certain aspects of the MiFID II suitability requirements, 3 May 2022 ESMA22-106-4032.

Also, the SFDR does not include the concept of "Substantial contribution to environmental objectives" whereas both include the concept of "contribution to environmental objectives" which leads to complexities.

There are also inconsistencies between SFDR and MiFID II. As noted again by the SMSG

> "Although article 8 products promote environmental or social characteristics, it is not required that they: (a) have a minimum percentage taxonomy aligned investments, (b) have a minimum percentage of sustainable investments in terms of SFDR or (c) consider PAI. Hence, it is possible that they are not eligible for meeting sustainability preferences as defined under MiFID."[40]

Finally, on a more general level, tensions exist between the environmental and social objectives. The EU legislative framework does not explain how to address them.

The desire of the EU legislator to promote sustainable finance at such a rapid pace might also lead to the issue of a lack of sufficient available investments. This regulatory complexity creates the risk of "green-bleaching" by which fund managers invest in sustainable activities but refrain from claiming to do so to avoid the risk of being accused of "greenwashing" if there are issues with their interpretation of the EU legislation. Greenwashing can be defined as the intentional or unintentional exploitation of policy priorities for communication purposes by reporting companies or investment firms or banks, without really aligning with the goals and expectations of these initiatives.

Commission Delegated Regulation (EU) 2021/1253 of 21 April 2021 implicitly admits this risk of scarcity of sustainable investment when it amended article 54 (10) of the Delegated Regulation (EU) 2017/565 as regards the integration of sustainability factors, risks and preferences into certain organisational requirements and operating conditions for investment firms, since it organises the process for "returning" to non-sustainable investments.[41] A possible result of this scarcity of available investments and the risk of being blocked in the "sustainable finance" might be that investors do not opt in to sustainability preferences in the first place.

A final issue is the profitability of ESG investments compared to classic investments. There is no clear answer yet to this question since academic studies have yielded various and sometimes opposite results. However, the scarcity of sustainable investments, made even worse by the regulatory risks attached to "greenwashing", imply that only few will qualify as sustainable creating the risk

---

[40] SMSG, Advice to ESMA, SMSG advice to the ESMA Consultation Paper on Guidelines on certain aspects of the MiFID II suitability requirements, 3 May 2022 ESMA22-106-4032.

[41] Commission Delegated Regulation (EU) 2021/1269 of 21 April 2021 amending Delegated Directive (EU) 2017/593 as regards the integration of sustainability factors into the product governance obligations, OJ EU L 277/137, 2 August 2021.

of overvaluation of those assets leading potentially to losses for the investors and financial stability issues. The number of sustainable investments is growing so that this question should solve itself over time, but the risk of overvaluation remains. ESMA noted in 2022 that

> "Concerns over 'green' asset overvaluation lingered, as the return on equity of less-polluting firms went into negative territory in 2020, while long-dated green bonds traded at a premium relative to other bonds."[42]

Ultimately, the issue of their profitability for investors is key.

E. Conclusion

The EU legislator has developed an ambitious agenda on sustainable finance and developed it at a very rapid pace. However, the consequences of both the speed and the nature of this agenda might not always have been analysed in sufficient detail.

As to the speed of the change, the SFDR has essentially tried to create demand from investors although the issue of the supply of investment products should have been fixed beforehand. This has created a significant gap between supply and demand. This gap will not be bridged until the CSRD is implemented in the Member States, which will be at the earliest in 2025 for the largest companies for their financial years starting on or after 1 January 2024. In the meantime, the risk of assets being overvalued due to scarcity remains high. As to the nature of the agenda, the risk of labelling certain activities as not being green although they contribute to decarbonisation, such as nuclear energy, or contribute to an orderly transition from fossil fuel, such as gas, remains high. Any mistake in the analysis could lead to underinvestment and high energy costs for both industry and consumers. Sustainable finance has to be implemented considering all aspects including its economic and social consequences as well as sovereignty issues. This is already what is happening in the US where, due to geopolitical developments, some investors think that it is necessary to adopt a more holistic approach to ESG.[43]

Finally, the sustainable finance agenda is indicative of a change from a market-based economy towards a more dirigiste approach the EU institutions and Member States finance sustainable investments while also promoting them to the private sector. The involvement of the private sector is necessary to meet Paris Agreement goals since public funding alone will not suffice. This approach is

---

[42] ESMA, TRVRisk, Monitor ESMA Report on Trends, Risks and Vulnerabilities No. 1, 2022, ESMA document number: 50-165-2058 Publication date: 15 February 2022.

[43] G. Tett, "ESG exposed in a world of changing priorities", *Financial Times*, 3 June 2022, at: https://www.ft.com/content/6356cc05-93a5-4f56-9d18-85218bc8bb0c (21 June 2024).

different from the successful ordo-liberalism approach of post-War Germany. Whether or not this more dirigiste approach is going to be economically and socially successful remains unclear, but it is already the most significant and visible consequence of the sustainable finance agenda.

Country Report Germany

Jens Ekkenga

A. Overview of the Initial Situation

I. Influences of ESG-compliant ownership governance on corporate governance

Under modern EU law, professional (financial) investors and insurance companies in particular have the task of obtaining meaningful data from the mandatory publications of large companies operating in the real economy based on their perception of their "corporate social responsibility" and of evaluating them from a sustainability perspective. Subsequently, the investors are to be induced to work towards ESG-affine management (*corporate governance*) through proactive use of the association's internal opportunities for exerting influence. The latter is to be achieved through the use of voting rights (*ownership governance*) wherever possible, but also includes a wide range of informal channels of influence which have been widely discussed for some time under the heading of "investor relations" and appear in a new light under ESG aspects. Germany has created a regulatory program under stock corporation law for this "sustainability dialog" and has *established institutionalized channels of influence* for investment funds[1] and institutional investors[2] for this purpose in sections 134a et seq. of the German Stock Corporation Act (AktG). The regulations cover not only voting behavior in the shareholder structure of the respective portfolio companies, but also the "exchange of opinions with the corporate bodies and stakeholders of the company" (item 3). The boundaries between the two categories are fluid, as shown by recent tendencies to include the shareholders' meeting as an initiator rather than a decision-maker. Accompanying resolutions of the Annual General Meeting that only contain recommendations for the management are already included in the "Say-on-Pay" provision of Section 120a AktG. They currently relate to the compensation of management board members, but according to

[1] For reasons of simplification, the term will henceforth be used as a blanket term, i.e. without differentiating between the (external) management company, the special fund (fund management company) and the depositary.

[2] According to the legal definitions in Section 134 a (1) Nos. 1 and 2 of the German Stock Corporation Act (AktG), they also originate from the insurance industry and customer-servicing asset management.

recent trends could be extended to include a voting system on matters of climate protection ("Say on Climate") and human rights ("Say on Human Rights").[3]

However, the location of the new regulations in *stock corporation law* is widely criticized in Germany as being non-systemic and inappropriate, because the fiduciary management of membership rights in portfolio companies by investment funds and institutional investors is not, strictly speaking, "actually" a matter of private law, but is one of the supervisory law monitored by the authorities.[4] The German legislator was probably primarily concerned with not affecting the institutional status of the funds as non-entities in the real economic sense. According to general principles of conflict-of-law qualification, the same would have to apply in a cross-border context so that the scope of application of the regulations would also be open to *foreign investors* holding shares in German AGs (in English "stock corporation; hereafter called "AG"). However, the definitional formulas of Sec. 134a AktG explicitly limit the group of addressees to investment funds domiciled in Germany – a basic legislative decision that has been met with criticism in view of the predominantly international nature of the overall matter[5] – and raises the as yet unresolved follow-up question as to what supranational mechanisms can help to bring national legal systems into line with each other in this respect. Obviously, this question is of particular urgency when dealing with investors from countries outside the EU, namely from the UK and the USA.[6] In addition, the clarification of the investment statute in cross-border situations is still one of the *terrae incognitae* of German commercial conflict law.[7]

II. ESG-compliant investment strategies of investment funds as a link between ownership governance and funding governance

German regulations on collective asset management by investment funds and insurance companies are not limited to the use of voting rights from shares, referred to as "engagement policy" ("Mitwirkungspolitik") in Section 134b (1) of the German Stock Corporation Act (AktG), but also extend to the design of portfolios through asset management that is as ESG-compliant as possible (*fund governance*). Section 134c AktG obliges insurance companies as "institutional investors" in this context to disclose their "investment strategy" in accordance with the comply-or-explain principle, whereas the design of the fund management of investment funds is not primarily governed by stock corporation law but by the regulatory provisions of the German Code on Investment Funds (KAGB). There are, however, no apparent objective reasons for this separation

[3] *Holle/Harnos* AG 2021, 853 et seq.
[4] *Tröger* ZGR 2019, 126, 141 f., 147 f.; *Baums* ZHR 183 (2019), 605, 607.
[5] *Baums* ZHR 183 (2019), 605, 608.
[6] *Baums* ZHR 183 (2019), 605, 608 et seq.
[7] First thoughts by *Freitag* ZHR 184 (2020), 139 et seq.

of systems. From the very beginning, there has been criticism in the literature that the comply-or-explain mechanism under Section 134 b of the German Stock Corporation Act (AktG) is partially ineffectual because the option of justified withholding of information on the company's own participation policy is not permitted for mandatory disclosures by investment funds.[8] The disclosure rules of the Sustainable Finance Disclosure Regulation 2019/2088/EU (SFDR) – the regulatory objective of which is primarily to create market transparency in a steering-neutral manner – have, moreover, further intensified this crowding-out effect. The information required there in Art. 3 et seq. on the fund products offered or advertised also includes information on the influence of the funds on the use of the investments in the portfolio companies. This is particularly evident in Art. 10 (1) UA 1 lit b) SFDR, according to which investment funds as issuers of "light green" or "dark green" fund products, as described in Art. 8–10 SFDR respectively,[9] are subject to an extended disclosure obligation. They include, among other things, disclosures on "information on the methodologies used to assess, measure and monitor the environmental or social characteristics or the impact of the sustainable investments selected for the financial product." When CSR reporting – that already includes all investment companies regardless of their size – [10] is extended to comprehensive "*sustainability reporting*", the previous incentive concept is likely to become obsolete once and for all. This is because the opening for an "explained silence" contained in Art. 19a (1) (2) CSR Directive 2013/34/EU in its current version will then no longer apply as such.[11]

III. Links between fund management (funding governance) and fund unit sales (product governance and financial service governance)

As a regulatory matter, fund governance is closely related to the distribution of fund units, which has been subdivided into a staggered market opening and monitoring procedure since the start of *product governance regulation* by the European Markets in Financial Instruments Directive (MiFiD II). Germany has transposed these directive requirements into national law in the primarily regulatory "Wertpapierhandelsgesetz" (WpHG – German Securities Trading Act). Pursuant to Section 80 (9) WpHG, the market opening – also referred to as "product clearance" – requires a target market determination for graded defined customer groups, which, according to Art. 9 (9) of DelDir 2017/593/EU as amended by Art. 1 No. 2 of the new DelDir 2021/1269/EU, includes the

[8] *Baums* ZHR 183 (2019), 605, 609 with reference to Section 3 Abs. 2 KAVerOV, Art. 37 DelReg 231/2013.

[9] *Hanke* ZIP 2022, 62, 63 et seq.

[10] Cf. Art. 36 (7) Directive 2013/34/EU.

[11] European Commission, Art. 19a the proposal for a new Corporate Sustainability Reporting Directive (CSRD) from 21.4.2021, COM(2021) 189 final.

consideration of "any sustainability-related objectives". However, so-called "*sustainability preferences*" for or against an ESG-compliant investment – as legally defined in Art. 2 No. 7 of DelReg 2017/565/EU – cannot yet be concretely proven in the planning and preparation stage of fund distribution, since customer contact is still lacking that would allow exploration of concrete acquisition interests in the "know-your-customer" procedure. German literature therefore considers equating the "customer interest" to be served with a *typified collective interest*, which is characterized, among other things, by a predefined "sustainability preference" that is abstracted from the level of consideration of the fund investor as the ultimate beneficiary.[12]

As a result of the differentiation between abstract and concrete "sustainability preferences", problems of demarcation and reconciliation arise that, in turn, affect the relationship of product governance regulations with funding management, on the one hand, and with customer business in the retail business markets, on the other. In essence, there are three problem areas:

(1) Investment funds are excluded from the scope of MiFiD II (Art. 2(1)(i) RL 2014/65/EU) and are thus not bound to serve sustainability preferences in the sense of the product governance rules. However, they must accept that the fund units issued by them are distributed as "financial instruments" (Section 2 (4) no. 2 WpHG) in accordance with the requirements of Section 80 (9) to (12) WpHG, so that the as yet unresolved question arises as to whether and to what extent collective investor protection under the product governance rules ultimately has an impact on the content of the funding governance principles at hand.[13]

(2) In the ongoing distribution of fund units upon completion of the formal product release, the product governance rules partly overlap with the so-called *conduct of business rules* in the financial service vis-à-vis the individual fund customer. The assessment and selection criterion of a "generally valid-idealized" sustainability preference takes its place here alongside of a personal sustainability preference, which the "investment firm with the direct client relationship" must clarify by way of the so-called customer exploration ("know your customer") phase and fulfill in order to meet its so-called "ultimate responsible" criteria in the distribution chain (Section 12 (12) of the German Implementing Regulation on Section 80 of the German Securities Trading Act – WpDVerOV; for the EU, Art. 10 (10) DelDir 2017/593). In order to reliably implement this system, a clear distinction would have to be made between the product governance rules in fund unit sales and the service governance rules in the customer business. This distinction has not yet been made in Germany.[14]

---

[12] *Ekkenga* WM 2022, 1765, 1767.
[13] In more detail *Ekkenga* WM 2022, 1765, 1770 et seq.
[14] *Ekkenga* WM 2022, 1765, 1770 et seq.

(3) Insofar as the product governance rules on target market planning and the establishment of distribution channels for implementing this planning are relevant, the aim must be to identify the *supra-individual abstract preferences of the "typical" fund investor.* With regard to the "sustainability-related objectives", a differentiation must be made according to customer groups that apply to a pre-planned target market. In Germany, a lively and often contentious discussion has developed on the determination of such "typical" interests of different customer groups. The traditional model of the rational investor (*homo oeconomicus*) has increasingly receded into the background. Instead of the "investor", the average customer appears as the "buyer" of a financial product, who participates to a large extent in the collective protection rules for consumers of consumer goods and is unable to protect him/herself by making rational decisions (*homo inferior*). "Product governance" was consequently synonymous with unconditional risk avoidance in pursuit of protecting the end customer (behavioral finance) before the onset of the Green Deal.[15] How this ideal-typical customer preference relates to the newly emerging preference of a *homo oecologicus*[16]-oriented investor towards the common good remains a completely open question of systemic importance.

B. Governance Mechanisms at the Intersection of Corporate Governance and Shareholder Governance

I. The concept of management control through the use of voting rights instead of the capital market

From a German perspective, the concept of *management control through the use of voting rights* leads back to the world of thought at the beginning of the last century, which was initially characterized by the idea that the common good of large companies and their financing by long-term committed "entrepreneurial shareholders" were mutually dependent,[17] and which found its legislative end with the reform of stock corporation law in 1965.[18] In view of diverse experiences with the notorious inefficiency of direct shareholder democracy[19], German stock corporation law has always followed the legal idea of dualistic corporate governance, in which the task of management control is shifted to a specialized

---

[15] *Buck-Heeb* BKR 2017, 89, 96 et seq.; *Ekkenga,* in: Festschrift 25 Jahre WpHG, 2019, p. 975, 990.

[16] *Möllers* ZHR 185 (2021), 881, 892.

[17] *Rathenau,* Vom Aktienwesen – Eine geschäftliche Betrachtung, 1917, p. 26 et seq.; in addition *Fleischer* JZ 2017, 991, 992 ff.; *the same.* AG 2017, 509, 516.

[18] *Fleischer* JZ 2017, 991, 993.

[19] From the immense amount of older literature for example *Mertens* AG 1990, 49, 51 et seq.; latest *Weber/Kebekus* ZHR 184 (2020), 324, 331 et seq.

corporate body – the supervisory board – which is elected by the shareholders and represents their protective interests vis-à-vis the management board. In contrast, combating the "rational apathy" of individual shareholders by promoting "*shareholder activism*" at the voting base is a regulatory concept that is particularly suitable for stock corporations with a constitution of monistic association. From the outset, this concept is difficult to reconcile with the supervisory board system because the mediatization of important control functions with the help of a separate control body that is autonomous in its decision-making, is inevitably accompanied by a loss of decision-making authority at the expense of the shareholders' meeting as the decision-making body. In particular, the Annual General Meeting does not have the authority to pass resolutions on operational management matters without a corresponding request from the Executive Board (cf. Section 119 (2) AktG). Under German law, therefore, the mandatory organizational rules stock corporation law (Section 23 (5) AktG) embeds an obstacle in the system for a voting operation with a control and steering effect, which, according to the EU concept of sustainable ownership governance, has an impact right down to the details of management.

Conversely, German law binds the AG management to basic *decision-making prerogatives of the shareholders' meeting*, which fix the external frame of reference of the business operations in the long-term and relate, in particular, to the "corporate purpose" (profit-making or activities serving the common good) and "business purpose" ("Unternehmensgegenstand": e.g. determination of the industry, performance of holding functions) (cf. Section 23 (3) no. 2 AktG). In this respect, a *readjustment of the organs' competences* could become necessary if an attempt is made to escape the direct or indirect constraints of ESG-compliant economic conditions by mediatization techniques, for example, by outsourcing parts of the business that do not comply with the taxonomy to a non-listed subsidiary. The closest solution to this problem would probably be to make the AG-management responsible for ESG-compliant management of the subsidiary. The grounds for broad discourse on the more detailed description and concretization of such group management responsibility has been laid in Germany since the 1980s; this would be a good starting point.[20]

No less urgent is the question – which has not yet been addressed at all in professional circles – of a *readjustment of group management responsibility* in the reverse constellation of a dependency situation in which the listed AG finds itself due to a (public) takeover by an unlisted company. The question is of systemic importance because the financial intermediary – such as an investment fund – would evade its responsibility as the legally appointed ESG control agent by

[20] Basically *Hommelhoff*, Die Konzernleitungspflicht: Zentrale Aspekte eines Konzernverfassungsrechts, 1982.

transferring its shares to a non-ESG main shareholder.[21] For Germany, this could lead to the controlling majority shareholder being obliged to show *special consideration* towards ESG-sensitive minority shareholders. However, this entails the risk of an indirect, creeping extension of the ESG obligation to non-listed companies at the top of the group (including small and medium-sized enterprises = SMEs), which was not intended by the legislator. For Germany, there is also the completely open question of whether there can be a justifying "group interest" of ESG-inconsistent measures and decisions, especially within a contractual group with multiple foreign contacts (cf. Sec. 308 (1) Sentence 2 AktG). Alternatively, consideration should be given to strengthening the minority positions of individual activists, for example, by generously expanding the channels of influence and sources of information needed to maintain the sustainability dialog (see supplementary I., 1).

So far, ESG expectations are completely open to German *credit institutions*, which are explicitly committed to the sustainability objective under supervisory law (Section 25a (1) sentence 3 no. 1 KWG) and which have been counted among the socially responsible players in the financial markets for many decades ("social responsibility").[22] Although they could achieve ESG-beneficial effects through their depositary voting rights – which in Germany give them considerable decision-making leeway by law (Section 135 (3) AktG) – they are not included in the group of controlling agents appointed under EU law. As *lenders*, they exert influence on operational management by contractually ensuring compliance with a wide range of benchmarks – so far mainly with the aim of securing creditworthiness. As the internationally widespread and predominantly standardized contractual terms (covenants) become increasingly intermixed with "*green*" or "*sustainable*" *objectives*, lending practice is increasingly approaching the *earmarks* of "green" bond and project financing.[23] If the signs are not deceptive, this indicates a noticeable, if not fundamental change in previous contractual practice. The scope and depth of the rights of influence recently claimed by banks give rise to the question of whether debt financing on the basis of modern credit covenants is about gradually assuming the regulatory density of "*de facto control agreements*" which, according to German conviction, require shareholder approval due to their far-reaching significance.[24]

---

[21] First thoughts by *Möslein/Sorensen*, Europ.Comp.L. J. 15 (2018), 221, 227 et seq.; continuing *Ekkenga* WM 2020, 1664, 1669.

[22] For this already *Hopt*, Der Kapitalanlegerschutz im Recht der Banken, 1975, p. 526 et seq.

[23] *Kropf* WM 2021, 1017.

[24] Regarding the previous legal situation *Ekkenga*, Handbuch der AG-Finanzierung, 2nd ed., 2019, chapter 15 mn. 292 ff.

II. Extension tendencies based on the "stewardship" doctrine under UK law

Section 134b (1) AktG defines a broad framework of *institutionalized channels of influence* which, in addition to voting behavior of the shareholders, also include investor dialog with the corporate bodies and "stakeholders of the company" (para. 3). The extension picks up on development trends in the modern stewardship debate in the UK.[25] It leaves behind the focus on the participation of the legally appointed financial intermediaries and also includes other "stakeholders" who, according to more modern Anglo-Saxon findings, can be functionaries of an activist participation culture. In Germany, the mandate of monitoring important matters of the portfolio companies which is based on the concept of sustainability via an exchange of opinions with the corporate bodies and stakeholders (Section 134 b (1) nos. 2, 3 AktG), is something completely new. The regulation indicates the privileged granting of exclusive powers of interference ("engagement"), which the financial intermediaries can sensibly only make use of if they gain correspondingly privileged access to non-public and possibly sensitive corporate data. The internal competency structure in the relationship triangle between the management board/supervisory board/shareholders – which is systemic in Germany – will probably have to be completely readjusted as a result, whereby the question also arises as to what position the banks will have inside and outside the shareholder structure in the future (information privilege for banks by virtue of the principle of equal treatment?). The modern stewardship debate goes even further. According to this debate, other lenders (especially green bond creditors) should also be included in the sustainability dialog. Whether this legal idea is compatible with the German concept of a strict separation of powers between the management board, supervisory board and shareholders' meetings seems extremely doubtful. The discussion surrounding this controversy is still in its infancy as such.[26]

III. The (lack of) suitability of investment funds as functionaries of sustainable ownership governance

The assumption underlying the Shareholder Rights Directive that investment funds, as mandate holders of an ESG/SRI-friendly participation policy, are more predestined than other shareholders to intervene in management matters of portfolio companies[27] is the subject of controversial debate in Germany.[28] The

[25] *Davies,* Festschrift Hopt II. (2020), p. 131 et seq.; *Leyens*, Festschrift Hopt II. (2020), p. 709 et seq.

[26] *Roth/Ekkenga* AG 2021, 409 et seq.

[27] EU-Directive 2017/828 recitals 13 and 14.

[28] *Arnold* ZHR 185 (2021), 281 et seq.; *Klöhn* ZHR 185 (2021), 182 et seq.; *Brellochs/Stark* ZHR 185 (2021), 319 et seq.; *Ekkenga* WM 2020, 1664 et seq.

basic conception goes back to common knowledge about numerous efficiency advantages that a collective management of mass collected lot sizes brings with it.[29] What is overlooked is that economies of scale become weaker the more complex the administrative task becomes. Complexity, in turn, increases to the extent that fund management is required to pursue a competent participation policy in the individual portfolio companies beyond the actual portfolio management. This is particularly true for *mutual funds with a highly diversified investment structure*, because the more widely diversified the denomination, the less profitable it is for the fund to invest in the constructive use of voting rights or in accompanying initiatives accordingly; the costs incurred for this increase with the number of portfolio companies, regardless of whether and to what extent the fund is tailored to ESG/SRI-affine companies from the outset. Fund management and ownership governance are thus not compatible objectives; rather, optimizing one necessarily comes at the expense of the other.

The opposing thesis that investment funds are rather unsuitable for association-based participation in the management of the portfolio company is confirmed in German *supervisory law* insofar as the *scope of action institutionally assigned* to funds is not assigned to the real economy, but specifically to the financial economy as such. The Shareholder Rights Directive has not changed this, as can be seen not least from the fact that the matter is located in stock corporation law (instead of in supervisory law for financial service providers).[30] It therefore still applies that the "capital management company … in the performance of its tasks … acts exclusively in the interests of the investors" (cf. Section 26 (1) KAGB). The exercise of voting rights does not make an exception; rather, in accordance with Art. 37 (1) of Delegated Regulation 231/2013, the exclusive primacy of the benefit for the fund and its investors likewise applies here.[31] How this regulatory regime is compatible with the new stock corporation law remains unclear[32]: On the one hand, funds at the association level are explicitly encouraged in the relevant "Analysis Guidelines for General Meetings" specifically to "promote best practice for responsible corporate governance and of SRI/ESG issues …".[33] On the other hand, there has so far been consensus that an institutionalized coupling of the use of voting rights to recommendations of third parties – in particular to those of proxy advisors – is not compatible with

[29] *Köndgen/Schmies,* in: Ellenberger/Bunte, Bankrechts-Handbuch, 6th ed., 2022, sect. 93 mn. 5 et seq.; *Sei*, in: Gehwald/Naumann, Investmentfonds – eine Branche positioniert sich, 2011, p. 13, 17 et seq.

[30] *Baums* ZHR 183 (2019), 605, 609.

[31] In Germany, the regulation applies directly to AIF capital management companies and, by virtue of reference in Section 3 (2) KAVerOV, also to UCITS capital management companies.

[32] A planned coordination between both sets of norms has obviously been neglected, cf. *Baums* ZHR 183 (2019), 605, 609.

[33] BVI, BVI Analysis Guidelines for Annual General Meetings 2020, p. 6 (available online; as of July 2020).

German supervisory law as far as the handling of potential conflicts of interest is concerned.[34] However this debate is pursued in detail, the crucial point is and remains that funds can only fulfill their function as financial intermediaries in any way if – unlike the "anchor shareholders" – they do *not* pursue any operational corporate objectives outside the financial sector (expressly Section 1 (1) KAGB). From a German perspective, therefore, the almost proverbial passivity of the exercise of voting rights by professional investors[35] is not a systemic or developmental error[36] but, on the contrary, a system-supporting element of market-mediating organisms with a capital accumulation function or, more succinctly: the *imperative of real economic neutrality.*

It is not claimed that the investment funds would be entrusted with operational management tasks in their portfolio companies in deviation from this; there is no mention of this in the Agenda, and such a situation is not remotely expected in practice.[37] However, in accordance with the European Directive 2004/25 on takeover bids, German capital market law already qualifies a minority shareholder as the holder of a controlling position with ambitions of domination if he/she continuously coordinates the use of his/her voting rights with those of other members ("Common Ownership") and thus becomes part of a community of interests and actions, provided that shares to the extent of at least 30 % are involved ("*Acting in Concert*", cf. Sections 29 (2) Sentence 1, 30 (2) WpÜG). Nevertheless, the related obligation to acquire all outstanding shares of the portfolio company (Sec. 35 WpÜG) cannot apply to mutual funds because it would be completely incompatible with the requirement of a broad diversification of individual investments (cf. e.g. Sec. 206 KAGB: maximum 5 % of the investment volume per issuer). ESMA has also recognized this. It therefore proposes to consider ways of providing asset managers with a *blanket exemption from the mandatory takeover offer.*[38] From a legal point of view, this would indeed be easy to implement. From a legal ethical point of view, however, it remains unclear why outside shareholders are prevented from exiting at a legally predefined minimum price merely because the shareholder base is largely made up of interacting fund companies (instead of other anchor shareholders).

In Germany, there are more far-reaching concerns about system shifts as a possible consequence of increasing concentration in the shareholder structure, which the institutional demand for common ownership among portfolio share-

[34] *Eckner,* in: Beckmann/Scholtz/Vollmer, Investment, Kennz. 405.1, § 3 KAVerOV mn. 54 with reference of *Zetzsche,* Report of the Chairman of the Best Practice Principles Group Developing the Best Practice Principles for Shareholder Voting Research & Analysis, May 2014; see also Poelzig ZHR 185 (2021), 373 et seq..

[35] So instead of other *Tröger* ZGR 2019, 126, 132 et seq., 137 et seq.

[36] But so *Tröger* ZGR 2019, 126, 136: "Marktversagen"(in English called "Market failure").

[37] Applicable: Monopolkommission, 22. Hauptgutachten 2018, p. 187 (mn. 432); *Weber/Kebekus* ZHR 184 (2020), 324, 350.

[38] ESMA 30-22-762 from 18.12.2019, p. 68 et seq.

holders almost invariably entails.[39] The more voting rights that are pooled or committed to specific objectives, the more the power of the "confederates" grows vis-à-vis the stock corporation, and the more reason the latter has to demand special consideration from the fund companies by virtue of their *fiduciary duty as members*, even below the threshold of corporate law.[40] As a result, however, the funds tend to be forced into the balancing act of representing corporate interests at the issuer level and at the same time looking after the individual interests of their end-beneficiary fund investors. As the Monopolies Commission in Germany recently explained in detail, the two spheres of interest are not only incongruent, but also characterized by the *contrast between unilateral individual returns at the corporate level and multilateral total returns at the fund level.*[41] Since the potential for increasing total return as the object of the "portfolio interest" to be represented by the investment fund is all the greater the more competition unfolds between competing portfolio companies,[42] the funds' loyalty to the policies of individual portfolio companies can thus result in a tangible *conflict of interest* from which neither the EU Action Plan nor the ownership governance rules provide a way out.[43]

C. Core Elements of Sustainable Fund Management in German Law (Fund Governance)

I. (No) "impact funding" by virtue of being tied to a "green" portfolio interest

Under German investment law, positive advertising with "sustainability" remains a voluntary action parameter in the quality competition between individual fund categories with more or less pronounced return or sustainability potential. There is no genuine "green portfolio interest" to which fund management is bound *a priori.*[44] Rather, the investment fund's interests remain bound by the investment conditions (Section 26 (1) KAGB), so that there cannot be an institutionally created conflict of objectives between "ESG" and return without corresponding stipulations in the investment conditions (162 (1) No. 1 KAGB); this is not likely to change in the further course of the "Green Deal". It is true that, according to the supervisory practice of the BaFin, the fund management is obliged to comply

[39] Cf. *Weber/Kebekus* ZHR 184 (2020), 324, 336 et seq.

[40] *Weber/Kebekus* ZHR 184 (2020), 324, 350 et seq.

[41] Monopolkommission, 22. Hauptgutachten 2018, p. 194 et seq. (mn. 462, 463).

[42] Monopolkommission, 22. Hauptgutachten 2018, p. 194 (mn. 462).

[43] For possible complications in terms of antitrust law, see in this connection Monopolkommission, 22. Hauptgutachten 2018, p. 196 et seq. (mn. 470 et seq.).

[44] The term "portfolio interest" originates from the more recent corporate governance discussion and refers to the qualification and substantive weighting of the fund's interests vis-à-vis the interests of the co-shareholders, cf. *Weber/Kebekus* ZHR 184 (2020), 324 et seq.

with certain "sustainability quotas" in the operational funding if there would otherwise be a risk of misleading the investing public in violation of the prohibition (Section 4 (1) KAGB).[45] However, such restrictions are in principle only the *consequence* of a privately autonomously chosen fund label, which becomes particularly clear if the sustainability ratio is explicitly included in the investment conditions or if a "sustainable" index is tracked. In agreement, BaFin only wants to make allocations to the fund category for sustainable investment assets if sustainability aspects constitute "the determining feature in the management of the investment fund".[46] The supervisory goal is not administrative steering, but combating greenwashing as such. In that vein, the financial products designated as "light green" within the meaning of Art. 8 SFDR – which are only advertised "inter alia" with environmental or social features – are not likely to fall under the quota regulation, but the "dark green" products of Art. 9 SFDR, which sustainable investments are explicitly "aimed at", do. With its plans to extend Ecolabel Regulation 66/2010 to fund shares, the EU Commission does not seem to want to touch this primacy of private autonomy.[47]

However, the administrative influence on fund management is noticeably intensified by the official practice of binary allocation of individual funds to a specific fund category, for whose designation BaFin sets binding standards by directive pursuant to Section 4 (2) KAGB.[48] For some time now, BaFin has been considering introducing such a classification for "sustainable investment funds" as well. The consequence would be an obligation for fund managers to comply with a lower limit for the allocation of environmentally and socialy beneficial individual securities for their portfolios qualified as "sustainable", which BaFin would like to assess at 75% of the fund volume.[49] There are similar efforts at the European level, albeit with different minimum thresholds at play.[50] Since

[45] The basis for authorization is Section 307 (7) sentence 1 KAGB.

[46] Cf. BaFin, Draft Directive on Sustainable Investment Funds, Consultation 13/2021, available online, last accessed 22-06-2022 (no longer mentioned in the abridged version of 2.11.2021, however). According to press release from 10.5.2022, BaFin has indeed put the draft directive on hold (available online, last accessed 22-06-2022). At the same time, however, it seems to intend to use the draft as a basis for its supervisory practice under section 5(4) and section 26(2) KAGB. On the function of the Benchmark Regulation in this context, see *Steuer* ZBB/JBB 2022, 31, 33.

[47] For more details, see *Lange* BKR 2020, 261, 270; *Rudkowski/Chrzan/Pott* VersR 2022, 601, 604. DWS, Deutsche Bank's fund subsidiary is also currently accused of greenwashing due to insufficient provision of ESG-appropriate securities in its portfolios; German and U.S. supervisory authorities are currently investigating the company. Details are constantly published on the internet.

[48] So-called "Fondskategorien-Richtlinie," reprinted in *Boxberger*, in: Weitnauer/Boxberger/Anders, KAGB, 3rd ed., 2021, according to Sec. 4 mn. 9.

[49] Cf. BaFin, Draft Guideline for Sustainable Investment Funds, Consultation 13/2021, available on the web, last accessed 22-06-2022 and on this *Tran/Izzo-Wagner* RdF 2022, 16, 17.

[50] According to initial drafts of the European Supervisory Authorities (ESA), funds that are advertised and marketed in the broadest sense under sustainability aspects should have a sus-

any even approximate narrowing of sector diversification favors the emergence of cluster risks,[51] the establishment of rigid sustainability quotas tends to run counter to the hitherto overriding objective of achieving the best possible balance between investment returns and loss risks. Elements of an "impact investing" that is far from the market then become all the more apparent the lower the entry threshold for a green fund classification is set.

Particularly questionable in this context is the allocation to a "green" fund category on the basis of advertising statements over which the fund has no influence and which cannot be attributed to it as a consequence of a privately, autonomously designed distribution system. The classification of fund products "in sales"[52] on the occasion of ESG-related designations raises follow-up questions from this perspective, because "sales" in the legal sense can – pursuant to Section 293 (1) sentence 3 KAGB *e contrario* – also include initiatives of intermediaries, advisors, banks or other third parties who do not act on behalf of the management company or at its instigation. So far, there is a lack of tangible approaches in science and practice as to how this attribution problem can be solved.[53] BaFin has so far not shown any awareness of this issue in its guideline texts. In any case, there is probably a consensus that sustainability quotas imposed on the fund "from outside" must not lead to the original content of the investment conditions being devalued and the "old investors" among the fund holders being ignored as a result.

II. System boundaries

In the diction of the EU Commission, investment funds can only fulfill their role as controlling agents if they align their investment strategy with long-term investments, because short-term commitments provide neither an incentive nor the economic foundation to meaningfully exercise member voting rights. Short-term securities such as listed equities mutate into long-term securities under this investment strategy with the consequence that their circulation in secondary markets is restricted. For fund managers with an active investment strategy, this is characterized by the *non-use of the exit option*,[54] even if this means accepting real price losses and opportunity losses resulting from the omission of profit-taking through short-term selling.[55] In return, the investment fund is rewarded – and

---

tainability quota of approx. 66 % of the fund volume. See *Hanke* ZIP 2022, 62, 69 et seq. with further references.

[51] *Köndgen/Schmies,* in: Ellenberger/Bunte, Bankrechts-Handbuch, 6th ed., 2022, sect. 93 mn. 135 et seq.

[52] So Art. 2 (1) so-called "Fondskategorien-Richtlinie," reprinted by *Boxberger* op. cit fn. 48.

[53] Further *Wallach* ZBB/JBB 2016, 287, 290 et seq.

[54] However, this does not apply to index funds, as exit options are not available to them from the outset, see *Hell* NZG 2019, 338, 340.

[55] *Tröger* ZGR 2019, 126, 144 et seq.

in that process also apparently the calculation of the reform movement – with a "sustainable" return prospect, because ESG-affine engagements will pay off in the long run, while flexible reactions of the fund management to price changes are in doubt, rather, or, in any case likewise favor ESG-averse investments.[56] However, there is no explicit regulation on this complex, and the obligation to restrict from exits can so far only be plausibly explained by its long-term nature as a functional condition of effective ownership governance.

According to the German understanding on the issue, openings for an *ESG/SRI-affine investment strategy* are only available from the outset where the investment conditions specifically permit this. This is because the fund management cannot ignore the fiduciary commitment of the funds to the interests of their fund clients, which is agreed in the *investment contract*.[57] In Germany, this is the starting point of a fundamental criticism that focuses on the insufficient differentiation between individual fund types. The new regulation tacitly favors tradable *index funds* (also: ETFs) whose investment strategy consists in the faithful reproduction of a predefined and basically unchangeable basket composition (indexing) and for which, as a result, the exit option is not open from the outset.[58] *Actively managed investment funds* are thus at a disadvantage, because their business thrives precisely on the fact that they try to beat the index through continuous stock picking and frequent rebalancing, thereby gaining a competitive advantage over passively managed index funds.[59] There is therefore reason to believe that the trend of increasing domination of the markets for fund shares by investment funds with a static investment structure – which has been observed for some time anyway – will intensify even further, coupled with the negative consequences for competition in the performance markets[60] and for the functioning of securities trading respectively.

In view of the undisputed importance of professional investors as functionaries and guarantors of smooth securities trading, the *planned prioritization of long-term investments* by European law represents nothing less than a turning point in economic history as such. For the first time, a set of rules is being sought and, in some cases, already in place, which aims to restrict short-term trading movements and is thus ultimately directed *against* the market-controlling price elasticity of supply and demand. The looming consequences have already been visible for some time in the increasing spread of passively managed index funds

[56] For this *Roe*, Stock Market Short-Termism's Impact, European Corporate Governance Institute (ECG) – Law Working Paper No. 426/2018 – Harvard Public Law Working Paper No. 18–28; *Strand,* 22 (2015) Colum.J.Eur.L. p. 15, 59 *Gorman,* 72 (2017) N. Y. U. Ann. Surv. Am. L. 113; krit. Critical from a German perspective *Freitag* AG 2014, 647, 648.

[57] For this *Bueren* ZGR 2019, 813, 847 et seq.

[58] *Weber/Kebekus* ZHR 184 (2020), 324, 333; *Klöhn* ZHR 185 (2021), 182, 188.

[59] *Köndgen/Schmies*, in: Ellenberger/Bunte, Bankrechts-Handbuch, 6th ed., 2022, sect. 93 mn. 22.

[60] For this vividly *Weber/Kebekus* ZHR 184 (2020), 324, 338 et seq.

(ETFs)[61] and the displacement of actively managed mutual funds brought about by the new rules: As fixed platforms of a long-term investment *without* an exit option, ETFs reduce[62] the quantity of circulating shares (free float), which favors the trend toward price-distorting market constrictions and the danger of erratic price fluctuations.[63] The massive price plunge on "Black Monday", i. e. August 24, 2015, which led to epochal collapses of globally leading stock indices, is attributed by experts among others, to the triumph of ETFs.[64]

For the day-to-day business of actively managed investment funds, the forecast is that the systematic and widespread prevention or obstruction of short-term buying and selling decisions will noticeably weaken the *liquidity of secondary trading* – with the foreseeable risk that the supply dynamic will gradually freeze and the increasing market tightening will lead to mispricing, which will, in turn, have a direct impact on the redemption value of units in open-ended investment funds to the detriment of fund investors via price discounts. Meanwhile, the German legislator consistently requires a special review of the net asset valuation per share (Section 168 (1), (2) KAGB), among other instances, when organized share trading no longer has sufficient liquidity left to be able to generate meaningful stock exchange prices (Section 169 (3) KAGB in conjunction with Art. 71 (2) lit. b) DelReg 231/2013). If the volatility of the underlyings increases as a result of progressive market tightening, ETF investors will also feel the consequences, in the form of higher risk premiums which reduce the selling prices.[65] If – as is often the case – notoriously inflated prices are mapped due to stagnation, this could be reflected in equally inflated subscription offers for new issues, with the result that the allocation mechanism of organized markets for individual stocks would be undermined across the board.

D. Core Elements of Sustainable Fund Unit Sales in German Law (Product Governance)

I. Product approval and monitoring of sustainable financial instruments

The regulations on formal product approval and monitoring in fund shares sales date back to the Second European Financial Markets Directive 2014/65/EU

[61] See German Federal bank, monthly report Oct. 2018, p. 83 et seq.

[62] This refers to physically replicating ETFs as opposed to synthetically replicating funds, see *Glander/Mayr*, in: Baur/Tappen/Mehrkhah/Behme, Investmentgesetze, 4th ed., 2019, sect. 206 KAGB mn. 4.

[63] In addition from more recent times *Hilton/Möller/Doering* CF 2019, 278, 281 with further references.

[64] Cf. *Feldschmid*, Kritik an ETFs – gerechtfertigt?, https://investmentsparen.net/blog/news/5862-kritik-an-etfs-gerechtfertigt/ (05.09.2023).

[65] *Hilton/Möller/Doering* CF 2019, 278, 285.

(MiFiD II). Under the impact of the financial crisis as a result of the "Lehman Brothers" bank insolvency, the original intention was to drive speculative financial products with a particularly high risk content out of the market. Even the creators of a financial product, as so-called "conceptual designers", are obliged under the terms of Section 63 (4) and Section 80 (9) and (11) of the German Securities Trading Act (WpHG) to preconfigure distribution channels for "customer groups" described as models and, depending on the "product design", to define suitable target markets for which the financial product is then released for distribution after formal review. Further gatekeepers are the "sales companies", which are responsible for continuously monitoring product sales in cooperation with the concept developer for compliance with the target specifications and planned market limits and for reacting with defensive and safeguarding measures in the event that certain market barriers are breached (Section 63 (5), Section 80 (10), (12) WpHG[66]). The original purpose was thus the classic protection of investors – albeit in a previously unknown radical fashion – namely on the basis of maximum protection requirements, which are borrowed from the idea of consumer protection law and consistently abstract from the individual protection requirements of the concretely affected capital market participants (investor protection as "collective consumer protection").[67] The sustainability criterion, on the other hand, has so far only been mentioned in passing in BaFin's German administrative guidelines.[68]

This is likely to change in the foreseeable future, because under the new regime of two delegated EU acts from 2021, the coordinates in the previous governance system have shifted in an almost spectacular way. Protecting the clumsy public investor from excessive risk of loss is no longer the only, not even the priority governance criterion in this equation. In addition to the investor-protecting "danger prevention," a positive design objective has now been added, namely featuring the servicing of the *sustainability preferences* already mentioned in the introduction under I, 3. This refers to the individual decision of the customer or potential customer as to whether and to what extent he/she is primarily interested in financial instruments with sustainable promotion potential in the broadest sense (Art. 2 No. 7 DelReg 2017/565/EU as amended by Art. 1 No. 1 DelReg 2021/1253/EU with reference, inter alia, to the legal definition of "sustainable investment(s)" in Art. 2 No. 17 SFDR).[69] The fact that the decision

[66] In-depth *Ekkenga,* in: MünchKommHGB, Vol. 6. Bankvertragsrecht, 4th ed., 2019, mn. 86 et seq.

[67] *Ekkenga* loc. cit. mn. 4, 87

[68] No. 5.2.1. no. 6 no. 5 der "Mindestanforderungen an die Compliance-Funktion und weitere Verhaltens-, Organisations- und Transparenzpflichten" i. S. d. §§ 63 ff. WpHG für Wertpapierdienstleistungsunternehmen", so-called MaComp.

[69] The term "potential" customer is likely to mean the prospective investor during the contract initiation phase, not the "target customer" as defined by the product release and monitoring rules.

can theoretically also turn out against a "green" investment is not thereby denied; however, negative sustainability preferences may be ignored when modeling customer groups in the context of target planning.[70] As a further consequence, a fund product with a high sustainability factor can be prioritized in product sales even if it yields suboptimal returns. This is true regardless of whether a prior customer survey would reveal that the customer prioritizes his/her return goals over public common goals. This is because "sales" within the meaning of the product governance rules only means the marketing of fund shares by the provider (cf. Section 293 (1) sentence 1 KAGB). The rules on individual customer exploration ("know your customer") developed for financial services on behalf of customers, on the other hand, are directed at securities service companies (§ 63 (10), § 64 (3) WpHG) and are generally not applicable to fund companies and their sales intermediaries[71] (for more details, see below under II.).

In Art. 9 (9) and Art. 10 (2) of the DelDir 2017/593/EU in the version of the new Art. 1 No. 2, a. and No. 3 a) RL 2021/1269/EU, the EU Commission even goes one step further by classifying "sustainability" fundamentally higher than "risk avoidance". With this step, the negative selection of "unsuitable" customers or financial products to be carried out in the context of target market determination and sales planning is overridden "where financial instruments consider sustainability factors". In plain language, this means that financial products with a particularly high risk factor should also be sold to unsuitable customers, provided that this promotes sustainable finance. The steering effect is not expressed here in the form of a market restriction, but in the form of a *market opening for comparatively low-yield and/or high-risk financial instruments* from the production of ESG-affine issuers. The residual value of traditional, consumer-oriented customer protection in product approval and monitoring will then depend on how the extremely broad *legal definition of the term "sustainability factor"* in Art. 2 No. 24 SFDR is dealt with in the future. It is to be expected that the further discussion will be decisively shaped by the answer to this still completely open key question.[72]

II. Inclusion of fund shares in the ESG-oriented product release and monitoring procedure?

At first sight, however, investment funds whose sponsors are excluded from the scope of MiFiD II (Art. 2 (1) lit. i) RL 2014/65/EU) do not seem to be affected by the product release and monitoring rules at all. In line with this, Section 3 (1) sentence 1 no. 18 WpHG clarifies that investment funds are not "investment

[70] Cf. the Commission's wording in recital 7 of DelDir 2021/1269/EU.
[71] Applicable *Wallach* ZBB/JBB 2016, 287, 290 et seq.
[72] Similar *Waschbusch/Kiszka/Runco* BKR 2021, 609, 612.

service providers" and consequently do not belong to the group of addressees of "conceptors" as defined in Section 80 (9), (11) WpHG (= "manufacturers" within the meaning of the Delegated Directive 2017/593/EU), nor to that of sales intermediaries as defined in Section 80 (10), (12) WpHG.[73] As confirmed by sect. 5 (2) KAGB with its reference to sect. 20 (2), (3) KAGB on the one hand and to § 80 WpHG on the other hand, this applies equally to mutual funds (UCITs) and to alternative investment funds (AIF) *unless* the sponsoring company is also engaged in customer service, in particular, in investment advice or financial portfolio management. However, a closer look reveals that fund shares – which are all covered by the catalog of "financial instruments" within the meaning of the WpHG (Sect. 2 (4) No. 2 WpHG) – may well be subject to product release and monitoring obligations under EU law. The Directive in Art. 10 (2) UA 3 of the DelDir 2017/593/EU leaves no doubt about this. According to this Directive default, investment funds that are not subject to Directive 2014/65/EU (MiFiD II) must also carry out target market planning – not *de jure* (by law), but *de facto* (in fact) – because the respective investment firms involved in product distribution (Art. 1 (1) of the DelDir 2017/593/EU) are dependent on the corresponding input.[74]

E. Core Elements of Sustainable Customer Service in German Law (Financial Service Governance)

I. Customer service by financial advisors and distributors

Under German law, the same rules of conduct apply to *financial advisors acting on behalf of clients* as they are obliged to perform their services in the best interests of the client (Section 63 (1) WpHG). A core element of financial advice is to provide the client with the best possible information so that the client is able to make his or her purchase decision on an informed basis (Section 63 (7) sentence 1 WpHG). Since the financial advisor is required to act in accordance with the specific preferences expressed by the client (know your customer, Section 63 (10), Section 64 (3) WpHG), the financial advisor acts as an intermediary in a market-supporting and steering-neutral capacity, providing the publicly available data for specific applications and thus contributing to *individual publicity* that promotes transparency.[75] Pursuant to Art. 6 (2) SFDR, the provision of in-

[73] *Kumpan*, in: Schwark/Zimmer, KMRK, 5th ed., 2020, sect. 3 WpHG mn. 58.

[74] *Winkel*, in: Krimphove, MaComp, 3rd ed. 2021, BT 5.3.7. under mn. 73; *Busch* WM 2017, 409, 410; *Lercara/Kittner* RdF 2018, 100, 104; other opinion wrongly *Bley* WM 2018, 162, 166.

[75] Discord cf. instead of others *Zahrte*, in: MünchKommHGB, Vol. 6: Bankvertragsrecht, 4th ed., 2019, mn. 3 with further references.

formation must relate, among other things, to the consideration or relevance of *sustainability risks* within the meaning of Art. 2 No. 22 SFDR.

A second core element of financial advice, as underlined by the legal definition in Section 2 (8) No. 10 of the German Securities Trading Act (WpHG), consists of making selection decisions with the aim of providing the customer with a *purchase recommendation*. Recommendations generate market-opening effects, for example, when they are directed toward the purchase of ESG-compatible financial products that would not be a resounding market success from a return perspective. The counterpart to the market-opening recommendation is the market-closing *issuance of warnings*. In Germany, such warnings have always been an integral part of the advisor's duties under the general rules of conduct (Section 63 (10) sentence 3 WpHG). They have the effect of narrowing the market, for example, when they force profitable financial instruments out of trading because they are not "sustainable" enough. Financial advice thus becomes a mixture of functions, consisting of elements of information provision and gatekeeping.

Although information duties of the sales companies are not mentioned expressively in the new version of Art. 54 DelReg 2017/565/EU, they can be derived without constraint from Art. 10 (10) of the DelDir 2017/593/EU, which has been implemented into German law in Sec. 12 (12) WpDVerOV.[76] According to this clause, the "ultimate responsibility" for compliance with the capital market product monitoring regulations is imposed on the so-called "final distributor" with direct customer contact. Previously, the end distributor had to issue warnings in order to protect customers with low risk tolerance from acquiring speculative financial securities.[77] A purchase request expressed nevertheless may be served, but is subject to increased due diligence and justification requirements.[78]

Under the new regime, on the other hand, the end distributor will probably have no choice but to warn its customers against acquiring fund shares that have an opportunity/risk profile suitable for them personally, but which do not fit the range of products offered by a target market for customers with a high sustainability preference due to a lack of sufficient ESG proximity. The resulting increase in barriers to market entry is based – and this is, incidentally, a significant, albeit little-noticed difference from investment advice – not on the individually adjusted sustainability preference of the customer as a product buyer, but on the sustainability preference of the "catalog customer" developed in the product planning and approval process, as the product providers are obliged to model the

[76] On the invalidity of this regulation, however, see above under C. II.

[77] Cf. above under C. II, as well as on the duty to warn and inform as an element of product distribution monitoring *Ekkenga* loc. cit. mn. 97, 421.

[78] For details, see *Winkel*, in: Krimphove, MaComp, 3rd ed., 2021, section BT 5.3.6. mn. 66 et seq. with reference to the European guidelines of ESMA, there also on the – practically little used – planning of so-called "negative" target markets with a selection function.

catalog customer as such. In his/her capacity as "ultimately responsible party", the final distributor therefore does not act in pursuit of *concrete individual* customer interests, but as a "gatekeeper" in product marketing, i. e. as a trustee of the fund issuer and its sales companies in the mission to implement the sales plans designed in the *common good.* The situation is similar, *mutatis mutandis* with the issuance of forced recommendations of sustainable financial instruments. From the perspective of the end distributor, they are not acquisition recommendations in retail customer service, but advertising measures in the interest of the product providers. In German practice, the term "advisory-free (customer) business" has become established specifically for this purpose.[79]

Up to now, however, the success parameters in sales and customer service have been characterized by a certain synchronization, so that the potential for conflict contained therein seemed manageable. That is, a financial product with an opportunity/risk profile predefined by planners can only be successfully marketed if the customers' desired returns are met over the medium to long-term. Service offers which do not correspond to this will fall victim to performance-based selection and, in case of doubt, make way for "independent fee-based investment advice" (Section 64 (1) No. 1 WpHG), which is not integrated into the sales organizations.[80] Capital market law supports this allocation process primarily by requiring the service providers concerned to disclose potential sources of conflict in good time (Section 63 (2) WpHG).[81] With the addition of the sustainability criterion as a potentially conflicting target variable, however, the two-sided functional relationship of the end distributors involved in providing advice now expands into a completely new type of *functional conglomerate*: from now on, their task is not only to serve the marketing interests of issuers and the return interests of investors simultaneously, but also – on some meta-level – to act as trustees of potentially incompatible, in some cases even conflicting interests of the common good. The conflicting goals of "sales success versus ESG" and "return success versus ESG" will thus become part of the financial service system of the future.

II. Possible recipes for resolving conflicts of interest

Financial advisors, who by virtue of their involvement in product distribution are subject to a product monitoring obligation and bear "ultimate responsibility" for the trouble-free operation of "green" or "socially beneficial" distribution channels, will, in future, have to answer the fundamental question of how they can nevertheless satisfy the rules of conduct in the individual interests of their

---

[79] *Ekkenga,* in: MünchKommHGB, Vol. 6 Bankvertragsrecht, 4th ed., 2019, mn. 324.
[80] *Ekkenga* loc.cit. mn. 135.
[81] In detail *Ekkenga* loc. cit. mn. 383 ff., 458 et seq.

commissioning clients. How this balancing act can be achieved is still a matter of debate in Germany.[82] The technical discussion has hardly begun, and the time is not yet ripe for the development of detailed proposals. Initial attempts at approximation may start with the recognized rules of conduct on the management of conflicts of interest in the securities client business. Possible solutions include conflict avoidance, conflict disclosure and conflict resolution at the discretion of the parties involved.[83]

Pursuant to Art. 34 (2) lit. b DelReg 2017/565/EU, Sec. 80 (1) No. 2 WpHG, the sales company shall primarily strive to *avoid conflicts*. It could consist of the distribution company tailoring its *sales strategy* to target customers with little or no positive sustainability preference by limiting its customer service to order execution without advice.[84] It could then concentrate on return and risk aspects as part of the upstream customer exploration pursuant to Section 63 (10) WpHG and would be relieved of the obligation of having to entice the customer – contrary to his/her conviction – into a capital investment that may have a low return but is ESG-compatible. At the same time, the distributor would fulfill its product monitoring obligation, which requires to regularly review the suitability of the sales strategy for reaching the target market (Section 80 (10) sentence 2 WpHG).[85] This last provision must consequently also apply to target markets that address rather ESG-averse customers. The distributor does not have to carry out such target planning, but is not prevented from doing so either.[86]

The alternative is some kind of "imposed advisory service": the sales strategy is narrowed down to offers to customers who are prepared to accept ESG-related recommendations from the distributor and, as it were, to be checked for an "appropriate", i.e. positive, sustainability preference. The way to achieve this is through the establishment and exclusive use of ESG-compliant distribution channels for customer groups with a clearly pronounced sustainability preference, excluding non-advisory business, but including order execution (execution only). In its most consistent form, this concept would have the consequence that the advising sales company – in order to be able to fulfill its product monitoring obligation pursuant to Section 80 (10) sentence 2 WpHG – would have to refuse

[82] See *Krohn*, Nachhaltige Unsicherheit, FAZ from 19.7.2022, p. 23.

[83] *Ekkenga*, in: MünchKommHGB, Vol. 6 Bankvertragsrecht, 4th ed., 2019, mn. 458 with further references.

[84] According to the target market concept of the leading professional associations, the following can be selected for the sale of fund shares: investment advice, advice-free business within the meaning of section 63(10) of the Wertpapierhandelsgesetz (WpHG – German Securities Trading Act), and execution-only (section 63(11) of the WpHG), see Minimum Standard loc. cit. fn. 38 p. 7; also *Winkel*, in: Krimphove, MaComp, 3rd ed. 2021, BT 5.3.5. mn. 63.

[85] According to the ESMA Guidelines Product Governance of 2.6.2017, 35-43-620, no. 49, the distribution company must place a "main focus" on the distribution strategy, see *Winkel*, in: Krimphove, MaComp, 3rd ed. 2021, BT 5.3.5. mn. 62.

[86] Recital 7 of DelDir 2021/1269/EU, see above under C. II.

the sale of high-yield but ESG-remote securities if it did not succeed in wringing the concession of an improved sustainability preference from the customer. This approach, which amounts to *conflict resolution* through mandatory self-restraint by the investment service provider[87], is likely to correspond most closely to the new fundamental idea of sustainable product marketing as expressed in Art. 9 (9) and Art. 10 (2) of DelDir 2017/593/EU. In contrast, the neutral solution of a *conflict disclosure*, which is subsidiarily permitted in Art. 34 para. 4 DelReg 2017/565/EU, Sec. 63 para. 2 sentence 1 WpHG, is likely to be ruled out from the outset. It would amount to making the prospective buyer aware of possible losses in return as a consequence of a primarily ESG-affine investment strategy. The incentives thus conveyed would be good for capital market function protection[88], but would ultimately go against the spirit of the green deal narrative.

[87] To this aspect *Ekkenga*, in: MünchKommHGB, Vol. 6 Bankvertragsrecht, 4th ed., 2019, mn. 458.

[88] *Ekkenga* loc. cit. mn. 3.

Country Report Austria

Philipp Fidler / Martin Winner

A. Introduction

In Austria, a comprehensive discussion of ESG-regulation ("environmental – social – governance") has yet to emerge. In fact, corporate governance in general is not a highly debated topic within the academic community. Typically, a discussion of contemporary issues of corporate governance evolves with a certain delay and, in most cases, only after German literature has pointed out the problem. Hence, the Austrian debate mostly relies on impulses from the German corporate governance debate. This is also true for the current developments regarding the ESG-criteria, especially on whether and to what extent these criteria can be integrated into the corporate governance of public companies. Moreover, institutional investors have not been in the spotlight of the national academic discussion either – at least up to now. Maybe this status quo will change in the future. However, as of today, Austrian investment law remains a blind spot in academic research and cannot build on much preliminary work to speak of. This is mirrored by a reluctance to address regulatory issues, apart from the necessary transposition of directives by the European Union (EU). We aim to fill this gap in research and provide further studies, starting with this report.

In sum, there is neither a literary debate on sustainable governance in Austria, nor, ostensibly, any intention on the part of the national legislator to advance the issue on its own. To the extent that the EU has not enacted relevant legislation, there are no national ESG-specific rules to complement them – with the (small) exception of the (revised) Austrian Corporate Governance Code from January 2021, whose Preamble states that the "Governance Code aims to establish a system of management and control of companies and groups that is accountable and is geared to creating sustainable, long-term value".[1] Furthermore, Austria lacks a soft law "Stewardship Code" that explicitly addresses institutional investors. The development in Austria, if any, is thus still predominantly market-driven.

For the purposes of this country report, we will focus on selected issues of sustainable governance. Our topics focus on "shareholder governance" and

[1] Austrian Code of Corporate Governance, January 2021, p. 9 (preamble); https://www.corporate-governance.at/uploads/u/corpgov/files/code/corporate-governance-code-012021.pdf (24 October 2023).

"fund governance". In our view, the ESG-compliant governance strategies have to fit the specific market framework and the predominant governance model in a given jurisdiction in order to be successful. Otherwise, the legislator cannot successfully address the steering of capital and the subsequent use of those funds in a (portfolio) company. Given that backdrop, we will first start by providing an overview of the characteristics of the Austrian capital market (B.). We go on to address the main topics of this country report, namely the legal framework for sustainable ownership and shareholder governance (C.) and sustainable funding and fund governance (D.).

B. Market Framework for Sustainable Governance (ESG)

I. Size and Depth of the Austrian Capital Market

The Austrian capital market is very small. In November 2022, the Vienna Stock Exchange listed 63 companies on the regulated market. The market capitalization of these companies was about €137.35 billion in June 2022; the market capitalization of the companies included in the ATX, the Vienna Exchange's main index, stood at about €110.27 billion.[2] The market capitalization in 2020 corresponded to about 30.49 % of Austria's GDP.[3] For comparison: Denmark, a much smaller country than Austria by population and, correspondingly, with a smaller economy as measured by GDP, nonetheless has a market capitalization of about $460.01 billion[4] – more than three times of the Vienna Stock Exchange. The weak performance of the equity market is a characteristic element of the Austrian economy, albeit hardly worthy of imitation. It is the historic outcome of a largely bank-driven funding system for companies. Hence, any instrument trying to propagate ESG investment via capital market regulation will have less impact on the Austrian economy than on other markets with deeper securities markets.

In addition to the low market capitalization of the Vienna Stock Exchange, the Austrian capital market also has a particularly concentrated shareholder structure in comparison with other countries. According to a study by the OECD, the three largest shareholders of a listed company jointly hold more than 60 % of the shares on average.[5] According to another study, more than 80 % of

[2] https://de.statista.com/statistik/daten/studie/1019266/umfrage/marktkapitalisierung-der-im-atx-notierten-unternehmen/ (24 October 2023). Similar figures come from the World Bank: market capitalization in 2020 at approximately $132.08 billion; www.theglobaleconomy.com/rankings/stock_market_capitalization_dollars/Europe (24 October 2023); see also *De La Cruz/Medina/Tang*, Owners of the World's Listed Companies, OECD Capital Market Series, 2019, 8, Table 2: Market capitalization in 2017 at approximately $150.04 billion.

[3] www.theglobaleconomy.com/rankings/Stock_market_capitalization/Europe (24 October 2023).

[4] *De La Cruz/Medina/Tang* (fn. 2), 8, Table 2.

[5] *De La Cruz/Medina/Tang* (fn. 2), 19, Figure 19.

listed companies in Austria are considered to be controlled entities – typically with non-financial companies, the state or private individuals (so-called "family companies") as controlling entities.[6] This high degree of equity concentration is especially striking when compared to the ownership structure in countries like the USA and the UK, which operate the most liquid capital markets in the world. Typically, non-dominant shareholders hold the majority of the shares, although more recently even those countries experience a trend towards more equity concentration on account of the notorious rise in institutional ownership and investors.[7] The impression that one or more core shareholders typically exert control over an Austrian company is also consistent with what regulators (e.g., Austrian Takeover Commission or the Financial Markets Authority) are observing in practice. In Austria, the only listed company which can be considered as a "Berle-Means-Corporation" is Wienerberger AG – 100 % of whose shares are in free float.[8] This type of company, however, is an exception; as already pointed out, the free float of Austrian public companies only amounts to 40–50 % on average.

It follows from the concentrated shareholder structure that the management of the company (executive and supervisory board) cannot determine the investment process of a public company without the influence of third parties. Rather, core shareholders with strategic interests in the company have immense influence on their decisions. Hence, the opportunities for institutional investors as "ESG activists" are rather limited if the core shareholder or the controlling shareholder group does not support the initiative.[9] The controlling shareholders can use their influence within the company to counteract any attempt at "sustainable shareholder activism". However, there is currently no data available on whether the concentrated equity structure actually hinders the implementation of the ESG-agenda in Austrian public companies.

II. Composition of the Free Float

Not every shareholder is meant to be involved in the corporate agenda. If the shareholders lack knowledge about the management and needs of the company, the specifics of its financial situation or whether their stake is high enough, then there is no reason to believe that these shareholders will use their voting rights or their influence to enforce the ESG-agenda. At this point, we do not consider

---

[6] *Aminadav/Papaioannou*, Corporate Control around the World, Journal of Finance 75 (2020), 1191, 1209 and Table I (1205 et seq.). See also *Gugler/Peev/Winner*, Austria, in Gugler/Peev (eds.), The European Corporation: Ownership and Control after 25 Years of Corporate Governance Reforms (2023) 55.

[7] See *De La Cruz/Medina/Tang* (fn. 2), 20 et seq.

[8] www.wienerberger.com/de/investoren/aktie.html (24 October 2023).

[9] See *Taufner*, Aktionärsaktivismus in Österreich, Österreichisches Bankarchiv 2020, 690 (691).

the controlling shareholder, who exerts his influence in the company on a regular basis, but rather the type of shareholder who primarily considers his stake as a financial investment. As for this type of shareholder, conventional wisdom holds that institutional investors are generally more suitable for shareholder engagement than retail investors, who have no incentive to bear the costs of that engagement or probably could not do so even if they wanted to. The – presumably – greater knowledge and bigger financial resources on the part of institutional investors and asset managers are also the underlying rationale for the latest EU regulation, which assumes that they are better equipped to intervene in the company's business than retail shareholders (more detailed in Section III.). It follows then that the composition of the free float matters just as much as its size and the size of the capital market in general.

The available data shows that the Austrian capital market follows the international trend of a steady rise in institutional ownership. In 2020, Austrian private investors (retail) held only 19 % of the free float of companies listed on the ATX Prime.[10] Domestic non-financial companies held just under 14 %. In contrast, institutional investors held more than 66 % of the entire free float.[11] The vast majority of institutional investors comes from abroad – the statistically most important domiciles are the USA (just over 28 %) and the UK (just under 16 %). Hence, these two countries dominate the Austrian free float. In contrast, the share of Austrian institutional investors has fallen steadily in recent years to just under 17 % of the total free float in 2020 (of which 9 % are investment funds, 5 % banks and 3 % insurance companies).

The Austrian fund industry thus plays only a minor role on the domestic capital market. Although domestic mutual funds are the largest group of institutional investors in Austria when compared to insurances and banks, its share of free float market capitalization in the ATX Prime is still only around 5.9 %. By contrast, institutional investors from the UK and the USA together hold just under 35 % of market capitalization.

The data indicates that an EU-wide regulation of engagement by institutional investors for sustainable governance may not have substantial effects on the Austrian capital market, since a significant number of institutional investors are domiciled outside the EU, including the UK in the post Brexit-era. If European legislation overly relies on institutional investors as "active ESG agents on behalf of the public", there is a serious chance that the regulatory framework will miss

---

[10] The ATX Prime is a private-law market segment of the Vienna Stock Exchange and is designed as an "all-share index"; the index is composed of all securities listed in the prime market segment.

[11] https://www.wienerborse.at/listing/aktien/investoren/institutionelle-investoren-und-oesterreichische-aktien/?c16842%5Bfile%5D=ycv1ZbiZQALzbAyRmVt0kw&cHash=ec0ff8d4f9a310e692764e35a8c5526e (24 October 2023). All data in the following paragraphs is taken from this report.

most of its targets, at least in Austria. This conclusion seems to apply to most of the other member states as well. However, it seems that this is hard to remedy for the EU as the scope of EU-wide regulation is limited, leaving little space for extraterritorial effects for investors who are incorporated outside of the European Economic Area.

III. Investment Strategy of Institutional Investors and Asset Managers

Institutional Investors and Asset Managers are not a homogenous group but rather pursue different – and sometimes radically different – investment strategies. Again, not all of these strategies are suitable for pursuing the ESG-agenda. As the latter, according to the European Commission, is construed as a long-time engagement plan for shareholders, it generally requires institutional investors to pursue a long-term investment strategy for portfolio companies. Hence, institutional investors must not make use of the "exit" option but must instead use "voice" for the EU's ideas to come into fruition. Short-term "buy-and-sell" strategies – an investment strategy chosen by many actively managed hedge funds – are not compatible with this idea.

A rough proxy for the dominant investment strategy on the Austrian capital market is found in the categories "index"[12], "growth"[13] and "value".[14] Those are the three most-followed strategies by institutional investors, at least on the Austrian market. "Index investors" amount to 22.6 % of institutional ownership, "growth investors" to 30.5 % and "value investors" to 30.7 %.[15] A second indicator for the investment strategy is the turnover rate of shares held by institutional investors. The turnover rate is predominantly either moderate (40.5 %) or low (52.2 %). As a result, the majority of institutional investors have a low turnover rate, which indicates the potential for a long-term and ESG-compliant investment strategy. While the extent to which institutional investors with a purely passive investment strategy ("index trackers") contribute to this percentage is not broken down, one would nevertheless expect the tendency for their investment horizon to be long-term.

[12] "Index" means an investment strategy which strives to match the performance of an equity index (e.g., the MSCI EAFE Index or the S&P 500), while at the same time keeping trading costs at a minimum.

[13] "Growth" investors place the greatest emphasis in their selection process on the growth prospects of a company's earnings.

[14] "Value-oriented" investors prefer stocks that are trading at undervalued levels relative to some valuation such as a stock's intrinsic value. Value-investors tend to have longer-term investment horizons.

[15] https://www.wienerborse.at/listing/aktien/investoren/institutionelle-investoren-und-oesterreichische-aktien/?c16842%5Bfile%5D=ycv1ZbiZQALzbAyRmVt0kw&cHash=ec0ff8d4f9a310e692764e35a8c5526e (24 October 2023).

A basic precondition for ESG-compliant influence on corporate policy would be therein satisfied. However, it is not possible to say with certainty whether this potential for ESG-compliant investment strategies is significant on the Austrian capital market.

IV. Investment Funds with Sustainable Investment Strategies

The current regulatory approach of the EU tries to shift capital to companies with a sustainable business strategy. Moreover, consumers direct their preferences more and more towards investment funds that choose an ESG-compatible investment strategy. The beneficiaries of these funds expect asset managers to actively monitor their portfolio companies on whether their business strategies comply with the ESG-agenda. Investment Funds with sustainable investment strategies are likely to play a key role in the EU Commission's regulatory plans.

The Austrian market for such investment funds – while generally remaining small – reached historic highs in 2021.[16] As of December 31, 2021, the volume of "sustainable investments" amounts to a total of €63 billion.[17] This sum corresponds to a year-over-year increase of 62 %. For the definition of "sustainable investments", the authors of the study followed the classification of the Disclosure-Regulation.[18] Hence, mutual and special funds, which fulfil the criteria according to Art. 8 and 9 Disclosure-Regulation, are classified as sustainable investments. Furthermore, the study adds customers' deposits in sustainable banks to the overall sum of sustainable investments. However, mutual and special funds are responsible for most sustainable investments made in Austria, with an overall sum of €61.42 billion, which marks a year-over-year increase of 61 %.[19] From this sum, €38.39 billion were held by mutual funds, and €23.03 billion by special funds.[20] For comparison, the overall market of the Austrian funds industry amounts to €218.8 billion. Thus, sustainable mutual and special funds have a 28.2 % share of the overall market, which means that almost every third Euro invested in Austrian funds is subject to sustainable investment.

Sustainable mutual and special funds use different investment strategies in order to pick financial instruments or securities according to the ESG-criteria. Those strategies employed by management companies or asset managers are largely the same. For example, 99 % of all sustainable investment funds apply a strategy of "exclusion criteria", which means that asset managers systematically exclude certain companies, sectors or countries from their investment deci-

---

[16] Forum Nachhaltige Geldanlagen, Marktbericht Nachhaltige Geldanlagen, 2022, 20.

[17] Forum Nachhaltige Geldanlagen (fn. 16), 20.

[18] Regulation (EU) 2019/2088 on sustainability related disclosures in the financial services sector.

[19] Forum Nachhaltige Geldanlagen (fn. 16), 22.

[20] Forum Nachhaltige Geldanlagen (fn. 16), 21.

sions.[21] In 2021, the most common exclusion criterion is carbon, followed by human right abuses, violation of employment rights and companies active in the armaments, tobacco, alcohol or gambling industries.[22] Another common investment strategy is norm-based screening, which ranks second among the investment funds industry and is used for 96% of all mutual and special funds in Austria.[23] Norm-based screening means that asset managers, for example, regularly survey whether the portfolio company is making investments according to the UN Global Impact Principles. The filter, which the asset managers apply during the selection of assets, either comes from external ESG research providers or is provided by the fund's own analysts (so-called "sustainability analyses").

With the sustainable funds industry on the rise, the demand for sustainability labels and standards is also increasing. In Austria, 99 of 175 sustainable funds – which the authors of the study recorded in 2021 – were equipped with a sustainability label.[24] This amounts to a share of 57%. It is especially common for Austrian investment funds to advertise their fund units with the "Austrian Eco-Label" ("Österreichisches Umweltzeichen"), a certification awarded by the Austrian Ministry for Climate Protection, Environment, Energy and Mobility. According to the Ministry,[25] this eco-label provides guidance for consumers aiming to invest money according to ecological, social, and ethical criteria. The Ministry awards the eco-label only once a state-accredited organisation has issued a positive opinion. The Ministry hopes that the eco-label will accelerate positive ecological change so that sustainable investment fund units steer financial flows "in the direction of sustainability". Yet, despite the Austrian Ministry trying to imitate the regulatory approach of the European Commission, no connection can be observed to the regulation under EU law as expressed in the Commission's Action Plan on Financing Sustainable Growth.[26]

C. Sustainable Ownership und Shareholder Governance

I. The Emergence of "Stewardship" and "Shareholder Activism"

The "stewardship concept"[27] is the intellectual starting point for sustainable ownership and shareholder governance, because it aims to hold asset managers

[21] Forum Nachhaltige Geldanlagen (fn. 16), 22.
[22] Forum Nachhaltige Geldanlagen (fn. 16), 23.
[23] Forum Nachhaltige Geldanlagen (fn. 16), 22.
[24] Forum Nachhaltige Geldanlagen (fn. 16), 21.
[25] https://www.umweltzeichen.at/de/f%C3%BCr-interessierte/der-weg-zum-umweltzeichen/antragsinfos-zur-richtlinie-uz49-nachhaltige-finanzprodukte (24 October 2023).
[26] EU Commission, Action Plan: Financing Sustainable Growth of 8.03.2018, COM/2018/097 final.
[27] The origins can be found in the "UK Stewardship Code", which is now available in three

(fund managers) and institutional investors (such as pension funds) accountable for (co-)enforcing good corporate governance.[28] The current regulatory approach by the European Commission expands the stewardship concept into the ESG-area by "activating" the immense voting power of institutional investors on behalf of ESG aims. Their accumulated horizontal stake in companies worldwide (so-called "common ownership") has already incited some authors to proclaim the "new era of collective investment in capital".[29]

At least for Austrian law, the idea that the purpose of the public companies themselves also encompasses other objectives than maximising shareholder value can be traced back to the beginning of modern company law. For instance, the Stock Corporation Act of 1937 already required directors to manage the company considering, inter alia, the common good.[30] In substance, this obligation has been taken up in the current regulation (Section 70 Stock Corporation Act of 1965). Hence, under Austrian company law, the executive board may certainly consider the ESG-agenda in its investment decisions; one may also argue that there is an obligation to do so, at least if one understands this as a merely procedural obligation which does not determine the content of the decision.

In contrast, the new "sustainable" version of the stewardship concept aims not at the managers but at special types of shareholders, namely institutional investors and asset managers. Part of this concept is the expectation that these shareholders will – inter alia – monitor the company, attend the annual general meeting and use their voting rights to enforce the ESG-agenda. The stewardship concept is thus related to "shareholder activism" or at least active shareholders. Shareholder activism – unlike the stewardship concept – often has a negative connotation in continental Europe.[31] Shareholders acting in an activist manner are said to be trying to achieve their "short-term goals" through the "aggressive" and targeted exercise of their shareholder rights as well as through informal measures.[32] However, the typology of shareholder activism is actually more nuanced.[33] Shareholder activism can also focus on the ESG-Agenda and therefore dovetail with the EU's regulatory approach. Consequently, since the emergence of the sustainability and ESG-agenda, the image of shareholder activism has changed. Regulators no longer perceive shareholder activism as a risk but rather

versions (2010, 2012, and 2020), see *Davies*, in: Festschrift Klaus Hopt, 2020, 131 et seq. For the current version, see Financial Reporting Council, The UK Stewardship Code 2020: https://www.frc.org.uk/library/standards-codes-policy/stewardship/uk-stewardship-code/ (24 October 2023).

[28] *Winner*, Der UK Corporate Governance Code – Grundsätze und Funktionsweise, ZGR 2012, 246 (256).

[29] *Florstedt*, Aktionärsvoten zur Vergütung und Common Ownership, ZIP 2019, 1693 et seq.

[30] See *Kalss/Burger/Eckert*, Die Entwicklung des österreichischen Aktienrechts, 2003, 322.

[31] See *Langenbucher*, Kommunikation als Governance-Instrument in der börsennotierten Aktiengesellschaft, ZHR 185 (2021), 414 (418).

[32] See Die Presse, 27.4.2017: Aktive Aktionäre sind im Vormarsch.

[33] *Taufner* (fn. 9), 691 et seq.

as an opportunity. The "green variant of classic shareholder activism" – an approach now known as "sustainable shareholder activism" – intends to ensure that annual general meetings become the "venue for engaged debates on sustainability and corporate governance".[34]

Shareholder activism is a well-known international phenomenon, especially in the US and the UK. It became ascendant long before the rise of ESG-related shareholder governance. In contrast, the Austrian capital market has not very often experienced shareholder-led campaigns against the management. However, at least a few "activist shareholders" have made it into the media in comparatively recent times, such as a group of activists that successfully obtained a seat on the board of directors of a real estate company, even against the resistance of the controlling shareholder.[35] The proxy advisors ISS and Glass Lewis supported the "activist shareholders" by issuing voting recommendations in their favour.

However, cases of shareholder activism in Austria have not had an ESG-component, as far as we can ascertain[36] and practice has not yet delivered spectacular events such as the case of the activist investor Engine No. 1, which recently came to fame because the investment firm won two board seats at Exxon Mobil's annual shareholder meeting. One possible exception is found in the – publicly perceptible – activities of "Petrus Advisers", a well-known hedge fund which is notorious for its activist campaigns that target Austrian public companies. For example, *Klaus Umek* of Petrus Advisers recently sent a public letter to the CEO of CA Immo Anlagen AG, a real estate developer, in which he addressed, among other things, the company's ESG strategy.[37]

II. Implementation of SRD II – Reporting and Transparency Obligations of Institutional Investors and Asset Managers

Apart from such individual cases, the stewardship concept is not discussed in the literature in depth. However, the topic has recently been boosted by the implementation of the Shareholder Rights Directive (Directive 2017/828; "SRD II" for short). The SRD II standardizes new transparency and disclosure obligations

---

[34] See *Jaspers*, Sustainable Shareholder Activism in Publikumsgesellschaften – "Level Playing Field" in Deutschland, Österreich und der Schweiz, NR 2022, 154 (154); similar *Hell*, Die Shareholder Proposal Rule des US-amerikanischen Kapitalmarktrechts als Instrument des nachhaltigkeitsorientierten Aktionärsaktivismus, ZVglRWiss 119 (2020), 314 et seq.

[35] Juve-Report from 20.3.2015: Etappensieg für Investoren mit Herbst Kinsky und Löffler, www.juve.de/verfahren/anfechtung-der-conwert-hv-etappensieg-fuer-investoren-mit-herbst-kinsky-und-loeffler (24 October 2023).

[36] *Taufner* (fn. 9), 692.

[37] See boerse-express from 1.11.2022: Offener Brief von Petrus Advisers (Klaus Umek) an CA Immo Anlagen (Silvia Schmitten-Walgenbach); https://boerse-express.com/news/articles/offener-brief-von-petrusadvisers-klaus-umek-an-ca-immo-anlagen-silvia-schmitten-walgenbach-519265 (24 October 2023).

for institutional investors and asset managers and, in so doing, has created a regulatory framework for the stewardship concept in Austria for the first time. Recital (15) of the SRD II justifies the new transparency obligations with the argument that institutional investors and asset managers are often significant shareholders of listed companies in the EU and can therefore play an important role in the corporate governance of these companies and, more generally, in their strategy and long-term corporate success. According to the recital, experience in recent years has shown that institutional investors and asset managers frequently refrain from engaging with their portfolio companies. There is a link to ESG objectives in that, according to the recital, the long-term non-financial performance of companies could also be jeopardized if the capital market exerts pressure on the company to achieve short-term success.

The strategies pursued by the SRD II for fostering engagement can be found in its chapter 1b. According to Art. 3g SRD II thereof, institutional investors and asset managers must either draft a participation policy and publicly disclose its implementation or explain why they do not comply with these requirements ("comply or explain"). It is therefore not mandatory to develop an engagement policy. On the other hand, the European legislator has not chosen a mere "comply or explain" model for the disclosure of the investment strategy. According to Art. 3h SRD II, institutional investors must publicly disclose, inter alia, how their investment strategy contributes to the medium to long-term performance of their portfolio companies and their arrangements with asset managers with relevance for the institutional investor's investment horizon. Finally, according to Art. 3i SRD II, asset managers must also disclose to their institutional investors on an annual basis whether their investment strategy is compatible with the investment contract and how they contribute to the medium to long-term performance of the institutional investor's assets. This provision is not comply-or-explain but mandatory.

Austria has implemented these SRD II requirements in Sections 185–187 Stock Exchange Act 2018 ("BörseG 2018"[38]). Thus, unlike in Germany, the new provisions have not been introduced in company law.[39] However, the Stock Exchange Act is even less suitable for the transposition from a systematic point of view, because it is primarily intended to provide the legal framework for the market infrastructure. The internal transparency and reporting obligations of institutional investors and asset managers have little to do with this. In addition, these provisions do not purport to regulate the behaviour of these market participants in their capacity as shareholders of an issuer, but are concerned with

[38] Bundesgesetz über die Wertpapier- und allgemeinen Warenbörsen 2018 (BörseG 2018), BGBl. I Nr. 107/2017.

[39] For criticism see *Baums*, Institutionelle Investoren im Aktienrecht, ZHR 183 (2019), 605 (606 et seq.).

accountability obligations towards their own investors and beneficiaries, which, in turn, enter into effect in order to achieve positive results for the portfolio companies.[40] From a systematic point of view, it would have been preferable to introduce these rules in the relevant substantive legislation (regulation of UCITs, alternative investment funds, institutions for occupational retirement provision, investment firms, and certain insurance companies).[41]

In Austria, for several years now, there has been an informal legal requirement that European Union law should be implemented narrowly (no "gold-plating"). In line with that requirement, the national legislator has opted for a restrictive implementation of SRD II. In most cases, such as with additional information requirements, optional rights were not exercised, but only the mandatory (minimum) requirements of SRD II were implemented. The scope of application of the disclosure and transparency obligations pursuant to Sections 185–187 Stock Exchange Act is therefore narrow. First, this concerns the personal scope of application: based on the definition in SRD II, "institutional investors" are only life insurers, reinsurers and institutions for occupational retirement provision (Section 178 no. 2 Stock Exchange Act). The obligations under Sections 185–187 Stock Exchange Act thus only concern a smaller selection of investors than those referred to in normal parlance by the term "institutional investors". However, this narrow concept of institutional investors is in part ameliorated by the fact that institutional investors not covered often use an asset manager which is then itself subject to the obligations according to Section 185 Stock Exchange Act (that is Art. 3g SRD II).[42]

Much more decisive for the effectiveness of the rules, however, is the geographic scope of application. That is, institutional investors and asset managers are only covered by the rules implementing SRD II if Austria is the home member state in the sense of the sector-specific legal acts of the EU. It has already been pointed out that Austrian institutional investors and asset managers account for only a small part of the market capitalization (above B. II.). To the extent that foreign investors are subject to the rules of another member state, this is supposedly no problem because the implementation by the respective member state should be equivalent. However, a major regulatory gap arises in the case of institutional investors from the U.S. and the U.K. (especially hedge and investment funds), which, due to their great importance for the Austrian and, more broadly, the European capital markets, call into question the entire regulatory approach of SRD II.[43] This also means that the influence of US and UK regulation of the

[40] *Baums* (fn. 39), 607.

[41] Also *Baums* (fn. 39), 607.

[42] See already *Gassner/Winner*, in: Kalss/Oppitz/U. Torggler/Winner (eds.), BörseG/MAR § 185 BörseG, 2019, mn. 7.

[43] *Koch*, Der Kapitalanleger als Corporate Governance-Akteur im Rahmen der neuen §§ 134a ff. AktG, BKR 2020, 1 (3).

issue may become more important than those of the EU rules if the shift towards non-EU investors continues.

III. Current Market Practice on Engagement Policy – Case Study

Although the scope of application of Sections 185–187 Stock Exchange Act is narrow, it has nevertheless resulted in or, at worst, coincided with a more transparent market practice in Austria. As an example, one can cite the publications of Erste Asset Management GmbH (in short "EAM"). As of December 31, 2021, EAM manages assets worth €76.8 billion;[44] this also makes EAM the largest Austrian fund investor in the ATX Prime.[45] Around €15.3 billion (just under 20 % of EAM's assets) are managed according to strict sustainability criteria.

In order to implement its participation policy according to Section 185 Stock Exchange Act (Art. 3g SRD II), EAM developed a "Voting Policy"[46] based on the "Sustainability International Voting Guidelines" of ISS Governance and an "Engagement and Voting Policy".[47] It exercised voting rights for 463 of its portfolio companies in 543 general meetings in 2021.[48] The voting volume amounted to €6.7 billion. Voting rights are exercised by EAM in Austria directly and internationally via ISS (Institutional Shareholder Services), but only if EAM holds a share portfolio of more than €2 million or 5 % of the outstanding shares. When exercising voting rights is not possible because EAM does not hold shares in the company but other classes of securities (for example bonds), alternative engagement strategies are employed.[49] According to its own statements, EAM also seeks active dialog with companies, for example, as a "stakeholder".

The portfolio companies, in which EAM exercises its voting rights, are primarily based in the USA (219 companies) and Austria (33 companies). This is followed by Germany with 26 companies and, remarkably, Cayman Island with 20 companies. In many cases, EAM votes against management proposals or motions for resolutions in order to comply with the principles of the Sustainable Voting Policy.[50] This voting behaviour relates to shareholder proposals regarding, for example, capital measures or votes on the election of members of the executive or

[44] Erste Asset Management Engagement & Voting Report, 2021, III; https://cdn0.erstegroup.com/content/dam/at/eam/common/files/ESG/EAM_Engagement_Report_EN_2021.pdf (24 October 2023).

[45] Institutional Ownership of the ATX Prime in 2020: https://www.wienerborse.at/listing/aktien/investoren/institutionelle-investoren-und-oesterreichische-aktien/?c16842%5Bfile%5D=ycv1ZbiZQALzbAyRmVt0kw&cHash=ec0ff8d4f9a310e692764e35a8c5526e (24 October 2023).

[46] https://cdn0.erstegroup.com/content/dam/at/eam/common/files/ESG/VotingPolicy/EAM_Voting_Policy_EN.pdf (24 October 2023).

[47] https://www.erste-am.at/content/dam/at/eam/common/files/EAM_Voting_Policy.pdf (24 October 2023).

[48] For the following see Erste Asset Management Engagement & Voting Report, 2021, 27 f.

[49] Erste Asset Management Engagement & Voting Report, 2021, 5.

[50] Erste Asset Management Engagement & Voting Report, 2021, 31.

supervisory board. EAM also supports shareholder proposals that address ESG concerns, such as on emissions reductions or other decarbonisation strategies, diversity and inclusion proposals, and board composition (primarily affecting US-based portfolio companies).

The annual reports also contain case studies of the engagement with individual companies, unsurprisingly with a strong focus on local engagement but also with a certain focus on ESG issues.[51] Of course, such publications provide the reader only with biased insights into EAM's voting strategy. From the point of view of transparency, it is, however, laudable that EAM also discloses its voting behaviour in its entirety on its website.[52]

IV. Barriers to the Implementation of an Engagement Policy

It is one thing to develop an engagement policy to enforce ESG concerns at the portfolio company level, but another to implement such a policy properly. There are several barriers to effective implementation. For example, EAM has set value-based limits for the exercise of voting rights (share portfolio of more than €2 million or 5 % of the outstanding shares).[53] If these limits are not exceeded, an important means of influence is lost. As a result, although EAM's voting volume of €6.7 billion is 2.6 times the average market capitalisation of an ATX company, it still constitutes only a small part of the total assets under management of €76.8 billion. Moreover, the engagement policy – in contrast to the voting policy – focuses on Austrian portfolio companies, where EAM's access and level of information are most pronounced.[54]

There may be at least two factual barriers to an active engagement policy.

First, costs are obviously a limiting factor for institutional investors' engagement. To what extent this actually determines their behaviour is difficult to determine. It should be noted, however, that Austrian funds are typically not index trackers for which low management costs are the most important factor, as such funds cannot differentiate themselves from their peers through the selection of portfolio companies. Rather, they are actively managed funds for which management costs are, of course, also an important factor. Such funds appear, nevertheless, to be subject to less immediate cost pressure.

Second, the institutional investor vote is unlikely to change the balance on ESG issues. This is due to the concentrated shareholder structure mentioned above, because a majority shareholder may be inclined to block any ESG related

---

[51] See, e. g., for OMV Erste Asset Management Engagement & Voting Report, 2021, 9.

[52] https://www.erste-am.at/de/institutionelle-anleger/nachhaltigkeit/publikationen-und-richtlinien#/modalComponent/isOpen/true/url/%2Fde%2Fconfiguration%2Fleads%2Fesg-voting.modal (24 October 2023).

[53] Erste Asset Management Voting Policy, 2021, 2.

[54] Erste Asset Management Voting Policy, 2021, 4.

resolutions on the annual meeting.[55] One would not expect institutional investors to invest heavily in research if their votes have no discernible impact. Of course, this does not apply to other, more market-oriented forms of engagement, which are not implemented via a shareholder resolution. For example, institutional investors can enter into a dialogue with the company management, make their concerns publicly perceptible or even threaten with disinvesting – a threat which Austrian funds can credibly raise as they are managed actively.

In addition, various principles of company and capital market law may be responsible for legal obstacles to a comprehensive engagement policy.

First, the Austrian Takeover Act (ATA[56]) imposes a potentially major obstacle through its rules on acting in concert pursuant to Section 1 no. 6 ATA. If the Austrian Takeover Commission, i. e. the supervisory authority for public offers, determines that shareholders are acting in concert, then the voting rights of the shareholders are aggregated (Section 23 para 1 ATA), which may, in turn, trigger the obligation to make an offer pursuant to Section 22 ATA. In some agreements, it is also conceivable that the shareholders must disclose their pooled voting rights to the capital market according to Section 133 no. 1 Stock Exchange Act. Shareholders act in concert if they cooperate based on an agreement in order to obtain or exercise control over the target company, in particular, by coordinating the use of their voting rights. Acting in concert is presumed if several legal entities have reached an agreement on the exercise of their voting rights in the election of members of the supervisory board, although this presumption may be rebutted in individual cases, for instance, if the board member is "independent" and "professionally qualified", because in that case, the parties acting in concert only seek the ideal appointment to the supervisory board. Furthermore, it is irrelevant whether the shareholders exercise control in the shareholders' meeting or whether they attempt to exert pressure on the company's executive board through an "investor dialog".[57] In a well-known decision concerning a real estate company, the Takeover Commission stated that shareholders can also exert their influence under company law outside the general meeting in order to persuade the management bodies to conclude a certain transaction.[58]

Hence, the term "acting in concert" covers a broad field of possible cooperation between the shareholders.[59] It is irrelevant for which purposes or invest-

---

[55] See Section B. I.

[56] Bundesgesetz über Übernahmeangebote (Übernahmegesetz – ÜbG) BGBl. I Nr. 127/1998 idF. BGBl. I Nr. 78/2023.

[57] On the market practice in Austria, see for example *Gall/Hagenauer,* Dialog mit Investoren, RdW 2019, 816.

[58] ÜbK GZ 2016/1/2-317 mn. 136 (*conwert Immobilien Invest SE).*

[59] See also ESMA, Public Statement – Information on shareholder cooperation and acting in concert under the Takeover Bids Directive (amended version as of 8 February 2019); https://www.takeover.at/uploads/u/pxe/A4_Rechtliche_Grundlagen/ESMA_Leitfaden/ESMA_Inform

ment strategies control is exercised. It follows then, that if several shareholders come together to develop a joint commitment to ESG activities in a portfolio company, they could, in principle, be qualified as parties acting in concert for the purposes of takeover legislation. This is because the instruments used to enforce ESG concerns can easily take the form of a control-relevant agreement under Section 1 no. 6 ATA. An example of "sustainable shareholder activism" is the reorganization of German energy suppliers with the aim of separating the fossil and renewable energy businesses (RWE – Innogy; E.ON – Uniper). Should shareholders attempt to implement such structural measures based on a joint agreement, this behaviour would, according to voices in the literature, also be relevant for the purpose of the mandatory bid rule under takeover law.[60] This would almost certainly put a stop to such practices, as institutional investors cannot risk triggering the bid obligation. In practice, however, acting in concert in the context of "sustainable shareholder activism" has not been an issue for the Austrian Takeover Commission so far. This is probably because the concentrated shareholder structure in Austria makes it unlikely that the shares subject to such an agreement will exceed the threshold for the obligation to launch a takeover offer. We recommend that ESMA amends its whitelist in order to exempt sustainable shareholder activism from the legal sanctions followed by acting in concert.

A second corporate law hurdle to the implementation of the ESG agenda may result from the principle of equal treatment of shareholders (Section 47a Austrian Stock Corporation Act ["AktG"[61]]). This requirement could prevent the management board from providing ESG activists in the context of an investor dialog with the information they need to implement their agenda if this information is not already in the public domain. However, the prevailing view is that the executive board may provide information to selected investors if these investors are of particular importance, e.g., because the company cannot implement the measure without their support.[62] What is required, therefore, is an objective justification for the selective disclosure of information. Accordingly, the disclosure of information must be appropriate, proportionate and serve as the least invasive means of achieving the intended objective.

Third, the role of shareholders under Austrian corporate law is comparatively weak in that they generally cannot decide on management issues unless the executive board decides to submit the issue to the general meeting (Section 103 para 2 Austrian Stock Corporation Act), which boards rarely do in practice. The basic idea of that provision is to protect the management from the influence of

---

ation_on_shareholder_cooperation_and_acting_in_concert_under_the_Takeover_Bids_Directive_-_White_List__8.2.2019.pdf (24 October 2023).

[60] *Jaspers* (fn. 34), 163.

[61] Bundesgesetz über Aktiengesellschaften (AktG), BGBl. Nr. 98/1965 idF. BGBl. Nr. 24/1985.

[62] *Kalss*, Gesellschaftsrechtliche Informations- und Auskunftsrechte, in: Kalss/U. Torggler (eds.), Big Data, 2017, 7 (42).

the majority shareholder or the group holding the majority, which is the predominant shareholder structure in Austria.[63] As a result, engagement cannot take the form of putting decisions on management issues on the agenda of the general meeting. This is true even for companies with widely dispersed shareholdings.

V. Proxy Advisors

Proxy advisors are playing an increasingly important role in the Austrian market. However, their influence in Austrian portfolio companies is limited due to the concentrated shareholder structure. Anecdotal reports indicate that their recommendations have shifted the balance in cases where the general meeting's resolution required a super-majority. There are complaints by listed companies that international proxy advisors do not understand Austrian factual and legal environment (nor do they make the investment necessary for understanding the Austrian environment). It is, however, difficult to know whether such claims are justified or simply constitute an expression of dissatisfaction due to losing proxy contests. On the other hand, the conflict of interest arising from the proxy advisor's second role as preparer of corporate governance ratings and corporate governance advisor to listed companies is not discussed in detail either in the academic debate or in practice.

As far as we can ascertain, Austrian institutional investors use proxy advisors. As far as our case study EAM is concerned, EAM has established its own Voting Policies, but these are based on ISS International Sustainability Proxy Voting Guidelines.[64] ISS casts the votes abroad on behalf of EAM, while EAM itself participates in Austrian general meetings.[65] EAM mentions in its Voting Policies that it may use the services of ISS as a proxy voting advisor,[66] but does not disclose in its Engagement and Voting Report whether and to what extent it actually follows ISS recommendations when casting votes. Given the close link between the EAM Voting Policies and the ISS Proxy Voting Guidelines, this should be possible, in any case; of course, it would also be cost-efficient.

VI. The Role of Debt Financing

When corporate governance is discussed in Austria at all, it is exclusively from the perspective of equity investors. The role of typical debt providers such as banks or other institutional investors in corporate governance has not yet become an issue. Debt financing and sustainability are therefore usually only associated with

[63] See above Section B. I.

[64] https://www.issgovernance.com/file/policy/active/specialty/Sustainability-International-Voting-Guidelines.pdf (24 October 2023).

[65] Erste Asset Management Engagement & Voting Report, 2021, 27.

[66] Erste Asset Management Voting Policy, 2021, 2.

the issuance of "green bonds". In May 2022, for example, the Republic of Austria launched the first green bond with an issue volume of €4 billion. In the meantime, some private issuers have also used this means of financing. Most issuers are credit institutions, but there are also several non-financial companies; a total of 71 green bonds are currently listed on the Vienna Stock Exchange.[67]

D. Sustainable Funding und Fund Governance

I. Regulatory Approach for Investment Funds

At the European level, investment funds fall under either the UCITS[68] or the AIF[69] regime, with both sectors subject to European harmonisation. With regard to the current Sustainable Finance agenda of the European Union, investment funds are primarily subject to the Disclosure-Regulation[70] and the Taxonomy Regulation.[71] In simple terms, the Disclosure-Regulation contains various transparency obligations for financial market participants regarding sustainability risks at the company level and the sustainability of financial products. The fund industry has already developed its own terminology for the product categories of the Disclosure-Regulation, which distinguishes, for example, between "light green Article 8 products" and "dark green Article 9 products".[72] The regulatory approach goes beyond mere information and disclosure obligations: Article 2 no. 7 Delegated Regulation (EU) 2021/1253 additionally requires investment firms offering investment advice and portfolio management to take into account the individual sustainability preferences of clients. The term "sustainability preference" refers to a client's decision as to whether certain "sustainable" financial instruments – also in the sense of the Disclosure-Regulation and the Taxonomy-Regulation – should be included in his investment decision.[73] An accurate assessment in the literature states that the purpose of asking for sustainability preferences is to build up in the investor "the feeling of a moral obligation to become aware of his own ecological

[67] Data: www.wienerborse.at/marktdaten/anleihen/suche/?c7928%5BWBAG__ID_BOND_TYPE%5D=1013 (24 October 2023).

[68] Directive 2009/65/EC on the coordination of laws, regulations and administrative provisions relating to undertakings for collective investment in transferable securities (UCITS).

[69] Directive 2011/61/EU on Alternative Investment Fund Managers.

[70] Regulation (EU) 2019/2088 on sustainability related disclosures in the financial services sector.

[71] Regulation (EU) 2020/852 on the establishment of a framework to facilitate sustainable investment, and amending Regulation (EU) 2019/2088.

[72] See *Flor/Kreisl*, Es grünt so grün … Zur Umsetzung der TaxonomieVO – eine Bestandsaufnahme, Zeitschrift für Finanzmarktrecht 2022, 321 (322 und 325 et seq.); *Majcen*, Terminkontrakte im ESG-Portfolio, Österreichisches Bankarchiv 2022, 820 (821 et seq.); *Hanke*, Der Vertrieb von ökologisch nachhaltigen Anlageprodukten, ZIP 2022, 62 (63 et seq.).

[73] See *Hanke* (fn. 71), 66 et seq.

responsibility and to invest accordingly".[74] According to Austrian market participants, the integration of ESG-factors into investment advisory services is likely to play a key role in the demand for sustainable financial assets.[75]

The European legislator, moreover, has therefore adopted a strong "nudging" approach[76] with regard to financial intermediaries such as investment funds, which, although not yet directly intervening in the investment strategy of investment fund management companies, indicates a clear preference for sustainable assets and investments. Furthermore, with reference to investment fund management companies, only such "long term investments" are in any way capable of bringing about the transformation of the financial economy through ESG-compliant use of membership rights.[77]

II. ESG-Activism of the Fund Management

"Fund governance" in the sense of the Sustainable Finance Doctrine stands for an investment strategy that favours capital investment in environmentally and socially responsible, "well-managed" companies or "good corporate citizens" in the real economy (ESG), focusing on fund-managing financial intermediaries.[78] As mentioned above, these financial intermediaries are subject to sector-specific regulation based on EU harmonisation acts (UCITS Directive; AIF Directive). Austria implemented these EU legal requirements in the InvFG 2011[79] and the AIFMG[80].

An important issue of this study is whether ESG activism by fund management is possible under the current regulatory regime. Investment funds are designed according to the principle of risk diversification and thus take structural aim at diversification of the assets invested. Additionally, funds have to protect the investments made in case of insolvency of the management company. An investment fund is therefore characterized by the principles of risk diversification, third-party management and collective investment.[81] However, the broader the diversification, the less incentive management companies have to influence their portfolio companies actively, because their economies of scale are largely lost in this investment strategy.

---

[74] *Schön*, "Nachhaltigkeit" in der Unternehmensberichterstattung, ZfPW 2022, 207 (229).

[75] Forum Nachhaltige Geldanlagen (fn. 16), 27.

[76] See again *Schön* (fn. 73), 228.

[77] *Ekkenga*, Zur (Um-)Lenkung der Kapitalströme durch Investmentfonds zwecks Förderung "nachhaltiger" Investitionen – ein Systemüberblick unter Berücksichtigung ausgewählter Problemschwerpunkte, WM 2022, 1765 (1765).

[78] See *Ekkenga* (fn. 76), 1767.

[79] Bundesgesetz über Investmentfonds (InvFG 2011), BGBl. I Nr. 77/2011.

[80] Alternative Investmentfonds Manager-Gesetz (AIFMG), BGBl. I Nr. 135/2013 idF. BGBl. I Nr. 9/2020.

[81] See *Macher*, Praxishandbuch Investmentfonds, 2010, mn. 1/4.

However, as far as can be seen, the principle of risk diversification should not pose a serious obstacle to potential ESG activism by fund managers, even under the provisions of the UCITS Directive. In Austrian investment fund law, which is strongly influenced by EU law, the principle of risk diversification is based on a "three-tier-model".

On the first tier, the law exhaustively lists all investment categories in which a UCITS may invest (Section 67 InvFG 2011).[82] These asset classes include securities, money market instruments, fund units, deposits and derivatives. This does not create any regulatory hurdles because the category of listed "securities" also includes the asset classes typically associated with ESG activism, that is, equities and bonds. Neither does the principle of risk diversification prohibit setting up special funds, such as those with a focus on ESG criteria.[83] As a result, the fund management does not necessarily have to prioritize the negative correlation in the performance of the individual investments as long as the lower degree of diversification resulting from the fund's narrow focus is disclosed in the prospectus and the fund terms and conditions.[84] The mix of broadly invested and specialised funds offered on the capital market would otherwise be inadmissible under supervisory law.

The model's second and third tier are intertwined. In the second tier, eligible quantitative investment limits apply to eligible assets, which can be selected by the fund management. At the same time, those quantitative investment limits reflect the third tier of supervisory law, namely the principle of risk diversification, which, in turn, serves as a general requirement for the investment policy of mutual funds. Austrian literature refers to the general clause as "flexible system",[85] which means that risk diversification is not a strict rule, but rather consists of different elements working together. One of these elements is found in the quantitative investment limits that are intended to prevent excessive investments in individual issuers. According to Section 74 InvFG 2011, securities of the same issuer may only be acquired to the extent of up to 10 % of the fund assets. Index funds, on the other hand, may invest up to 20 % of the fund assets in shares or debt instruments of the same issuer according to Section 75 InvFG 2011, as long as the index is recognised by the supervisory authority. These requirements determine the point at which the assets of the UCITS are sufficiently diversified for regulatory purposes.

Section 78 InvFG 2011 is of particular relevance for ESG activism, as this provision also provides quantitative limits in pursuit of preventing a domi-

---

[82] *Macher*, in: Macher/Buchberger/Kalss/Oppitz (eds.), Investmentfondsgesetz, 2nd ed. 2013, § 66 InvFG mn. 13.

[83] *Macher* (fn. 81) mn. 30.

[84] *Köndgen/Schmies,* in: Schimansky/Bunte/Lwowski (eds.), Bankrechts-Handbuch, 5th ed. 2017, § 113 mn. 136, 138.

[85] *Macher* (fn. 81) mn. 14 et seq.

nant influence by the fund on an issuer. The general requirement according to Section 78 para 1 InvFG 2011 (see Art. 56 UCITS Directive) is that a management company may not acquire voting shares for any of the UCITS it manages which would allow it to exert a significant influence on the management of an issuer. According to the Austrian legislator, having a significant influence would contradict the concept of mere portfolio management.[86] However, there is an additional limit that is not based on a provision in the UCITS Directive: Section 78 para 2 no. 1 InvFG 2011 limits the investment with 7.5 % of the share capital of the issuing stock corporation; the management company may not acquire more than this for the fund assets of an individual UCITS. Hence, the management company must regard its participation as a financial investment rather than as an entrepreneurial participation. In the case of debt securities and non-voting preference shares, the limit is 10 % (Section 78 para 2 items 2 and 3 InvFG 2011), as mandated by Art. 56 UCITS Directive. However, even this quantitative investment limit is unlikely to have much impact on ESG activism in practice, as even with around 5 % of the voting rights, the management company still has ample opportunity at its disposal to make ESG-related demands of or put pressure on the management of the portfolio company in question.

Furthermore, the wording of Section 78 para 2 InvFG 2011 refers to the "fund assets of a UCITS". In a narrow interpretation, the holdings of several UCITS funds managed by the same company are therefore not aggregated when determining the maximum limit.[87] This is also supported by the fact that the wording of Art. 56 para 2 UCITS Directive states that a "UCITS may not acquire more than" the respective limit and does not refer to acquisitions by the investment or management company itself. This reading does not effectively prevent a management company from building up a dominant influence over individual issuers, since, at least in the case of larger and well-known issuers, it is not excluded from the outset that the management company acquires shares for several UCITS it manages and thus cumulatively reaches or even exceeds the investment limit of 7.5 %.

However, the general prohibition against acquiring shares that enable the management company to exercise a significant influence on the investee company according to Section 78 para 1 InvFG 2011 remains. In our opinion, it must be assumed that for the purposes of this qualitative limit, the holdings of different UCITS managed by the same company must be added together. Although neither Austrian law nor the German language version of the UCITS Directive are clear in this respect, a look at the English language version of the UCITS Directive is helpful: "An investment company or a management company acting in connection with all of the common funds which it manages (...) shall

[86] Erläuterungen zur Regierungsvorlage 1254 Beilagen zu den stenographischen Protokollen des Nationalrates 24. Gesetzgebungsperiode 45.

[87] Explicitly stated by *Leitgeb*, in: Bollenberger/Kellner (eds.), InvFG, 1st ed. 2016, § 78 mn. 2.

not acquire any shares [...]". This speaks in favour of aggregation, which is the only way to achieve the goal of avoiding a dominant influence on issuers. This is clearly the reading of the UCITS Directive by the German legislator. That is, pursuant to Section 210 para 2 KAGB[88], a UCITS capital management company may only acquire shares of the same issuer amounting to a maximum of 10% of the voting rights for all domestic UCITS it manages. This requires the aggregation of holdings by different UCITS.[89] In contrast to the Austrian legislator, there is no general qualitative criterion analogous to Section 78 para 1 InvFG 2011. It seems that the Austrian legislator has missed the point: Art. 56 UCITS Directive expects the national legislator to set quantitative limits on investments not at the level of individual UCITS, but aggregated at the level of the investment company.[90] In summary, in Austria, the influence of funds – ESG or not – on companies is not limited by a strict cap but by a qualitative barrier, namely the prohibition of holdings that grant "significant influence", which, at least in theory, gives investment funds greater scope for pro-ESG activities, although, to our knowledge, its limits have not yet been tested.

Apart from these absolute investment limits, which are intended to prevent excessive influence on the management of the issuer, the supervisory regime for UCITS investment funds is open to the exercise of voting rights. In accordance with Section 26 para 1 InvFG 2011, the management company must devise effective and appropriate strategies for the exercise of voting rights so that these exclusively benefit the UCITS fund. The Austrian legislator has thus always been aware of the fact that management companies can exert considerable influence on the capital markets through the financial instruments in their portfolios.[91] The management company's strategies must ensure that the exercise of voting rights is in line with the investment objectives and the investment policy of the UCITS (Section 26 para 2 item 2 InvFG 2011). In addition, the Austrian fund industry undertakes compliance with certain quality standards, which are laid down in a special "Code of Conduct" ["CoC"][92] and, inter alia, place specific requirements on the exercise of voting rights. As responsible shareholders, the investment companies declare their intent to exercise their voting rights independently and exclusively in the best interests of their investors on all matters

---

[88] Kapitalanlagegesetzbuch vom 4. Juli 2013 (BGBl. I S. 1981 idF. BGBl. 2023 I Nr. 411).

[89] See, e.g., *Kayser/Holleschek,* in: Emde/Dornseifer/Dreibus (eds.), KAGB, 2nd ed. 2019, § 210 mn. 6.

[90] This can also be deduced from the fact that Art. 56 para 1 subpara 2 UCITS Directive mentions that "Member States shall take account of existing rules defining the principle stated in the first subparagraph in the law of other Member States". Obviously, this presupposes that the Member States include (quantitative) limits on an aggregate level in their national legislation, as Germany has done in Section 210 para 2 KAGB.

[91] *Buchberger,* in: Macher/Buchberger/Kalss/Oppitz (eds.), InvFG 2nd ed. 2013, § 26 mn. 2.

[92] Accessible at https://www.voeig.at/voeig/internet_4.nsf/sysPages/qualitaetsstandards.html (24 October 2023).

that could have a lasting effect on their interests.[93] The interests of investors are regularly determined by the investment objectives and investment policy described in the information documents. On that account, the exercise of voting rights must also be in line with the investment objectives and the investment policy in order to comply with the will of the investors as much as possible.[94]

For UCITS funds with an ESG investment strategy, it would therefore not pose a regulatory problem if the fund management actively pushed for the pursuit of a sustainable investment strategy among its portfolio companies, but rather, this conduct is simply required by supervisory law. For example, if a UCITS fund invests in companies with an ESG agenda in accordance with its investment policy, this strategic orientation must also be reflected in its voting behaviour.[95]

III. Contrast between ESG-interests and Investor Preferences?

The exercise of shareholder voting rights from UCITS funds ultimately also follows from the management company's duty to safeguard investor interests. Pursuant to Section 29 InvFG 2011, the management company has the duty to act in the best interests of the UCITS and its unit holders. However, conflicts between individual investor and ESG interests may arise, namely to the extent that the deliberate exclusion of ESG-averse portfolio companies leads to a loss of returns for the fund-holders. If the fund management accepts such losses and forgoes "sin stocks" with considerable returns,[96] it runs the risk that the fund-holders may bring claims for damages resulting from the breach of contract. Austrian literature has not yet addressed this potential conflict of interest.

Whether the fund management actually breaches its duty to protect interests in an individual case depends largely on the information in the rules and the prospectus of the fund in question. In the case of an ESG fund that integrates sustainability factors into its investment process from the outset or even actively pursues a sustainability objective ("light green" and "dark green" funds according to Art. 8 and 9 Disclosure-Regulation), investors can of course not claim that the fund would have achieved a higher return with shares of a major tobacco company, for example.

In case of equity funds with a broad investment objective, on the other hand, the management company must maximize the investors' return without restriction. However, the acquisition of shares in "sustainable companies" is by no means without exception contrary to the management company's duty to safeguard the investors' interests. Indeed, it is not necessarily the case that an ESG-oriented investment strategy actually delivers worse results. Countless empirical

[93] Point III.6. CoC.
[94] *Buchberger* (fn. 89) mn. 13.
[95] *Buchberger* (fn. 89) mn. 13.
[96] See already *Bueren*, Sustainable Finance, ZGR 2019, 813 (853).

studies are currently trying to determine the (relative) performance of ESG-affine investment strategies. We can only cite one arbitrarily selected recent meta-study, which concludes for the period starting in 2015 that managers of companies justify sustainable investments with better operating results on the one hand, yet, the return of ESG investments at the portfolio level, on the other hand, does not differ from "conventional" investment strategies.[97] From a legal perspective, it therefore remains a difficult question in individual cases whether ESG interests conflict with the interests of fund-holders.

E. Conclusion

Austria is not currently attempting to promote the transformation to a sustainable real economy through its own initiatives on the capital market. The legislator limits itself to the implementation and enforcement of EU regulation. An in-depth and, above all, overarching academic discussion on matters of sustainable finance likewise remains lacking.

However, as we discussed in the sections above, recent studies show that investors on the capital market are increasingly switching to sustainable investments. This progressive redirection of capital flows should make direct interventions in the market process – should they be planned at the European level – at very least, less urgent, but probably also unnecessary. One can already observe that institutional investors, including management companies and other asset managers, are becoming actively involved in their portfolio companies in line with the ESG agenda. Whether such involvement is sufficient, is, of course, a question of personal assessment. But it is safe to say that the supervisory regime of the sector-specific legal acts (UCITS, AIF) currently poses few if any institutional barriers to ESG activism. In order to achieve the EU's policy objectives, it will be much more important what type of investment strategy is envisaged under the individual investment fund's rules. This is driven, in part, by a shift in demand.

At this stage, little empirical evidence exists on the behaviour of institutional investors and their ability to influence their portfolio companies. In Austria, share ownership is traditionally concentrated in the hands of a small group of shareholders (concentrated shareholder structure). According to widespread opinion, this could be an obstacle to sustainable shareholder activism by institutional investors that cannot be removed by legal rules. However, regulation under EU law – especially in the form of SRD II – has already made the exercise of voting rights by institutional investors more transparent, among other effects. It would not be surprising if a shift in market practice increasingly provokes legal questions and triggers a more intensive discussion in Austria in the future.

[97] *Utz et al.*, Journal of Sustainable Finance & Investment (2022) 1 (2).

Country Report Denmark

Hanne S. Birkmose / Karsten Engsig Sørensen

A. Introduction

The Danish take on the recent regulatory developments at the EU level in regard to sustainable finance and ownership seems to have been minimalistic, meaning that EU regulatory acts have been transposed where needed, yet no large-scale plans for supplementary regulation at a national level have materialised. The EU legislative acts have, moreover, only recently entered into force, which is why there is no case law yet at hand for helping interpret the rules.

For our contribution to this book, we have focused on topics that are being triggered by the sustainable finance agenda, but which have a basis in issues that are developed in Danish theory, practice or legislation. For the first part, the focus will be mainly on the role of institutional investors or asset managers acting in their capacity as shareholders, whereas the second part will focus mainly on these entities acting in their role as investors and financial intermediaries.

B. Sustainable Ownership/Shareholder Governance

I. Stewardship in Danish law[1]

Whilst we did not see the same post-crisis debate in Denmark on active ownership and shareholder engagement as took place in some other European countries, the Danish Committee on Corporate Governance indeed adopted a Stewardship Code in 2016.[2] The initiating steps of the Danish Code were taken by the Committee on Corporate Governance[3] and it was subsequently supported by the Minister, who highlighted how shareholder engagement by institutional

[1] This section is largely inspired by Marina Birsch Madsen and Hanne S. Birkmose, "The Danish Stewardship Code: The Past, the Present and the Future", in Dionysia Katelouzou and Dan W. Puchniak (eds.), "Global Shareholder Stewardship" (Cambridge University Press 2022).

[2] Committee on Corporate Governance, "Stewardship Code" (November 2016) https://corporategovernance.dk/sites/default/files/180116_stewardship_code.pdf (5 September 2023) [hereinafter Danish Code].

[3] Letter to the Minister of Business and Growth from the Danish Committee on Corporate Governance (10 June 2014) (On file with the authors).

investors can ultimately benefit the competitive edge held by Danish companies.[4] In the Code's preface, the Committee announced a heightened focus on the role of institutional investors in listed companies as one of the reasons behind the development of the Danish Code. The Danish Code was heavily inspired by the original version of the UK Stewardship Code (UK Code[5]),[6] and consisted of seven principles as such. The aim of the Danish Code was to promote long-term value creation in Danish listed companies and therein contribute to maximising long-term return for investors.[7] In this respect, the Danish Code shared a mutual purpose with the Danish 'Recommendations on Corporate Governance',[8] which seeks to 'support value creation and accountable management, thus strengthening the long-term competitiveness of the companies.'[9] Moreover, it aimed to increase transparency in terms of how exactly individual investors choose to pursue stewardship activities. This was emphasised by the application of the comply-or-explain principle, which is based on voluntariness and leaves it up to the individual investor to determine the extent of compliance with the principles.[10]

The Danish Code was directed specifically at 'Danish institutional investors who invest in shares of companies that are publicly listed in Denmark. The Code is directed at shareholders and asset managers, as well as investors who perform both roles and directly or indirectly manage third party funds'.[11] As no uniform definition of an institutional investor existed prior to the adoption of the Code, the Committee clarified its target group by stating that the Danish Code was relevant primarily to 'investment funds, insurance companies, investment firms, pension funds and financial institutions'.

---

[4] See Ministry of Industry, Business and Financial Affairs, "Aktivt ejerskab skal understøtte en sund udvikling i danske virksomheder" [Active Ownership is to Support a Healthy Development in Danish businesses] (25 January 2016) https://em.dk/nyhedsarkiv/2016/januar/aktivt-ejerskab-skal-understoette-en-sund-udvikling-i-danske-virksomheder/ (5 September 2023).

[5] Financial Reporting Council, "The UK Stewardship Code" (September 2012) https://www.frc.org.uk/getattachment/d67933f9-ca38-4233-b603-3d24b2f62c5f/UK-Stewardship-Code-(September-2012).pdf (5 September 2023) [hereinafter UK Code 2012].

[6] Danish Code (n 2) p. 3. It is mentioned in the preface that 'the Committee has sought to ensure that the Code is in line with leading foreign stewardship principles, notably including The UK Stewardship Code.'

[7] Ibid.

[8] Committee on Corporate Governance, 'Recommendations on Corporate Governance' (August 2019) https://corporategovernance.dk/sites/default/files/190911_recommendations_version_260819.pdf (5 September 2023) [hereinafter Recommendations on Corporate Governance]. *See* Danish Code (n. 2) 3.

[9] Recommendations on Corporate Governance, *ibid.* p. 3.

[10] On the somewhat more coercive approach adopted by the UK Stewardship Code, see Dionysia Katelouzou and Peer Zumbansen, "The New Geography of Corporate Law Production: Charting the Transnational Political Economies of Corporate Governance.", University of Pennsylvania Journal of International Law, vol. 42, 2020.

[11] Danish Code (n. 2) p. 4. The code is thus limited to *Danish* institutional investors' *domestic* investments.

The Danish Code consisted of seven principles and featured the Committee's explanatory comments on those individual principles. These comments served as a guideline and source of inspiration in the investors' subsequent work with the principles.[12] The themes covered by the seven principles were similar to those in the UK Code.[13]

At the time of the introduction of the Danish Stewardship Code, the EU was also preparing the adoption of the amended version of the Shareholder Rights Directive (hereinafter the SRD II).[14] During the public consultation that preceded the adoption of the Code, some responses to the consultation noted that the 'timing' of the Danish Code should perhaps have been considered more carefully given the (at that time) ongoing negotiations in the EU regarding the future amendment of the Shareholder Rights Directive.[15] As the SRD II also took inspiration from the UK Code, it is entirely questionable whether the result would have been much different if the Committee had waited around for the SRD II to be adopted.

The SRD II was transposed into Danish law in June 2019.[16] However, a number of the provisions did not enter into force until later.[17] This approach was chosen to give the affected parties more time to adjust to the new legal framework accordingly. The provisions on the transparency of the institutional investors and asset managers were transposed as amendments to several existing acts,[18] including the Financial Business Act and the Alternative Investment Fund Managers Act.[19] The Act transposing SRD II is structured such that section 1 contains the different provisions to be implemented in the Companies Act; section 2

---

[12] Danish Code (n. 2), p. 5.

[13] Birkmose and Madsen (n. 1), p. 155.

[14] Council Directive 2017/828/EU of 17 May 2007 amending Directive 2007/36/EC, as regards the encouragement of long-term shareholder engagement [2017] OJ L 132/1.

[15] A list of the respondents can be found here: Committee on Corporate Governance, https://corporategovernance.dk/sites/default/files/media/document/hoeringsnotat_med_links_-_anbefalinger_for_aktivt_ejerskab.pdf (5 September 2023).

[16] Lov 2019-04-09 nr. 369 om ændring af selskabsloven, lov om kapitalmarkeder, lov om finansiel virksomhed og forskellige andre love (Gennemførelse af ændringer i aktionærrettighedsdirektivet om tilskyndelse til langsigtet aktivt ejerskab) (Act No 369 of 9 April 2019 on the amendment of the Company Act, the Capital Markets Act, The Financial Business Act and different other acts (Transposition of changes in the Shareholder Rights Directive on the encouragement of long-term active ownership)) (our translation). See in greater detail, Birkmose and Madsen (n. 1), p. 167–169.

[17] The provisions on transparency of institutional investors and asset managers came into force for financial years starting on 1 January 2020. Consequently, the first reporting will take place in 2021. The provisions on identification of shareholders do not come into force until 3 September 2020.

[18] SRD II (n. 14), ch. 1b also includes provisions on transparency of proxy advisors. These, however, are beyond the scope of this Chapter.

[19] Consolidating Act No. 937 of 6 September 2019 and Consolidating Act No. 1047 of 14 October 2019.

contains the provisions to be implemented in the Capital Markets Act, and so on. Hence, the provisions transposing articles 3g–3i of the SRD II are found in several sections. More precisely, they are found in section 3, No. 3 (aimed at asset managers) and No. 4 (insurance companies), section 4, No. 3 (asset managers regulated by the AIFM Directive), section 5, No. 2 (UCITS funds which have not delegated the management to an investment management company), section 6, No. 2 (pension funds), section 7, No. 1 (ATP), and section 8, No. 1 (LD). The transposition is generally true to the wording of the SRD II, which is why provisions found in the different acts are essentially comparable overall.

Danish acts did not use the term 'institutional investor' anywhere in black letter law prior to the transpositions, despite it being an established term. Due to the regulatory approach involved, the term is still not a part of the transposition of the SRD II. Rather, the different provisions found in the different acts use sector-specific terms that are natural to the specific acts that transpose Directive 2009/138/EC[20] and Directive (EU) 2016/2341[21], as, these make up the SRD II's 'institutional investor' scope, as it were.[22] As a result, despite the transposing acts refraining from using the term 'institutional investors', the scope is nevertheless the same as in the Directive. However, it was stated in the preparatory document that it is important to the Danish regulators that national undertakings which are naturally seen as institutional investors should be included as well.[23] Consequently, the scope is widened as compared to the SRD II, as the so-called 'Arbejdsmarkedets Tillidspension (ATP)' and 'Lønmodtagernes Dyrtidsfond (LD)'[24] are given the same duties as SRD II's institutional investors. The term 'asset manager' was also not found in any Danish acts prior to the implementation of the SRD II. However, rather than using established terms, this term is now defined in the relevant acts, including the Financial Business Act, section 3(1)(70) and the Alternative Investment Fund Managers Act, section 3(1)(54). The definitions follow the definition found in the SRD II, Article 1(2)(b).

According to the Danish provisions – which transpose the SRD II – institutional investors and asset managers must both develop and publicly disclose a policy for active ownership in listed companies. The requirements on the content

[20] Directive 2009/138/EC of the European Parliament and of the Council of 25 November 2009 on the taking-up and pursuit of the business of Insurance and Reinsurance [2009] OJ L335/1 (Solvency II).

[21] Directive (EU) 2016/2341 of the European Parliament and of the Council of 14 December 2016 on the activities and supervision of institutions for occupational retirement provision [2016] OJ L354/37.

[22] Institutional investors are defined in SRD II (n. 14), art 2(b)(d).

[23] Proposal no. 157 of 6 February 2019 for the Act on the amendment of the Companies Act, the Capital Markets Act, the Financial Business Act, and different other acts (transposition of changes in the Shareholder Rights Directive on the encouragement of long-term active ownership) [our translation], sec. 2.2.3.

[24] ATP and LD are both Danish labour market supplementary pension funds.

of the policy closely follow the wording of the SRD II, and institutional investors must publish an engagement policy regardless of whether investments are made through an asset manager.

Moreover, institutional investors as well as asset managers have to disclose, on an annual basis, how their engagement policy has been implemented, along with a general description of their voting behaviour, a statement about the most significant votes, and a statement on the use of the services of proxy advisors. Institutional investors and asset managers also must disclose how they cast votes at the general meetings of companies in which they hold shares. Such disclosure, however, may exclude votes that are insignificant due to the subject matter of the vote or the size of the holding in the company. This option follows from SRD II Article 1(3). Recital 18 of the preamble states that '[s]uch insignificant votes may include votes cast on purely procedural matters or votes cast in companies where the investor has a very minor stake compared to the investor's holdings in other investee companies'. This understanding of 'insignificant votes' is peculiar in relation to the latter, since, offhand, it seems more relevant to look at the investor's stake in the shares of a given company relative to the full share capital involved and therefore the investor's potential influence in the said company. Despite this, the same wording is found in the Danish preparatory document.[25] Recital 18 also states that '[i]nvestors should set their own criteria regarding which votes are insignificant on the basis of the subject matter of the vote or the size of the holding in the company and apply them consistently'. This is also repeated in the Danish preparatory document,[26] and no further guidance is given on the matter. Disclosure of how the votes have been cast does not have to be made on an annual basis. Neither the SRD II nor the Danish provisions specify the frequency with which such information has to be disclosed.[27] However, in order to ensure the relevance and timeliness of such information, it is to be expected that such information has to be disclosed at 12 month intervals, at minimum. This could be done in connection with the publication and the implementation of the policy.

Meanwhile, the transparency provisions that transpose Article 3g of the SRD II are subject to the 'comply or explain' principle. According to section 344 of the Danish Financial Business Act, the Danish Financial Supervisory Authority shall supervise compliance with the provisions of the Financial Business Act and therefore also compliance with the 'comply or explain' provisions.[28] Sanctions in cases of noncompliance with the 'comply or explain' approach include reprimands and orders, but not pecuniary sanctions. What's more, there are no

[25] Proposal no. 157 (n. 23), explanatory notes for section 3, No. 4 and section 4, No. 3.
[26] Ibid.
[27] SRD II (n. 14) art 3g (1)(b).
[28] Similar supervisory provisions apply for other types of institutional investors.

formal requirements laid down for the disclosure process.[29] However, as the information has to be made freely available to the public on the institutional investor's or the asset manager's website, this medium is expected to be the preferred form for the required disclosure.

The SRD II also includes provisions that ensure transparency on matters relating to the relationship between institutional investors and asset manager investors. In these matters, the transposition of Articles 3g(2) and 3h in Danish law follows the wording of SRD II.[30]

The Danish provisions transposing the Directive's Chapter 1b on transparency became effective for financial years beginning 1 January 2020 or later.[31] Consequently, the institutional investors and asset managers had to report on their stewardship for the first time in 2021. As mentioned above, this approach was chosen to give institutional investors and asset managers sufficient time to adjust to the 'comply or explain' provisions that are now found in hard law provisions.[32] This transition period seems to have been most relevant to institutional investors and asset managers that had not previously applied the Danish Code as it allowed them to discuss whether to adjust their practices to comply with the stewardship provision either in whole or in part, or to explain why they are not complying in whole or in part.[33] Institutional investors and asset managers that were signed up to the Danish Code could continue their practice whilst preparing for the necessary amendments, such as the scope of the policy. This is due to the fact that from 2020 onwards, the policy is supposed to cover their entire portfolio and not only investments in Danish listed companies.

As for the targeted institutional investors and asset managers of the two frameworks, they are largely identical. The Danish Code was addressed to Danish institutional investors who invest in shares of companies that are publicly listed in Denmark. The term 'institutional investor' was left undefined in the Danish Code, but from the introduction to the Code, it was clear that the understanding of the term was very broad as it included 'shareholders and asset managers,

---

[29] Further on the transposition of Article 3g of the SRD II and the enforcement trends across Member States, see Dionysia Katelouzou and Konstantinos Sergakis, "Shareholder Stewardship Enforcement" in Dionysia Katelouzou and Dan W. Puchniak, *Global Shareholder Stewardship* (Cambridge University Press 2022).

[30] Supra (n. 16) Section 3, No. 4; Section 4, No. 3; Section 5, No. 2; Section 6, No. 2; Section 7, No. 1; and Section 8, No. 1.

[31] Ibid., sec. 9.

[32] On the symbiosis of soft and semi-hard stewardship requirements in the EU, see Dionysia Katelouzou and Konstantinos Sergakis, "When Harmonisation is not Enough: Shareholder Stewardship in the European Union." European Business Organization Law Review (2021) 22.

[33] The exact number of investors and asset managers that have not signed up to the code is unknown, partly because it is difficult to extract only those that invest in Danish listed companies from the Danish Financial Supervisory Authority's registers. However, the list of signatories shows a clear lack of asset managers, and so the number is probably as high as a couple of hundred.

as well as investors who perform both roles and directly or indirectly manage third party funds'.[34] The transposed provisions on stewardship are also aimed at Danish institutional investors and asset managers, but the provisions apply regardless of whether they invest in Danish listed shares or foreign listed shares. Moreover, due to the widening of the scope of the SRD II in Danish law, institutional investors and asset managers that are covered by the transposed provisions on stewardship are more or less similar to the institutional investors invited to sign up to the Stewardship Code, other than the scope of the former being marginally narrower.[35]

A review of the legal requirements in relation to the content of the policy on active ownership also reveals a great deal of overlap. This is hardly surprising seeing as both frameworks were greatly inspired by the UK Code.[36]

Due to the adoption of SRD II in Danish law, the Committee on Corporate Governance agreed with the Minister for Industry, Business and Financial Affairs in January 2020 that the Danish Stewardship Code would be phased out in 2020. However, as of mid-2023, the Committee has still not issued any statement withdrawing the Code, and as such, it therefore still formally applies and is found on the Committee for Corporate Governance's website.[37] It is interesting, though, that Denmark has chosen to go a different path than other countries and phase out the Code, rather than maintaining the Code and developing engagement mechanisms through this more flexible instrument.[38] The fact that the Code is being phased out also comes with the consequence that the most recent developments of the UK Code are not reflected in the Danish rules on stewardship.[39]

II. Shareholder activism in practice

We have argued elsewhere that there is great potential at hand for shareholder engagement in Denmark, on account of the vast powers that are granted shareholders in the Nordic corporate governance model.[40] In addition to the appoint-

---

[34] Danish Code (n. 2) p. 4.

[35] An example of an institutional investor not covered by the transposed provisions is the so-called group 2 insurance companies, per contra the wording of the Danish Financial Business Act, sec. 159.

[36] See explicitly the Danish Code (n. 2) 3. See also Birkmose and Madsen (n. 1) p. 155.

[37] https://corporategovernance.dk/anbefalinger-for-aktivt-ejerskab (5 September 2023).

[38] See Katelouzou and Sergakis supra (n. 32) p. 225 et seq.

[39] See https://www.frc.org.uk/getattachment/5aae591d-d9d3-4cf4-814a-d14e156a1d87/Stewardship-Code_Dec-19-Final-Corrected.pdf (5 September 2023).

[40] Hanne S. Birkmose and Karsten Engsig Sørensen, "Shareholder Democracy in Denmark: Contrasting Law on the Books and Law in Practice", sec. 1.3 in Harpreet Kaur, Chao Xi, Christoph Van der Elst, and Anne Lafarre (eds), *The Cambridge Handbook of Shareholder Engagement and Voting* (Cambridge University Press, 2022).

ment and removal of members of the board of directors,[41] shareholders have exclusive rights to decide on a number of other issues. In addition, under Danish law, the general meeting is considered omnipotent, meaning that it can decide on any matter concerning the company where such power is not explicitly given, by law, to either the board of directors or the executive management, including issues that relate to the day-to-day management of the company.

Hence, the Danish Companies Act relies on shareholders to exert their influence at the general meeting. Shareholders' influence on the corporate governance affairs of listed companies, however, – including institutional investors and asset managers – partly depends on their formal rights at the general meeting. In general, the rules are quite generous to shareholders. No matter the size of the shareholding, shareholders may speak at the general meeting, pose questions to the board of directors concerning the business of the company and submit proposals to be included in the agenda. The latter allows shareholders not only to react to the agenda set by the board of directors, but also to take an active role in issues to be discussed at the general meeting or proposals to be deliberated. Resolutions decided by the general meeting are binding, as the board must comply with any lawful decision made by the general meeting. This framework grants shareholders extensive powers that enable them to not only monitor and control corporate governance arrangements, but also to shape the rules governing the company. In practice, however, shareholders rarely call a meeting. Although they occasionally propose issues for the meeting agenda, those proposals are almost always voted down by a vast majority. As a result, one may conclude that the potential for shareholder democracy and activism is not being readily utilized by shareholders in Denmark. This is particularly the case for institutional investors.

Data from the general meetings of the 'GM seasons' 2017/2018 and 2018/2019 show that although there has been a slight increase in engagement by institutional investors, the overall level of engagement remains low. The data comprises agendas and minutes of annual general meetings and extraordinary general meetings from Danish companies.[42] The data shows that in the GM season 2018/2019, shareholders put an item on the agenda 31 times in large cap companies;[43] only once did a shareholder propose an amendment to an item on the

[41] The general meeting may remove the board at any time and without reason; see CA §§ 120 and 121.

[42] See Birkmose and Madsen (n. 1), p. 164–167 for the AGM seasons 2017/2018 and 2018/2019 (only large cap companies); and Birkmose and Engsig Sørensen (n. 40) for the GM season 2018/2019 (all listed companies). A methodological challenge in conducting a review based on publicly available data from the companies lies in the fact that no uniform approach currently exists. Some companies publish only a record of decisions, whereas others publish an extensive protocol. Hence, the aggregate level of shareholder engagement at the general meetings may be higher than the data actually show.

[43] These are the largest companies with the most liquid shares in Denmark. Usually, the GM takes place in the spring, as listed companies with a financial year from 1 January to 31 December

agenda; 130 addresses to the general meeting were made; and 137 questions were posed to management. For all listed companies, we identified shareholder proposals in the AGMs of 17 of the 126 companies considered. Although the total number of shareholder proposals stood at 47, nineteen were proposed in one company (Danske Bank A/S). It is very unusual to see such a high number of shareholder proposals in a single company. In this case, the number stems from Danske Bank's widely publicised involvement in a money laundering scandal in 2018. The 47 shareholder proposals should be considered in comparison with the 478 board-promoted proposals during the same period. Nevertheless, it still corresponds to approximately 10 per cent of all resolutions put forward at AGMs during the period being proposed by shareholders. Moreover, shareholders addressed the board of directors in the meetings of 27 companies, for a total of 144 addresses; and 127 oral questions were asked in 27 of the 126 companies considered. In most cases, the questions were posed by associations representing shareholders[44] or by individuals. Questions posed by institutional investors were less common. As a result, the Danish institutional investors' share in the shareholder engagement visible at the general meeting is quite limited accordingly.[45] Institutional investors made up 14 % of the addresses and asked 4 % of the questions in large cap companies. In none of the AGMs considered, however, were shareholder proposals actually put forward by institutional investors.

Issues related to corporate social responsibility (CSR) were among the more popular topics addressed by shareholder proposals (7 proposals in 47 companies),[46] while sustainability was not an issue raised by companies or shareholders in the general meetings considered.

There are clear indications, however, that the awareness of these issues is indeed growing, in particular, in response to the EU sustainable finance agenda. First, starting with the annual financial reports for 2021, a number of companies, including listed companies, have to report on sustainable economic activity, according to the Taxonomy Regulation, art. 8.[47] Second, the 2020 Danish Corporate Governance Code includes a recommendation according to which the board of directors is supposed to adopt a policy for the company's corporate social responsibility, including social responsibility and sustainability. That policy should, furthermore, be available in the management commentary and/or on

---

are required to submit their annual report (approved by the AGM) to the Danish Business Authority within four months after the end of the financial year, cf. the Danish Financial Statements Act, s 138.

[44] The two dominating associations are the Danish Shareholders' Association (Dansk Aktionærforening) and an association by the name of Critical Shareholders (Kritiske Aktionærer).

[45] None of the minutes revealed engagement by non-Danish institutional investors.

[46] Birkmose and Engsig Sørensen (n. 40) sec. 13.3.2.

[47] Council Regulation (EU) 2020/852 of 18 June 2020 on the establishment of a framework to facilitate sustainable investment, and amending Regulation (the Taxonomy Regulation).

the company's website.[48] Although it is not new that the Corporate Governance Code includes a recommendation on the company's CSR policy, it is new that it specifically mentions social responsibility and sustainability. Large companies are also required to supplement the management commentary with a non-financial social responsibility report (CSR report), according to the Financial Statements Act, § 99 a. Third, the 2021 GM season showed examples of large Danish institutional investors putting shareholder proposals on the agenda of listed companies' general meetings, also in terms of ESG-related issues.[49] Finally, these developments, combined with the mentioning of ESG in the provisions transposing the SRD II, art. 3 g, may also serve to accelerate the ESG and sustainability focus. Still, it remains to be seen how it will be ultimately reflected in AGM practice.

III. Obstacles to a meaningful "engagement policy"

An increasing number of shares are held by foreign investors.[50] In recent years, foreign institutional investors, in particular, have increased their ownership of Danish shares. In 2018, foreign investors, presumably mainly institutional investors, held 54 per cent of the total capital listed.[51] Yet for years, the pattern has been that foreign investors are less likely than Danish investors to participate and vote in general meetings.

There may be several explanatory factors at play here, but part of the problem is that foreign investors have often had trouble appointing a proxy holder. A proxy holder has to have a written proxy on hand which is dated and signed by the shareholder.[52] A proxy can be indefinite, but the shareholder nevertheless

---

[48] Listed companies have to report on their compliance with the Corporate Governance Code according to the Financial Statements Act, sec. 107 b. Reporting is subject to the comply or explain-principle though.

[49] See Louise Celia Corpela, Anders Ørjan Jensen and Julie Müller Cornelius, "Generalforsamlingen 2022 – status, fokus og trends.", *Revision og Regnskabsvæsen* No. 1, 2022, sec. 5.2.

[50] The percentage of share capital held by foreign investors more than doubled from 2006 to 2016. See Klaus Søgaard, Michael Brichmann, and Louise Celia Korpela Martiny, "Generalforsamlinger i børsnoterede selskaber – Udvalgte emner og problemstillinger (del 2)", Revision & Regnskabsvæsen, 2017, pp. 15. See also Jesper Lau Hansen and Carsten Lønfeldt, "Corporate Governance in Denmark" in Per Lekvall (ed.), The Nordic Corporate Governance Model (SNS Förlag 2014) p. 117 et seq.

[51] See the review by VP Securities available at https://www.vp.dk/News-and-Insights/News-List/2018/6/VP-Annual-General-Meeting-Analysis-Active-ownership-and-digitisation-set-the-scene (5 September 2023); regarding 2019, data from the Danish National Bank show that of the 25 largest listed companies (the so-called C25 index) were owned by foreign investors in November 2019; *see* www.nationalbanken.dk/da/statistik/find_statistik/Documents/V%C3%A6rdipapirstatistik/V%C3%A6rdipapirer%2020200107.pdf (5 September 2023); the largest percentage of foreign ownership is found in large cap companies. *See* Søgaard, Brichmann and Korpela Martiny, *ibid* p. 15 et seq.

[52] Danish Companies Act, sec. 80.

have the option to recall it at any time.[53] Proxies can be blank – i.e. without any voting instructions – leaving the decision on how to vote up to the proxy holder. Institutional investors often hold shares through nominee accounts. Consequently, it is the nominee who is registered by name in the share register of the company. Current Danish practice assumes that the registration of a nominee named does not suffice in terms of the nominee being entitled to exercise the rights attached to shares with the exception of economic rights.[54] In that vein, a nominee is not able to vote at general meetings unless the de facto shareholder has given notice of his or her acquisition of the shares to the company, established his or her title to them, and has provided the nominee with a valid proxy. This practice often results in a large number of voting instructions being dismissed for noncompliance.[55]

To remedy this problem, new legislation was adopted in April 2022 that changed the rules on proxies in the Danish Companies Act.[56] According to the new rules, a nominee will no longer be regarded as the proxy of the de facto shareholder and will thus no longer have to present valid voting instructions. The nominee will have the right to exercise voting rights on the shares despite the fact that most ownership related rights belong to the shareholder as long as the shares are registered under the name of the nominee in the company's register of shareholders. The nominee exercising voting rights must see to it that the necessary instructions from the shareholders are in place. If requested by the company, the nominee must document that he/she possesses the necessary instructions, which can be in the form of a SWIFT-notice or something similar. The new rules entered into force on the 1st of July 2022 and will make it easier for a nominee to vote according to voting instructions from the shareholder. The law, however, does not change the duty of the intermediary to facilitate that the shareholder him/herself (or another proxy appointed by the shareholder) can exercise voting rights. All in all, the expectation is that this legislation will make it easier for foreign investors to exercise their voting rights and thus get more actively engaged.

Another possible obstacle to shareholder engagement is the mandatory bid rule. According to § 44 of the Danish Capital Market Act, a mandatory bid is imposed on anyone that controls – directly or indirectly – a third of all the voting

[53] Danish Companies Act, sec. 80(2).

[54] Bunch and Corfixsen Whitt, "Selskabsloven med kommentarer" (3rd edn., Karnov Group 2018) sec. 52.

[55] See VP Securities, "Memorandum: The Possibility of Simplifying the Proxy Voting Process in Denmark", p. 2 www.vp.dk/News-and-Insights/News-List/2018/2/Memorandum-The-possibility-of-simplifying-the-proxy-voting-process-in-Denmark (5 September 2023). The same figure – a third of all voting instructions – is mentioned in the proposal for a new legislation remedying the problem, see below (n. 56) (proposal L 117 dated 9 February 2022, p. 16).

[56] See L 117 B adopted 19 April 2022 altering inter alia the Danish Companies Act § 80 and § 104.

rights in a listed company unless it can be proven that such a shareholding does not confer control over the company. This duty also applies to a group of persons or companies that acts in concert and controls a third of the voting rights in a listed company. If a group of shareholders coordinates their behaviour at the general meeting and, together as a collective unit, controls a third of the voting rights, it raises the question of whether they could trigger a mandatory bid duty. If that were the case, this would certainly pose an obstacle to such collaboration.

Acting in concert does not require a formal agreement between the shareholders, as an implied agreement suffices. Most of the cases involving implied agreements have included related parties, but in principle, an implied agreement could also be established between non-related shareholders. The aim of the agreement (implied or explicit) is supposed to be to control the company. Although this will normally include an agreement to control a broader range of issues or activities in the company, it could likewise theoretically be an agreement restricted to one or a few issues – provided that these issues are substantive – such as, for instance, the election of the board of directors. Hence, it cannot be excluded that shareholders collaborating at a general meeting may – given the right circumstances – may be acting in concert.[57] There is, however, no case law to substantiate this. It is, however, assumed that the white list published on 12 November 2013 by ESMA may be useful as a guide for interpreting the concept of acting in concert in Danish law, and consequently, the activities mentioned in the white list may be less likely to trigger a mandatory bid duty.[58]

However, even when shareholders collaborate to the extent that they are seen to be acting in concert, this event in and of itself will not trigger a mandatory bid. This would also require there to be a transfer of shares, e.g., wherein one of the collaborating shareholders acquires additional shares during the time in which they are acting in concert. In 2013, the Danish FSA suggested changing the rules such that a mandatory bid would be effected even if no transfer of shares took place. This would have the effect that shareholders acting in concert (and controlling a third of the votes) would trigger the mandatory bid duty even if they did not acquire additional shares.[59] This change would therefore make it more

---

[57] See the discussion in Karsten Engsig Sørensen, "Samarbejde om opnåelse af kontrol med børsnoterede selskaber", *Nordisk Tidsskrift for Selskabsret* 2009:3 pp. 131–163.

[58] Right after ESMA adopted the white list the Danish FSA indicated that it would use this for interpreting the Danish takeover rules, see VEJ no. 9687 from 15/09/2014. This is also assumed in the legal literature, see Marina Bitsch Madsen, "Når samarbejde bliver dyrt: nye regler om "at handle i forståelse" og tilbudspligt", *Nordisk Tidsskrift for Selskabsret* 2014:2, p. 86 and Dan Moalem, Matthias V. W. Nielsen & Lennart Meyer Østenfjeld, "Overtagelsestilbud – nye praksis og nye regler", Nordisk Tidsskrift for Selskabsret 2014:4 p. 4. However, Jesper Lau Hansen, "Kapitalmarkedsloven med kommentarer", 2022, p. 381 finds the white list less useful since it is not very precise when it comes to collaboration on electing board members.

[59] See the proposal L119 dated 23 October 2013, that inter alia aimed to change the Danish Securities Trading Act which at the time contained the mandatory bid rule.

likely for a shareholder collaboration to trigger a bid. However, this part of the proposal received significant criticism during the public hearing, and eventually the proposal was given up and did not ultimately become a part of the final law adopted. On that note, the minister in charge pointed out that it was important not to impede shareholder engagement.[60]

IV. On the inclusion of debt investors in the activist programme

As mentioned above in Section I.1, the Danish Stewardship Code is being phased out, and it may be argued that it leaves the Danish framework less flexible and with less room for transposition of international trends. One such trend – which is not currently reflected in the Danish stewardship framework – is the UK development, where institutional investors and asset managers are encouraged to use their influence not only as equity investors, but regardless of how the capital is invested.[61] To date, there has been no debate on the role of institutional investors and asset managers in Denmark in relation to debt investment or alternative investments.

This, however, in no way means that investors other than equity investors have no influence on the companies in which they are investing, as dialogue with company stakeholders is indeed key to Danish corporate governance practice. The very first Danish Corporate Governance Code from 2001 included a recommendation (II.1), according to which the boards are supposed to adopt a stakeholder policy which lays down the company's relationship to its stakeholders, containing *inter alia,* the company's business concept (idégrundlag), fundamental values, and objectives. Moreover, according to the recommendation (II.2), the supervisory board should ensure that the interests and roles of the stakeholders are respected in accordance with the company's policy on such issues. Here, it was mentioned that it was natural to ensure that the executive board and the company's stakeholders are participating in active exchange for the purposes of developing and strengthening the company. Today, recommendation 1.1.1 states that 'the [Danish Corporate Governance] Committee recommends that the management – through ongoing dialogue and interaction –, ensures that shareholders, investors and other stakeholders gain the relevant insight into the company's affairs and that the board of directors obtains the possibility of hearing and including their views in its work' and recommendation 1.1.2 states, furthermore, that 'the Committee recommends that the company adopts policies on the company's relationships with its shareholders, investors and if relevant other stakeholders ...'.

[60] See the account in Marina Bitsch Madsen, (n. 58), pp. 82–83.
[61] The UK Stewardship Code 2020, p. 6 https://www.frc.org.uk/investors/uk-stewardship-code#the-uk-stewardship-code (5 September 2023).

At the same time, the Corporate Governance Code does not mention anything on dialogue between investors and stakeholders. This may not be surprising, as the addressees of the Code are Danish companies with shares admitted to trading on a regulated market in Denmark. However, the Danish Stewardship Code did not include anything on dialogue either. It did, however, include a recommendation on collaboration with other investors.[62] Judging from the comments which follow the recommendation, it nevertheless seems clear that the reference to investors should be seen as other equity investors (shareholders).

Although the Corporate Governance Code does mention dialogue with stakeholders, we do not find that any efforts are being made in Denmark to make dialogue between investee companies and shareholders or other stakeholders more concrete.

V. On the relationship between "dialogue conducting/engagement" and equal information treatment of shareholders

As mentioned above, the Danish Corporate Governance Code encourages dialogue between management and shareholders, and it is generally assumed that such dialogue often takes place in practice.[63] Such dialogue may potentially create a conflict with the duty of confidentiality imposed on the management of the investee company, along with the duty to treat shareholders equally and a prohibition on insider trading. These issues have been discussed in Danish legal literature although not specifically in relation to ESG and sustainability.

According to § 132 of the Danish Companies Act, members of management – including both members of the executive management and the board of directors – are bound by a duty of confidentiality. They may not share information with outsiders including shareholders if doing so would be harmful to the company. The focus is on trade secrets which are most likely to cause such harm.[64] Since the reach of the provision is somewhat ambiguous, it is assumed that the board of directors themselves may decide on what information can be shared and if the board or the executive management may only share information that the board has accepted, it is less likely that the provision is infringed upon.[65]

If there is no board decision specifying what information may be shared, all individual members of the board have to decide on their own. The starting point

---

[62] Principle 4.

[63] The reports that the Danish institutional investors have published as part of their SRD II obligations indicate that this is quite common. See also our paper entitled 'Engagement policies and the promotion of sustainability', available at ssrn.com.

[64] See for instance Jan Schans Christensen, "Kapitalselskaber", 2021 p. 492 and Peer Schaumburg-Müller, "Selskabsloven med kommentarer", 2020, p. 799.

[65] *See* Paul Krüger Andersen, "Aktie- og anpartsselskabsret", 2021 p. 393 and Schaumburg-Müller, "Selskabsloven med kommentarer", 2020, pp. 795–796.

will be that trade secrets may not be shared, yet there is nevertheless room built-in in there for exceptions. First, sharing sensitive information may be justified in case of its necessity for running the company. If, for instance, the board is considering a merger, it makes little sense to plan for such a merger if the board is not convinced that the major shareholders are likewise interested in such a merger. In that vein, sharing information about the possible merger would in this case be justified and thus not violate the duty of confidentiality.[66] More controversial is the question of whether a member of the board of directors may share information with the shareholder who elected him or her. It has been argued that a director may have a wider discretion for offering information to such a shareholder, in particular, if the shareholder undertakes treating the information confidentially.[67] However, this view has been challenged and thus it cannot be said for certain that a relaxation of the duty of confidentiality is indeed in place.[68]

If information is shared with some and not all shareholders, there could potentially be an infringement of the duty to treat shareholders equally. Although this duty is generally recognised in Danish law,[69] there has been little discussion about how this duty may affect dialogue with shareholders as such. It is, however, assumed that the duty enjoys broad general application and thus includes information-sharing, although the duty may well be less strong in protecting the shareholders' non-economic rights.[70]

Although it may be assumed that providing shareholders with different information may be an infringement of the duty to treat shareholders equally, a number of exceptions can enter into play that allow varied dissemination of information. First, the articles of association may allow for a different treatment of shareholders by allocating different classes of shares different rights, and a decision by the general meeting may allow different treatment of shareholders in specific questions. Neither of these exceptions seems very practical. More relevant is the exception for justified deviations from the duty. If the company can find objective reasons for offering different shareholders different infor-

[66] See Schans Christensen, supra (n. 64) p. 492.

[67] See Jesper Lau Hansen: "Informationsmisbrug", 2001 pp. 442–456 and Carsten Fode & Mette Neville: "SMV-bestyrelsen – hele vejen rundt", 2018, pp. 292–293.

[68] See the discussion in the government report 1498/2008 pp. 334–335, where the view that a member of the board may share sensitive information with selected shareholders is presented as a minority view. The discussion about sharing information with those who have elected a member of the board has, in particular, been discussed in relation to employee representatives. Whereas it is assumed that they cannot freely share sensitive information with the workers in the company, they are likely to be able to share such information with a trade union organising these workers.

[69] The duty to treat shares equally is codified in § 45 of the Danish Companies Act. Although the EU Company Law Directive only stipulates such a duty in relation to the rules on capital, it is assumed that the Danish duty existed before the adoption of the Second Company Law directive, and that it has a broader impact accordingly, *see*, *supra* (n. 64) p. 143–152 and Erik Werlauff: "Selskabsret", 2019 pp. 439–442.

[70] Schans Christensen, supra (n. 64) p. 148.

mation, this may be acceptable. Again, favouring larger shareholders with information about certain upcoming strategic decisions may be justified by the fact that their opinion will have significant bearing on the decision of whether to go ahead or not. As mentioned, the question has hardly been discussed in theory and there are no decisions addressing how the duty of equal treatment may affect disclosure of information to shareholders.

Any dialogue with shareholders in listed companies must also respect the rules in the Market Abuse Regulation (MAR) on unlawful disclosure of inside information.[71] These rules do not prohibit all disclosure of inside information to outsiders such as shareholders. In that way, an exception is made where the disclosure takes place in the normal course of the members' employment, profession or duties.[72] This means that to some extent, the allowance for disclosing information depends on the management setting and regulation applied in national law.[73] For Danish law, it is assumed that there is in fact some room for members of management to disclose inside information even to persons or organisations outside the company. This is based primarily on the Danish Supreme Court's decision in U2009.2142 H, which was the case that had previously resulted in the preliminary reference that gave us Case C-384/02, *Grøngaard & Bang*. The Supreme Court found that it had not been an unlawful disclosure to share the information on the planned merger with the trade union, including information on the exchange rate of the shares of the two companies involved, as, this information was indeed relevant for assessing the impact that the merger or alternatives to this merger could have for the employees of the company. It was thus assumed that the disclosure of the information was a normal part of the employee representatives' function as an employee representative. It was also relevant that the information was imparted in confidentiality, whereby the union was made aware that they had to observe the obligation under MAR Art. 10.[74] The judgment seems to allow for disclosure where it serves the interest of the company or allows the members to perform their duties. In particular, it may be possible to give information to large shareholders about intended plans if these plans can only be realised with the acceptance of these shareholders. In any case, however, the information disclosure should be limited to what is strictly necessary for achieving the justified goal.[75]

---

[71] See MAR, regulation 596/2014 Art. 10 and 14(c).

[72] See Case C-384/02, Grøngaard & Bang, para. 26.

[73] See Paul Krüger Andersen, Nis Jul Clausen & Jesper Lau Hansen: "Børsretten", 2019 p. 582.

[74] On this duty see also Konstantinos Sergakis, *The Law of Capital Markets in the EU: Disclosure and Enforcement* (Palgrave 2018) p. 165.

[75] See further David Moalem, "Om forbuddet mod uberettiget videregivelse af intern viden", *Nordisk Tidsskrift for Selskabsret* 2010:1 pp. 119–148 and Krüger Andersen, Jul Clausen & Lau Hansen, supra (n. 73) p. 587.

Taken all together, it seems that Danish law allows for some flexibility in sharing information with shareholders, yet management nevertheless needs to keep these rules in mind when they engage in such dialogue so as not to exchange information that goes beyond what is needed for safeguarding the interest of the company and in the case of a listed company, the interest of the market.

C. Sustainable Funding / Portfolio Governance

I. Generalities on the reorganization of funding management under ESG aspects

When SRD II was transposed into Danish law, no debate took place on the transposition of art. 3 h, and the preparatory work only included very little, which could be relevant for the content of an investment strategy. It is only stated here that the exercise of active ownership should be seen in connection with the institutional investor's or asset manager's investment strategy, whether, for example, the institutional investor/the asset manager offers an active or a passive investment strategy.[76] This could imply that a passive investment strategy will be followed by a reluctant attitude towards active ownership. This is not necessarily the case, however.[77] It may not be surprising that Art. 3 h does not include any material on the investment strategy, as it is purely a disclosure provision. Similar to SRD II, Art. 3 g, Art. 3 h is also transposed in existing regulations, such as the Financial Business Act, the Investment Fund Act, and the Alternative Investment Fund Management Act.

From this starting point, Art. 3 of the Sustainable Finance Disclosure Regulation (hereinafter the SFDR) may have a positive impact on the inclusion of sustainability in the investment strategy, as it requires that financial market participants and financial advisers focus on the integration of sustainability risks in their business models. However, the overall approach by the Danish Financial Supervisory Authority seems to be that no national regulation will supplement the European framework, whereafter the Regulation will stand on its own. An exception to this is made where national regulation is needed for transposing the Regulation's provisions, e.g. delegated directives, or where the Danish FSA finds that guidelines may be necessary for supporting the European mandatory framework. Concerning Art. 3, the latter may be relevant, as the Regulation does not grant the Commission any delegated power in relation to this provision. For the time being, we have found very little material regarding the interpretation of

[76] Proposal no. 157 (n. 23), explanatory notes for sec. 3, No. 2.

[77] See among others Jill E. Fisch, "The Uncertain Stewardship Potential of Index Funds", in Dionysia Katelouzou & Dan W. Puchniak (eds) *Global Shareholder Stewardship*, (Cambridge University Press, 2022) and the same author, "The New Titans of Wall Street: A Theoretical Framework for Passive Investors", University of Pennsylvania Law Review, Vol. 168, p. 17, 2020.

the SFDR Art. 3 in Denmark, though, as no guideline has thus far been issued. However, the Danish FSA has published an assessment of the SFDR Art. 3 in the Danish Financial Sector, which gives some indications on the interpretation of this provision by the Danish FSA.

According to SFDR Art. 3, financial market participants and financial advisers are required to publish information on their websites about their policies on the integration of sustainability risks in their investment decision-making process, respectively, in their investment advice or insurance advice. This provision applies from 10 March 2021 and as mentioned, it does not await the adoption of any delegated acts. Consequently, as early as May 2021, the Danish FSA initiated an assessment of the SFDR Art. 3 in Danish banks and pension funds covered by the scope of the SFDR, cf. Art. 2, no. 1, letters d and j, and Art. 2, no. 11, letter c, respectively.[78] The aim of the assessment was to examine whether selected banks (8) and pension funds (4)[79] complied with the requirements of the SFDR Art. 3 and, secondly, to identify best practices in the field by, wherever possible, comparing how banks and pension funds met the obligations of Art. 3. The result showed that several of the firms reviewed had implemented the obligations under Art. 3 insufficiently and that there was thus significant room for improvement.

The SFDR neglects either to set out formal requirements on how the policies are supposed to be formulated or to specify where on the websites of the respective firms that the information should be located. However, Art. 3 presupposes that firms publish at least one text which creates transparency regarding their calculation of sustainability risks. This information is designed to provide investors with an understanding of how the respective enterprise works with sustainability risks or, alternatively, why they refrain from doing so.[80] The assessment included three different aspects accordingly.

First, the assessment looked at whether the firms in question describe how sustainability risks are integrated and whether they describe their assessment of the impact of sustainability risks on the value of their investments. All the undertakings reviewed stated that they incorporate sustainability risks into their investment decision-making process or advice, but the FSA found that the level of detail in the descriptions of this integration varies widely.[81] Only two undertakings were found to be providing customers with a nuanced description of where and how they integrate sustainability risks across their investment area or advice. According to the FSA, the most useful and comprehensive Art. 3 policies clearly addressed where and how the firms integrate sustainability risks. This

[78] Danish Financial Supervisory Authority, *Assessment of the Sustainable Finance Disclosure Regulation Article 3 in the Danish Financial Sector* (2021).

[79] The eight banks and four pension funds were selected on a risk-based approach, *ibid.* p. 3.

[80] Ibid. p. 5.

[81] Ibid. p. 5–6.

included nuanced and concrete descriptions of the actions undertaken for minimising sustainability risks carried out by the enterprises, or alternatively, the lack of such actions, as the aim is to ensure that the end-investor is properly informed about where and how, specifically, the enterprise takes the risks identified into account.[82] Regarding the second part of the assessment of whether the content of the policies met the requirements of Article 3 of the SFDR, the FSA found that in order to comply with Art. 3, the policy must, at minimum, include considerations as to whether sustainability factors can have a negative impact on the value of the specific investments of the respective enterprise. To this end, generic and general descriptions of sustainability risks as a phenomenon are not sufficient. Rather, best practice requires the firm to provide a nuanced and entity-specific assessment of how different sustainability risks are managed across the given types of investments of the undertaking, thus providing end-investors with proper information regarding the exposures of the undertaking.[83] Regarding the content of the policies, the FSA also reviewed which documents include the sustainability risk integration policy. The FSA noted that all the firms reviewed provided more than one document to the FSA and that they specified that several of these documents formed the basis of their policy for the integration of the respective sustainability risks. The FSA found that the documents in many cases indicated an insufficient conceptual distinction between sustainability risks and the impact on sustainability factors, respectively, as well as an insufficient understanding of the fact that Art. 3 pertains exclusively to sustainability risks.[84] This led the FSA to conclude that the policy for the integration of sustainability risks must be easily accessible and identifiable to the end-investors, and that this obligation can be met through the publication of either an independent policy on the integration of sustainability risks or through an independent section with an illustrative title in a broader policy on the area.[85]

In addition to the various aspects described above, the FSA also examined compliance with the publication requirement of the article, i. e. on the respective enterprise websites. The FSA found that 11 out of the 12 reviewed firms submitted a website link to the policies on the integration of sustainability risks. However, the FSA also stated that in order to comply with the disclosure requirement, the policies are supposed to be published in a logical and easily accessible location on the company websites in order to facilitate identification thereof by the end-investor.[86]

Finally, the FSA examined the extent to which the policies were implemented in the internal processes of the respective undertakings. To this end, the FSA

---

[82] Ibid. p. 6.
[83] Ibid. p. 7.
[84] Ibid. p. 8.
[85] Ibid. p. 8.
[86] Ibid. p. 9.

asked these firms to submit a description of how the policies in question are applied in their internal processes as well as to submit relevant documents in connection thereof. However, the FSA found that it did not have sufficient documentation to form an overall opinion on this issue. For that reason, the FSA plans to focus on this area in future supervisory efforts.[87]

The overall conclusion on the assessment was that the FSA found that there was significant room for improvement among the undertakings reviewed on several points, particularly as regards more nuanced identification of sustainability risks for the given investments of the undertakings as well as where and how exactly these risks are integrated into the investment decision process or investment advice.[88] However, at the time of the publication of the assessment, the FSA stated that it would not apply any supervisory reactions since it was a new legislative area. Rather, the firms reviewed would receive individual feedback and elaboration on their shortcomings from the FSA to guide them in their continuing work on Art. 3.[89]

II. On the conflicting relationship between ESG-compliant and prudential portfolio strategies

The business model of institutional investors, including pension funds and mutual funds, for the most part follows the traditional principles of financial regulatory law, according to which they have to align their investment strategy with the principles of quantitative and qualitative risk diversification. The aim of these principles is to ensure sufficient diversification of the investment objects with the result that the investment is spread over a number of portfolio companies and likewise that they feature different risk profiles so that no cluster risks can emerge. Such investment strategy is generally considered to be in line with the fiduciary duties of the institutional investors, including the prudent person principle, which, in case of pension funds, are found in the Solvency II Directive and the Delegated Regulation (EU) 2015/35.[90] The importance of the prudent person principle in relation to the potential conflict between ESG interests and client interests is discussed below in Section II.3.

---

[87] Ibid. p. 9.

[88] Ibid. p. 10.

[89] Ibid. p. 2.

[90] Directive 2009/138/EC on the taking-up and pursuit of the business of Insurance and Reinsurance (Solvency II) and the Commission Delegated Regulation of 10 October 2014 supplementing Directive 2009/138/EC of the European Parliament and of the Council on the taking-up and pursuit of the business of Insurance and Reinsurance (Solvency II). EIOPA has issued 'Guidelines on system of governance' which guides Member States in the implementation and interpretation of the Directive.

In relation to the overall investment strategy the Solvency II Directive, Art. 132 (2), second sub-paragraph states that '[a]ll assets, in particular those covering the Minimum Capital Requirement and the Solvency Capital Requirement, shall be invested in such a manner as to ensure the security, quality, liquidity and profitability of the portfolio as a whole …' This wording is not transposed into the Danish legislative text, but the preparatory works refer to the main content of the provision in relation to the discussion of the prudent person principle. Moreover, the Financial Business Act, Art. 132 (4) also states that without prejudice to paragraph 2, '[a]ssets shall be properly diversified in such a way as to avoid excessive reliance on any particular asset, issuer or group of undertakings, or geographical area and excessive accumulation of risk in the portfolio as a whole.' The black letter regulation of other types of institutional investors also includes provisions on diversification, including the Financial Business Act Art. 157–157b and the Investment Fund Act, Chapter 14 and 15.

In particular, in relation to the financial sector, the Danish FSA has held out that climate-related risks should be handled like any other financial risk and that the FSA generally expects the financial sector to follow the applicable rules for good governance structures in managing financial risks as a result of climate change.[91] Consequently, risk management must be proportional to the nature, scope and complexity of the individual financial undertaking's business model. This means that the enterprises must address all risks affecting them and that their governance must incorporate management of these risks in their strategy, risk profile, risk appetite, policies, and guidelines accordingly. Hence, the financial risks which stem from climate change, for example, should be included in the risk management calculation just like any other financial risk. Although the brief from the Danish FSA only specifically concerns risks stemming from climate change, there is no reason to believe that other types of sustainability risks should be handled any differently.

In sum, the reorientation of portfolio management to ESG concerns has not really been addressed by the Danish FSA and without any amendments to the underlying regulatory regime, the risks that follow from a given (ESG) investment strategy must be handled like any other risk. It may well feature the consequence that it will be less profitable for the fund to make constructive use of voting rights due to the quantitative risk diversification requirement. However, it is not an issue which has been discussed in Denmark. Moreover, it may also involve a conflict with ESG-aligned strategies due to the qualitative risk diversification requirement. In the worst case, it could imply that pension funds may not be able to offer investment products which fall under the SFDR, Art. 9, due

---

[91] See Finanstilsynet, "Climate change and sustainable finance in the financial sector", December 2019, available at https://www.finanstilsynet.dk/Nyheder-og-Presse/Pressemeddelelser/2019/Julebrev_baeredygtighed_131219 (5 September 2023).

to the fact that the investment universe available for such products would be too narrow for the funds to comply with the prudent person principle.

III. On the conflict relationship between ESG interests and client interests in portfolio management

When it comes to the relationship between ESG interests and client interests in portfolio management and the potential conflict it holds, it is once again the overall duties of the financial undertaking which are relevant – these being mainly the fiduciary duties of the financial undertakings, and in case of the pension funds, in particular, the prudent person principle.

Starting with the latter, the prudent person principle was transposed into the Danish Financial Business Act § 158. The provision does not refer to the prudent person principle, but rather states that '[i]nsurance companies shall invest their assets in such a way as to safeguard the interests of the policyholders and beneficiaries to the best of their abilities.' However, the preparatory work makes clear references to the principle. Moreover, the prudent person principle has since been extended to apply to the Danish labour market supplementary pension funds, ATP and LD.[92]

The overall aim of the principle is reflected in the Solvency II, Art. 132 (2), third subparagraph, which states that '[a]ssets held to cover the technical provisions shall also be invested in a manner appropriate to the nature and duration of the insurance and reinsurance liabilities. Those assets shall be invested in the best interest of all policy holders and beneficiaries taking into account any disclosed policy objective.' In respect to this paragraph, the Danish preparatory work states that in order to fulfil this requirement, the pensions funds must adopt an investment strategy for each individual pension product and the derived obligations, meaning that the investment strategies must reflect that which the pension fund's clients have been promised.[93] Although it is not clear how the reference to the 'the best interest of all policy holders and beneficiaries' should be interpreted, the Danish FSA has held out that it includes an obligation to create the greatest possible long-term return considering the pension fund's risk appetite.[94] It is generally accepted that it does not mean that the pension fund must optimize the return in any case, as, it will – as a starting point – entail a high

---

[92] ATP-loven § 26 and LD-loven § 6.

[93] Proposal no. 114 of 21 January 2015, explanatory notes to § 1 no. 43. See *also* Tomas Krüger Andersen and Torben Christensen, "Prudent person-princippet – reguleringen af institutionelle investorers investeringer", *Nordisk Tidsskrift for Selskabsret*, 2022:1, footnote 35.

[94] This interpretation predates the transposition of the Sovency II directive, but it follows from the preparatory work that it still stands, ibid. See also Krüger Andersen and Christensen, ibid. p. 14.

risk.[95] The preparatory work mentions that when assessing whether a pension fund complies with the prudent person principle, the FSA will assess whether the individual pension fund has laid down an appropriate investment strategy which establishes a clear framework for the risk accepted in relation to each product, ensures a suitable degree of risk diversification, and prevents risk that conflicts with the interests of the policy holders. Moreover, the FSA has stated that the FSA will assess whether the investment strategy and the actual investments support the pension fund's long-term objective, including securing the best possible return. These criteria do not originate directly in the Solvency II Directive and are therefore seen as the Danish legislator's understanding of what lies in the best interest of the policy holders.[96] It should be mentioned that the Financial Business Act § 158 (2) grants the Danish FSA the power to lay down more detailed regulations on the application of subsection one by the adoption of an executive order. The FSA has so far not made use of this authority.

The importance of the prudent person principle has not been discussed specifically in relation to the current sustainable finance agenda in Denmark, but the FSA has previously issued statements on ethical investments and climate change and sustainable investment. Based on these statements, it seems to be the opinion of the FSA that the overall aim also in relation to ESG related risks is to comply with the prudent person principle. Hence, if a pension fund can choose between two investments with the same expected return, it is unproblematic to choose the one with the highest ESG score. On the other hand, a pension fund cannot include ESG considerations if it results in an expected lower return.[97] Later, the question was discussed in one of the Danish Parliament's committees, and there, the Minister for Industry, Business and Financial Affairs stated that a pension fund can incorporate ESG considerations in the investment strategy as long as the investment strategy reflects what the beneficiaries have been held out. Consequently, in this case, CSR considerations can be included in an investment even if another investment, seen in isolation, would have yielded a higher return as long as the pension fund seeks the best possible return within the limits of an investment strategy agreed upon with the beneficiary.[98] Finally, it was said that it would also be possible to include ESG considerations if it is part of a fund's well-diversified portfolio as long as the portfolio on an overall level is appropriate, including how it regards the relationship between risk and return. The interpretation and extent of the latter statement is not clear, and it leaves Danish pension

[95] Krüger Andersen, ibid.

[96] Krüger Andersen, ibid. p. 9.

[97] Krüger Andersen, ibid. p. 15–16.

[98] The minister of business' reply to the Danish parliament's 'Erhvervs- Vækst- og Eksportudvalg' of 26 February 2017. See, Besvarelse af B 44 spørgsmål 1 stillet af Folketingets Erhvervs- Vækst- og Eksportudvalg d. 13. februar 2018.

funds with little clarity in relation to the incorporation of ESG considerations into their investment strategy.[99]

As a result, it seems that Danish pension funds are restricted in their freedom to invest in a sustainable or ESG-compliant manner when it is not explicitly arranged with their beneficiaries. In this case, they must aim to generate the highest possible return with respect to the risk profile for the individual products. They can thus only include ESG considerations in the investment strategies which are laid down for an individual product and which are worked out with the beneficiary for the purpose of following the policy objectives of a more sustainability-oriented investment sector. Securing this agreement between the pension fund and the beneficiaries is key to the whole process of the funds incorporating ESG considerations – a point made repeatedly by the Minister for Industry, Business and Financial Affairs.[100]

D. Concluding remarks

Denmark used to be a pioneer when it comes to promoting sustainable business. It was one of the first countries to introduce rules on non-financial (or sustainability) disclosure. In recent years, however, there seems to be less interest in introducing new rules for promoting this agenda, and instead Denmark has been focusing on implementing the rules adopted in the EU on this topic.

Given its status as a small country with no strong tradition of litigation, the law in this area has often evolved very slowly. As a consequence, there are some issues that may have been subject to scholarly debate but have not been conclusively decided in either black letter law or case law. However, the pragmatic approach normally used by Danish lawyers – including judges – is likely to result in solutions that will allow the promotion of the sustainability agenda within the boundaries set by EU law.

---

[99] Krüger Andersen, ibid. p. 16.

[100] https://www.ft.dk/samling/20201/almdel/eru/spm/676/svar/1814443/2455480.pdf (5 September 2023).

Country Report Ireland

Blanaid Clarke / Félix E. Mezzanotte

A. Introduction

Ireland is the domicile for 6.1% of worldwide investment fund assets positioning it as the third largest global centre and the second largest European centre.[1] Approximately €4.16 trillion in net assets are held in 8,841 Irish domiciled funds.[2] There are two broad categories of mutual funds in Ireland: undertakings for collective investment in transferable securities ("UCITS") within the scope of the UCITS Directive[3] and alternative investment funds ("AIFs") falling under the Alternative Investment Fund Managers Directive ("AIFMD")[4].

In 1932 when Berle and Means published their seminal text, *The Modern Corporation and Private Property*, on the separation of ownership and control, institutional investors played a minor role in corporate decision making. In his preface to a revised edition in 1967, Berle referred to the vastly increased number of shares held not by individuals but by intermediate financial institutions including pension trust funds and mutual funds. A consequence of these institutions, he noted, is that "they remove the individual still further from connection with or impact on the management and administration of the productive corporations themselves."[5] Today, there are often more than one layer of intermediaries impeding shareholders' ability to exercise influence over their investments and their governance rights. The rise of institutional investing and the recent popularity in index funds has changed the nature of share ownership across the globe. The "Big Three" asset manager/investment companies who specialize in index funds, Vanguard, State Street, and BlackRock, thus have significant influence over the companies in which they invest. Although traditionally they adopted a passive approach to governance, since 2017, they have

[1] EFAMA International Statistical Release, Quarter 4 2023 (March 2024). This country report reflects the state of the law as of October 2022.

[2] Irish Funds: Total Irish Domiciled Funds as at end of January 2024 https://www.irishfunds.ie/facts-figures/industry-statistics/total-irish-domiciled-funds/ (3 April 2024).

[3] Directive 2009/65/EC (referred to as "the UCITS IV Directive") as amended by Directive 2014/91/EU ("referred to as the UCITS V Directive") is now the main regulatory instrument.

[4] Directive 2011/61/EU.

[5] Adolf Berle and Gardiner Means, The Modern Corporation and Private Property. New York, Macmillan Co., 1933), 1991 edition published by Transaction Publishers at pp. xxxii and xxxiii.

launched policymaking initiatives to improve board gender diversity and reduce climate risk.[6] This chapter examines the impact on and implications of corporate governance on this form of ownership in the context of the Irish market and with particular reference to sustainable investments. Before doing so however, a brief introduction is provided to the regulatory environment in Ireland.

Directive EU/2017/828 amending the Shareholders Rights Directive 2007/36/EEC was introduced partly in response to perceived corporate governance failings in the wake of the Global Financial Crisis when institutional investors and asset managers were criticised for inadequate monitoring of investee companies, poor engagement and short-termism leading "to suboptimal corporate governance and performance."[7] The amendment marked an acknowledgment that the complex chains of intermediaries involved in the ownership of listed companies "render the exercise of shareholder rights more difficult and may act as an obstacle to shareholder engagement."[8] It was transposed into Irish Law by the European Union (Shareholders' Rights) Regulations 2020 ("SR Regulations") which amend the Companies Act 2014 ("2014 Act"). References in this paper to "the SRD" are to the amended version of Directive 2007/36/EEC.

In order to engage, institutional investors and asset managers need to receive timely, accurate and relevant information on their investee companies. Over the last number of years, there has been a focus on improving disclosure in relation to the non-financial aspects of a company's business. The Non-Financial Reporting Directive 2014/95/EU ("NFRD") requires companies within its scope[9] to disclose information on environmental, social and employee matters, human rights, bribery and corruption. It was implemented into Irish law through the European Union (Disclosure of Non-Financial and Diversity Information by certain large undertakings and groups) Regulations 2017. Once implemented, the Corporate Sustainability Reporting Directive[10] ("CSRD") will replace the sustainability reporting requirements in the NFRD and will be broader in scope including non-listed large companies, as well as listed SMEs. The CSRD will also render

---

[6] *D. Lund*, Asset Managers as Regulators, 171 University of Pennsylvania Law Review (2022), forthcoming (https://ssrn.com/abstract=3975847) (5 September 2023).

[7] Second recital. The definition of "institutional investor" in Art. 2(e) includes EU life insurers and EU pension funds. The definition of "asset manager" in Art. 2(f) includes the following types of entities where they invest on behalf of institutional investors: (a) MiFID firms providing portfolio management services; (b) certain AIFMs; (c) UCITS management companies; and (d) self-managed UCITS Directive 2007/36/EC was most recently amended by Directive 2023/2864/EU.

[8] Para 4.

[9] These are large public-interest entities with an average number of employees in excess of 500, and public-interest entities that are parent companies of a large group with an average number of employees in excess of 500 on a consolidated basis.

[10] Directive 2022/2464/EU amending Directive 2013/34/EU, Directive 2004/109/EC, Directive 2006/43/EC and Regulation (EU) No 537/2014, as regards corporate sustainability reporting COM/2021/189 final.

the sustainability reporting requirements more consistent with the broader sustainable finance legal framework (which includes Regulation (EU) 2019/2088 on sustainability-related disclosures in the financial services sector ("SFDR") and the Taxonomy Regulation (EU) 2020/852). Finally, there are then six amending Delegated Acts on investment and insurance advice, fiduciary duties, and product oversight and governance. These Acts incorporate sustainability considerations into frameworks for the UCITS Directive, AIFMD, MiFID II, Solvency II, and the Insurance Distribution Directive.

The Central Bank of Ireland ("Central Bank") regulates and supervises financial services firms and takes the necessary enforcement actions to ensure compliance with the relevant regulations. Established under the Central Bank Reform Act 2010, it is a single fully integrated body with responsibility for both central banking and financial regulation. It is the national competent authority in relation to the EU UCITS and AIFs regimes and, to this extent, it supervises the incorporation and activities of UCITS and AIFs as well as of fund service providers including fund management companies such as UCITS fund management companies and AIF fund managers ("AIFMs"). These companies are subject to legal and regulatory requirements contained in the Central Bank's UCITS Regulations and the Central Bank's AIF Rulebook, as well as the Central Bank's Guidance for Fund Management Companies (CP 86 Guidance).[11]

B. Sustainable Ownership and Shareholder Governance

I. Exercising Voting Rights

In its recitals, the SRD justifies the Commission's emphasis on shareholder engagement. It describes "effective and sustainable shareholder engagement" as "one of the cornerstones of the corporate governance model of listed companies, which depends on checks and balances between the different organs and different stakeholders". It emphasizes its positive effect on the financial and non-financial performance of companies including as regards environmental, social and governance ("ESG") factors. The difficulties the SRD seeks to resolve stem from the complex chains of intermediaries which are described as impeding the exercise of voting rights in a number of ways. Firstly, companies may not be able to identify their shareholders and thus communicate with them. Secondly, shareholders' votes may not be correctly transmitted to the company. Thirdly, institutional investors and asset managers may not engage with their investee companies or may be unduly influenced by short term market pressures. Their

[11] Central Bank of Ireland, 'Fund Management Companies – Guidance, December 2016' (hereinafter CP 86 Guidance).

lack of transparency about their investment strategies and their engagement policies and how these are implemented reduces investor awareness and engagement and has a detrimental effect thus on accountability. Chapter Ib of the SRD seeks to respond to these transparency concerns.

Section 1110H of the 2014 Act deals with engagement policies for asset managers. In keeping with Article 3g of the SRD, Section 1110H(1) and (2) requires asset managers to either develop and publicly disclose an engagement policy in accordance with Section 1110H or to publicly disclose "a clear and reasoned explanation for its failure to do so". This follows the comply or explain model which has become a hallmark of corporate governance regulation since the UK's *Cadbury Code* in 1992. Echoing Article 3g (1)(a) of the SRD, Section 1110H(3) of the 2014 Act provides that the engagement policy must describe how the relevant asset manager: integrates shareholder engagement in its investment strategy; monitors investee companies on relevant matters, including strategy, financial and non-financial performance and risk, capital structure, social and environmental impact and corporate governance; conducts dialogues with investee companies; exercises voting rights and other rights attached to shares; cooperates with other shareholders; communicates with relevant stakeholders of the investee companies; and manages actual and potential conflicts of interest in relation to its engagement. An example of how this requirement has been implemented by a MiFID authorized firm is the active ownership approach written in accordance with the SRD and with referred to by Irish Life Investment Managers ("ILIM") in its Voting Policy.[12] The policy notes at the outset:

> "As a Responsible Investor, ILIM adopts an Active Ownership approach to promote better corporate behaviour in investee companies in terms of sustainability and management of Environmental, Social and Governance risks. ILIM exercises voting rights and constructively engages with investee companies, encouraging better standards and management processes covering material ESG risks."

ILIM's Voting Policy notes that it will vote when it has proxy-voting authority other than in the case of countries where voting is logistically difficult or where the costs are disproportionate relative to the size of its holding. ILIM The Policy states that it "generally votes in favour of shareholder proposals that seek to manage risks and opportunities related to ESG issues and which promote good corporate citizenship". ILIM's Responsible Investment Team oversees and implements the Voting Policy including monitoring voting implementation undertaken on ILIM's behalf by ISS, its proxy voting advisor. ISS uses ILIM's Global Proxy Voting Guidelines which sets out its considerations and expectations in relation to ESG matters and related voting decisions. ILIM points out however that it may choose to vote contrary to the ISS recommendation where for ex-

[12] https://vds.issgovernance.com/repo/7675/policies/ILIM%20Voting%20Policy-%202023.pdf.

ample it is actively engaging with a company and has agreed a course of action that requires voting in a particular way on a specificc resolution. It also describes its processes of monitoring, engagement and escalation indicating that the latter may include voting against director re-election, voting against the board Chair and voting against the approval of the annual financial statements. This is done on a case-by-case basis. ILIM's voting and engagement policies are acknowledged to reflect the policy agreements in place with ISS and Vigeo Eiris shareholder advisory service. Finally, ILIM also publishes a Responsible Investment Policy contains additional Sustainability Principles and which applies to all assets it manages on behalf of its clients consistent with the terms of their Investment Management Agreements.

Section 1110H(4) of the 2014 Act implements Article 3g (1)(b) of the SRD requiring asset managers who have developed engagement policies to publicly disclose annually how its these policies has been implemented. This should include a general description of voting behaviour; an explanation of the most significant votes taken; information on the use of any proxy advisory services; and information on how it has cast votes in the general meetings of investee companies.

There is thus no provision for mandatory voting or indeed "activist" use of voting rights and no statutory stewardship duties. While the provision is also framed as a "comply or explain" one, the general expectation is that relevant asset management firms will comply and implement their engagement policies. In keeping with the SRD, if the asset manager does not make this disclosure on the implementation of its engagement policy in any given year, Section 1110H(6) of the 2014 Act provides that it must publicly disclose a clear and reasoned explanation for its failure to do so.

In terms of the voting process, under the 2014 Act, shareholders holding 5 % of a company listed on a regulated market or 10 % of any other company have a statutory right to requisition an extraordinary general meeting. Shareholders holding 3 % of a company listed on a regulated market company can make proposals and add items to an Annual General Meeting agenda. Shareholders are entitled to put questions to management at general meetings. Notices of general meetings of public limited companies must inform shareholders of their right to ask questions and ensure such questions are answered. A leadership principle in the *UK Corporate Governance Code* which applies to Irish listed companies states that "In order for the company to meet its responsibilities to shareholders and stakeholders, the board should ensure effective engagement with, and encourage participation from, these parties."[13] A related provision provides that the chair should seek regular engagement with major shareholders "to understand their

[13] Financial Reporting Council, UK Corporate Governance Code 2018, General Principle D. The UK Corporate Governance Code 2024 which comes into effect in 2025 contains the same General Principle.

views on governance and performance against the strategy" and he or she should ensure that the board has a clear understanding of shareholders' views.[14] Committee chairs are also charged with engaging with shareholders on significant matters related to their areas of responsibility.

The provisions of the Companies (Miscellaneous Provisions) (Covid-19) Act 2020 facilitating virtual meetings still apply. Despite this, most annual general meetings ("AGMs") in 2021 were conducted using a physical meeting with restricted attendance and "some form of one-way video or audio broadcast for shareholders."[15] There was also a marked decline in shareholder voting participation at AGMs in 2021 compared to the previous year. Thomson Reuters reported:

> "The main examples of shareholder activism in Ireland have been directed towards executive remuneration with numerous companies experiencing significant minority votes against their remuneration policies or repots in recent years. There have been some instances of shareholder activism directed towards corporate activity such as encouraging divestment and share buyback ... Separately to board remuneration, some activism has related to board composition and governance, including, in particular, calls to separate the roles of chairman and chief executive officers ... To date, shareholder activism in Ireland has not evidently been focussed on CSR issues."[16]

In response to such activism, the *UK Corporate Governance Code* provides that if 20 % or more of votes have been cast against the board recommendation for a resolution at a shareholder general meeting, the company must: explain how and when it will consult shareholders to understand the reasons behind the voting result; publish an update on the views received from shareholders and actions taken within six months of the shareholder meeting; and then provide a final summary in the annual report.[17] This seeks to add weight to such shareholder dissent allowing the market an opportunity to discipline boards that fail to respond to investors' concerns.

The Irish Association of Investment Managers ("IAIM"), the representative body for investment managers in Ireland in its response to the Irish Government's consultation on the EU's Renewed Sustainable Finance Strategy[18] stated that very few investment managers supplied data on the integration of sustainability criteria and options to invest in sustainable financial assets but that it would welcome such disclosure. It agreed (though not "strongly agreed") that

---

[14] Provision 3.

[15] *Mason Hayes Curran*, 2021 AGM Season Report.

[16] E.Grace and N.McGrath, Shareholder activism in Ireland: overview, Thomson Reuters Practial Law (2021).

[17] Provision. 4.

[18] IAIM response EU Sustainable Finance strategy Consultation May 2020 Final https://www.iaim.ie/wp-content/uploads/2020/07/IAIM-response-EU-Sustainable-Finance-strategy-Consultation-May-2020-Final.pdf (3 April 2024).

the EU should take further action to encourage investor engagement, including making use of their voting rights, with companies conducting environmentally harmful activities inconsistent with environmental objectives and the EU-wide trajectory for greenhouse gas emission reductions in order to encouraging these companies to adopt more sustainable business models. In order to address short termism, it stated that the focus should be on engagement between asset managers and institutional investors and it agreed that Member States should be required to have an independent monitoring framework to ensure the quality of information disclosed in remuneration reports published by listed companies, UCITS management companies and AIFMs. It also suggested that voting frameworks across the EU should be further harmonised at EU level to facilitate shareholder engagement and votes on ESG issues stating that

> "Anything that makes it easier to vote, would be welcomed – specifically with regards to the infrastructure for actually processing the votes. Currently, the process can be too onerous and complicated and can deter engagement for that reason."[19]

The IAIM was not in favour of EU action to allow investors to vote on a company's environmental and social strategies or performance. It opined that while further clarification on voting type was needed, "there is enough in the existing framework". It also recommended that investors engage with investee companies to encourage the adoption of more sustainable business models though it rejected the idea of forced divestment from companies which are not on the EU trajectory for GHG emissions. The IAIM's web page states that it is in the process of formulating a Stewardship Code although this is not believed to be imminent. However, many of the asset managers and owners who have signed up to the *UK Stewardship Code* have Irish subsidiaries and a number of these have indicated that in order to align with the approach taken by their UK Group companies, they have used the Financial Reporting Council's guidance and their twelve principles of stewardship in creating their own Stewardship Policies.[20]

The Irish Funds Industry Association ("IFIA"), which represents fund managers, depositaries, administrators, transfer agents, and other specialist firms in the sector, has published a *Corporate Governance Code for Collective Investment Schemes and Management Companies*[21] which applies to Irish regulated funds and their manager with a view to ensuringe that funds operate efficiently and in the interests of investors. It has also published a *Corporate Governance Code*

---

[19] P. 7.

[20] See for example Brewin Dolphin Ireland https://www.brewin.ie/wp-content/uploads/sites/13/2023/10/stewardship-policy-2021-final.pdf (3 April 2024).

[21] https://files.irishfunds.ie/1432820468-corporate-governance-code-for-collective-investment-schemes-and-management-companies.pdf (3 April 2024).

for Fund Service Providers.[22] The IFIA has described shareholder engagement on environmental issues as a very important tool for investors and one which is currently taking place with good effect.[23] It has recommended monitoring the application of the SRD to assess whether it effectively encourages long-term engagement, before taking any further actions. It is supportive of collaborative investor engagement through investor alliances such as Climate Action 100+ being more formalised arrangements. It agreed with ESMA's recommendations in its Report on Short-termism that the legal boundaries of investors acting in a coalition to drive ESG related changes should be clarified. It also supports EU actions to facilitate cross-border communication between companies and investors, cross-border voting and appropriately facilitating the filing of shareholder resolutions, which is not possible in many EU Member States. Finally, it emphasized the importance of facilitating investors acting as stewards of their investee companies and noted that engagement by investors who embed ESG in their practices can yield better outcomes in terms of transition than complete divestment.

II. Obstacles to Mutual Fund Engagement

The broad diversification policies adopted by mutual funds can make meaningful engagement with their investee companies more time-consuming and expensive. Other impediments are generally acknowledged to include: shareholder apathy; imperfect information; the free-rider problem; a lack of incentives; short-termism; liquidity and thin equity; financial constraints; managerial manipulation of agenda; intermediated ownership; herd behaviour; the role of proxy advisers; fiduciary duties (discussed in Part III(2) below); acting in concert restrictions; restrictions on voting rights; and market abuse regulations. This section of the chapter will focus on the latter three regulatory challenges.

1. The Mandatory Bid Rule

The application of the mandatory bid rule ("MBR") in Directive 2004/25/EC on takeover bids ("Takeovers Directive") to potential "concert parties" is one of the most cited regulatory obstacles to shareholder engagement. The Takeovers Directive regulates the conduct of takeover bids of EU listed companies and was transposed into Irish Law by an amendment to the Irish Takeover Act 1997 ("1997 Act") and the European Communities (Takeover Bids (Directive 2004/25/EC)) Regulations 2006 ("2006 Regulations"). The Irish Takeover Panel ("Panel") was

---

[22] https://files.irishfunds.ie/1432808933-01072014-Corporate-Governance-Code-for-Fund-Service-Providers.pdf (3 April 2024).

[23] Irish Funds Response to European Commission Consultation on the Renewed Sustainable Finance Strategy https://irishfunds-secure.s3.amazonaws.com/1594829573-Irish-Funds-Renewed-Sustainable-Finance-Strategy-Consultation-Response.pdf (3 April 2024).

established pursuant to the 1997 Act to monitor and supervise takeovers and it was designated under the 2006 Regulations as the competent authority for the purposes of the Takeovers Directive. The Panel applies the Irish Takeover Panel Act, Takeover Rules, 2022 ("Takeover Rules") to regulate the conduct of takeovers of companies for which it has jurisdiction to supervise under the Takeovers Directive and /or the 1997 Act.[24] Takeovers outside the scope of the Takeovers Directive but still regulated pursuant to the 1997 Act include takeovers of Irish registered companies listed on the London Stock Exchange, the New York Stock Exchange or NASDAQ.

There are currently two applicable definitions of concert parties in the Takeovers Rules depending on whether the Takeovers Directive applies or not. If it does, the relevant definition is "natural or legal persons who cooperate with the offeror or the offeree company on the basis of an agreement, either express or tacit, either oral or written, aimed either at acquiring control of the offeree company or at frustrating the successful outcome of a bid".[25] If it does not apply, the relevant definition refers to parties who "pursuant to an agreement or understanding (whether formal or informal) between them ... actively co-operate in the acquisition by any one or more of them of securities in the relevant company concerned or in the doing, or in the procuring of the doing, of any act that results in an increase in the proportion of such securities held by any one or more of them and "acting in concert" shall be construed accordingly."[26]

The latter does not include concerted action in relation to the frustration of a bid but it is wider in the sense it relates to the acquisition of any securities and not just concerted action aimed at the acquisition of control. Rule 3(3) of Part A of the Takeover Rules sets out a detailed list of persons "deemed to be acting in concert" for the purpose of the Takeover Rules. These include group companies with associated companies; fund managers and controllers wither the persons on whose account they manage the investments on a discretionary basis; and financial advisers with their clients.

Article 5 of the Takeovers Directive requires Member States to introduce a MBR though the definition of "control" is left to individual Member States. Control in Ireland relates to "the holding, whether directly or indirectly, of securities of the company that confer, in aggregate, not less than 30 % (or such other percentage as may be prescribed) of the voting rights in that company".[27] Rule 9(1) of the Irish Rules provides that except with the consent of the Panel, if any person, or any persons acting in concert, acquire control of a relevant company,

[24] See the Notes to the Takeover Rules: *4. Companies and Transactions to which the Act, the Regulations and the Rules apply* for a detailed description of the jurisdictional rules. The 1997 Act also regulates "other relevant transactions" and schemes of arrangement.

[25] Article 2(1)(d) of the Takeovers Directive.

[26] Section 1(3) of the 1997 Act.

[27] Section 1(1) of the 1997 Act.

they must make an offer to the holders of each class of equity share capital of the relevant company. While it is unclear from the drafting of Article 5 which of the concert parties would have to make the bid, Rule 9(1) imposes the obligation on "such one or more of those persons as the Panel shall direct". Unlike the MBR in the Takeovers Directive, a bid is also required under Rule 9 where any person, or any persons acting in concert, who already control a relevant company consolidates this control by acquiring within any 12 month period additional securities which increases by more than 0.05 % the aggregate percentage of the voting rights conferred by the securities held by them.[28] An exception under Rule 9 allows a single holder of securities[29] who holds securities conferring more than 50 % of the voting rights to acquire additional securities of that company without incurring a bid obligation. Rule 9(4) provides that the consideration for the offer will be "not less than the highest value of the consideration per share paid by the offeror or any person acting in concert with it" for shares of the offeree of that class" during the 12 months prior to the announcement of the firm intention to make an offer.

In most Member States, the coming together of two parties considered to be concert parties would be sufficient to trigger the mandatory bid but in Ireland it is triggered when control is acquired or consolidated ie when either one of the concert parties then increases their shareholding in the company.[30] The situation of shareholders voting together may not of itself trigger a mandatory bid but in certain circumstances, this might indicate that there is a group acting in concert.[31] The Panel when reviewing shareholder collective action in this context has regard to ESMA's statement on shareholder co-operation in the context of the Takeovers Directive. This sets out a "White List" of activities, identified by members of the Takeover Bids Network, which shareholders can generally engage in without running the risk of being deemed to be acting in concert.[32] The existence of this list reduces the risk posed to activist shareholders that a MBR would be imposed. The list includes: shareholders discussing matters to be raised with the company's board and making representations to the board about company policies, practices or particular actions that the company might consider taking; and exercising shareholders' statutory rights to add items to the agenda of a general meeting. It was not possible however to adopt a common position on all activities and the list for example does not include any activity relating to cooperation in relation to board appointments.

---

[28] This requirement applies whether or not such class confers voting rights.

[29] This includes persons regarded as such for the purposes of Rule 5.1(a)(ii).

[30] Note 1 on Rule 9.

[31] Note 2 on Rule 9.

[32] ESMA Public Statement, Information on shareholder cooperation and acting in concert under the Takeover Bids Directive June 2014 (last updated 8 January 2019).

2. Differential Voting Rights

A second potential barrier to shareholder engagement is the use of capital structures which deviate from the "one share one vote" principle and limit or remove voting rights for some classes of shareholders while promoting them for others. Such structures impede shareholder engagement for the class of shareholders with less or no voting rights. There is no prohibition in Ireland on such structures and this is a matter for each company itself. Loyalty shares which give shareholders additional votes per share if the shares are held for a specified period of time have a similar effect but are less common in Irish listed companies.

3. Market Abuse Regulation

The Market Abuse Regulation (Regulation (EU) 596/2014) ("MAR") restricts the disclosure of market sensitive information and thus impedes the ability of companies to have meaningful discussions with their shareholders on an individual basis. The Market Abuse Directive 2014/57/EU which provides for criminal sanctions for market abuse and the MAR were transposed into Irish law by way of the European Union (Market Abuse) Regulations 2016. The Central Bank has issued industry letters to issuers informing them of the key findings from its 2020 market abuse supervisory work and setting out its expectations in relation to MAR compliance standards.[33] Pursuant to Part 23 of the Companies Act 2014, the Central Bank has also issued the *Central Bank (Investment Market Conduct) Rules* setting out market abuse related requirements and *Guidance on the Market Abuse Regulatory Framework*. The latter deals with the selective disclosure of such information. It states that "an issuer may, depending on the circumstances, be justified in disclosing inside information to certain categories of recipient" and this includes major shareholders of the issuer and the issuer's lenders.[34]

III. The Role of Nominee Directors

In Ireland, parent companies or significant shareholders who wish to influence the management of a company, will have an opportunity to do so through the usual shareholder engagement opportunities discussed above, tabling resolutions of their own and exercising their voting powers. In addition, they may seek representation on the board. As corporate directors are prohibited in Ireland, they must nominate a natural person to fulfil this role and then expect their nominee to look after their interests as well as the companies' interests. In addition to being bound by confidentiality rules and the market abuse restrictions identified above, nominees must fulfil their statutory duty to act in the interests of the

[33] https://www.centralbank.ie/regulation/industry-market-sectors/securities-markets/market-abuse-regulation (2 April 2024).

[34] Section 3.2.

company. If a conflict arises thus between the interests of their nominator and the company, the latter must prevail. However, as Sections 228 (3) and 228(4) clarify "a director of a company may have regard to the interests of a particular member of the company" where the director has been appointed or nominated for appointment by that member.[35] This right is stated to be without prejudice to the director's duty under Section 228(1)(a) to act in good faith in what they consider to be the interests of the company.[36]

Furthermore, a director must not agree to restrict their power to exercise independent judgment.[37] In *Boulting v Association of Cinematograph Technicians*[38], Lord Denning stated that there is nothing wrong with a director being nominated by a shareholder to represent their interests 'so long as the director is left free to exercise his best judgment in the interests of the company which he serves. But if he is put upon terms that he is bound to act in the affairs of the company in accordance with the directions of his patron, it is beyond doubt unlawful.' This case was cited in the Privy Council case *Central Bank of Ecuador and ors v Conticorp SA and ors*[39] where the sole director of a Bahamian company IAMF Ltd. which held itself out as an independent investment management fund was found to have breached his duties as a director by acting only in accordance with the instructions of IAMF's owners and controllers. The Privy Council noted that the director 'simply did as he was told, no more and no less, even it appears if it consisted in signing back-dated documentation. He took the risk, at the very least, that the instructions he received and followed might not be proper'. The Irish courts are likely to adopt a similar approach. If adhering to ESG considerations is considered as acting in the interests of the company, the nominee directors are required to pursue this objective. Another limitation on the influence of a parent or major shareholding is the provision in the *UK Corporate Governance Code* that the board should identify and manage conflicts of interest "including those resulting from significant shareholdings, and ensure that the influence of third parties does not compromise or override independent judgement."[40] The representation of a significant shareholder is considered as one of the circumstances which are "likely to impair, or could appear to impair, a non-executive director's independence".[41]

---

[35] This applies where the member is entitled to make the appointment or nomination under the company's constitution or a shareholders' agreement.

[36] Section 228(3) of the Companies Act 2014.

[37] Section 228(1)(e). The only exceptions are where: this is expressly permitted by the company's constitution; the case concerned falls within section 228(2); or the director's agreeing to such has been approved by a resolution of the company in general meeting.

[38] [1963] 2 QB 606, 626–627.

[39] [2015] UKPC 11.

[40] Provision 5.

[41] Provision 6.

IV. Proxy Advisors

The role of proxy-advisors and their involvement in voting process has raised concerns about conflicts of interest as they may be responsible for the production of corporate governance ratings for the issuing companies or be engaged by them as underwriting advisors.

The 2020 Regulations introduces new obligations for proxy advisors providing services to shareholders with respect to shares admitted to trading on an EU regulated market. Regulation 110K requires a relevant proxy advisor to apply and publicly report annually on its application of a code of conduct or to publicly disclose annually a clear and reasoned explanation for its failure to do so. Where a code is applied, it must publicly disclose annually: the ways in which the code of conduct was departed from; an explanation for the departure; and any alternative measures adopted by the relevant proxy advisor. It must disclose information in relation to the preparation of its research, advice and voting recommendations, including: whether it has dialogues with the relevant companies and their stakeholders and the object of the and the extent and nature of those dialogues; and its policy regarding the prevention and management of potential conflicts of interest. It must also identify and, as soon as practicable, disclose to its clients: "(a) any actual or potential conflicts of interest or business relationships that may influence the preparation of the relevant proxy advisor's research, advice or voting recommendations, and (b) the actions the relevant proxy advisor has undertaken to eliminate, mitigate or manage the actual or potential conflicts of interest."

MiFID authorised firms are required to take all appropriate steps to identify, manage or prevent potential or actual conflicts of interest that arise when providing its services. Many firms draw up and publish online their Conflicts of Interests policies.

V. Extra-Territorial Effect

There is an obvious risk that the exclusion of institutional investors domiciled outside the EU from the SRD will weaken the new regime and impede the imposition of participation duties and related disclosure obligations.

Regulated entities domiciled outside the EU including those UK entities post Brexit are not entitled to passport into the EU pursuing business in Member States on a Freedom of Establishment and Freedom of Services basis. The Central Bank have advised firms that intend to continue or intend to commence providing services in the EU to ensure that they hold the appropriate authorisation.

A third country asset manager is not a "relevant asset manager" for the purposes of the SRD but it may be indirectly within scope of the requirements. Where they have been delegated responsibilities by asset managers regulated by the Central Bank, they may be required to provide details of their shareholder engagement policies and procedures to assist asset managers falling within the scope of the SRD to implement their policies. Similar indirect responsibilities apply pursuant to the NFRD and the Delegated UCITS Directive and the Delegated AIFMD Regulation.

VI. Engagement by Bondholders

Although bondholders do not have voting rights, they do have an opportunity to engage with the companies by communicating their views to them. Art 3g (1) (a) of the SRD requires institutional investors and asset managers to describe in their engagement policy how they monitor investee companies on relevant matters and also "conduct dialogues" with them and communicate with other relevant stakeholders of the investee companies.

There has been significant growth in investment in assets such as fixed income bonds, real estate and infrastructure and the *UK Stewardship Code* encourages its signatories to consider how to exercise stewardship effectively in these circumstances.[42] Signatories are asked to disclose their conflicts policy and how this has been applied to stewardship. In particular, they should explain how they have identified and managed any instances of actual or potential conflicts related to stewardship. Such conflicts may arise inter alia because of ownership structures and bond and equity managers' objectives.[43] Harnessing such bond-holders as a force for good in driving the ESG agenda is of course key.

VII. Equality of Information for Shareholders

The impact of MAR restricting dialogue between management and major shareholders was dealt with above. Another relevant consideration is whether it is possible to discriminate in the treatment of large and small shareholders or whether the principles of "equal treatment interest of non-involved (small) shareholders" and the "equal opportunities in capital markets" affect this. Article 46 of Article 85 of Directive 2017/1132/EU on Company Law provides that the laws of the Member States must ensure "equal treatment to all shareholders who are in the same position." This is the position under the common law and in *PTSB Holdings v MacManus*[44] Barrett J. stated "It is trite but perhaps necessary to observe that the principle of equality of equal members is a pervasive principle of Irish company law". Failure to adhere to such a principle may give rise to an action under section 212 of the 2014 Act on minority protection.

---

[42] P. 4

[43] P. 10.

[44] [2015] IEHC 500.

In addition, a General Principle under the 1997 Act provides that "All holders of the securities of an offeree of the same class must be afforded equivalent treatment". The Takeover Rules develop this Principle further. Rule 20.1(a) in particular provides that "Information about companies involved in an offer or contemplated offer and which is tendered by or on behalf of an offeror or the offeree during the course of an offer shall be made equally available by it to all the holders of shares in the offeree of the class or classes the subject of the offer as nearly as possible at the same time and in the same manner." Meetings of representatives of the offeror or offeree with select shareholders are allowed but Rule 20.1(b) provides that they must be chaperoned by financial advisers who must confirm to the Panel that any material new information or significant new opinions are not disclosed.

C. Sustainable Funding / Portfolio Governance

I. Portfolios, Diversification and Engagement with Investee Companies

According to portfolio theory, an efficient portfolio maximises risk-adjusted returns by diversifying risk.[45] In the context of sustainable investments, the concern has been that the use of screening strategies (e.g. negative screening or best in class approaches) to select sustainable assets in portfolios will reduce the portfolio's risk diversification and, thereby, the portfolio's value will fall due to higher risk.[46] While it is submitted that screening strategies necessarily restrict the universe of stocks available for selection in the construction of portfolios,[47] the risk and return effects in ESG portfolios arising from this drop in risk diversification have however been contested.[48] This said, ESG screening is only one among several sustainable investment strategies. Other highly popular strategies have been recognised as well including strategies based on the integration of sustainability risk and engagement strategies.[49]

In the context of engagement strategies, portfolio diversification is also a relevant factor. Engagement is easier or less costly in portfolios that contain a lower number of companies, and vice-versa. Therefore, the greater engagement

[45] *Schoenmaker/Schramade*, Investing for long-term value creation, Journal of Sustainable Finance & Investment 2019 9(4), 356–3, 359.

[46] *Verheyden/Eccles/Feiner*, ESG for All? The Impact of ESG Screening on Return, Risk, and Diversification, Journal of Applied Corporate Finance 2016 28(2), 45–55, 51–55 (citing *Markowitz*, Portfolio selection, Journal of Finance, 1952 7(1), 77–91).

[47] *Verheyden/Eccles/Feiner* (Fn. 46).

[48] *Verheyden/Eccles/Feiner* (Fn. 46), 54–55.

[49] Global Sustainable Investment Alliance, Global Sustainable Investment Review 2020, 2021, 10–12.

costs engendered by more diversified portfolios may curtail returns.[50] The incentives and disincentives to exercising voting rights have also been analysed in the context of passive, relative to, active investment funds. Since passive funds, such as Index Funds, necessarily track or mimic their benchmark index, they lack the ability to exit the target companies that remain included in the benchmark index. This fact creates an incentive for the fund to engage.[51] But the exercise of voting rights by passive funds may nevertheless undermine their cost advantage, a factor that discourages engagement. It has also been claimed that actively managed funds pursue short-term financial returns, and that this strategy thwarts sustainable investment objectives.[52] Beyond the evaluation of the financial incentives driving a fund's engagement with investee companies, the legal approach to this issue concentrates on the question to what extent current legislation in Ireland creates an obligation, born by asset managers and institutional investors, to engage with investee companies. This question has been addressed earlier in section II(1) of this chapter.

It is reiterated that Chapter 8B of the 2014 Act does not mandate the type of engagement policy that an institutional investor or fund manager should develop, implement and disclose on a comply or explain basis. It is also noted that these rules apply to Irish-based investment funds, including UCITS and AIFs (and their FMCs), regardless of the characteristics of the fund in terms of type (e.g., passively or actively managed), strategy (e.g., adopts long- or short-term strategies), or design. Once the fund has determined its engagement policy, this action sets the scope within which the overall engagement strategy of the institutional investor and asset manager will be conducted. Financial incentives relating to the costs and benefits of engaging with investee companies, and more particularly of exercising voting rights, will be weighed and managed by each fund having into account their own business models and strategies and, as it will be examined in the following section, having into account the best interest of the fund and of investors.

---

[50] Engagement is costly but it can also generate financial returns, *Gantchev*. The costs of shareholder activism: Evidence from a sequential decision model, Journal of Financial Economics 2013, 107, 610–631. Evidence suggests, however, that successful ESG engagements have generated long-term valued especially when the theme of engagement is related to climate change, *Hoepner/Oikonomou/Sautner/Starks/Zhou*, ESG Shareholder Engagement and Downside Risk, European Corporate Governance Institute – Finance Working Paper No. 671/2020, 27 December 2021.

[51] *Mallow*, Asset Management, Index Funds, and Theories of Corporate Control,November 2019, 7–8, 11–12, SSRN https://papers.ssrn.com/sol3/papers.cfm?abstract_id=3483573 (5 September 2023).

[52] These arguments emerged from the questionnaire sent to the authors of this chapter for the purpose of this country study (in file with the authors).

II. Promoting the Best Interest of the Client in Portfolio Management

The requirement of acting in the best interest of the client has been consistently and widely adopted in Irish statutory rules. According to the European Union (Markets in Financial Instruments) Regulations 2017 (MiFID 2017 Regulations),[53] investment firms bear a duty to 'act honestly, fairly and professionally in accordance with the best interest of its clients'[54] and to comply, especially, 'with the principles set out in Regulations 32 and 33.'[55] Regulation 32 contains product governance rules and rules on information disclosure to clients, such as duties to disclose information to clients on product costs, fees and charges. Moreover, the investment firm shall ensure that 'all information, including marketing communications, addressed by the investment firm to clients or potential clients is fair, clear and not misleading.'[56] Regulation 33 sets out appropriateness[57] and suitability requirements.[58] Transposed UCITS and AIFM rules have also prescribed best interest requirements.[59] According to the CP 86 Guidance, 'Fund management companies are under regulatory obligations to act in the best interests of the investors in the investment funds under management.'[60] The client's best interest principle also admits a general law basis in Ireland, although these legal principles will not be developed in this chapter.

As noted earlier, sustainability issues have become increasingly important for investors. Profit-driven investors will most likely look at sustainable investment strategies only if they contribute to maximise their short-term financial returns.[61] But evidence has shown an increasing influence of not only financial but also moral- or ethical-based motivations driving investor's choices.[62] Survey data have indicated that investors are willing to pursue mixed strategies whereby they

[53] S. I. No. 375 of 2017 (hereinafter 'MiFID 2017 Regulations').

[54] MiFID 2017 Regulations (Fn. 53), reg 31(1)(a).

[55] MiFID 2017 Regulations (Fn. 53), reg 31(1)(b).

[56] MiFID 2017 Regulations (Fn. 53), reg 32(3)(a).

[57] MiFID 2017 Regulations (Fn. 53), reg 33(5)–(9).

[58] MiFID 2017 Regulations (Fn. 53), reg 33(3)–(4).

[59] S. I. No. 352/2011, European Communities (Undertakings for Collective Investment in Transferable Securities) Regulations 2011, reg 24(1) and schedule 5; S. I. No. 257/2013 European Union (Alternative Investment Fund Managers) Regulations 2013, Part 3, Operating conditions for AIFMs, Chapter 1, General requirements, reg 13(1).

[60] CP 86 Guidance (Fn. 1).

[61] *Gary*, Best Interests in the Long Term: Fiduciary Duties and ESG Integration, University of Colorado Law Review, 2019 90, 733 (750–754); *Friede/Busch/Bassen*, ESG and Financial Performance: Aggregated Evidence from More than 2000 Empirical Studies, Journal of Sustainable Finance & Investmend 2015 5(4), 210–33.

[62] *Schanzenbach/Sitkoff*, Reconciling Fiduciary Duty and Social Conscience: The Law and Economics of ESG Investing by a Trustee, Stanford Law Review 2020 72, 381 (398) (depending on the purpose of the investment, the authors differentiate between 'collateral benefits' or 'improved risk-adjusted returns'); *Gary* (Fn. 61), 750–754.

invest sustainably even if this entails foregoing returns.[63] The question remains to what extent an asset manager that pursues sustainable investment strategies reflects the best interest of the fund or of the investors (or clients), and what the manager's actions entail from the perspective of fiduciary duties. The 2018 report '*The Fiduciary Duty in the 21 Century – Ireland Road Map*'[64] sums up the fiduciary responsibilities of asset managers by indicating that '[t]here are currently no provisions in Irish fund or investment management legislation or regulation which expressly require that ESG factors be taken into account – or be disregarded – by the manager when managing an asset portfolio. The requirement that does exist is to act in the best interests of the client and, linked to that, to have appropriate due diligence processes for selecting and monitoring investments.'[65] The key legal constraints stem from contractual arrangements (mandates) and from the fund documentation itself and the Report notes that there are no other obligations on fund managers to take account of ESG issues in their investment processes.[66] Outside those instruments, the overarching principle applies: the asset manager is expected to make sustainable investments only when such investments prove to be in the client's best interest. In these situations, the asset manager 'should disclose this to their investors and be able to explain how the ESG investment strategy accords with their duty to act in the best interests of their clients.'[67]

Given the above, it follows that an asset manager in Ireland is obliged to account for an investor's sustainability interests to the extent that this is explicitly stated in the fund documents, the client's mandate or consent. Absent such statements, the asset manager would not be obliged to choose sustainable investments in portfolios unless doing so promotes the best financial interest of the client. However, this understanding, which adheres largely to a contractarian view, must now be adjusted to a new legal and regulatory landscape. New requirements have been introduced in Ireland flowing from the multiple reforms completed

[63] University of Cambridge Institute for Sustainability Leadership, Walking the talk: Understanding consumer demand for sustainable investing, 2019, Cambridge UK; Principles of Responsible Investments, Understanding and Aligning with Beneficiaries Sustainability Preferences, 2021, 9.

[64] This report was published by the UN's Environment Programme Finance Initiative, the Principles for Responsible Investment and the Generation Foundation in collaboration with SIF Ireland, 'Fiduciary Duty in the 21st Century – Ireland Roadmap', 2018, https://www.unpri.org/download?ac=9792 (5 September 2023) (written by *Sullivan/Heuston/McGann/Martindale/Kearney/Feller*) (hereinafter UNEP FI Report). The report defines 'fund management' as collective portfolio management (i.e., the activity of managing collective investment schemes or funds to include the discretionary investment management function) and 'investment management' as individual portfolio management (i.e., discretionary management portfolios on a client-by-client individual mandate basis).

[65] UNEP FI Report (Fn. 64), 14.

[66] UNEP FI Report (Fn. 64).

[67] UNEP FI Report (Fn. 64).

by the EU institutions on sustainable finance. Such requirements have further restricted the business conduct of investment service providers operating in Member States. Due to recent changes to the MIFID II suitability requirements – that apply in Ireland since 02 August 2022, the client's sustainability preferences must be identified – as stated by the client during the assessment of suitability – and serviced by MiFID investment firms.[68] In the same direction, upgraded MIFID II product governance rules require that manufacturers and distributors identify target markets of end users including their sustainability objectives.[69] On 01 August 2022, Delegated Regulations modifying the UCITS Directive and the AIFM Directive entered into effect, and consequently, Irish-based FMCs must integrate sustainability risk into their operations and investment strategy as part of the duties they owe to the fund they manage and the fund's investors.[70] Sustainability-related information disclosure regulations imposed by the SFDR[71] and the EU Taxonomy Regulation[72] further underpin the process of integrating sustainability risk and factors into the financial sector in Ireland. While the combined effect of all these recent reforms have significantly increased the regulatory burden faced by Irish-based financial market participants, the new rules will ensure that asset managers integrate sustainability into their operations including the product approval process as examined below.

D. Sustainable Finance / Product Governance

I. Sustainability in Product Governance Rules

In Ireland, the MiFID 2017 Regulations transposed the EU product governance regime into Irish law. More particularly, Regulations 23(1)(b) to (e) and Regu-

[68] Commission Delegated Regulation (EU) 2021/1253 of 21 April 2021 amending Delegated Regulation (EU) 2017/565 as regards the integration of sustainability factors, risks and preferences into certain organisational requirements and operating conditions for investment firms, OJ L 277/1, 2.08.2021.

[69] S. I. No. 363 of 2022, European Union (MARKETS IN FINANCIAL INSTRUMENTS) (AMENDMENT) (NO. 3) Regulation 2022 '(published on 15 July 2022).'

[70] Commission Delegated Directive (EU) 2021/1270 of 21 April 2021 amending Directive 2010/43/EU as regards the sustainability risks and sustainability factors to be taken into account for Undertakings for Collective Investment in Transferable Securities (UCITS) (Text with EEA relevance), C/2021/2617, OJ L 277, 2.8.2021; Commission Delegated Regulation (EU) 2021/1255 of 21 April 2021 amending Delegated Regulation (EU) No 231/2013 as regards the sustainability risks and sustainability factors to be taken into account by Alternative Investment Fund Managers, C/2021/2615, OJ L 277, 2.8.2021.

[71] Regulation (EU) 2019/2088 of the European Parliament and of the Council of 27 November 2019 on sustainability related disclosures in the financial services sector (OJ L 317, 9.12.2019) (hereinafter 'SFDR').

[72] Regulation (EU) 2020/852 of the European Parliament and of the Council of 18 June 2020 on the establishment of a framework to facilitate sustainable investment and amending Regulation (EU) 2019/2088 (OJ L 198, 22.6.2020) (hereinafter 'EU Taxonomy Regulation').

lations 23(2)–(3) of the MiFID 2017 Regulations treat this issue as part of the investment firm's organisational requirements, and Regulations 32(1)–(2) do this in the section dedicated to 'general principles and information to clients.' In addition, Schedule 4 (Regulation 32) of the MiFID 2017 Regulations contains a rich set of rules further distilling the obligations of manufacturers and distributors.[73] Generally speaking, the product governance rules in Ireland adhere closely to the EU regime, and the recent EU sustainability-related reforms have been introduced through modifications to the Schedule 4 (Regulation 32).[74]

A brief description of relevant rules is provided. Devising or creating financial instruments encompasses 'the creation, development, issuance or design of financial instruments (or more than one of those things).'[75] The manufacturer, when devising or otherwise creating financial instruments for sale to clients, shall 'maintain, operate and review a product approval process' for each financial instruments before they are marketed or distributed to clients.[76] This product approval process includes the determination of 'an identified target market of end clients within the relevant category of clients for each financial instrument'[77] making sure that 'all relevant risks to the identified target market are assessed and that the intended distribution strategy is consistent with the identified target market.'[78] The manufacturer shall also 'make available to any distributor all appropriate information on the financial instrument and the product approval process, including the identified target market of the financial instrument.'[79]

The product approval process shall account for potential conflict of interest each time a financial instrument is devised or otherwise created, and make sure that the end clients' interest is not adversely affected.[80]

This product approval process also involves continuing obligations whereby the manufacturer shall regularly review the financial instruments that it offers or markets and the distribution strategy of such instruments.[81] In relation to an investment firm that distributes (offers or recommends) financial instruments manufactured by others, this firm shall have in place adequate arrangements to obtain the information from the manufacturer and to understand the characteristics and the identified target market of each financial instrument.[82] In the practice of business, these Irish statutory rules are usually complemented by ESMA's *MiFID II Product Governance Guidelines* that contain detail rules aimed

[73] MiFID 2017 Regulations (Fn. 53). sch4, s1 (manufacturers) and s2 (distributors).
[74] S. I. No. 363 of 2022 (Fn. 69).
[75] MiFID 2017 Regulations (Fn. 53), sch 4 (s1(1)).
[76] MiFID 2017 Regulations (Fn. 53), reg 23(1)(c)(i).
[77] MiFID 2017 Regulations (Fn. 53), reg 23(2)(a).
[78] MiFID 2017 Regulations (Fn. 53), reg 23(2)(b).
[79] MiFID 2017 Regulations (Fn. 53), reg 23(1)(c)(ii).
[80] MiFID 2017 Regulations (Fn. 53), reg 23(1)(b) and sch4, s1(3)–1(4).
[81] MiFID 2017 Regulations (Fn. 53), reg 23(1)(d).
[82] MiFID 2017 Regulations (Fn. 53), reg 23(1)(e).

to ensure that products are effectively reaching the identified target market.[83] Regulations 32(1) and 32(2) of the MiFID 2017 Regulations have added further product governance rules. To some extent, they reiterate the obligations born by manufactures and distributions already spelled out under Regulation 23 of the same Regulations. Distributors have also the obligation to monitor that the financial instruments remain consistent with the needs of the identified target market.[84] Importantly, Regulation 32 sets out the obligation of investment firms to disclose relevant information to their clients, including information on product costs, fees and charges.[85]

Sustainability considerations have been brought into product governance by way of modifications made to Schedule 4 (Regulation 32) of the MiFID 2017 Regulations. Manufacturers and distributors are required to match the financial instrument with the sustainability investment objectives of potential clients as revealed by the identified target market of that instrument.[86] In the context of the manufacturer-distributor interaction, the investment firm 'shall present the sustainability factors of the financial instrument in a transparent manner and provide distributors with the relevant information to duly consider any sustainability related objectives of the client or potential client.'[87] The continuous obligation of manufacturers and distributors to monitor the evolving market conditions to maintain consistency between the financial instrument and the identified target market will also include maintaining consistency with changing sustainability investment objectives.[88] Negative target markets will not apply to financial instruments with sustainability properties.[89]

To conclude this section, two final observations are made. First, the Centra Bank has been granted wide powers to take enforcement action in the event of product governance failures. Among them, Regulations 91 and 92 of the MiFID 2017 Regulations allow the Central Bank to suspend the marketing or sale of financial instruments in various circumstances, among them, where 'the investment firm has not developed or applied an effective product approval process or otherwise failed to comply with Regulation 23(1)(b) to (e).'[90] To what extent the Central Bank has utilised these powers is a separate question that requires fur-

[83] ESMA, 'Final report Guidelines on MiFID II product governance requirements' 27 March 2023 ESMA35-43-3448.

[84] MiFID 2017 Regulations (Fn. 53), reg 23(1)(d).

[85] MiFID 2017 Regulations (Fn. 53), reg 32(7)–(11).

[86] S. I. No. 363 of 2022 (Fn. 69), substituting para. 1(10) and 1(13) of schedule 4 MiFID 2017 Regulations.

[87] S. I. No. 363 of 2022 (Fn. 69), adding para. 1(15A) to schedule 4 MiFID 2017 Regulations.

[88] S. I. No. 363 of 2022 (Fn. 69), substituting para. 1(16) and para. 1(10) of schedule 4 MiFID 2017 Regulations.

[89] S. I. No. 363 of 2022 (Fn. 69), substituting para. 2(4) of schedule 4 MiFID 2017 Regulations.

[90] MiFID 2017 Regulations (Fn. 56), Part 11, ch1, reg 92(4)(s) (transposing article 42 (EU) 600/2014 granting product intervention powers to NCAs).

ther enquiry. Second, a widely adopted practice in Ireland has been the outsourcing of investment service provision. In this so-called 'delegation' or 'outsourced' model, FMCs delegate the provision of MiFID investment services, linked to the UCITS and AIFs funds they manage, to MiFID investment firms (especially the portfolio management functions and/or the product distribution functions) by way of contractual agreements or mandates. Since these FMCs typically do not provide MiFID investment services or activities (but instead delegate such provision), the MiFID 2017 Regulations do not, as a general rule, apply to them.[91] To this extent, these FMCs are not legally bound to comply with the product governance rules examined in this section. In contrast, the MiFID 2017 Regulations do apply to the outsourced Irish-based MiFID investment firms. Since the latter, however, are required by such Regulations to coordinate closely their product distribution strategy with FMCs, which act as manufacturers, it has been strongly recommended that FMCs comply anyway, voluntarily, with the MiFID 2017 Regulations on product governance for practical and, especially, commercial reasons.[92]

II. Rule Compliance and Greenwashing Risk

The Central Bank's supervisory policy has aimed to mitigate climate risk effectively and making sure that climate and wider sustainability-related obligations are complied with.[93] In this context, the Central Bank has created a Climate Risk and Sustainable Finance Forum (the Climate Forum), bringing together stakeholders 'to share knowledge and understanding of the implications of climate change for the Irish financial system. This initiative aims to enable the sharing of best practice on embedding climate risk and sustainable finance considerations within firms.'[94] Moreover, this Climate Forum is expected to facilitate new knowledge, understanding and strategies for regulation and supervision. Reflecting on the recent EU sustainability-related reforms, the Central Bank has stressed that recent reforms to MiFID II and to the UCITS and AIFM Directives require 'a strong focus on effective implementation'[95] as these reforms represent 'major developments with significant new requirements for regulated entities.'[96]

---

[91] Irish Funds Industry Association, MiFID II – Implications for the Irish Funds Industry Questions and Answers, 25 June 2018 version, 2nd edition, 4 (introduction), 5 (Q1.1), and section E (in file with the authors).

[92] Irish Funds Industry Association (Fn. 91).

[93] Central Bank of Ireland, 'Supervisory Expectations of Regulated Firms Regarding Climate and Other ESG Issues' (speech by Gabriel Makhlouf, Governor) 03 November 2021, 3.

[94] Central Bank of Ireland, Supervisory … (Fn. 93).

[95] Central Bank of Ireland, Consultation on the Renewed Sustainable Finance Strategy, 14 July 2020 (written by Gerry Cross, Director Financial Regulation – Policy and Risk) and Vasileios Madouros (Director of Financial Stability), section 1 'A focus on implementation'.

[96] Central Bank of Ireland, Consultation … (Fn. 95).

A tool frequently used by the Central Bank to monitor rule compliance has been thematic reviews. Such reviews were conducted in relation to structured retail products whereby key product governance weaknesses were identified.[97] Other reviews evaluated compliance by MiFID investment firms with the suitability requirements,[98] compliance by FMCs with the CP 86 Guidelines,[99] and compliance by Irish-based UCITS Management Companies with regulation on performance fees.[100] Similar steps are expected to take place in relation to compliance with the newly implemented sustainability-related rules.

In Ireland, tackling greenwashing risk has also become a top policy priority, with the Central Bank playing a critical role in ensuring 'the orderly functioning of markets and wider market integrity, particularly in the development of sustainable finance and the prevention of "greenwashing".'[101] Defined in simple terms, greenwashing constitutes a conduct whereby a firm's performance, or a financial product, is presented (e.g., marketed) as sustainable when, as a matter of fact, it is not.[102] The Central Bank is expected to take action to tackle greenwashing practices in the Irish financial markets by monitoring due compliance by financial participants with the new sustainability-related disclosure obligations. Furthermore, the Central Bank is empowered to supervise compliance and enforce core legislation including MiFID II, the UCITS Directive, and the AIFM Directive as transposed into Irish law.

Special attention is drawn to the Central Bank's consumer protection powers as they enable very distinctive enforcement actions. Drawing from such powers, the Central Bank may direct – or issue a direction to – financial service providers when it is satisfied that one or more providers have committed widespread or regular relevant defaults, and such defaults cause customers to suffer loss or damage. By way of this direction, the CBI may seek appropriate redress for the

---

[97] Central Bank of Ireland, Letter to CEO. Themed Inspection: Structured Retail Products in MiFID authorised Investment and Stockbroking Firms and Credit Institution, (Helena Mitchell, Head of Consumer Protection, Supervision Division) 1 September 2016.

[98] Central Bank of Ireland, Letter on Common Supervisory Action on MiFID II Suitability Requirements, 1 December 2021 (letter prepared by Sandra Shanley, Head of Function, Consumer Protection – Investment Firms and Client Assets Division, Central Bank of Ireland).

[99] Central Bank of Ireland, Thematic review of fund management companies' governance, management and effectiveness, 20 Aug 2020 (prepared by Gerry Cross and Colm Kincaid) (18-month review covering 358 Irish FMCs).

[100] Central Bank of Ireland, Thematic Review of UCITS Performance Fees, 4 September 2018 (produced by Patricia Dunne Head of Securities and Markets Supervision).

[101] Central Bank of Ireland, Consultation … (Fn. 95), 3.

[102] ESMA, Sustainable financial markets: translating changing risks and investor preferences into regulatory action, 12 February 2020, European Financial Forum 2020 Dublin (Speech by Steven Maijoor, Chair European Securities and Markets Authority), ESMA32-67-642. More recently, the ESAs produced a report on how to understand and approach greenwashing practices, see ESMA, 'Progress Report on Greenwashing' 31 May 2023, para 13, ESMA30-1668416927-2498.

benefit of the affected customers.[103] It is noted that the definition of 'relevant default' contains practices that are closely linked to investor protection and greenwashing conduct:

(a) charging a customer an amount which the regulated financial service provider is not entitled to charge, (b) *providing a customer with a financial service which the customer has not agreed to receive, (c) providing a customer with a financial service which was not suitable for the customer at the time when it was provided, (d) providing a customer with inaccurate information which influences the customer in making a decision about any financial service, (e) a failure of any system or controls of the regulated financial service provider,* or (f) a prescribed contravention.[104]

On the side of private enforcement, Article 44 of the Central Bank (Supervision and Enforcement) Act 2013 grants a private right of action. It prescribes that '[a] failure by a regulated financial service provider to comply with any obligation under financial services legislation is actionable by any customer of the regulated financial service provider who suffers loss or damage as a result of such failure'[105] This private right of action is granted to customers of financial service providers that suffer harm as a result of a failure by the providers to comply with statutory obligations arising from financial services legislation including MiFID II, UCITSD and AIFMD.[106] It remains to be seen whether new legislation such as the SFDR is also included within the scope of these powers. The existence of this statutory private right of action does not preclude other rights that may emerge from either common law – such as breach of contract or tort claims in relation to false or misleading sustainability-related representations or disclosures – or other specific statutory provisions contemplating civil liability for losses caused by misstatements in prospectuses.[107] Decisions by the Irish courts in related to sustainability or ESG issues have been limited, lawsuits brough by activists (environmental NGOs) being litigated in court on the basis of causes of actions found in environmental law.[108]

---

[103] S. I. No. 26/2013 – Central Bank (Supervision and Enforcement) Act 2013, Part 6 – Customer Protection, art 43(1).

[104] S. I. No. 26/2013 (Fn. 103), art 43(2) (indented letters added).

[105] S. I. No. 26/2013 (Fn. 103), art 44.

[106] *Breslin/Corcoran*, New Private Right of Action for Damages in Financial Services Litigation, Dublin University Law Journal 2015 38(1), 17, (47); *Clarke*, Ireland in: Busch/van Dam (eds), A Bank's Duty of Care, Oxford: Hart Publishing, 2017, 285, (319–322).

[107] *Breslin/Corcoran* (Fn. 106), 319–322. Also, *Stapleton/Cremin/Dobbyn*, Ireland: Environmental, Social and Governance Law 2022, in: ICGL 2022, 13 December 2021, s2.5; *Kennedy/Clarkin/Collins/King*, Ireland, in: Securities Litigation, Ryan/Selendy (eds), Law Business Research Ltd, 2017, 47–53

[108] *Stapleton/Cremin/Dobbyn* (Fn. 107), 47–53.

Country Report France

Pierre-Henri Conac

A. Introduction

France has a large asset management industry and a long tradition of supporting and encouraging socially responsible investments. On many aspects, France has been, and sometimes even remains, ahead of European Union (EU) legislation on those issues. The French legislator expressed support for such policy as early as 2001 and has been in favour of shareholders' engagement since 2003.

The legal framework relating to investment funds choosing to support Environmental, Social and Governance (ESG) objectives is well developed. All French investment funds which are Undertakings for the Collective Investment in Transferable Securities (UCITS) or AIF (Alternative Investment Funds) can qualify as ESG funds.[1] However, employee funds have a special regime for them and have been allowed to adopt an ESG approach as early as 2001.[2] Furthermore, funds controlled by the French State are managed according to ESG principles. The rules regarding French asset managers and investment funds are located in the Monetary and Financial Code and in the General Regulation of the securities supervisor, the *Autorité des marchés financiers* (AMF). The legal regime is completed by company law provisions on public limited liability companies (*Sociétés anonymes* or SA) which are located in the commercial code.

B. Sustainable Ownership/Shareholder Governance

I. General aspects on the use of voting rights by investment companies

1. Employee investment funds

France has a long tradition of investments funds dedicated to employees. This dates back to De Gaulle who promoted employee participation in the profits of

[1] On AIF, see I. Riassetto & M. Storck, "Les organismes de placement collectif", Tome 2. *Les fonds d'investissement alternatifs*, Joly Editions, 2022, 1772 pp.

[2] On the evolution of the French regime, see I. Parachkevova, "Les obligations des fonds d'investissement au sein des sociétés cotées", *Revue des sociétés*, 2015, p. 75; E. Forget, "L'investissement éthique. Implications en droit des sociétés", *Revue des sociétés* 2015, p. 559; I. Riassetto & M. Storck, "L'engagement actionnarial des sociétés de gestion de portefeuille", *Mélanges en l'honneur d'Alain Couret*, Dalloz, 2022, p. 625.

the company as early as 1959 and then again in 1967. It served as a way to bridge the gap between capitalism and socialism. At this time, codetermination was not politically achievable in France due to the joint opposition of employers' representatives and workers' unions.

Employee participation in profits takes several forms. It can consist of direct individual payments but also of ownership in special employee funds which invest in shares. In this manner, a large investment fund industry investing in shares for the benefit of employees has developed in France. Employee investment funds are referred to as a company common contractual fund (*fonds commun de placement d'entreprise* or FCPE). FCPEs are themselves classified into two categories. A first category is required to invest more than one-third of its resources in the shares of the company where the employees work. A second category is called "diversified" FCPEs where a maximum of one-third of the resources can be invested in the shares of the company where the employees work.

Those funds tend more to have an ESG focus. They were the first in France to be allowed to integrate ESG concerns. A law of 19 February 2001 on employee then introduced provisions encouraging the inclusion of social and environmental criteria in their investment policies. Art. L. 214–39 of the Monetary and Financial Code provided at the time that: "The regulations (*of the FCPE*) shall specify, where applicable, the social, environmental or ethical considerations that the management company must respect in the purchase or sale of securities, as well as in the exercise of the rights attached to them. The fund's annual report shall report on their application, under conditions defined by the *Commission des Opérations de Bourse*." The *Commission des Opérations de Bourse* (COB) was the securities supervisor at the time and was replaced by the *Autorité des marchés financiers* in 2003. Art. L. 214–39 of the Monetary and Financial Code was remarkable because it mentioned "social, environmental or ethical considerations" as part of the investment policy of the FCPE even if adopting such policies was, and remains, noncompulsory. In addition, it referred to the "exercise of the rights attached" to those securities which implies exercising one's right to vote. Currently, this provision is found in Art. L 214–164 V. of the monetary and financial code. Its content is essentially unchanged compared to 2001.

As a further commitment to ESG, as of 2018, employee funds can invest in "solidarity funds" (*fonds solidaires*) whose assets are invested in solidarity companies (*entreprises solidaires*) whose shares are not admitted to trading on a regulated market.[3] The regime of the *Entreprise solidaire d'utilité sociale* (ESUS) was created in 2014.[4]

[3] Art. L. 3332–17 and L. 3332–171 of the Labour Code. Law n°2008–776 of 4 August 2008 modernising the economy *(de modernisation de l'économie)*, JO 5 August 2008, text 1.

[4] Law n°2014–856 of 31 July 2014 relative à l'économie sociale et solidaire, JO 1 August 2014, text 2.

2. All-purpose investments funds

a) "Duty" to vote

In France, as early as 1996, a French Senator, Philippe Marini, proposed the introduction of a legal obligation of voting and transparency for institutional investors.[5] Then, in 1997, the French securities supervisor, the *Commission des opérations de bourse*, in Article 8 of its Regulation No. 96–03, required UCITS managers to give precedence to the interests of unit holders when voting. The manager was not obliged to vote but could only do so by giving primacy to the interests of investors. This article also provided for an obligation of transparency, as the manager had to report on "its practice with regard to the use of voting rights in the annual report of the UCITS". These provisions were later repealed and included in the general regulation of the *Autorité des marchés financiers* (AMF). Despite the lack of legal obligation, the main French asset managers professional association, the *Association française de la gestion financière* (AFG), adopted a new recommendation in 1996 in its UCITS Code of Ethics (*Réglement de déontologie des OPVCM*). Its Article 15 recommended the use of voting rights for the first time and imposed an obligation of transparency in this regard.[6]

In 2003, a report by the *Institut Montaigne*, inspired by the 1994 US Dept. of Labor position[7], proposed establishing a duty to vote for institutional investors.[8] Following on his idea, senator Philippe Marini succeeded in incorporating the obligations of UCITS managers into the law with respect to voting. During the legislative process on the "financial security" law of August 1, 2003 (*Loi de sécurité* financière or LSF), he proposed, on behalf of the Senate Finance Committee, an amendment which became Article L. 533–4,8° of the Monetary and Financial Code, according to which portfolio management companies (*sociétés de gestion de portefeuille*) were obliged to "exercise the rights attached to the securities held by the UCITS[9] they manage, in the exclusive interest of the shareholders or unit holders of these UCITS and to report on their practices with respect to the exercise of voting rights under the conditions set by the AMF's general regulation. In particular, when they do not exercise these voting rights, they shall explain their reasons to the unit holders or shareholders of the UCITS". According to Article L. 533–4,8° of the Monetary Code, the debtor of the voting/transparency

[5] Ph. Marini, "Report on the modernization of company law", Doc. fr, 196, p. 94.

[6] AFG, "*Règlement de déontologie des OPCVM*", 3-4-1997 art. 15, al. 2.

[7] "The fiduciary obligations of prudence and loyalty to plan participants and beneficiaries require the responsible fiduciary to vote proxies on issues that may affect the value of the plan's investment". Rules and Regulations, Department of Labor, Interpretative bulletin relating to statements of investment policy or guidelines 94–2, July 29, 1994, p. 4 et 5; Code of federal regulations, Table 29, Chapter XXV, 2509-94-2, 1994.

[8] Institut Montaigne, "Mieux gouverner l'entreprise", March 2003, 106 pp.

[9] Until the implementation of the 2011 AIFM directive, French investment funds were all called "UCITS" (coordinated UCITS and non-coordinated UCITS).

obligation has to be the management company and not the UCITS itself.[10] This duty was, and still remains, a "comply or explain" approach. The content of this article was transferred in 2007 as a part of the implementation of the Markets in Financial Instruments Directive of 2004, without any change, into a new Article L. 533–22 of the Monetary and Financial Code.

This "duty" to vote was strengthened as part of the implementation of delegated directive 2010/43/EU of 1st July 2010, implementing Directive 2009/65/EC on UCITS, whose Article 21 "Strategies for the exercise of voting rights" required that "Member States shall require management companies to develop adequate and effective strategies for determining when and how voting rights attached to instruments held in the managed portfolios are to be exercised, to the exclusive benefit of the UCITS concerned".[11] Meanwhile, in 2013, alternative investment funds (AIFs) were added to the list as part of the implementation of the Alternative Investment Fund Managers (AIFM) Directive of 2011.[12]

The directive (EU) 2017/828 of 17 May 2017 as regards the encouragement of long-term shareholder engagement was implemented in France by the so-called PACTE Act of 2019.[13] Article L. 533–22 I. of the Monetary and Financial Code holds that "The portfolio management companies mentioned in Article L. 532–9 (*UCITS, AIF ....*), with the exception of those that exclusively manage AIFs covered by I of Article L. 214–167, AIFs covered by IV of Article L. 532–9, AIFs covered by the second paragraph of III of the same Article L. 532–9 or which manage other collective investments mentioned in Article L. 214–191, draw up and publish a shareholder engagement policy describing the way in which they integrate their role as shareholder into their investment strategy. Each year, they publish a report on the implementation of this policy." The obligation to have an "engagement policy" also applies to "investment firms that provide investment services mentioned in Article L. 321–1(4) (as they) are subject to the provisions of Articles L. 533–22 and L. 533-22-1 in the same way as the portfolio management companies mentioned therein".[14] Life insurance companies and reinsurance companies are also subject to Article L. 533–22 of the Monetary and Financial Code as long as they invest in shares admitted to trading on a regulated market

[10] Apart from self-managed investment companies.

[11] Commission Directive 2010/43/EU of 1 July 2010 implementing Directive 2009/65/EC of the European Parliament and of the Council as regards organisational requirements, conflicts of interest, conduct of business, risk management and content of the agreement between a depositary and a management company, OJ L 176/42, 10.07.2010.

[12] Directive 2011/61/EU of the European Parliament and of the Council of 8 June 2011 on Alternative Investment Fund Managers and amending Directives 2003/41/EC and 2009/65/EC and Regulations (EC) No 1060/2009 and (EU) No 1095/2010, OJ L 174/1, 01.07.2011.

[13] Law n°2019–486 of 22 May 2019 *relative à la croissance et la transformation des entreprises*, JO 23 may 2019.

[14] Art. L. 533-22-4 of the Monetary and Financial code.

or do so indirectly through a portfolio management company or investment firm subject to Article L. 533–22.[15]

For that reason, France anticipated the "voting policy" of directive 2017/828 of 17 May 2017 back in 2003 as regards the encouragement of long-term shareholder. Since the PACTE Act of 2019, the duty to exercise the rights attached to the securities held by the UCITS and AIF which they manage in the exclusive interest of the investors has been transferred from Article L. 533–4,8° to Article R. 533–16 of the Monetary and Financial Code. These duties are also detailed in the AMF General Regulation through positions and recommendations. The AFG association publishes an annual report on the exercise of voting rights by portfolio management companies.[16]

b) ESG policy

Well ahead of the EU legislator, the French legislator subsequently introduced references to Environmental, Social and Governance issues. Article 224 of the law 2010–788 of 12 July 2010 on the national commitment to environment (so-called "Grenelle II") introduced a specific provision on ESG in Article L. 214–12 of the Monetary and Financial Code. This new article held that "Management companies shall make available to subscribers of each of the undertakings for collective investment in transferable securities that they manage information on the manner in which their investment policy takes into account criteria relating to compliance with social, environmental and governance quality objectives. They shall specify the nature of these criteria and the way in which they are applied according to a standard presentation fixed by decree. They shall indicate how they exercise the voting rights attached to the financial instruments resulting from these choices." This reform was clearly designed to promote ESG investments as such. In 2011, this provision was transferred into a new Article L. 533-22-1 of the Monetary and Financial Code complementary to Article L. 533–22.[17]

At the same time, the scope of application was extended to all type of UCITS, including investment funds without legal personality (*fonds communs de placement*). That being the case, Article L. 533-22-1 of the Monetary and Financial Code is the key reference for ESG voting policy and disclosure by investments funds and institutional investors. In 2012, a decree was adopted as Article D. 533-

[15] Art. L 310-1-1-2 of the Insurance code.

[16] AFG, "Exercice des droits de vote par les sociétés de gestion en 2021", *Données d'enquête* 2021 – 20e édition.

[17] Ordonnance n° 2011–915 du 1er août 2011 relative aux organismes de placement collectif en valeurs mobilières et à la modernisation du cadre juridique de la gestion d'actifs, JO 2 August 2011, text 5.

16-1 of the Monetary and Financial Code.[18] As a result, in 2012, all management companies of UCITS were requested to disclose whether or not their investments funds were ESG. This created pressure to embrace ESG since the other funds could suffer from reputational damage accordingly.

Article L. 533-22-1 of the Monetary and Financial Code was amended in 2015 and 2019.

In August 2015, the French legislator passed a law on the energy transition in favour of green growth (*Loi relative à la transition énergétique pour la croissance verte or LTECV*), whose Article 173-VI led to two significant changes.[19] The first change was an extension of the scope of Article L. 533-22-1 to essentially all large French institutional investors: "Insurance and reinsurance companies governed by the Insurance Code, mutual insurance companies or unions governed by the Mutual Insurance Code, provident institutions and their unions governed by the Social Security Code, open-ended investment companies, the *Caisse des Dépôts et Consignations*, supplementary pension institutions governed by the Social Security Code, and the supplementary pension institution for non-tenured employees of the French State and public authorities, the public institution managing the mandatory supplementary public pension scheme and the *Caisse nationale de retraites des agents des collectivités locales ...*". The second change was to include a requirement to disclose also "the means implemented to contribute to the energy and ecological transition". They shall specify the nature of these criteria and the way in which they are applied, in accordance with a standard presentation set by decree". This reform forced investment funds and institutional investors to support the climate transition as it would otherwise be difficult to explain to investors, especially retail investors, as well as to the general public, that they have no policy on the means implemented by them for contributing to the energy and ecological transition.

The implementing decree provided precisions as to the content of the information expected. Article L. 533-22-1 paragraph 4 held that: "The decree provided for in the third paragraph shall specify the information to be provided for each of the objectives, depending on whether or not the entities mentioned in the same paragraph exceed the thresholds defined by the same decree. Taking into account exposure to climate risks, in particular the measurement of greenhouse gas emissions associated with the assets held, as well as the contribution to compliance with the international objective of limiting global warming and achieving the objectives of the energy and ecological transition, are among the information relating to the taking into account of environmental objectives. This

[18] I. Riassetto, "OPCVM ISR: information sur les critères ESG", "Revue de Droit Bancaire et Financier", July-August 2012, p. 59.

[19] Law n° 2015–992 of August 17, 2015 on the energy transition for green growth (*Loi relative à la transition énergétique pour la croissance verte*), JO 18 August 2015.

contribution is assessed in particular with regard to indicative targets defined, depending on the nature of their activities and the type of their investments, in accordance with the national low-carbon strategy mentioned in Article L. 221–1 B of the Environmental Code. Where applicable, the entities mentioned in the third paragraph of this article shall explain the reasons why their contribution is below these indicative targets for the last closed financial year." The focus of the legislator was on climate change and the fight against global warming. The requirements are in Article D. 533-16-1 of the Monetary and Financial Code.

This report by asset managers is also known as the "Article 173 report". There are two types of legal structures which are covered. For the investment fund industry, the requirement applies to the management company (*société de gestion de portefeuille*) and, above a certain level, to each investment fund. An "Article 173 report" must be produced for each investment fund with net assets of €500 million or more. As to the management company, information concerns the strategy of the portfolio management companies in terms of taking ESG into account in their investment policies and, where applicable, risk management (general approach, means of information, list of products concerned, involvement of the company in ESG, risk management). This information relates to the entity's consideration of ESG criteria in its investment policy concerns and the technical methods used for taking ESG criteria into account in the investment process (ESG criteria used, sourcing, methodology for rating issuers, methodology for selecting securities, results of the application of the methodologies, review of investment and risk management policies in light of the analysis of the results).

In 2019, Article L. 533-22-1 of the Monetary and Financial Code was amended by the law of 8 November 2019 "regarding energy and climate" (*Loi Energie et Climat* or LEC) in order to add a specific disclosure as to climate change and biodiversity to those provisions.[20] The goal was to fully implement the recommendations of the Task Force on Climate-Related Financial Disclosures (TCFD) by structuring the disclosure of information around the key notions of governance of climate and biodiversity-related issues, scenario-based analysis and risk management. Management companies of investment funds must disclose "information on the risks associated with climate change as well as biodiversity risks". They must also disclose "the means implemented to contribute to the energy and ecological transition, as well as a strategy for implementing this policy". Previously, the information was more general in nature and focused on "exposure to climate risks". This change is in line with the "double materiality" standard adopted by the European Financial Reporting Advisory Group (EFRAG). The focus is also on the "strategy for implementing this policy". In addition, this information "concerns in particular the level of investments in favour of the climate

[20] Art. 29, Law n°2019–1147 of 8 November 2019 *relative à l'énergie et au climat*, JO 11 November 2019, text 1.

and the contribution to the respect of the international objective of limiting global warming and to the achievement of the objectives of the energy and ecological transition". The disclosure requirements are thus more demanding since 2019.

The 2019 LEC Act also extended those requirements to "credit institutions and investment firms for their activities of portfolio management on behalf of third parties and investment advice".[21] The financial institutions covered since 2015 remain subject to Article L 533-22-1 of the Monetary and Financial Code through specific references in their Codes. This is the case of insurance companies[22], mutualist companies[23], provident institutions[24] as well as various state-controlled institutions.

Despite the fact that those disclosure requirements are indeed extensive, the regulation is still based on the "comply or explain" approach, yet the "comply" dimension is notably stronger. The 2019 LEC anticipated the 2019 sustainability-related disclosures in the financial services sector (SFDR).[25] The SFDR is a minimum harmonisation text (*Recital 28*) so that France will be able to require and maintain more extensive information in this field.

3. *ESG labelled investments funds*

In 2016, the French government created a special label for Socially Responsible Investments (*Investissement socialement responsable* or ISR).[26] This label replaced a private one created in 2009 by Novethic. There are also some other labels endorsed by the government (eg Greenfin created in 2015), but the ISR label is the most important. This label is managed by the Ministry of Economy and Finance and can be granted to UCITS or portfolio management companies which satisfy certain criteria. Since 2020, it can be chosen by alternative investment funds (AIFs), real estate investment funds, *Société Civile de Placement Immobilier* (SCPI) and *Organisme de Placement Collectif Immobilier* (OPCI). Those investors have to apply the "Principles for Responsible Investment" (PRI) developed by the United Nations.

---

[21] Art. L. 511-4-3 of the Monetary and Financial Code.

[22] Art. L. 310-1-1-3. – The undertakings referred to in Article L. 310-1-1, paragraph 1 and Article L. 310-1-1, paragraph 1 III which reinsure the commitments referred to in Article L. 310–1, paragraph 1 are subject to the provisions of Article L. 533-22-1 of the Monetary and Financial Code; Art. L. 385-7-2. – Article L. 533-22-1 of the Monetary and Financial Code is applicable to supplementary occupational retirement funds.

[23] Art. L. 114-46-3 of the Mutual Code "The companies governed by this Code are subject to the provisions of Article L. 533-22-1 of the Monetary and Financial Code."

[24] Art. L. 931-3-8. of the Social Security Code: "Article L. 533-22-1 of the Monetary and Financial Code shall apply to provident institutions (*institutions de prévoyance*) and their unions."

[25] Regulation (EU) 2019/2088 of the European Parliament and of the Council of 27 November 2019 on sustainability-related disclosures in the financial services sector, OJ L 317/1, 09.12.2019.

[26] Décret n° 2016–10 du 8 janvier 2016 relatif à la création du label "Investissement socialement responsable".

They must contribute directly or indirectly to the financing of the energy and ecological transition.[27] In order to satisfy this requirement, 90 % of the assets represented in the portfolio of the investment fund must come from ESG issuers. In addition, for those funds which existed before they opted for the ISR label, they must either remove the 20 % less ESG issuers or have a significantly better ESG average for the portfolio than before opting for the label. In addition, ISR labelled funds must publish a voting policy and allocate resources and take actions such as filing ESG resolutions in the shareholders' general meeting, although there is no minimum number of resolutions to be filed every year. The ISR label has been criticised by a 2020 report by the Ministry of Finance who considered it too vague.[28] A 2022 report also criticised the ISR label as too "generalist" and called for the creation of a more specific label Climate Transition (*Transition Climat*).[29]

ISR labelled funds have increased significantly notably due to the fact that Article 72 of the 2019 PACTE Act required life insurance companies to offer at least one fund in units of accounts (*contrat d'assurance vie en unités de compte*) with an ESG label approved by the government. Life insurance funds in units of accounts are very popular in France.

4. State-controlled funds

The French government has promoted socially responsible investments through the funds it controls for a long time. For instance, a law of 17 July 2001 established a Retirement Reserve Fund (*Fonds de Réserve pour les Retraites*) with the aim of financing the pension system. It contains provisions encouraging the inclusion of social and environmental criteria in the investment policies. Most publicly controlled investment funds are subject to Article L. 533-22-1 of the Monetary and Financial code and support in practice ESG policies. This is the case of the *Caisse des dépôts et consignations*[30] and various public sector funds.[31]

---

[27] Décret n° 2015–1615 du 10 décembre 2015 relatif au label "Transition énergétique et écologique pour le climat".

[28] J.-P. de Saint-Martin Sébastien Piednoir, Inspection générale des finances, Bilan et perspectives du label "Investissement socialement responsable" (ISR), December 2020.

[29] Rapport Perrier, "Faire de la place financière de Paris une référence pour la transition climatique: un cadre d'actions", Paris, 2022.

[30] Art. L. 518-15-3 of the Monetary and Financial Code: "L'article L. 533-22-1 est applicable à la Caisse des dépôts et consignations".

[31] Art. L. 942-6-1 of the Social Security Code: Article L. 533-22-1 of the Monetary and Financial Code is applicable to institutions for supplementary occupational retirement and to institutions for supplementary retirement, to the institution for supplementary retirement of non-tenured employees of the State and public authorities (*institution de retraite complémentaire des agents non titulaires de l'Etat et des collectivités publiques*), to the public establishment managing the compulsory additional public retirement scheme (*établissement public gérant le régime public de retraite additionnel obligatoire*) and to the National Retirement Fund for local authority employees (*Caisse nationale de retraites des agents des collectivités locales*)."

Participations on the part of the French State in State-Owned enterprises (SOEs) or in listed companies are held overwhelmingly by a Government Shareholding Agency (*Agence des participations de l'Etat* or APE) which depends on the Ministry of Economy and Finance. As part of the policy supporting ESG, the APE takes an active role. Since 2015, the APE has endorsed Corporate Social Responsibilities (CSR) principles and promoted them in the companies in which it holds shares. A Corporate Social Responsibility (CSR) Charter setting out the priorities for the APE as a Shareholder was published in early 2021. Currently, the APE asks the companies in its portfolio to adopt a corporate purpose (*raison d'être*) and to incorporate their CSR commitments which must be factored into their strategic plan and be subject to tangible and quantifiable undertakings. Special focus has been placed on companies' climate policies, gender parity in management bodies (*conseil d'administration*) and the implementation of responsible procurement policies. The APE also insists on its expectations as regards reducing greenhouse gas emissions and the reduction of carbon emissions. All listed companies and major unlisted companies in the APE portfolio have committed to complying with the 2015 Paris Agreement and have set themselves a goal compatible with the agreement accordingly. This is also enforced in the meanwhile. For instance, the capital increases of the national railway company (SNCF) in 2020 and airline Air France-KLM in 2021 were contingent on commitments to reducing their greenhouse gas emissions.

II. Factual/economic obstacles to a meaningful "engagement policy" as defined in Art. 3g EU Directive 2017/828 by mutual funds

There are no real economic obstacles to a meaningful "engagement policy" by investments funds, especially since most of them are management companies owned by large banks which can easily cover the costs. In addition, some investors have teamed up their efforts. For instance, a group of ESG-minded investors established a Responsible Investment Forum (*Forum de l'investissement responsible* or FIR) in 2001. It is a multi-stakeholder association whose purpose is to promote responsible investment. It brings together investors, fund managers, specialists in social and environmental analysis, consultants as well as unions, Non-Governmental Organisations (NGOs) and some scholars. Many members come from the public sector, such as the *Caisse des Dépôts et Consignations*, have a close relationship to it or are insurance companies. Some are small management companies who support or specialise in ESG investments. They influence votes and promote legislative reforms in the field of shareholder engagement. For instance, they partnered with the socialist Think Tank "Terra Nova" in 2021 to call for a legislative reform on "Say on climate".[32]

[32] Olivier Laffitte, avocat et Alexis Masse, président du Forum pour l'investissement responsible, "Le 'Say on Climate': une solution urgente et pragmatique", 6th of April 2021.

It follows that the obstacles for a meaningful "engagement policy" are mostly legal. A first obstacle is to identify other investment funds as their identity might not be known. In many French companies, a declaration of crossing a threshold below 5 % of the voting rights or of the shares, with at least 0.5 % increments, has to be made to the issuer. Since this requirement is imposed by the articles of association, it is not required to share the information with minority shareholders and investment funds. The information is only made public when a 5 % threshold in voting rights or shares is crossed, as this is requested by the Directive of 2004/109/EC of 15 December 2004 on the harmonisation of transparency requirements in relation to information about issuers whose securities are admitted to trading on a regulated market.

Another legal obstacle is the limited access to the shareholders' list. The French Commercial Code provides the right for any shareholder to obtain – at least 15 days prior to a shareholder meeting – any shareholders' list (nominative shareholders, bearer shareholders who have immobilised their shares, domicile) and the number of shares held by each shareholder.[33] This includes the right to make a copy of the list. Copies can be made by taking notes, pictures, etc ... However, this right is not very useful. The reason is that having access 15 days before the shareholders' meeting is far too late for actually contacting them. Many institutional shareholders have already voted at this stage and minority shareholders, moreover, have often already made up their mind as to their vote.

Shareholder activism is generally not well received in France especially when it originates from foreign investors. However, requesting the filing of a resolution can hardly be considered as acting in concert as such. The European Securities and Markets Authority (ESMA) issued a public statement on this point in 2013 which made clear that tabling "draft resolutions for items included or to be included on the agenda of a general meeting" or "agreeing to vote the same way on a particular resolution put to a general meeting" constitute part of a "White list" of activities which in and of itself, will not lead to those shareholders being regarded as persons acting in concert and thus the risk of having to make a mandatory bid.[34] The position of the AMF is similar. This is implicitly recognised by a think tank essentially representing law firms and their clients which suggested in 2019 that the AMF should adopt guidelines for determining exactly what behaviour by activist shareholders constitutes acting in concert.[35]

[33] Art. L. 225–116 and R. 225–90, R. 225–91, R. 225–92 of the Commercial code.

[34] ESMA, Public Statement, Information on shareholder cooperation and acting in concert under the Takeover Bids Directive, 12 November 2013 ESMA/2013/1642.

[35] Recommendation n° 10, Club des juristes, "Activisme Actionnarial, Groupe de travail présidé par Michel Prada, ancien Président de l'Autorité des Marchés Financiers (AMF)", November 2019, https://think-tank.leclubdesjuristes.com/wp-content/uploads/2019/11/Activisme-actionnarial-Le-Club-des-juristes-nov.2019.pdf (28 November 2023).

Investors who exchange and coordinate among themselves in order to vote the same way on an ESG resolution have so far never been considered as "acting in concert". One reason is that investors are not acting in concert as long as there is no binding commitment, and each party can change its opinion and vote at its discretion.[36] Cooperation with other shareholders is explicitly mentioned in Article R. 533–16 4°) of the Monetary and Financial Code. Many investment funds simply follow the recommendations of ISS or Glass Lewis or the FIR and cannot be considered to be "acting in concert" under Article 5 of the Takeover Directive. In addition, the risk is very low that ESG activist investors coordinate themselves such that they would represent more than 30 % of the capital.

French company law does not regulate "Say on climate" resolutions as such and it is left to the board of directors to decide whether or not they are valid under the commercial code since it sets the agenda of the shareholders' general meeting.[37] The key issue is whether they constitute an infringement on the management of the company and on the powers of the board of directors which is codified by law. The commercial code allows for some flexibility in this area, but one indisputable point is that the general shareholder's meeting cannot be in charge of business decisions which can only be made by management. Hence, the validity of such proposed resolutions depends on their drafting. Many of them have been rejected by the board of directors for being too intrusive into the management affairs of the company. Others which were drafted in a more general way have, however, indeed been accepted. Some companies have also drafted their own resolutions on combatting climate change outlining their policy on the issue. No court decision has so far been issued on the validity of the "Say on climate" resolutions and to what extent.

Since 2020, some investors and NGOs have requested that a resolution on the climate policy of specific listed issuers, – especially those active in the oil and gas industry – be subject to a vote of the shareholders' general meeting ("Say on climate"). One obstacle is that those shareholders need to hold around at least 0.5 % of the capital, which is a very high threshold in large listed companies.[38] A think tank, the *Haut Comité Juridique de la Place financière de Paris,* issued a report on "Say on climate" resolutions on the 15th of December 2022 which concludes that their validity provided they do not interfere in the management of the company.[39]

Activists ESG investors in France have been so far unsuccessful at passing such resolutions. This is due to the fact that NGOs do not own a significant amount of shares and investment funds are usually satisfied with "Say on climate" res-

[36] Art. L 233–10 of the Commercial code.
[37] Art. L. 225–105 of the Commercial code.
[38] Art. L. 225–105 of the Commercial code.
[39] The report is available at: https://www.banque-france.fr/sites/default/files/rapport_54_f.pdf (4 September 2023).

olutions proposed by issuers. However, even if the resolution filed by ESG activist investors is not ultimately adopted by the general shareholders' meeting, there might still be a noticeable impact. For instance, an activist resolution was rejected in 2021 in the case of the energy company, TotalEnergies Some large asset managers were involved, such La Banque Postale, Crédit Mutuel AM, Assurances du Crédit Mutuel or a small investment firm, Meeschaert. This led to a dialogue between TotalEnergies and those investors which resulted in another resolution which took those requests into account, and was proposed in 2022 and ultimately largely adopted. A majority of shareholders, including large asset managers (Amundi, AXA IM, BNP Paribas AM and BlackRock) approved this "climate" resolution presented by the company in 2022.

In practice, most large investment funds tend to side with the management.

III. Restriction of investment strategy to portfolio companies in free float?

Most French companies listed on the regulated market Euronext Paris have a controlling shareholder, although this is less the case for companies that are members of the main index (CAC 40). Refusing to invest in shares of companies without enough free float would significantly limit the scope of investments in shares, which, in turn, would hurt investors. Consequently, this does not constitute a barrier to ESG investing, but, in theory, nevertheless affects their impact. However, most companies, especially the large ones, value the option of having resolutions adopted with large majorities at their shareholders' general meetings. They usually also aim to avoid adverse publicity resulting from criticisms from NGOS. They tend, to a large extent, to engage with activist ESG investors in order to better understand their expectations. The impact of such funds, moreover, is not proportionate to the size of their shareholdings, as companies aim to avoid reputational damage.

IV. On conflicts of interest as a result of collaboration on activist voting

There are few proxy advisors active in France. Some of them are national, like Proxinvest which has been acquired by Glass Lewis in December 2022. Proxinvest has been historically a very professional and independent proxy adviser. Otherwise, the two most active proxy advisers are Institutional Shareholder Services (ISS) and Glass Lewis, which will now act in France through Proxinvest. There are no conflicts of interests. On the contrary, French issuers complain that ISS and Glass Lewis do not take their remarks sufficiently into account.

Glass Lewis and ISS adopt balanced positions, at least from the point of view of issuers. For the 2019 proxy season, Glass Lewis announced a partnership with the Sustainability Accounting Standards Board (SASB), whereby they would be considering their definitions of materiality when conducting our analysis on certain environmental and social shareholder proposals. As to ISS, it adopts a case-by-case approach on votes on management proposals that asks shareholders to approve the company's climate transition action plan, taking into account the thoroughness and rigor of the plan.[40]

NGOs also act as *de facto* proxy advisors as they run press campaigns in favour or against specific resolutions, especially the ones dealing with the issuer climate strategy. They also sometimes interfere in shareholders' general meetings.

V. On the need for cooperation with lending banks

The management of the portfolio companies has the duty to manage the assets in the best interest of its shareholders. Article L. 214–9 of the Monetary and Financial Code provides that "The UCITS, the depositary and the management company shall act honestly, loyally, professionally, independently and in the sole interest of the UCITS and the unitholders or shareholders of the UCITS. (...)". There is a similar provision for AIF and their managing companies.[41] The same principle applies also to investment services such as portfolio management. Article L. 533–11 of the Monetary and Financial Code provides that "When providing investment and related services to clients, investment service providers other than investment management companies shall act honestly, fairly and professionally, in the best interests of their clients".[42] This requirement is not limited to the exercise of voting rights covered by Article D. 533–16.

This principle implies that management companies have to act first in the interest of their investors and should not enter into a situation with a bank that could create a conflict of interest. In France, in practice, large asset managers are owned by banks so that the risk of conflict of interest is limited.

VI. On the inclusion of fund companies domiciled outside the EU

Investment fund and management companies domiciled outside the EU are not subject to French law when it comes to their ESG policy and their structure.

VII. On the inclusion of debt investors in the activist programme

Debt investors in France do not behave as activists. Some large public and private issuers have issued so-called "green bonds". The first green bond was issued in July 2007 by the EIB (European Investment Bank) under the name "Climate

[40] ISS, Continental Europe, Proxy Voting Guidelines, Benchmark Policy Recommendations, Effective for Meetings on or after February 1, 2022 Published December 13, 2021.

[41] Art. L. 214-24-3 of the Monetary and Financial Code.

[42] I. Riassetto, "Le devoir du gestionnaire d'OPC d'agir dans l'intérêt des porteurs de parts", *Droit bancaire et financier, Mélanges AEDBF-France VI*, 2013, p. 581.

Awareness Bond".[43] However, there are currently no rules in place stating what qualifies as a "green bond". Asset managers apply their own methodologies. Those bonds have often been issued in order to invest in a specific project such as renewable energy. Whist the size of this market has been growing in France, it remains limited due to a lack of sufficient low-carbon assets in the balance sheets of issuers. A large part is purchased by ISR funds which then have a duty to their investors to follow up with issuers. However, bondholders have very limited to no influence at all on the management of a company.

Recently, "sustainability-linked bonds" (SLB) were created. They finance the company and not a specific project. The issuer pays a higher yield if certain predefined ESG objectives are not achieved.

VIII. On the relationship between "dialogue conducting/engagement" and equal information treatment of shareholders

The regime in France is governed by the provisions implemented from the directive 2017/828 of 17 May 2017 as regards the encouragement of long-term shareholders.

However, all communication is subject to the provisions of the Market Abuse Regulation 596/2014 of 16 April 2014 on market abuse (market abuse regulation). The regulation applies to ESG investors which does not, however, mean that there is no dialogue taking place. Such dialogue usually takes place ahead of the shareholders' general meeting.

C. Sustainable Funding / Portfolio Governance

I. On the conflicting relationship between ESG-compliant and prudential portfolio strategies

The potential conflict between ESG-compliant and prudential portfolio strategies has not been raised in France. This is probably due to the fact that ESG investment funds are still limited in number as regards investments in shares. As for investment in bonds, the issuers are often large corporations or public institutions which limits the overall risk of default. In that vein, the ESG-bond funds risk is essentially similar to that of non-ESG bond funds.

[43] N. Rodes, O. Vietti & S.Déo, "Green bonds: il est urgent de ne plus attendre", *Revue d'Economie Financière*, n°138, 2020, p. 287.

II. On the conflict relationship between ESG interests and client interests in portfolio management

This conflict of interest is not addressed in French legislation. The management of a portfolio company has a duty to manage the assets in the best interest of its shareholders as provided for by Article L. 214–9 of the Monetary and Financial Code provides. According to Article R. 533-16-1, portfolio management companies are also obliged to exercise their rights, especially voting rights, attached to the securities held by the UCITS and AIF they manage, in the exclusive interest of the investors.

A leading author considers that if an investment fund pursues an ESG strategy, then it has a duty towards his or her investors to fulfil this specific commitment, even if this means that it could impact the performance of the company. The ESG commitment could go as far as going against the social interest of the company.[44] This is possible as long as the fund does not commit an "abuse of minority". This is also provided for by Article 34 of the Rules of Ethics of the AFG.[45] In France, minority shareholders holding one-third of the votes in a public limited liability company (*Société Anonyme* or SA) can block a decision at an extraordinary shareholder meeting. French courts have held that minority shareholders can abuse their voting right by voting against a resolution if the vote is contrary to the social interest of the company and has been cast for the sole purpose of serving the interests of the minority shareholders to the detriment of all the other shareholders.[46] An abuse of majority is unlikely because it implies that the investment fund reaches a very high percentage. As part of these rights, French courts have explicitly recognised the right of portfolio management companies to file a derivative suit (*action sociale ut singuli*) against the managers of a listed issuer.[47]

The issue of whether ESG funds underperform is debated so that it is not clear to everyone involved that there is a conflict at hand. The evidence is not clear enough to draw a conclusion but tends so far to conclude that ESG funds do neither better or worse than regular funds[48] This might have to do with the fact that the concept of what is ESG is might be too broad. Asset managers adopt various criteria which are not similar and might be too vague.

---

[44] I. Riassetto & M. Storck, "Les organismes de placement collectif", Tome 2. *Les fonds d'investissement alternatifs*, Joly Editions, 2022, p. 753; I. Riassetto, "Fonds éthiques et sociétés commerciales", *Liber amicorum. Dominique Schmidt*, ed. Joly, 2005, p. 400, esp. p. 420.

[45] AFG, "Règlement de déontologie des OPCVM", art. 34. In exercising its rights, the asset manager must avoid any behaviour that could be considered an abuse of the minority.

[46] P. H. Conac, "The Shareholders' Duty Not to Abuse Rights, in Shareholders' Duties", ed. Hanne S. Birkmose, Wolters Kluwer, 2017, p. 363.

[47] T. com Paris, 1-3-2019, Banque et droit n° 185, May-June 2019, p. 85, note F. Bussière.

[48] G. Capelle-Blancard, "Mesurer les performances extra-financière: le véritable défi de l'ISR", *Revue Banque, June 2021*, p. 27.

As anecdotal evidence, a comparison can be drawn between two indexes. Euronext Paris issued in February 2021 an ESG index for investments in the largest firms called CAC 40 ESG. The performance of this index from its creation on the 26th of February 2021 to 25th of January 2023 is 13.44 %. The performance of the "regular" CAC 40 for the same period was 17.8 %. This has to take into account that the CAC 40 includes oil and gas company, such as TotalEnergies, which performed very well during this period.

III. On the fundamental suitability of active mutual funds for shareholder activism

The issue of active ESG funds not being able to act as long-term investors is not discussed in France. Since the universe of ESG-eligible companies according to Euronext, such as those included in the CAC 40 ESG, is rather vast, this means that ESG funds might sell their shares instead of voicing their concerns. However, if stricter criteria are applied as a consequence of the application of the 2019 SFDR, the ESG investable universe would become much smaller.

IV. On the compatibility of shareholder activism with the tasks of mutual funds as financial intermediaries

There is no legal limitation for investment funds to participate and vote. However, there are limitations in terms of participation to the management of the company except for private equity funds.

V. Specifically on the suitability of passive investment funds (index funds, ETF)

Passive investment funds specialising in ESG exist in France. No debate has taken place about whether they might lose their cost advantage because they are under an obligation to exercise their voting rights following ESG standards. This does not seem to be a problem for those Exchange Traded Funds (ETF) specialising in ESG.

The AMF adopted a Position-Recommendation 2020–03 on ESG investments funds in 2020 which includes a "Position" on the use of total return swaps in order to create "synthetic tracking".[49] Position 9 is applicable to certain collective investments that communicate on the consideration of non-financial criteria in their management and stipulates that "communication on the consideration of non-financial criteria by funds making very significant use of total return swaps

[49] AMF Position/Recommendation Doc-2020-03, Information to be provided by Collective Investment Schemes incorporating Non-Financial approaches, Document created on 11 March 2020, amended on 27 January 2022.

must be proportionate and restricted to the limited communication category". In addition, they must meet some additional conditions mentioned in Position 9 designed to avoid the risk of greenwashing.

VI. Specifically on the suitability of alternative investment funds

There is no legal incompatibility between ESG objectives and alternative funds. Some activist investors have supported ESG campaigns against issuers.

VII. Implications of the ECB's low interest rate policy in an ESG context

There is certainly a conflict of objectives between the European Central Bank (ECB) low interest rate policy and the optimisation of asset management in the spirit of the ESG doctrine. However, since long-term interest rates have increased significantly in 2022, this conflict is becoming less important.

D. Sustainable Trading / Product Governance

I. General aspects of the reorganisation of securities trading under ESG aspects

The existing rules on product planning and the distribution of investment funds in France are identical to those required by the Second European Financial Markets Directive 2014/65/EU (MiFID II). As France strongly supports the Capital Markets Union (CMU) and efforts toward supervisory convergence, the AMF tends to abstain from developing its own doctrine and instead strives to achieve common positions adopted at ESMA or else reforms of Level 1 or Level 2 directives and regulations.

Portfolio management companies (*sociétés de gestion de portefeuille*) of UCITS and AIF are not "investment firms" in the sense of MiFID II. That is, they are not subject to MiFID II rules on product governance and are explicitly excluded in the French Monetary and Financial Code.[50] MiFID II was not extended to apply to them in terms of subjecting them to product regulation and putting them at a competitive disadvantage compared to other Member States who would also not have extended MiFID II to them. However, portfolio management companies are subject to distribution rules when they distribute their own UCITS and AIF and provide an investment service, which they can do if the Member States so provide, "by way of derogation" (Article 6 of UCITS Directive and AIFM Directive), such as portfolio management or investment advice.

---

[50] Art. L. 533–24 of the Monetary and Financial Code.

MiFID II and French law make no distinction between ESG and non-ESG investors when it comes to product distribution, but only between professional and non-professional (retail) investors. However, if an investment fund is labelled ISR, it should be distributed towards investors who have expressed ESG preferences in accordance with Article 9 para. 9 of the Delegated Directive 2017/593/EU as amended by Article 1 No. 2 of the Delegated Directive 2021/1269/EU. This article requires that "Member States shall require investment firms to identify at a sufficiently granular level the potential target market for each financial instrument and specify the type(s) of client whose needs, characteristics and objectives, including any sustainability related objectives, the financial instrument is compatible. As part of this process, the firm shall identify any group(s) of clients whose needs, characteristics and objectives the financial instrument is not compatible, except where financial instruments consider sustainability factors. (...)".

1. Distribution of investment funds with an ESG label

Article L. 214–26 III of the Monetary and Financial Code stipulates that an asset manager must provide a key investor with an informational document and the information contained in this document must be "clear, correct and not misleading". Since the 2019 PACTE Act, the AMF is charged the quality of the information provided by management companies for the management of collective investments on their investment strategy and their management of the risks related to the effects of climate change."[51]

The AMF adopted a Position-Recommendation 2020–03 on ESG funds in 2020 in order to avoid greenwashing, especially to protect retail investors.[52] The key element is that investment funds which label themselves as ESG must show a "significant" commitment to ESG objectives and that those commitments must be measurable. The AMF is, however, neutral as to the exact means by which the manager demonstrates the sustainability of their approach.

Position 2 specifies that only collective investment products which comply with certain characteristics can make non-financial characteristics a key aspect of communication. Those characteristics are as follows:

a) the approach adopted is binding in that it provides measurable objectives in the regulatory documents for the consideration of non-financial criteria;

b) the commitment to take non-financial criteria into consideration must be significant. The Position-Recommendation 2020–03 provides several criteria.

---

[51] Art. L. 621–1 of the Monetary and Financial code.

[52] AMF Position/Recommendation Doc-2020-03, Information to be provided by Collective Investment Schemes incorporating Non-Financial approaches, Document created on 11 March 2020, amended on 27 January 2022.

c) The non-financial analysis, non-financial indicator or non-financial rating coverage rate must be higher than 90 %. This rate may be estimated based either on the number of issuers or the net asset value of the collective investment product.

The ISR also features requirements for receiving the label which vary depending on the type of funds, but which are set at a high level between 70 % and 90 % of the assets.[53]

In order to make it easier for fund managers to modify their product ranges to enable the consideration of non-financial characteristics, the AMF streamlined the product modification procedure in 2020 by no longer requiring that such modifications constitute a change subject to its authorisation.[54]

If a financial product is designated as an ESG investment fund, then it should only be distributed exclusively to investors who have expressed a "sustainability preference".

2. Distribution of investment funds without an ESG label

Beyond this, if the investment fund is not labelled ESG, it should not be excluded from distribution to investors who have expressed ESG preferences since they can still apply ESG policies despite not requesting an ESG label. There is no guidance on this. In addition, the issue of the articulation of product distribution and the consideration of "any sustainability-related objectives" have not been discussed in the French literature so far.

II. Sustainable distribution regulation in the fund industry Part 1: 'Formal product release

There has not been a specific change in the regulatory and supervisory practice of the AMF since the implementation of MiFID II.

III. Sustainable distribution regulation in the fund industry Part 2: Regular monitoring of the distribution of fund units

The AMF has not issued guidance on what constitutes the "typical" customer interest from a sustainability perspective, and what weight is given to the interest of maximum return. Courts tend to consider the "typical" customer as the "average" client. There are also no findings on how the fund industry should

[53] SRI label supported by the French authorities, Label guidelines, Publication Date: 23 July 2020 Commencement Date: 23 October 2020.

[54] AMF Position/Recommendation Doc-2020-03, Information to be provided by Collective Investment Schemes incorporating Non-Financial approaches, Document created on 11 March 2020, amended on 27 January 2022.

react to ESG-related changes after an issue of fund units has been completed as part of ongoing product monitoring.

IV. Sustainable distribution regulation in the fund industry Part 3: Impact of asset management on the attractiveness of offering fund shares

The AMF did not engage in the exercise of identifying the typical investor. It probably assumes that he or she would accept a possible level of underperformance. ESG investment funds are marketed without any reference to the risk of underperformance. This is unsurprising and more time will be needed to assess whether ESG funds under or over-perform or perform similarly to non ESG funds of the same category.

V. Sustainable distribution regulation in the fund industry Part 4: Product intervention and prohibitions

There is no experience so far in France with the AMF using its product intervention or product prohibitions powers in response to a fund failing to respect its ESG label.

VI. Sustainability in investment advice Part 1: Product governance in the individual client's interest

There is no evidence in France that the financial returns for individual investors is treated as subordinate if a financial product qualifies as "sustainable" but yields suboptimal profits. The AMF has not disclosed any investigation in this field. The AMF is currently much more concerned with potential issues of "greenwashing" due to the fact the ISR label allows for very different approaches to ESG in practice.

So far, there has been no civil action decided by the French Supreme Court (*Cour de cassation*) claiming damages for investors on account of incorrect advice linked to ESG preferences.

VII. Sustainability in investment advice Part 2: Product governance and greenwashing

The AMF is in charge of checking whether "greenwashing" is going on with investment funds. However, no investigation has been disclosed so far. This is due to the fact that the regulatory regime be it national or European, is considered vague. In addition, there are too many concepts at play: ISR, ESG, sustainable, responsible, ethical, impactful ... All of these factors make it difficult for the AMF to enforce disclosure.

The AMF has nevertheless started to do specific controls, so-called "spots", which are designed to be "educational" and for learning from the experience of investment funds.

VIII. Sustainability in investment advice Part 3: On the regulatory and liability significance of ESG quality labels

The French government has been trying to promote a semi-official standard with the ISR label. However, this standard is not exclusive and has been criticised as being too vague.

E. Conclusion

France has developed a regulatory framework, ahead of the EU, designed to promote ESG investment funds. However, the policy prescriptions were adopted rather hastily and before the industry could adapt. The key issue is that the concept of ESG is so large and vague that it has led to issues of "greenwashing" which has now caught the attention of the AMF and the French legislator. This creates an "expectation gap" with retail investors, who – contrary to professional investors – are not familiar with the various understandings of ESG by investment firms and are sometimes surprised to discover that shares held do not match what they would expect in terms of ESG. Legal developments at the EU level should lead to an improvement of the situation. In June 2020, the EU legislator adopted a Taxonomy Regulation which provides clarity on what constitutes environmentally sustainable ("green") and under which circumstances.[55] Applicable to the asset management industry, the SFDR of 2019 was supposed to also lead to an improvement of the overall situation. Meanwhile, the ESMA aimed to address this issue with a November 2022 Consultation On Guidelines on funds' names using ESG or sustainability-related terms.[56]

The development of ESG investment funds in France faces another challenge. French retail investors mostly invest in life insurance products that hold bonds as they tend to be risk averse. ESG-bond funds have less impact on companies than ESG-funds invested in shares. It will be difficult to change this situation since it is a profoundly cultural phenomenon.

Whether the push towards ESG investments is done at the expense of the profitability of the investment is not a question which is currently addressed

[55] Regulation (EU) 2020/852 of the European Parliament and of the Council of 18 June 2020 on the establishment of a framework to facilitate sustainable investment, and amending Regulation (EU) 2019/2088, OJ UE L 198/13, 22.6.2020.

[56] ESMA, Consultation Paper, On Guidelines on funds' names using ESG or sustainability-related terms, 18 November 2022 ESMA34-472-373.

in the French literature. The assumption by the French legislator is that ESG investments will not underperform in the medium to long-term. It is too early to assess this. However, if such underperformance were to occur, and as long as no promise of overperformance has been made, it can be expected that French courts would easily come to the conclusion that the retail investor prioritised ESG preferences over profitability.

Country Report Czech Republic

Kateřina Eichlerová

A. Overview of the Initial Situation

Sustainable finance is closely related to the ESG (Environment, Social, Governance) phenomenon, which was defined by the EU Commission in the "Action Plan: Financing Sustainable Growth" of 8 March 2018[1] and which refers to a balance between the factors of environmental sustainability, social sustainability, and corporate governance. This idea is not entirely new, but in the past, it was all based on voluntariness.[2] However, it cannot be overlooked that ESG principles can also be fulfilled to a minimum extent by complying with existing rules in the field of environment, occupational safety, etc., i. e. through compliance programmes.

How does ESG manifest itself in the Czech Republic? The Czech Republic is a strongly export-oriented country, hence, not only large Czech companies may be subject to the requirements of foreign legislation, e. g. UK legislation, e. g. in the area of public procurement. It follows then, that if Czech companies aim to compete on foreign markets, they must comply with these requirements.

There is also a strong presence of foreign investment in the Czech Republic, and this is the second way in which ESG is beginning to take hold, as Czech subsidiaries are fulfilling the concepts of foreign parent companies.

It should be mentioned that the main source of financing in the Czech Republic is not the regulated market but bank loans. Banks, earlier than investors on the capital market, can be seen setting conditions in line with ESG, such that projects which are not in line with ESG are not granted loans at all or are lent on significantly worse terms.[3]

---

[1] COM(2018)97 final.

[2] An example of an entrepreneur who applied social responsibility as early as the first half of the 20th century is found in a man named, Tomáš Bat'a, who tried to combine success in business and social responsibility towards employees (housing, education, old age security) in the region in which he operated. Bat'a contributed not only to the development of the company focused on shoe production, but also to the development of Zlín, where the company operated.

[3] The same approach is taken by some insurance companies and some outright refuse to insure entrepreneurs who are in the lignite mining business.

Many companies believe that ESG is a competitive opportunity for them to reach customers.[4] On the other hand, it cannot be overlooked that the appropriate and timely implementation of ESG into the internal organisation of companies, their relationships with suppliers and customers, all requires time, people and money, and not all companies comprehend this. Large companies are already well advanced in the implementation process, while SMEs do not yet know much about what awaits them with non-financial reporting. There is a debate about whether regulation of financial institutions and large companies will negatively impact their suppliers, who will be required to report derivatively from their large customer. Although it is declared that ESG should not have a negative impact on SMEs, it is not clear how this is to be achieved, as everything is linked to the question of who should bear the costs of mapping, analysing and reporting on ESG processes for SMEs. If it is up to them, it may be a costly affair for them, given their size. If it is up to their large customers to help them, then they may be faced with the question of whether it is worthwhile and whether they should switch to suppliers who can handle the task without their help.

In summary, large companies are in the process of preparing for a change in the legal framework, while SMEs are in a holding pattern. Those who do not expect the change in approach at bringing in new customers are fulfilling their existing obligations in a formal rather than material way.

B. Sustainable Ownership and Shareholder Governance

I. Overview

First of all, it is necessary to introduce the structure of company law in the Czech Republic. The basis of the legal regulation can be found in the Civil Code (CC, Act no. 89/2012 Sb., *občanský zákoník*) in the section on the regulation of legal persons (sec. 118 – 418 CC). This is followed by the Business Corporations Act (BCA, Act no. 90/2012 Sb, *o obchodních společnostech a družstev*), which regulates general issues of business corporations and their individual forms (unlimited partnership, limited partnership, limited liability company, joint stock company and cooperative). The specific business corporations are of course also affected by sectoral regulation according to the area in which it operates (banks, energy companies, etc.). Those corporations operating on the capital market are regulated through the Capital Market Enterprise Act (CMEA, Act no. 256/2004 Sb, *o podnikání na kapitálovém trhu*). There are the rules implementing EU

[4] Survey of the Confederation of Industry of the Czech Republic among 100 industrial companies from June 2022 (https://www.spcr.cz/images/Pruzkum_SPCR_udrzitelnost_vysledky_25072022.pdf) (5 September 2023).

Directive 2017/828.[5] The Sustainable Financing Goals are being pursued through a variety of legal means in line with European legislation. One of these is the legislation on shareholder engagement which combines both historical and new legal regulations.

Shareholder engagement has several manifestations. The identification of shareholders and communication between the company and the shareholder, including proof of votes, are regulated in sec. 121c to 121i CMEA. Rules regarding on the remuneration of company directors are regulated in sec. 121j to 121v CMEA. Sections 127e to 127n CMEA regulate the rules relating to the engagement policy and investment strategy. Sections 127l to 127n CMEA regulate the rules relating to the voting adviser. The regulation of "significant transactions" can be found in § 121v CMEA.

II. Information on shareholders

One of them is the right of a public company to know its shareholders. However, this right varies depending on whether the company has issued registered or bearer shares. In the case of registered shares, the company has a continuous overview of its shareholders because it is obliged to keep a list of shareholders. This has an informative and, to some extent, a legitimising function.[6] Other shareholders can request information about other shareholders [sec. 266 (1) of the BCA].

A public company may also issue registered shares as dematerialised shares, in which case, the articles of association may provide that the register of dematerialised securities maintained by the central depository has to replace the list of shareholders. A public company may also issue shares in bearer form as immobilised or dematerialised shares. In such a case, it is not necessary to keep a list of shareholders and the other shareholders are not entitled to a copy thereof. If a public company does not keep a list of shareholders itself, it does not have continuous access to information on who its shareholders are, but only in certain instances (the convening of a general meeting, the holding of a general meeting, distribution of profits).

Following the EU Directive 2017/828, sections 121c and 121d CMEA enshrine the right of a Czech listed public company to know its shareholders if its shares are dematerialised or immobilised shares. In the case of immobilised or dematerialised shares, the relaxation of the competitive environment has led to the existence of more central registers of dematerialised securities and more sep-

[5] Directive (EU) 2017/828 of the European Parliament and of the Council of 17 May 2017 amending Directive 2007/36/EC as regards the encouragement of long-term shareholder engagement.

[6] Under sec. 265 (1) of the BCA, a shareholder is presumed to be one who is entered in the list of shareholders.

arate registers of collective investment dematerialised securities and immobilised securities.[7] The central and separate registers may be linked to so-called downstream registers where the securities are registered in customer accounts. Hence, under the current rules, a public traded company obtains information on who its shareholder is from the issuance account statement maintained by the central depository or through information on the owner's account obtained through the central depository from downstream recordkeepers.

III. Engagement policy

The institutional investors[8] and asset managers[9] have specific information obligations above and beyond those of other capital market players or standard companies. These special information obligations – which are intended to contribute to their transparency – include the obligation to an engagement policy and an investment strategy regarding public traded company established in the EU held by an institutional investor or asset manager. Under Czech law, these are two documents: engagement policy and invest strategy. However, nothing prevents it from being treated as a single document.[10] It is not mandatory to prepare an engagement policy if the reasons for not doing so are explained.

The obligation to draw up an engagement policy is imposed on institutional investors and asset managers by Section 127f of the CMEA. The engagement policy is to be published free of charge on their websites. The engagement policy should cover four areas. First, it should include information on how the institutional investor's investment strategy reflects its engagement in the public company whose shares it owns or, similarly, how shareholder engagement in the target public traded company reflects the asset manager's investment strategy. Second, the policy should include how the institutional investor or asset manager monitors the long-term performance of the target public traded company. Thirdly, the policy should include how the institutional investor or asset manager communicates with the target public traded company, with other shareholders, and how voting rights are exercised accordingly. Fourthly, it should describe the

[7] Until 30 May 2016, there was only one central depository where all book-entry securities were registered.

[8] Under sec. 2 (2) subsec. a) CMEA an institutional investor is an insurance company authorised to provide life insurance and a reinsurance company authorised to provide life insurance reinsurance and employees' pension insurance institutions.

[9] Under sec. 2 (2) subsec. b) CMEA an asset manager is mainly 1. a securities trader, 2. a foreign person providing main and supplementary investment services in the Czech Republic through a branch, 3. some investment fund managers and foreign investment funds.

[10] An example is the asset manager's engagement policy and investment strategy Erste Asset Management GmbH, pobočka Česká republika (https://www.erste-am.cz/content/dam/cz/eam/Data_banka/Politika%20zapojen%C3%AD%20a%20investi%C4%8Dn%C3%AD%20strategie%20spr%C3%A1vce%20aktiv.pdf) (5 September 2023).

procedure for dealing with actual or potential conflicts of interest where the institutional investor or asset manager has other relationships with the target public traded company other than by virtue of share ownership, such as significant business relationships, and a conflict of interest cannot be ruled out on its part.

The institutional investor and asset manager is required, under Section 127g CMEA, to evaluate the engagement policy on an annual basis and publish a report on its website. The annual report is to include (i) a description of how the engagement policy was implemented, (ii) a general voting strategy, (iii) information on their significant votes at the target public traded company's general meeting, (iii) an explanation of those votes, and (iv) information on the use of voting advisors.

Under sec. 127h CMEA, the institutional investor and the asset manager need not publish the engagement policy and annual report on its fulfilment if they disclose satisfactory reasons for doing so (*comply or explain*).

The approach to developing an engagement policy varies. Some companies opt for general information such as that they act on a case-by-case basis according to the specific circumstances,[11] while others indicate in which companies they do not invest (banned weapons, coal mining) and in which circumstances they do not attend the general meeting (shareholding of less than 5 % or insignificant matters on the agenda)[12] or, conversely, in which circumstances they do attend (change of business, reduction of share capital, issue of bonds, demerger of profits or other own resources, the payment of losses).[13] Some indicate categories of involvement ranging from normal involvement to intermediate to advanced involvement, depending on the intensity of communication with the company (advanced involvement includes, for example, the option of requesting a general meeting).[14]

Failure to disclose the engagement policy or the annual report on its implementation is an offence for which the Czech National Bank may impose a fine of up to CZK 1 million on the institutional investor and asset manager.

---

[11] An example is engagement policy of AMISTA investiční společnost, a.s., www.amista.cz/files/wincome_podfond/wincap-politika-zapojeni.pdf (5 September 2023).

[12] An example is the asset manager's engagement policy and investment strategy of Erste Asset Management GmbH, pobočka Česká republika, www.erste-am.cz/content/dam/cz/eam/Data_banka/Politika%20zapojen%C3%AD%20a%20investi%C4%8Dn%C3%AD%20strategie%20spr%C3%A1vce%20aktiv.pdf (5 September 2023).

[13] An example is the engagement policy of WOOD & Company investiční společnost, a.s., www.woodis.cz/media/21753/wood-is-politika-zapojeni.pdf (5 September 2023).

[14] An example is engagement policy of group Generali, www.generaliceska.cz/documents/20183/26791/Politika-zapojeni.pdf/d3685a7b-30d0-44ee-ba33-c4165b966f2b (5 September 2023).

IV. Voting rights as a manifestation of shareholders' engagement

In principle, Czech stock law is very liberal. Public companies may issue different classes of shares – non-voting shares or multiple voting rights shares; the number of votes may not depend on the size of the investment, etc. (sec. 276 BCA). In certain cases defined by law, a shareholder may not exercise voting rights (sec. 426 BCA). These cases may be extended by the articles of association if there are important reasons at hand [sec. 426 lit. e) BCA].

A shareholder may be present at the General Meeting in person or by proxy (sec. 399 BCA). The law permits the articles of association to provide for the possibility of voting by technical means (e.g. video conferencing) or by correspondence for a shareholder who is physically absent (sec. 398 BCA). It is also permissible for the articles of association to provide for *per rollam* decision-making at the general meeting (sec. 418 BCA).

To facilitate the rights of shareholders in relation to the EU Directive 2017/828, a Czech public traded company is also obliged, under Section 121e CMEA in conjunction with Section 120 (7) CMEA, to inform shareholders through the central depositary and intermediary about the convening of a general meeting, the payment of a dividend, the payment of a dividend advance, the distribution of other funds of theirs and changes in the rights attached to shares.

Section 121i CMEA implements the obligation of a Czech public traded company to provide, upon request, information on whether and how the shareholder's votes were counted at the general meeting, i. e. whether the shareholder voted for, against or abstained.

The scope for institutional investors and asset managers to be involved in the decision-making of the general meeting is therefore considerable, but in many cases, the high diversification required in share ownership may be an obstacle, where passivity in the exercise of voting rights is, in principle, a sound economic decision.

V. Proxy advisors

The proxy advisors are important players in the developed capital market. They should be distinguished from individual advisers. Unless the articles of association provide otherwise, each shareholder is entitled to attend the general meeting with one other person who will regularly act as an adviser [sec. 399 (2) BCA]. The articles of association may limit or even extend the right to advisers to two persons, so that a shareholder may use an adviser for economic matters and an adviser for legal matters.[15]

[15] According to Article 11:08 of EMCA, "a shareholder and his representative may attend the general meeting together with one or two advisors. An advisor may make a statement on behalf of the shareholder at the general meeting".

However, proxy advisers within the meaning of the EU Directive 2017/828 and capital market regulations are institutional advisers who advise more than one shareholder. A proxy advisor is a legal person whose business is to advise and give recommendations to institutional investors on voting at a general meeting of a public traded company [sec. 2 (2) al. c) CMEA]. Their role is considerable. On the one hand, they save each institutional investor or asset manager the cost of analysing information about a given company. On the other hand, their recommendations have a significant impact on the behaviour of institutional investors or asset managers.[16] For these reasons, it is legitimate to demand not only transparency of proxy advisors but also a certain standard of conduct. Sections 127l to 127n CMEA oblige proxy advisers to follow a certain code of conduct or else to disclose a reasonable explanation for not following or deviating from it (*comply or explain*). They are then required to update this information annually. In terms of transparency, the proxy advisor is required to provide detailed information on its website on key issues relating to the quality and independence of advice and recommendations (publication of methodology, main sources of information, prevention of conflicts of interest, etc.).

VI. The remuneration policy and remuneration report

First of all, it is appropriate to state the basic rules of remuneration of members of boards in a public company and the option of their modification in the articles of association. Only then will I focus on the special rules concerning remuneration in public traded companies.

A public company under Czech law may have a one-tier or two-tier model. Under the one-tier model, directors are elected by the general meeting unless they are called to the office by the shareholder.[17]

Under the two-tier model, members of the management board and the supervisory board are elected by the general meeting unless they are called to office by the shareholder,[18] or in the case of supervisory board members in large public companies, by employees.[19] The articles of association may also provide that the members of the management board are elected by the supervisory board [sec. 438 (1) BCA]. If the supervisory board elects the members of the management board, the supervisory board then also approves of their performance con-

[16] *Kotásek*, in: Pokorná/Lasák/Kotásek et al., Obchodní společnosti a družstva, 2. ed., Praha, C. H. Beck, 2022, 453.

[17] The right to appoint and remove a member of the board of directors may be accompanied by shares [sec. 458 (1) BCA].

[18] The right to appoint and remove a member of the management board or supervisory board may be accompanied by shares [sec. 438a (1) and 448b BCA].

[19] Employees have the right to elect 1/3 of the members of the supervisory board if the company has more than 500 employees on the first day of the financial year [sec. 448 and 448a BCA].

tract, including the remuneration rules [sec. 438 (1) BCA]. In all other cases, the general meeting has to approve of the performance contract [sec. 59 (2) BCA].

The doctrine implies that it is possible to separate the approval of the performance contract from the election of a member of the management board. Hence, it is permissible to provide in the articles of association that the general meeting elects the members of the management board but the supervisory board approves of the performance contract, or, vice-versa, that the supervisory board elects the members of the management board but approves of the performance contract.[20]

If the remuneration agreement is not approved by the general meeting or the supervisory board, it shall not take effect and the performance of the function shall be free of charge [sec. 59 (2) and 59 (3) BCA]. Only if the approval is due to reasons on the part of the company and not the member of the elected body, is the member of the elected body entitled to the usual remuneration [sec. 59 (4) BCA].

Publicly traded companies are required to have a remuneration policy approved by the general meeting pursuant to section 121k et seq. CMEA. The remuneration policy is a binding document that applies to (i) members of boards and (ii) the Chief Executive Officer and (iii) their deputies, if they exist. The remuneration policy therefore applies not only to persons in a business relationship with the company (members of boards) but also to employees in top management positions – Chief Executive Officer. The Chief Executive Officer is defined in sec. 121m (1) CMEA with reference to Article 2(i)(ii) of the EU Directive 2017/828 as an individual directly subordinate to the board of directors to whom business management has been delegated at least to the extent of the day-to-day management of the issuer as a whole. The EU Directive 2017/828 allows Member States to extend the personal scope to other persons acting in similar positions. The Czech Republic has not made use of this option in the transposition, as the disclosure of remuneration is still perceived rather negatively.[21]

Czech law does not normally regulate the position of CEO. It defines the position only for the needs of business on the capital market or specific areas of business (e.g. banks).

For the sake of completeness, it should be added that business management is perceived by Czech doctrine and case law as decision-making on day-to-day management issues; it is therefore understood more narrowly than in the meaning of the Directive. Of course, business management does not exhaust the powers of the board of directors. I believe that, in the Czech context, the range

[20] *Hurychová,* Schvalování odměn členů řídících orgánů akciových společností, Obchodněprávní revue, 11–12 (2016), 305 f.

[21] *Hurychová/Tomášek,* "Mind the gap ..." aneb k poměru mezi odměnami vrcholné exekutivy a odměnami zaměstnanců akciových společností (pay ratio), Obchodněprávní revue, 1 (2021), 23 f.

of persons that will be affected by the given remuneration policy gets discussed accordingly. This will not be problematic for those companies where there is no vertical delegation of business management, but rather a horizontal delegation between the members of the board of directors.

The remuneration policy is a strategic document prepared by the board of directors and approved by the general meeting at least once every 4 years, or more frequently if there is a material change. The approved remuneration policy establishes a framework, which, in principle, must not be exceeded when paying remuneration to a specified group of persons. Performance contracts, other legal acts or internal regulations of the company shall cease to have a legal effect upon approval of the remuneration policy *ex lege* to the extent that they conflict with the remuneration policy [sec. 121m (3) and (4) CMEA].[22]

If the remuneration policy is not submitted to the general meeting for approval, the performance of the functions of the persons concerned shall be free of charge until the date of the general meeting to which the remuneration policy was submitted for approval [sec. 121k (1) CMEA].

If it is submitted but not approved, then the company may temporarily maintain its current remuneration practice, i.e. until the policy is approved; the revised remuneration policy then has to be submitted to the following general meeting for approval [sec. 121k (3) CMEA].

Even if the remuneration policy is approved and it is understood that remuneration is to be paid only in accordance with it [sec. 121m (1) CMEA], the company may deviate from the policy if it is necessary for the long-term interests and sustainability of the company or for the maintenance of its business operations, provided that the remuneration policy contains procedural rules for temporary deviation and a list of the rules from which such deviation may be made (sec. 121n CMEA).

The public traded company is obliged to publish the approved remuneration policy on its website for the period of its application [sec. 121k (4) CMEA].

The remuneration policy could be applied by companies even before the adoption of the relevant statutory regulation, or it may be applied by public non-traded companies on the basis of the internal autonomy of legal entities if the articles of association extend the scope of the general meeting to include the approval of the remuneration policy. The remuneration policy goes beyond the boundaries of business management, so that there is nothing to prevent this issue from being entrusted to the general meeting on a voluntary basis. After all, it is in principle nothing more than a sub-component of the financial plan, the approval of which may also be entrusted by the articles of association to the

[22] *Kotásek,* in: Pokorná/Lasák/Kotásek et al., Obchodní společnosti a družstva, 2. ed., Praha, C.H. Beck, 2022, 451. *Čech,* in: Černá/Štenglová/Pelikánová et al., Právo obchodních korporací, 2. ed., Praha, Wolters Kluwer, 2021, 601.

general meeting. The key point is that the general meeting is not empowered to change the parameters of the remuneration policy submitted, but, instead, can only accept or reject it.

The remuneration policy is followed by an annual remuneration report, which is to be published on the company's website for a period of 10 years [sec. 121o (4) CMEA].

The remuneration report is intended to provide up-to-date information on the remuneration of those to whom the remuneration policy applies, namely an overview of all remuneration, including all benefits in whatever form. The information is to be formulated in such a way that it is possible to compare the evolution of remuneration over time and in relation to employees.

The remuneration report shall be submitted for approval at the latest, at the general meeting which approves the financial statements for the financial year for which the remuneration report is prepared. If the general meeting does not approve the remuneration report, the board of directors has to explain in the next remuneration report how the result of the vote at the general meeting has been taken into account in drawing up the new report [sec. 121o (3) CMEA]. The remuneration report is verified by the auditor accordingly (sec. 121q CMEA).

The law requires that the remuneration report contains particular details of the remuneration granted for the past financial year to each person concerned [sec. 121p (3) CMEA].

The remuneration report should also include data on the annual change in the average remuneration of the company's other employees per employee with a fixed weekly working time, for at least the last 5 financial years [sec. 121p (2) CMEA]. The purpose is to be able to compare the remuneration of executives and other employees (*pay ratio*). However, it is not entirely clear how companies are to approach this part of the report, who is to be included in the range of employees, with what remuneration, etc.[23] This part of the report is not subject to verification by the auditor.

The approach of public traded companies to the preparation of remuneration policies and remuneration reports is not the same. Some companies, e.g. ČEZ, a.s.,[24] provide detailed information on the remuneration of specific persons, while others, e.g. Kofola Československo a.s., provide specific information on remuneration in relation to persons identified only by letters (member A to member F), not by their names.[25]

[23] *Hurychová/Tomášek*, "Mind the gap …" aneb k poměru mezi odměnami vrcholné exekutivy a odměnami zaměstnanců akciových společností (pay ratio), Obchodněprávní revue, 1 (2021), 23 f.

[24] www.cez.cz/webpublic/file/edee/ospol/fileexport-s/pro-investory/investor-relations/vh2022/cj/vh2022_08b_zprava-o-odmenovani-zprava-cz.pdf (5 September 2023).

[25] www.kofola.cz (5 September 2023).

VII. The significant transactions

The Directive 2017/828 also regulates the conclusion of so-called significant related party transactions. These rules have been implemented in sec. 121s to 121v CMEA. Who is a related party is given in sec. 2 (2) al. d) CMEA which follows from Commission Regulation no. 1126/2008. A significant transaction for which the approval of the general meeting is required is (i) the disposal or acquisition of assets of the company exceeding 10 % of the assets and (ii) an increase in the company's debt only or contingent debt exceeding 10 % of the assets (sec. 121s and 121t CMEA). The amount of assets is to be judged by reference to the latest annual accounts. Individual transactions shall be aggregated in one fiscal year. Transactions carried out in the ordinary course of business and at arm's length are excluded from approval as the other relevant cases (sec. 121v CMEA). The company is required to publish detailed information about a significant transaction on its website so that it can be assessed whether the transaction was reasonable and fair from the point of view of the company and its shareholders (sec. 121u CMEA).[26]

If a transaction is carried out without the consent of the general meeting, the company and its shareholders may invoke the invalidity of such legal action within a subjective period of 6 months and an objective period of 10 years (sec. 48 BCA).[27] The related party should have been aware of the obligation to have the transaction approved by the general meeting and on that basis, cannot be presumed to have entered into the transaction in good faith without the approval of the general meeting and without the assurances accordingly.

B. Certain aspects of Sustainable Funding and Portfolio Governance

The institutional investors and some asset managers have to publish on their website, free of charge, an investment strategy containing information on how the main elements of their strategy correspond to the structure and maturity of their debt, with an emphasis on long-term debt, and how they contribute to the medium and long-term performance of the investments. The investment strategy is to be updated annually. The preparation of investment strategy is mandatory.

[26] *Kotásek,* in: Pokorná/Lasák/Kotásek et al., Obchodní společnosti a družstva, 2. ed., Praha, C.H. Beck, 2022, 452.

[27] *Kotásek,* in: Pokorná/Lasák/Kotásek et al., Obchodní společnosti a družstva, 2. ed., Praha, C.H. Beck, 2022, 452. *Čech,* in: Černá/Štenglová/Pelikánová et al., Právo obchodních korporacích, 2. ed., Praha, Wolters Kluwer, 2021, 602. *Eichlerová,* Zastoupení podnikatele, Praha, Wolters Kluwer, 2022, 295.

In addition, under sec. 127j (2) CMEA, the institutional investor publishes on its website the key terms and conditions under which the asset manager, at its discretion, manages the institutional investor's securities:

(a) how the asset manager is incentivised to
1. design its investment strategy in accordance with the institutional investor's debt
2. make investment decisions based on an assessment of the medium and long-term performance of the company,
(b) determine how the asset manager engages with the company for improving its medium and long-term performance,
(c) determine how the performance of the asset manager is evaluated; and
(d) assess the manner in which the institutional investor
1. oversees the costs incurred by the asset manager in relation to the turnover of assets under management,
2. sets and monitors a target turnover or range of target turnover for the assets under management,
(e) fixes the duration of the arrangement.

Failure to disclose the investment strategy is an offence for which the Czech National Bank may impose a fine of up to CZK 1 million on the institutional investor and asset manager.

However, these documents are so far mostly very brief and not comparable to each other. In my view, therefore, they do not yet fulfil the function that the Commission hoped they would.

C. Sustainable Trading / Product Governance

Financial products are also regulated under Regulation 2019/2088. According to this regulation, financial products can be divided into three categories: (i) dark green (Article 8), (ii) light green (Article 9) and (iii) others (Article 6).[28]

Second EU Markets in Financial Instruments Directive (MiFID II) of the year 2019 includes protection against abusive practices including greenwashing.[29]

Under Commission Delegated Regulation (EU) 2021/1253 of 21 April 2021 amending Delegated Regulation (EU) 2017/565, investment firms, securities dealers and other financial service providers covered by MiFID II from August 2022, are required to ensure that the business they recommend or are scheduled

---

[28] *Mezzanotte,* Recent Law Reforms in EU Sustainable Finance: Regulating Sustainability Risk and Sustainable Investments, 2022, 28 f.

[29] *Mezzanotte,* Recent Law Reforms in EU Sustainable Finance: Regulating Sustainability Risk and Sustainable Investments, 2022, 28 f.

to conclude as part of a portfolio management service is consistent with the client's overall investment objectives, including their risk tolerance and any sustainability preferences. It means that they provide more detailed information on all the financial instruments they offer and their sustainability because without this, it is impossible to give investment advice or conduct portfolio management, particularly from a sustainability perspective.

Sustainability preferences shall mean the customer's or potential customer's choice as to whether and to what extent one or more of these financial instruments should be included in their investments:

1. a financial instrument for which the customer or potential customer determines that a minimum proportion is invested in environmentally sustainable investments within the meaning of Article 2(1) of Regulation (EU) 2020/852 of the European Parliament and of the Council (the Taxonomy Regulation);
2. a financial instrument where the customer or potential customer specifies that a minimum proportion is invested in sustainable investments within the meaning of Article 2(17) of Regulation (EU) 2019/2088 of the European Parliament and of the Council;
3. a financial instrument that takes into account the main adverse impacts on sustainability factors, i.e. those instruments that consider and reduce the significant negative environmental, social and employment impacts caused by these investments.

In addition, investment firms will now be required to indicate – in addition to a description of the types and range of financial instruments – the sustainability factors, if any, that have been taken into account in the selection of financial instruments.

It is hoped that this information will enable investors to make informed decisions and reorient their investments towards more sustainable technologies and businesses accordingly.

Detailed criteria for environmentally sustainable economic activities that must be met for investments to be classified as green and therefore sustainable are contained in Article 3 of the Taxonomy Regulation.

Country Report Italy

Marco Lamandini / Elia Cerrato García

A. Sustainable Finance. The EU acquis (in a nutshell)

The European acquis on Sustainable Finance for investment funds and financial intermediaries[1] is currently based on two main pillars:

(a) the EU Taxonomy Regulation (Regulation EU 2020/852 of the European Parliament and of the Council of 18 June 2020 on the establishment of a framework to facilitate sustainable investment) which establishes the EU taxonomy, i. e., a list of environmentally sustainable economic activities meant to provide not only companies and policymakers but also investors with clarity on what economic activities can be considered environmentally sustainable, for the purpose of protecting private investors from greenwashing, helping companies to become more climate-friendly and helping shift investments where they are most needed; and

(b) the Sustainable Finance Disclosure Regulation (Regulation (EU) 2019/2088 of the European Parliament and of the Council of 27 November 2019 on sustainability-related disclosures in the financial services sector and its implementing regulations of 4 June 2021 and 6 July 2021) (hereinafter, the SFDR), which aims to bring about a level playing field for financial market participants and financial advisers on transparency in relation to sustainability risks, the consideration of adverse sustainability impacts in their investment processes and the provision of sustainability-related information with respect to financial products. The SFDR requires asset managers such as Alternative Investment Fund Managers (AIFMs) and Undertakings for Collective Investment in Transferable Securities (UCITS) managers to provide specific and standardised disclosures on how ESG factors are integrated at both an entity and product level. A significant portion of the SFDR applies to all asset managers, whether or not they have an express ESG or sustainability focus.

The EU framework for financial intermediaries also includes references to ESG in other instruments, like e. g. Regulation (EU) 2019/2089 on EU climate Transition Benchmark and amendments on Level II implementing measures of UCITS, AIFMD, MiFID II, IDD and Solvency II. On 6 April 2022, the Euro-

[1] Listed companies and their ESG engagement, as well as their non-financial reporting requirements remain outside the scope of this paper.

pean Commission published the Regulatory Technical Standards (RTS)under the SFDR. These standards define the 'level 2' ESG disclosures required under SFDR. For banks, EBA published a Report on ESG risk management and supervision in June 2021 and the ECB adopted a Guide on climate and environmental risks in November of 2020. For AIFMD and UCITS, ESMA is working on the development of guidelines on sustainability-related terms in funds' names to ensure that sustainability characteristics or objectives are reflected in a "material", "fairly" and "consistently" way. So far, the provisional agreement resulting from the 2022 public consultation and inter-institutional negotiations contains two new mandates for ESMA to develop guidelines determining in which situations the "name" of an AIF ot UCITS is unclear, unfair or misleading.

We will briefly consider how the European framework was implemented in Italy. As it will be apparent from what follows, many questions as to potential clashes between ESG ambitions and conflicting financial goals have no clear answer from the Italian regulatory and supervisory experience nor from Italian case-law so far.

B. Sustainable Corporate Governance – Influence of ESG on corporate governance

In Italy, the regulatory framework for engagement policy and shareholder voting is established by the Consolidated Act on Finance or *Testo Unico della Finanza* (TUF) (Legislative Decree no. 58/1998, as subsequently amended and integrated) (hereinafter, the Italian Consolidated Act) and, by the general provisions of the Italian Civil code for corporations. The Italian Consolidated Act lays down also additional rules for publicly listed corporations.

Furthermore, soft law legal instruments also influence ownership governance of firms in Italy. In particular, the new Italian Corporate Governance Code was approved in its final version on January 31, 2020 (the 2020 Code)[2]. This Code, was promoted by issuers' associations and investors' associations, encompassing non-binding and voluntary best practice principles and recommendations applicable to publicly listed companies. The Corporate Governance Code is thus based on a comply-or-explain approach.

II. Sustainable investment strategies of "engaged" investment funds

Article 3g SRD II regulates engagement policies of institutional investors. Legislative decree no. 49 of 10 June 2019 implemented in Italy SRD II, inserting those

[2] Italian Corporate Governance Code, 2020, https://www.borsaitaliana.it/comitato-corporate-governance/codice/2020eng.en.pdf (5 April 2024).

provisions into the Italian Consolidated Act (in particular, in Title III, Chapter II, Section I-ter, Articles 124-quarter to 124-novies).

The rules on shareholders engagement and disclosure duties apply to institutional investors and asset managers investing in companies whose shares are listed in Italian regulated markets or in the regulated market of other Member States.

This means that, in terms of territorial outreach – in accordance with Article 124-quater(2) of the Italian Consolidated Act –, a foreign institutional investor investing in a company listed in the Italian stock market will likewise be subject to the relevant Italian rules on shareholder engagement.

Articles 124-quarter to 124-novies of the Italian Consolidated Act include specific rules regarding the transparency of investment policies of institutional investors, asset managers and proxy advisors. This encompasses the role of ESG factors in such policies.[3] Article 124-sexies, e. g., encourages the asset manager "to make investment decisions based on the assessments relating to the long and medium-term financial *and non-financial results* of the investee companies and to engage with these companies in order to improve the medium and long-term results". The breach of the provisions established in Articles 124-quinquies, 124-sexies and 124-septiesby institutional investors and asset managers, as well as to voting consultants in the event of a breach of Article 124-octies or of the relative implementing provisions will result in the imposition of a pecuniary administrative sanction ranging from 2,500.00 to 150,000.00 euros upon the terms provided for in Article 193-*bis* (1) of the Consolidated Act.

In addition, the Italian Corporate Governance Code is also consistent with SRD II. In fact, article 5 of the 2020 Code "nudges" (under comply or explain) issuers listed in the Italian Stock Exchange to be more sensitive towards long-term sustainability, especially regarding their remuneration policies. Remuneration policy shall contribute, according to the Code, to "the company's strategy, the pursuit of long-term interests and the sustainability of the company and illustrate how it does so". Along the same lines, the Corporate Governance Code recommends that the variable component of the remuneration policy for executive directors and managers should also be linked to a company's performance in terms of ESG requirements (article 5, para 27).

As to engagement policies in practice and the role of proxy advisors in the ESG context, a survey conducted by Consob along with Assogestioni regarding the integration of ESG criteria into the investment policies and stewardship activities shows that, when considering whether to implement engagement prac-

[3] Compare *Maugeri*, Sostenibilità ed engagement degli azionisti istituzionali, Riv. Soc. 2021, 1350; *Tedeschi*, La direttiva Shareholders Rights II e il nuovo ruolo degli investitori istituzionali nelle società per azioni quotate: dall'attivismo all'engagement nella prospettiva di efficienza e di continuità dell'impresa, Riv. dir. comm., 2020, II, 559; *Alvaro/Maugeri/Strampelli*, Investitori istituzionali, governo societario e codici di stewardship, Quaderno giuridico Consob n. 19, 2019, 11.

tices with investee companies, managers use primarily internal teams and less proxy advisors and external consultants.[4] This suggests that concerns about the dangers of possible conflicts of interest due to the involvement of proxy advisors appear to have not yet materialised (or at least not to have been detected) in Italy. Should such conflicts materialise, it should be recalled that proxy advisors which are incorporated in Italy or have a registered office in Italy are regulated and required to report information regarding the performance of their research, their advice and their voting recommendation to CONSOB on an annual basis. More importantly, pursuant to Article 124-octies(g)of the Italian Consolidated Act., proxy advisors must further disclose their policies on the prevention and management of potential conflicts of interests. CONSOB is also entrusted with supervisory powers over proxy advisors and pursuant to Article 114(5) of the ItalianConsolidated Act, may require proxy advisors to publish "in the manner it shall establish", the information and documents it considers to be necessary for informing the public. If the proxy advisors fail to comply with this requirement, "CONSOB shall publish the material at their expense".

Neither supervision nor case-law has yet addressed the full potential of the possible implications of ESG engagement policies in Italy over the way strategic and investment decision-making is taken by investment companies as well as how engagement strategies are actually enacted regarding listed companies.[5] Several questions thus still need to be tested.

This is so, for instance, forESG policies in the context of groups and for ESG preferences of controlling shareholder(s) or anchor shareholder(s) or coalition of such shareholders in closed companies. In turn, there is no case-law so far concerning possible friction between ESG policies and loan covenants. There is, on the contrary, growing attention to green bonds and social bonds and on selective

[4] *Linciano/Cafiero/Ciavarella/Di Stefano/Levantini/Mollo/Nocella/Santamaria/Taverna*, La finanza per lo sviluppo sostenibile. Tendenze, questioni in corso e prospettive alla luce dell'evoluzione del quadro regolamentare dell'Unione europea, 2021, https://www.consob.it/documents/1912911/1972319/fs_1.pdf/cd935bf5-f395-d36b-732c-068399d7a308 (4 April 2024), 47.

[5] The only case discussing the implications of ESG engagement in Italy is the pending climate litigation case against the Italian company ENI and its shareholders, the Italian Ministry of Economu and Finance (MEF) and Cassa Depositi e Prestiti S.p.A. (CDP), which have sufficient votes to exercise a dominant influence in ENIS's general meetings and, therefore, in the firm's policies. Based on the landmark ruling Milidefeusie et al v Royal Dutch Shell plc, the NGOs-claimant argues that ENI's own decarbonization strategy is not in line with the goals enshrined in the Paris Agreement and the best available climate science recommendations to limit climate impacts. The claimants further request to the Court of Rome to declare that ENI, MEF and CDP shall adopt an industrial strategy to reduce its GHG by 45% by 2030, and that the three defendants are jointly and severally liable for past and potential future damage to the fundamental rights to health, safety, and property. See Greenpeace Italy et. Al. v. ENI S.p.A., the Italian Ministry of Economy and Finance and Cassa Depositi e Prestiti S.p.A. (pending), https://climatecasechart.com/non-us-case/greenpeace-italy-et-al-v-eni-spa-the-italian-ministry-of-economy-and-finance-and-cassa-depositi-e-prestiti-spa/.

dialogues between engaged investors and managers of the investee company (as it will be discussed below). It remains still to be seen, moreover, to what extent investors will be granted private causes of actions against the institutional investors and their directors in the event of non-compliance with ESG engagement policy previously disclosed (and being part of the precontractual information which may have guided the investment decision). In the Italian literature, some authors surmise that recent openings of the Supreme Court (*Corte di Cassazione*) – albeit in a different context – may facilitate findings in favour of investors (Cass. 3 January 2019, no. 5 and Cass. 9 January 2019, no. 301).[6] Others, however, offer a more nuanced view.[7] The matter is thus still at the level of academic debate.

III. Connections between fund governance and product governance

"Product Governance" originates from MiFID II. Among its core elements is the regulatory obligation for financial service providers to *formally approve newly issued financial products and to continuously monitor product distribution, including distribution chains.*" ESMA's 2022 Consultation Paper sets out ESMA guidelines on sustainability-related amendments on certain aspects of the MiFID II product governance requirements, such as the target market categories to be considered and the negative target market assessment.[8] The original aim of the regulation was to prevent "dangerous" financial products with excessively high-risk potential from coming into circulation in the first place. However, in its Action Plan on the 8th of March 2018 (COM(2018) 97 final), the EU Commission announced that it also intended to include (retail) customer business with financial products in its ESG agenda. Commission Delegated Directive (EU) 2017/593 supplements Directive 2014/65/EU of the European Parliament and of the Council (MiFID II) by further specifying, among other things, product governance obligations. This Directive clarifies that sustainability factors and

---

[6] *Toniolo*, Vincolatività delle politiche di engagement e responsabilità civile degli esponenti aziendali rispetto a profili ESG: Note a Cass. 3 gennaio 2019, n. 5 e 9 gennaio 2019, n. 301, Rivista di Diritto Bancario 2021, III, 347 ss.

[7] *Annunziata*, Alcune note sul tema delle politiche di impegno dei gestori di patrimoni (tra SRD II e TUF) in: Studi in Onore di Sabino Fortunato, Vol. IV, Cacucci Editore, 2023, 2981-2999..

[8] ESMA: Consultation Paper: Review of the Guidelines on MiFID II product governance requirements, 8 July 2022. ESMA proposes adding a new paragraph 20 to the draft guidelines "to clarify that firms should identify sustainability-related objectives as part of the target market assessment". As regards a product's sustainability-related objectives", ESMA suggests adding a draft of the guidelines to paragraph 81, specifying products which consider sustainability factors, "the firm should always perform a negative target market assessment with respect to the five target market categories (client type, knowledge and experience, financial situation, risk tolerance and objectives and needs), but should not consider the sustainability-related objectives of the products when performing such a negative target market assessment".

sustainability-related objectives should be taken into account in both product oversight and governance process.

In Italy, the principles envisaged in MiFID II have been integrated into the Italian Consolidated Act, while Legislative decree 254/2016 – as regards the disclosure of non-financial information – incorporates the periodic disclosure requirements vis-à-vis sustainability information.

The Italian Consolidated Act integrates the principles envisaged in Articles 16(3) and 24(13) of MiFID II into articles 21(2-bis) and (2-ter). Pursuant to Article 21(2-ter), the investment company shall assess the compatibility of the financial product offered or recommended with the needs and interests of the client to whom it is offering the product. In addition, Consob Regulation on intermediaries (adopted with Resolution no. 20307 of 15 February 2018 and subsequently amended) comprises the general rules and principles that apply to intermediary producers and intermediary distributors.[9]

On the disclosure of non-financial information, Legislative decree 254/2016, which implemented EU Directive 2014/95 in Italy, requires public-interest entities (PIEs) to report periodically sustainability information, including the company's business activity impact on environmental, social, anti/corruption and human rights matters.[10] Likewise, the annual report of the board of directors can include non-financial statements. These companies should follow Consob guidelines provided for in Resolution 21850 of the 19th May of 2021 on how to address the risk of greenwashing.

C. Governance mechanisms (intersection of corporate governance and shareholder governance)

I. Interplay between sustainable corporate governance and sustainable shareholder governance

The Italian traditional corporate structure of listed firms is based on the shareholder-elected board of directors (*sistema tradizionale*), where shareholders hold the power to appoint and remove the members of the board of directors (management body) and a panel of statutory auditors. Auditors provide oversight on the compliance of firms with the law, the organisational requirements included

[9] Regolamento adottato dalla Consob con delibera 20307/2018, https://www.consob.it/o/PubblicazioniPortlet/DownloadFile?filename=/documenti/bollettino2018/d20307.pdf (4 April 2024).(English version: https://www.consob.it/web/consob-and-its-activities/laws-and-regulations/documenti/english/laws/reg20307e.htm?hkeywords=&docid=9&page=0&hits=20&nav=false) (4 April 2024).

[10] PIEs are defined in Article 16 of Legislative Decree 39/2010 as national companies issuing securities admitted to trading in national and European markets; banks; insurance and reinsurance companies with registers office in Italy.

in the firm's bylaws and the proper management and accounting principles.[11] The traditional model applies as a default rule unless the articles of association explicitly reject this structure. After the 2003 company law reform, firms can now choose between adopting a one-tier or a two-tier management and control system as an alternative to the traditional structure.[12]

Under the one-tier structure (*sistema monistico*), an oversight committee is appointed within the shareholder-elected board of directors, whose members must be non-executive and independent.[13] The shareholders' meeting appoints a board of directors (*consiglio di amministrazione*). The directors will manage the company, and appoint a controlling body from among its members (*comitato per il controllo sulla gestione*).[14]

Under the two-tier structure (*sistema dualistico*), a supervisory board (*consiglio di sorveglianza*) is appointed alongside the management board by the shareholders.[15] The supervisory board is vested with the power to appoint the members of the management board (*consiglio di gestione*).[16]

Corporate governance is also influenced by the financial intermediaries' regulation and the development of the stewardship principles.[17] By enhancing the monitoring role of institutional investors and asset managers as owners and in relation to their voting rights. Article 112 of Consob Regulation on intermediaries, as amended in 2022,[18] covers the strategies for exercising the right to vote on the part of intermediaries and relates it to Article 37 of Regulation 231/2013 as regards the sustainability risks and sustainability factors to be taken into account by AIFM.

In addition, articles 136 and 137 of Consob regulation on intermediaries, as amended in 2022, contain provisions on disclosure and reporting obligations in relation to ethical or socially responsible finance. Both provisions lay down that "qualified parties" and "insurance companies" shall disclose information as to

---

[11] Art. 2364 of the Italian Civil code sets out the decision-making authority of the shareholders' meeting. Art. 2409-bis confers the shareholders' meeting with the opportunity to appoint an external auditing body. Art. 2381 provides the possibility to delegate managing powers to a management committee.

[12] Art. 2380, 2409-octies, and 2409-sexiesdecies of the Italian Civil code.

[13] Art. 2409-sexiesdecies to 2409-noviesdecies of the Italian Civil code.

[14] Art. 2409-octiesdecies of the Italian Civil code.

[15] Art. 2409-octies and -novies of the Italian Civil code.

[16] Art. 2409-terdecies of the Italian Civil code.

[17] *Balp/Strampelli*, Empowering Institutional Investors In Concentrated Ownership Contexts: The Case Of Italy, 17 South Carolina Journal of International Law And Business, Fall 2020, Issue 1, p. 20.

[18] Regulation establishing the provisions for implementation of Legislative Decree no. 58 of February 24, 1998, on intermediaries (Adopted by CONSOB with Resolution no. 20307 of February 15, 2018 and subsequently amended by Resolutions no. 21466 of 29 July 2020, no. 21755 of 10 March 2021 and no. 22430 of 28 July 2022).

"any policies and objectives that may be pursued in exercising the voting rights related to the financial instruments held in the portfolio".

II. The Italian Stewardship Principles

Stewardship principles are another example of self-regulation which also influences corporate governance. The 2016 Italian Stewardship Principles target investment funds and asset managers for increasing "discussion and cooperation between Investment Management Companies and listed companies in which they invest."[19] Likewise, the Stewardship Principles have an indirect impact on listed firms since these firms "are called upon to promote dialogue with investors, asset managers and their respective advisors."[20]

The 2016 Italian Stewardship Principles for the exercise of administrative and voting rights in listed companies included recommendations promoting the dialogue and purposeful debate between issuers and investors on long-term objectives related to ESG and non-financial performance activities.[21] Principle 2 recommends that investment companies "monitor financial data and issues of corporate governance of investee listed issuers", with the aim of better protecting the interests of "the collective investment undertakings and portfolios managed", as well as to create an active dialogue with the respective administrative and/or auditing bodies. Nonetheless, the Corporate Governance Code does not provide guidance as to how such dialogues are to be conducted in practice;[22] there is a prevailing consensus supporting such dialogues (which do take place in practice), yet they must be also mindful and fully compliant with MAR requirements .[23]

III. Sustainability Investment Funds and Sustainability Ownership Governance in Italy

Consob has recently carried out a survey addressed to asset managers and institutional investors operating in Italy on the integration of ESG criteria into their investment choices and management analysis, and on engagement (hereinafter

[19] Guiding Principles, 2016 Stewardship Principles, p. 11.

[20] Id.

[21] The 2016 version of the stewardship principles amended 2013 Stewardship Principles. The first stewardship principles adopted in Italy were integrated into the 2011 EFAMA Stewardship Code.

[22] *Strampelli*, Institutional Investor Stewardship in Italian Corporate Governance, ECGI Working Paper Series in Law 2020, https://www.ecgi.global/sites/default/files/working_papers/documents/strampellifinal.pdf (4 April 2024).

[23] *Maugeri*, Sostenibilità ed engagement degli azionisti istituzionali (fn. 3), 1369, with additional references.

2022 Consob survey).[24] The aim of this action was to increase understanding of the advantages and barriers attached to the current regulation for market participants.

The answers to the consultation show that the strategy of engagement and voting is the most frequently found method applied to the entire asset portfolio, especially by larger managers.[25] With regard to the engagement activities carried out with respect to issuers, a greater number of managers mentioned employing engagement strategies. In particular, the use of internal teams for evaluating and decision-making in invested companies is more commonly practised than the use of proxy advisors. Some use a variety of approaches: (1) a mixed approach, based on internal analysis and external consultants; or (2) they interact with issuers when issuers do not provide the market with sufficient information to allow a full assessment of the quality of governance and their exposure to social and environmental risks.[26]

It should be noted that, in relation to factual obstacles to a meaningful engagement policy, the 2022 Consob survey concludes that the implementation of homogeneous policies regarding the integration of ESG factors is hard due to the "lack of a mandatory reporting standard and certified ESG data" available for asset managers. However, in relation to the engagement tools used by investment funds, the 2022 Consob survey also shows that exercising voting rights and participation in trade/industry associations appear to be the frequently employed tools due to the "repercussions" that engagement activities may have on investment choices.[27] In relation to the issues covered by the engagement, the survey shows that the majority of the respondents replied that the three ESG issues are taken into account in carrying out their engagement activities. Of the remainder who answered, three stated that they focus their engagement activities on governance and environmental issues, two that they limit their engagement activities to governance issues only, while one specified that the choice all depends on the nature of the issuer and the fund's mandate.[28]

---

[24] *Anchino/Ciavarella/Deriu/Fiore/Nocella/Tambucci/Turi*, Gestione del risparmio e sostenibilità: l'approccio dei gestori in ItaliaSurvey sull'applicazione di criteri ESG nell'ambito delle politiche di investimento e delle attività di stewardship da parte dei gestori di attivi, Consob/Quaderno di finanza sostenibile, nº 2, giugno 2022, https://www.consob.it/documents/1912911/1972319/fs2.pdf/36ecf8b3-9309-dec7-2245-e9c92d376d25 (4 April 2024).

[25] *Anchino* et al. (fn. 24). Engagement and voting strategies are adopted by all larger managers (with assets under management above 70 billion euros), who apply them to the entire assets in seven cases and to specific mandates/products in three cases, while they are applied only by six out of ten smaller managers (with assets under management below 70 billion euros). In addition, no larger managers report applying impact investing, norm-based screening, sustainability themed, and best-in-class strategies to their entire assets, unlike the smaller managers.

[26] *Anchino* et al. (fn. 24), 26–27.

[27] *Anchino* et al. (fn. 24), 23.

[28] *Anchino* et al. (fn. 24), 23–24, https://www.consob.it/documents/1912911/1972319/fs2.pdf/36ecf8b3-9309-dec7-2245-e9c92d376d25 (4 April 2024).

IV. Prudential Management of Sustainability Risks as Part of the Investment Strategies

The matter regarding the disclosure of the main elements of the investment strategy of institutional investors and of their arrangements with asset managers is regulated at the European level in Art. 3h Directive 2017/828. Art. 3(1) of SFDR sets out an obligation to publish information on "policies on the integration of sustainability risks in [their] investment decision-making process." Likewise, the Commission Delegated Regulation 2021/1255 and Delegated Directive 2021/1270 state that "all authorised fund managers are required from 1 August 2022 to integrate sustainability risks in their portfolio and risk management processes and overall governance structure".[29] Rn. 12 of SFDR stipulates, in turn, that "financial market participants and financial advisers", as part of their duties to act in the best interest of end investors, must conduct adequate due diligence prior to making investments" . The same Rn. further sets out that:

"in order to comply with their duties under those rules, financial market participants and financial advisers should integrate in their processes, including in their due diligence processes, and should assess on a continuous basis not only all relevant financial risks but also including all relevant sustainability risks that might have a relevant material negative impact on the financial return of an investment or advice. Therefore, financial market participants and financial advisers should specify in their policies how they integrate those risks and publish those policies".

Following the examples of the EBA with its 2021 Report on ESG risk management and supervision and of the ECB, with its Guide on climate and environmental risks, the Bank of Italy issued its "aspettative di vigilanza sui rischi climatici e ambientali", which lists 12 supervisory expectations to all financial market participants supervised by the Bank of Italy (and thus not only banks, but also investment companies, asset managers, SICAV and SICAF and several other financial entities comprised in the supervisory perimeter) on the prudential implications of ESG risks[30], with the adjustments required by means of the

[29] Commission Delegated Regulation (EU) 2021/1255 of 21 April 2021 amending Delegated Regulation (EU) No 231/2013 as regards the sustainability risks and sustainability factors to be taken into account by Alternative Investment Fund Managers; and Commission Delegated Directive (EU) 2021/1270 of 21 April 2021 amending Directive 2010/43/EU as regards the sustainability risks and sustainability factors to be taken into account for Undertakings for Collective Investment in Transferable Securities (UCITS).

[30] Banca d'Italia: Aspettative di vigilanza sui rischi climatici e ambientali, 1–14, https://www.bancaditalia.it/focus/finanza-sostenibile/vigilanza-bancaria/Aspettative_di_vigilanza_BI_su_ESG.pdf (4 April 2024) See also EBA: Report on ESG risks management and supervision, EBA/REP/2021/18, 2021, https://www.eba.europa.eu/publications-and-media/press-releases/eba-publishes-its-report-management-and-supervision-esg-risks (4 April 2024). 2023). In May 2022 the EBA has launched a discussion paper on the role of environmental risks in the prudential framework for credit institutions and investment firms. The paper uses a risk-based approach and assesses how prudential requirements can reflect forward-looking environmental risks as

proportionality principle. The "aspettative" serve as guidance, are not binding *per se* but nonetheless set a relevant benchmark for supervisory purposes for the proper management of physical and transition ESG risks. The expectations include robust governance for including climate and environmental risks into the corporate culture and strategy and in its portfolios' risk appetite framework (Principle 1); the adoption of appropriate ESG impact assessment metrics, including the adoption of sustainability KPIs and their ongoing monitoring (Principle 2); appropriate internal operational rules, including risk management actions targeting climate and environmental risks, documented internal preparatory actions in support of investment decisions addressing specifically climate and environmental risks associated with each relevant investment decision, IT capabilities for gathering and aggregating, on a systemic basis, all data necessary for the assessment of the exposure to climate and environmental risks (Principle 3); the mapping of climate and environmental credit, operational/reputational, liquidity risks associated with their activities (Principle 4); the regular performance of adequate data analysis and the development of metrics associated with climate and environmental risks (Principle 5); the inclusion of climate and environmental risks in the ICAAP and ILAAP assessment of regulatory capital and liquidity or, if not applicable, on the NAV of the managed portfolios and on the operative volumes (Principle 6; see also Principle 10 and 11); the regular updating of their methodologies and tools for ESG assessment (Principle 7) and their appropriate disclosure (Principle 12), the inclusion of climate and environmental risks in the lending process, in accordance with EBA Guidelines EBA/GL/2020/06 (e.g. by inserting heatmaps into the qualitative criteria for credit scoring) (Principle 8).[31]

Of particular interest is Principle 9, whereby "financial market participants take into account any possible impact of climate and environmental risks on the pricing of their investments, also in perspective, in order to minimize the risk of losses". The Bank of Italy further exemplifies Principle 9 adding that the inclusion of climate and environmental risks into the market risk may lead to the adoption of new investment policies, e.g. by way of the compilation of a phasing out list of investments in less sustainable sectors, taking into account,

well as, in connection to its 2021 Report on Management and Supervision of ESG risks, aims to offer risk-management tools that can be utilized by institutions. The final paper is expected in June 2023 and may affect future national developments on supervisory expectations. See EBA: Discussion paper on the Role of Environmental Risks in the Prudential Framework, 2022, https://www.eba.europa.eu/publications-and-media/events/discussion-paper-role-environmental-risk-prudential-framework (4 April 2024).

[31] EBA: Final Report – Guidelines on Loan Origination and Monitoring, 2020, https://www.eba.europa.eu/sites/default/files/document_library/Publications/Guidelines/2020/Guidelines%20on%20loan%20origination%20and%20monitoring/884283/EBA%20GL%202020%2006%20Final%20Report%20on%20GL%20on%20loan%20origination%20and%20monitoring.pdf (5 April 2024).

at the same time, the risk of minor diversification implicated by necessity by any exclusionary strategy.[32] In the asset management context, the Bank of Italy expects differentiated investment strategies in light of the varying weight given to ESG objectives in each relevant line of business (strategies best in class, adoption of climate benchmarks, bespoke exclusionary lists and so on).

In turn, also the Italian Corporate Governance Code, under point 1.C.1, entrusts the board of directors , with the power to determine the risk profile in accordance with the issuer's strategic objectives. In this context, it is recommended that "any risk that may affect the sustainability of the issuer's business in a medium-long term perspective" should be taken into account by the board in a manner that is consistent with "the interest of the issuer and the generality of its shareholders".[33]

V. Possible Sources of Error

It seems fair to acknowledge that the prudential approach has been inspired, in Italy, so far, by the belief that an ESG-compliant portfolio strategy may also attain the objectives of a sound portfolio management; yet it is left up to the responsibility of the asset managers to reconcile any possible conflict between ESG-compliant and wider risk diversification strategies in the specific circumstances of each investment decision. Meanwhile, neither regulation nor supervision nor case-law have yet addressed the full potential of such potential clashes in the Italian case.

In Italy, a mechanism that has been examined for reducing conflicts of interests is to increase the sustainability-related rating by means of third-party ratings that can provide an independent assessment of the investee's performance in relation to ESG-focused engagement. The way the ESG-oriented strategy is reconciled with the client interest is, so far, by way of transparency, and involves the development and public disclosure of engagement policies alongside the SRD II provisions. Article 124-septies (1) of the Consolidated ItalianAct requires asset managers to describe how their investment strategy and its implementation meet the arrangements between the parties. The regulation emphasises that, in this regard, asset managers shall inform about how these contribute to the long-term performance of the assets under management. Yet, many issues remain still unresolved, as already noted by the cross-country study of the OECD of 2017.[34]

---

[32] *Anchino* et al. (fn. 24), 14–15: Managers were asked through which strategies sustainability information is integrated into the investment and/or management process of holdings, following the classification adopted by EUROSIF (2018)15. The report shows that "all respondents adopt a mix of different types of investment strategies", although the strategy of integrating ESG factors is the only one adopted by all respondents.

[33] Italian Corporate Governance Code, https://www.ecgi.global/node/8009 (5 April 2024).

[34] OECD: Investment governance and the integration of environmental, social and govern-

D. Sustainable Fund Management in Italian law (fund governance)

I. Investment Strategies of Investment Funds

A study published in 2019 by Consob[35] raised concerns regarding possible conflicts between ESG interests and client interests, the suitability of an active engagement strategy, and the ESG standards for passive ETF. As regards the engagement policies, the authors noted that "the diversification of the portfolio and the reduced size of the participation held in each single company could in principle make the exit option more efficient than the voice option", given that "the latter indeed requires an expensive activity of acquiring and processing information on the items on the agenda of the various shareholders' meetings". In turn, as for passive investment funds like ETF, the same study noted that opinions in Italy are unsettled.

It is also noted that "passive investors are increasingly assuming a decisive role in the success or failure of the campaigns undertaken by speculative funds, whose usual model of 'activism' involves contemplating an investment in the capital of the target of no more than 10 %. It is precisely their long-term orientation, that increases the likelihood that the management of the investee company will take into account the point of view of "passive" investors rather than the aspirations of active (or activist) fund managers oriented towards the short-term. It seems fair to acknowledge, however, that neither regulation or supervision nor case-law currently offers decisive guidance on this matter, nor on the way in which ESG values will be concretely embedded in hedge funds strategies. As for pension funds, Legislative Decree 147/2018 – on the activity and supervision of pension funds, which implements IORP II Directive or EU directive 2016/2341 – envisions a set of rules for integrating ESG risk that are of relevance for the investment policy, decision-making process and risk management of pension funds.

ance factors, 2021 https://www.oecd.org/finance/Investment-Governance-Integration-ESG-Factors.pdf (5 April 2024). The study emphasises that "pension funds, insurers and asset managers should be equipped to understand and respond to potential risks and opportunities arising from ESG-related factors in order to safeguard the assets that they invest on behalf of their beneficiaries and clients" and "regulators must be confident that institutional investors meet the required standards of prudence and care when they include ESG considerations in their portfolio decisions". In relation to the policies that influence institutional investment governance, the study shows that they are influenced by various policy measures and voluntary initiatives. These can signal that institutional investors may – or even should – interpret prudential standards as supporting ESG integration (for example, reporting standards and stewardship codes). However, some policies may serve to discourage ESG integration (for example, triennial valuations). Meanwhile, lack of harmonisation and common definitions also stands as an obstacle to more widespread application of ESG analysis. Moreover, there is no definitive terminology for describing the components of ESG and interpretations of ESG vary within the investment communities and across jurisdictions accordingly.

[35] See *Alvaro/Maugeri/Strampelli*, Investitori instituzionali, governo societario e codici di stewardship, Quaderni Giuridici Consob 19(59) 2019.

The Decree also integrates precontractual disclosures on ESG when they are important to clients.

II. Possible Barriers to Fund Managers' ESG Portfolios

The 2022 Consob survey also noted that despite the growing awareness of sustainable finance issues on the part of all economic actors recorded in recent years, in practice, significant barriers remain in place that the market hardly can overcome on its own.

On the one hand, as ESMA has also noted, large fund managers may be able to use more sophisticated tools than smaller and mid-sized fund managers when assessing the impact of sustainability risks in fund managers' portfolios and management analysis and, proposes "to ensure convergent supervisory scrutiny of the effective implementation of sustainability risks by all fund managers across the EU".[36]

On the other hand, inefficiencies related to the ecosystem of non-financial disclosure disseminated by corporations and by so-called information intermediaries, such as ESG rating and scoring agencies that assess the ESG performance of issuers and products and the exposure to risks related to ESG factors, ultimately to hinder effective and proper consideration of ESG factors by financial system participants.[37]

E. Sustainable product governance of financial market participants (product governance)

I. Monitoring of Sustainable Financial Instruments

The Consob regulatory plan for 2022 included adapting national legislation to the EU package of measures included in the Capital Markets Recovery Package or Directive (EU) 2021/338, which has changed MiFID II regarding disclosure requirements, product governance and position limits, with the aim of facilitating market recovery from the pandemic crisis and for the purpose of integrating sustainability considerations. The amendments to be made include the transposition of Delegated Directive (EU) 2021/1269, which made changes to Delegated Directive 2017/593 regarding the integration of sustainability factors into product governance obligations. Then there was Delegated Regulation (EU) 2021/1253, which amended Delegated Regulation 2017/565 with respect to the integration

[36] ESMA: Supervisory briefing: Sustainability risks and disclosures in the area of investment management, 13–14, https://www.esma.europa.eu/document/supervisory-briefing-sustainability-risks-and-disclosures-in-area-investment-management (5 April 2024).

[37] *Anchino* et al. (fn. 24), 9–10.

of sustainability factors, risks and preferences into certain organisational requirements and operating conditions for investment firms' activities.[38] As part of the Capital Markets Recovery Package, Directive (EU) 2021/338 modifies MiFID II on the subject of investor protection. Apart from that, EU Regulation 2021/1257 delegated acts for the implementation of MiFID II, UCITS and IDD. Then, Directive (EU) 2019/2034 amended MiFID II as regards the provision of investment services by non-EU companies on the exclusive initiative of clients, regarding, among other things, the product governance regulations applicable to the provision of investment services, the conflicts of interest discipline, and the distribution of Insurance-based Investment Products (IBIPs).[39]

To this effect, CONSOB launched two public consultation campaigns:

(a) on 11 February 2022, on the proposed amendments to Consob Regulation 11971 regarding issuers, which aim at incorporating the requirements on sustainability under the Taxonomy Regulation and the SFDR, including the information required under Articles 5, 6 and 7 of the Taxonomy Regulation.

(b) on 17 February 2022, on the proposed amendments to Consob Regulation no. 20307 regarding intermediaries. In the context of product oversight governance, changes include whether manufacturers should consider the customers' sustainability interests and potential conflicts of interests between insurance distributors and insurance companies that are also distributors. In relation to the information that should be collected by manufacturers or distributors, the consultation addresses consumers' sustainability preferences in the process of approval of products and defining the target market for the appropriate designing of products in order to assess the adequacy of the investment before recommending it to a customer, and in relation to the information that manufactures and distributors should share about customer sustainability preferences.

II. Implications of ESG-compliant for Product Governance

The implication of ESG factors for product governance are still somehow in flux, and at the Italian level, they essentially reflect developments at the European level, which, in turn, are to some extent still evolving.[40] Yet, also in this context, it seems fair to acknowledge that many issues remain unresolved.

---

[38] Consob: Piano delle Attività di Regolazione, 2023, https://www.consob.it/documents/1912911/1982734/Piano_att_regol_2023.pdf/6b49d56a-98b9-0ec3-d13c-72bf85843c4f (5 April 2024), 2.

[39] Consob, Piano delle Attività di Regolazione, 2022, 2023, https://www.consob.it/documents/1912911/1982734/Piano_att_regol_2023.pdf/6b49d56a-98b9-0ec3-d13c-72bf85843c4f (5 April 2024), 8.

[40] See e.g. ESMA Q&A on Regulation 2019/2088; ESMA: Consultation of 27 January 2022 on sustainability under MiFID II; but also the delegated implementing acts adopted by the Commission.

For example, it still remains to be seen in Italy how restrictions to product distributions to certain clusters of investors and the regular monitoring of the approved distribution strategies will be addressed in practice according to the new framework, once fully in place. So far, Article 62 et seq. (following article 16(3) MiFID) of the Consob regulation on intermediaries – as last amended by Resolutions no. 21466 of 29 July 2020 and no. 21755 of 10 March 2021 – provides product governance rules that require intermediary manufacturers to "adopt, exercise and monitor an approval process for each financial instrument … and for any significant change to financial instruments as well as to "establish, implement and maintain appropriate procedures and measures to ensure that the implementation of financial instruments complies with conflict-of-interest obligations … and ensure that, in the implementation of financial instruments … no harm is caused to end clients or to the integrity of the market …".

It is noticeable, in this respect, that at the entity level, several Italian financial market participants, including listed companies adhering to the Code of Corporate Governance, have established a sustainability committee (in accordance with a report published by Consob in 2022, the number of listed companies that had established such a committee increased from 73 in 2020 and 89 in 2021 to 103 out of 148 companies which published an NFS, and anecdotal evidence shows that this trend is still on the rise).[41]

In turn, Article 66 contains product governance rules which impose "business control functions" on intermediary manufacturers, who shall make available to CONSOB – "upon request" – reports containing information about "the financial instruments created by the intermediary and the distribution strategy". In light of SFDR's entry into force, CONSOB published a CONSOB's Warning on the first application of Regulation EU 2019/2088 on the 4th of March 2021. The warning drew the attention of financial market participants, inviting them to supplement their periodic reports (to be filed with CONSOB itself) with an explanation of the measures adopted and the internal control systems put in place for complying with SFDR.[42]

As regards the product-level precontractual disclosures, CONSOB has also stressed that, as of 10 March 2021, Undertakings for Collective Investment in

[41] Consob: Report on non-financial reporting of Italian listed companies with the Addendum: Implementation of Article 8 of Taxonomy Regulation, 2022, https://www.consob.it/documents/11973/2358180/rnf2022.pdf/d5a19e2b-1508-dc96-d818-cbbf9a7a8928?t=1696863994874 (5 April 2024). Consob: Report on non-financial reporting of Italian listed companies, 2021, https://www.consob.it/documents/1912911/1920109/rnf2021.pdf/510ff9c1-4709-19be-de38-f91d0e9a6586 (5 April 2024), 8. See also Consob: Report on non-financial reporting of Italian listed companies, 2020, https://www.consob.it/web/consob-and-its-activities/abs-rdnf/-/asset_publisher/FsaeQgfwuj2D/content/report-dnf-2020/718268 (5 April 2024), 8.

[42] Consob, First application of Regulation (EU) 2019/2088: Consob's Warning, https://www.consob.it/web/consob-and-its-activities/newsletter/documenti/english/en_newsletter/2021/year_27_n-09_08_march_2021.html?nav=false (5 April 2024).

Savings (UCIs), IBIPs, Italian UCITS and open non-reserved alternative investment funds (AIFs) must update their documentation offerings in compliance with SFDR. As for distributors, Article 71 requires distributors to "adopt appropriate measures and procedures to ensure that the instruments and services they intend to offer or recommend are compatible with the needs, characteristics and objectives of a given reference market and that the distribution strategy envisaged is consistent with that market".

In addition, Article 73 states that intermediaries shall make available to Consob, periodic review of the procedures and measures adopted by the intermediary for governing financial instruments, including "information about the financial instruments offered or recommended and on the services provided by the intermediary and on the distribution strategy". As already noted, additional information and reporting requirements are set out in Articles 136 and 137 of Consob Regulation on intermediaries as regards products and services qualified as "ethical" or "socially responsible".[43]

It is also worth noting that Consob, in its Strategic Plan for 2022–2024, builds upon objectives outlined in its previous Strategic Plan for 2019-2021, aiming to pursuit of the best procedures for the transition to the sustainable finance paradigm.[44] Emphasising the increasing importance for financial supervisors to adopt proactive and evidence-based approach, Consob underscores several key initiatives, such as strengthening the supervision of non-financial reporting, analysing the sustainability reporting initiatives of companies' supervisory bodies, remuneration and engagement policies, and UCITS and AIF fund advertisements, supervising through joint ESMA action the compliance of managers with ESG regulations, both in investment decision-making and disclosure at entity and product level, as well as the integration of ESG issues in the product governance and suitability assessment procedures, and adopting a proactive dialogue with stakeholders and the representatives of the financial community.

This approach is in line with ESMA Guidelines on product governance requirements under MiFID II.[45] Yet, despite the above, and although it is claimed by some authors that Italy was a pioneer in the product governance of Sustainable and Responsible Investment (SRI) and thus in the integration of ESG con-

---

[43] See section C.I.

[44] CONSOB Piano Strategico 2022-2024 (aggiornamento dicembre 2023), https://www.consob.it/documents/1912911/1949521/ps_2224_dic_2023.pdf/f2946233-5e96-c503-63cf-e57db1122b3c, 19-20. See also Consob, Piano Strategico 2019–2021, https://www.consob.it/documents/1912911/1923551/ps1921.pdf/6c550c62-ecb2-0ffa-8a6e-87c6f79fab9b (5 April 2024).

[45] ESMA: Final Report of Guidelines on MiFID II product governance requirements, 2023, https://www.esma.europa.eu/sites/default/files/2023-03/ESMA35-43-3448_Final_report_on_MiFID_II_guidelines_on_product_governance.pdf (5 April 2024), 19(e).

cerns into investment policies[46], it remains to be seen in Italy how the challenges concerning ESG product distribution will actually be addressed in practice on the ground.

III. Greenwashing and Product Governance Implications

As for greenwashing, and its product governance implications and the potential liability attached to greenwashing practices, it seems possible so far to acknowledge from an Italian perspective that, indeed, in Italy, there has been at least one case of private litigation for "greenwashing" decided by the Tribunal of Gorizia, with interim measures of cease and desist pronounced on 26 November 2021 (such interim measures were revoked, though, on appeal, in March 2022).

Moreover, from a supervisory perspective, for the purpose of addressing the risk of greenwashing, Consob published the non-financial parameters that will be taken into account for identifying the entities whose non-financial statements (NFs) will be checked by the financial supervisor to prevent greenwashing. That is, pursuant to Article 6, paragraph 1 of Consob Regulation no. 20267 of 28 January 2018, implementing Legislative Decree no. 254 of 30 December 2016, Consob checks non-financial statements on a sample basis.[47] Consob Resolution 21850 on 19th of May 2021, furthermore, clarified in its point (1)(d) that, in relation to possible greenwashing, the selection of the entities to be checked by the supervisor "is also made taking into account the importance assumed by ESG factors when raising capital through the issuance of financial instruments intended to finance projects with environmental sustainability characteristics" and must likewise take into account the need for a "rotation of the selected companies".[48] The Italian legislation confers the powers to impose administrative sanctions

[46] UNEP, Financing the Future. Report on the Italian National Dialogue on Sustainable Finance, 2016 (25.06.2022), 27. The report also stated that "all financial products labelled as 'sustainable' or 'green' or 'ethical' have to provide further information to describe objectives, processes and results. Labelling schemes could enable companies to implement this requirement in ways that ease consumer decision-making."

[47] Consob, Report on non-financial reporting of Italian listed companies, 2021: "In order to stem possible greenwashing phenomena in the face of the growing attention of retail investors to sustainability profiles in the choice of their investments, in March 2020 CONSOB published a warning note no. 1/20 on the 'Provision of investment services and ESG issues' (pending full implementation of the Disclosure Regulation) relating to disclosure on sustainability in the financial services sector. With the aforementioned reminder, the Institute has reconstructed the indications already contained in the regulations in force that must be followed by intermediaries, including the additional information and reporting obligations provided for by articles 136 and 137 of the CONSOB Regulation on Intermediaries, relating to products and services qualified as 'ethical' or 'socially responsible'."

[48] Consob, Delibera n. 21850, Determinazione per le dichiarazioni non finanziarie pubblicate nell'anno 2020 dei parametri previsti dall'art. 6 del regolamento adottato con delibera n. 20267 del 18 gennaio 2018, https://www.consob.it/documents/1912911/1921350/d21850.pdf/05b3824e-2079-4ac1-2ab0-df4264d72b12 (5 April 2024).

on the supervisory authority as a public enforcement mechanism. Only time, however, will tell what use will be made of such powers.

F. Sustainable Financial Service in the Customer Business

From 1 January 2023, the rules of relevant information that investment funds will provide to customers (Key Information Document) were amended in the Issuer's Regulation (resolution no. 22551 of 21 December 2022). The PRIIPs Regulation (cf. Art. 32(1)) provided for an exemption from its obligations for managers as well as persons advising or selling units of UCITS. On the basis of PRIIPs' transitional regime, up until 31 December 2022, the drafting of the document containing the key information on the essential characteristics of the UCITS as well as the prospectus offered to investors (Key Investor Information Document or KIID),[49] provided for in Article 78 of Directive 2009/65/EC (UCITS Directive) and governed by Commission Regulation (EU) No 583/2010 of 1 July 2010, are required for the offer of UCITS.

ESAs' report of 28 of April 2022 contained a series of recommendations in order to review PRIIPs Regulation for including appropriate consumer testing and for including sustainable development objectives in the KID template. In particular, the report provides an example on how a new section covering any sustainable development investment objective could be integrated into the current KID template.

In Italy, as of 1 January 2023, UCITS managers will be required to prepare a KID for offers to retail investors, in line with the scope of the PRIIPs Regulation. The amendments mainly concerned the rules governing the marketing of units or shares of both Italian and EU UCITS. This change aims to avoid the duplication of information burden on managers and the overlapping of information for the end investor, ensuring that from 1 January 2023, retail investors in PRIIPs will only receive the KID and not also the KIID.[50]

In particular, the new Article 82a of the UCITS Directive provides that the KID, drafted in accordance with the relevant European framework, must be deemed to comply with the requirements applicable to the KIID under the Directive (EU) 2021/2261 (UCITS Directive) and as a result, Member States are required to ensure that competent authorities do not require managers to also draft the KIID. As a result, since the PRIIPs regulation requires the drafting of the KID for offers to retail investors, UCITS originators will no longer be required to draft the KIID in this circumstance.

---

[49] Article 34(1)(b) of the Issuers' Regulation.

[50] The KIID and the KID both have a summary disclosure of the key characteristics of the financial product as their target.

An exception included in the new regime involves the offers of UCITS funds addressed to qualified investors. In this situation, Article 82 of UCITS Directive managers can choose between the KID or the KIID.

In addition, the amendments to Annex 1 of the Issuers' Regulation ("Offer to the public for the subscription and/or sale of financial products and admission to trading on a regulated market of securities") concern "Procedures for the drafting of the prospectus for the offer and/or for the admission to trading of UCITS and related schedules". They aim to ensure that the information contained in Part II of the prospectus is consistent with the content of the KIID, in line with the provisions concerning pre-contractual information (Art. 79(1) of the UCITS Directive), as well as in line with the content of the KID (Article 6(1) of the PRIIPs Regulation).

Country Report Sweden

Erik Lidman

A. Introduction and disposition

The Swedish equity market structure is to a comparatively high extent based on listed companies having large shareholders who take an active and central role in the management of their companies and who collaborate with the large financial institutions, and to a large extent likewise that these shareholders take on broader societal responsibility for the business in their companies.[1] This is something that is also heavily reflected in the Swedish discussion on corporate sustainability. The Swedish legislative focus in the area centres around soft law and voluntary measures by owners and companies, and this regulation is presented in this report. In so far as can be judged by the performance of the Swedish market and business in terms of performance, growth and available sustainability benchmarks, this liberal approach seems to be working exceedingly well. It is nevertheless currently under heavy pressure due to the more dirigiste approach that is being taken in the EU's harmonisation efforts in the area. Hence, in addition to describing the national ESG-rules and regulations, a secondary focus in the report is on the overall approach to sustainability in corporate law and financial market regulation in Sweden, also featuring a critical perspective on current developments within the EU.

The disposition of the chapter is the following. In section B., a brief presentation is made of the Swedish market structure. In section C., I then continue on to describing why the national structure matters in the context of sustainable development and ESG. In section D.-F., I then address the general topics of this volume (sustainable ownership or shareholder governance in section D., sustainable funding in section E., and sustainable trading section F.).[2] In section G., I then offer a few critical reflections on the ongoing harmonisation of equity markets in the EU in the name of sustainability and ESG from a Swedish perspective.

[1] E.g. Lekvall (ed.), *The Nordic Corporate Governance Model*, SNS Publishing 2014; Thomsen, "The Nordic Corporate Governance Model", *Management and Organization Review* 2016, 189–204; Thomsen, "Nordic Corporate Governance Revisited", Nordic Journal of Business 2016, 4–12.

[2] Since the focus is on Swedish regulation, EU legislation with direct effect is not included in the report.

B. The Swedish market structure

What rights investors have (in general, but here specifically with regards to ESG), and what shareholders may or may not do within a national legal framework, is a somewhat complicated question in several legal systems. In some jurisdictions, such as Germany, there are fairly clear limits on how investors may influence and engage with a company, and there is a clear division of responsibilities and competences between management and investors.[3] In other systems, such as the US, no such division is as clearly made. However, the model has emerged in environments where the ownership of listed companies has been so widespread that investors have generally engaged little with their portfolio firms, which is why the boards typically have a much larger mandate in the company's overall governance in the first place. In some cases, the board nevertheless has an obligation to put certain issues up for decision-making at the general meeting, yet it is hardly uncommon for the general meetings decision to be advisory rather than binding.[4]

The Swedish (and Nordic) case differs significantly from what has been described above.[5] In the Swedish model, which has emerged in a market where ownership for the last one hundred years has typically been concentrated and most listed companies have had one or more major shareholders, there is no division in the mandate between the board and the shareholders of relevance here. Instead, the starting point in Sweden is that it is the shareholders who have the ultimate control over the company, and the board is obliged to adhere to any and all general meeting's decisions accordingly.[6] It is also the shareholders who independently nominate and elect the board and auditor (in companies on a regulated market through the nomination committees). The shareholders of a Swedish limited liability company (*aktiebolag)* are thus authorised to make decisions in almost all matters concerning the company through the general meeting.[7] The shareholders also have a number of exclusive competencies. In addition to the right to appoint the board (and firing board members), there is the right to set its compensation and elect auditors, including changes to the articles of association[8] and issues of liquidation, mergers and increases and de-

---

[3] See for instance Kraakman et al., *The Anatomy of Corporate Law: A comparative and functional Approach*, Oxford University Press 2017, 50.

[4] See Kraakman et al., *The Anatomy of Corporate Law: A comparative and functional Approach*, Oxford University Press 2017, 50–51.

[5] See Lekvall (ed.), *The Nordic Corporate Governance Model*, SNS Publishing 2014.

[6] See Andersson, Johansson, and Skog, *Aktiebolagslagen: en kommentar*, Norstedts Publishing 2018, Section 7:1.

[7] See ch. 7 sec. 1 in the Swedish Companies Act (2005:551).

[8] Which indirectly limits many other things that the board cannot do without the general meeting first changing the articles of association, including changes to the business model outside the scope decided by the shareholders and, as will be relevant in this chapter, diverging from the purpose of the corporation.

creases in the share capital.[9] The importance of active investors and the influence given to the general meeting are fundamental factors in corporate governance as well as in how listed companies are regulated – including in the ESG-field.

C. The Swedish market in an ESG-perspective

At the time of writing, Sweden has around 1100 listed companies on its three equity markets, with a combined market value of over 1.5 trillion dollars.[10] The IPO market is also going strong – 2021 was an IPO record year, with over 180 IPOs with a combined value of over 20 billion dollars.[11] This makes Sweden stick out as most Western European public markets have seen a decline in the number and value of listed companies, and the Swedish market was both the best-performing equity market of 2021 as well as the largest measured by number of listed companies, according to Bloomberg.[12] Sweden also had the 3rd largest market capitalisation in the EU, as well as the highest net-listings in the period 2010–2021.[13] In addition, Sweden made second place in the IMD World Competitiveness Ranking 2021,[14] number two in the WIPO Global Innovation Index 2021,[15] and number two in the Sustainable Development Report 2021.[16] It can also be noted that Sweden drew more ESG venture capital than any other European country, in absolute numbers, by a wide margin.[17] While not a perfect system, agency costs also seem to be low in international comparisons,[18] owners are highly engaged,[19] and minority shareholder protection is strong.[20]

---

[9] See for a comprehensive discussion Åhman, *Behörighet och befogenhet i aktiebolagsrätten*, Iustus 1997, 515 ff.

[10] According to data from Modular Finance, supplied by the Swedish Securities Council (25 October 2023).

[11] See www.di.se/nyheter/noteringsvag-pa-vag-mot-borsen-ser-ut-att-sla-alla-rekord/ (25 October 2023).

[12] bloomberg.com/news/articles/2021-09-11/swedish-ipo-frenzy-propels-stock-market-into-europe-s-big-league (25 October 2023).

[13] Data compiled from the OECD Capital Market Series dataset in May 2022.

[14] https://www.imd.org/centers/world-competitiveness-center/rankings/world-competitiveness/ (25 October 2023).

[15] https://www.wipo.int/global_innovation_index/en/2021/ (25 October 2023).

[16] https://www.sdgindex.org/reports/sustainable-development-report-2021/ (25 October 2023).

[17] https://www.bloomberg.com/news/articles/2021-12-16/venture-capital-record-makes-sweden-new-impact-hub-in-europe (25 October 2023).

[18] Cf. Nenova, "The value of corporate voting rights and control: A cross-country analysis", Journal of Financial Economics 2003, 325–351.

[19] Gilson, "The Nordic Model in an International Perspective: The Role of Ownership", in Lekvall (ed.), *The Nordic Corporate Governance Model*, SNS Publishing 2014.

[20] Gilson, "The Nordic Model in an International Perspective: The Role of Ownership", in Lekvall (ed.), *The Nordic Corporate Governance Model*, SNS Publishing 2014; Gilson, "Con-

Swedish companies also perform at a best-in-class level in terms of more specific sustainability measures. In the Commission's 2020 Sustainable Corporate Governance Initiative, shareholder dividends were used as a metric for short-termism and unsustainable corporate behaviour.[21] As a response to this, an empirical Swedish study was carried out based on data on Swedish listed companies between the years 2000 and 2019 (786 unique firms and 7,389 firm-years).[22] Based on the analysis, the authors concluded that there is no material evidence of short-termism among listed firms in Sweden, that 44 % of the Swedish firms do not pay out any dividend, and out of the remaining dividend-paying firms, a "large portion of dividends come from a few large firms which are highly profitable and have strong sustainability performance". Almost all of the top dividend payers had a typical Swedish ownership structure, with strong shareholders taking active roles in management.

The Swedish study then continued on to examining the sustainability performance of the top 20 dividend-payers using Financial and Sustainability Reports, ASSET4 performance ratings, and CSRHUB performance ratings (all important and generally accepted sustainability measurements). The overall assessment was that the top dividend-payers in Sweden performed very well in both sustainability reporting and sustainability performance. By way of reference, according to KPMB, about 77 percent of the 100 largest companies in each EU Member State report on sustainability performance, and 67 percent of the reporting companies disclose their information following the GRI standards.[23] For Sweden, the study found that 90 percent of the top 20 dividend-payers applied the GRI standards in 2019. Out of these firms, 80 percent have been seeking voluntarily limited external assurance on specified sustainability information in their sustainability reports (51 % for the 100 companies studied by KPMG). Nine of the 16 non-financial firms were also listed in the top sustainability indices (Dow Jones Sustainability Index and the FTSE4Good), and the average ASSET4 environmental Pilar score was 72.4 (compared to 64.89 in large European listed companies in general).[24]

---

trolling Shareholders and Corporate Governance: Complicating the Comparative Taxonomy", Harvard Law Review 2006, 1641–1679; Nenova, "The value of corporate voting rights and control: A cross-country analysis", Journal of Financial Economics 2003, 325–351.

[21] See European Commission, Directorate-General for Justice and Consumers, Study *on directors' duties and sustainable corporate governance: final report*, Publications Office, 2020, https://data.europa.eu/doi/10.2838/472901 (25 October 2023).

[22] Carlsson-Wall, Eugster, Hjelström, and Nilsson, *Corporate Governance and short-termism: an in-depth Analysis of Swedish data*, https://www.hhs.se/en/about-us/news/department-of-accounting/2021/corporate-governance-and-short-termism-an-in-depth-analysis-of-swedish-data/ (25 October 2023).

[23] KPMG, *Time has come – The KPMG Survey of Sustainability Reporting 2020*.

[24] Iamandi, Constantin, Munteanu, and Cernat-Gruici, "Mapping the ESG Behavior of European Companies. A Holistic Kohonen Approach" Sustainability 2019, 1–41 (studying 1165 large European listed companies).

More generally, the investment company RobecoSAM – which specialises in sustainability investments – ranks Sweden second out of 150 studied countries in their sustainability ranking,[25] and Sweden placed eight out of 180 countries in the 2020 Environmental Performance Index, which provides a summary of the state of sustainability using 32 performance indicators.[26] Sweden was ranked fifth of 156 assessed countries on the World Economic Forum's Global Gender Gap Report (surpassed by, among others, Iceland, Finland and Norway, who share the Nordic corporate governance model),[27] and Sweden ranks as the fourth least corrupt country in the World Bank corruption studies.[28] Sweden also ranked second in the Global Innovation Index in 2020,[29] and topped the Global Sustainable Competitiveness Index the same year.[30]

With regards to sustainability standards and ESG, it is important for this report to note that a central Swedish perspective (especially from a regulatory stand-point) is that it is the shareholders and equity financing that *drives* the green transition, with a demand for company management to consider climate risks, not the least since shareholders as investors are interested in companies' long-term results as being decisive for the present-day value of their shares and the future return on their investment. A well-functioning equity market is thus an important ESG-mechanism. A study by the European Central Bank, analysing data from 1990 to 2013 from 50 countries, illustrates this well.[31] It finds that for a given level of economic development, financial development and environmental regulation, CO_2 emissions per capita are lower in economies that rely more on market-based equity funding. The study points to two key explanations for the relationship between the use of equity financing and lower carbon emissions: "First, stock markets reallocate investment towards less polluting sectors" more effectively than other types of financial markets. Second, equity markets "also push remaining carbon intensive sectors to develop and implement greener technologies." The authors conclude that "carbon-intensive industries produce more green patents as national stock markets deepen." *Mats Isaksson*, former head of the Corporate Governance and Corporate Finance Division at the OECD thus concludes that, in general,

[25] https://www.robeco.com/en/key-strengths/sustainable-investing/country-ranking/ (25 October 2023).

[26] https://epi.yale.edu/ (25 October 2023).

[27] https://www.weforum.org/reports/global-gender-gap-report-2021(25 October 2023).

[28] https://www.transparency.org/en/cpi/2020/index/swe (25 October 2023).

[29] https://www.globalinnovationindex.org/Home (25 October 2023).

[30] https://solability.com/the-global-sustainable-competitiveness-index/the-index (25 October 2023).

[31] De Haas and Popov, *Finance and carbon emissions*, European Central Bank Working Paper No. 2318/2019.

"broad and deep public equity markets that present investors with the ability to diversify the firm-specific risks associated with technological innovation lower the overall societal cost of capital for research and development that result in new patents, products and processes that have a smaller carbon footprint."[32]

In the following sections, I focus on the topics that are the overall general focus of this volume (sustainable ownership, sustainable funding and sustainable trading). As can be seen, the regulation is relatively general and oriented towards disclosure, and much of it is simply not regulated in Sweden at a granular level. However, this is not due to a lack of political or legislative ambition with regards to sustainable development, nor has it resulted in poor sustainability performance. On the contrary, results point toward the opposite. However, there is a strong belief in the effectiveness of the public equity market and the general corporate governance system to contributing to the necessary problem solving, and even though the country has been ruled by socialists for most of modern history, dirigiste interventions in the markets in this sense have not been very common.

D. Shareholder governance

I. On shareholder engagement from a policy perspective in Sweden

A focus within the EU with regards to the harmonisation of corporate law and the internal market has, especially since the financial crisis of 2008, been to foster shareholder engagement, which has also been viewed as an important factor in long-term and sustainable equity markets.[33] The point of view of the Swedish regulator is generally that the most important way of ensuring shareholder engagement is to be mindful of market incentives for engagement and to remove practical and regulatory obstacles in place from attending general meetings, receiving information from the company, and from voting. Beyond this, it is also recognised *that not all investors have the means nor the incentives to engage and vote, and there is very little that can meaningfully be done to address this.* The problem here is of course the free-rider issue: for a shareholder with a small stake in a company (be it a private person or a highly diversified institution), it will simply not be rational to engage with the firm. For them, in the vocabulary of Hirschman, the exit would be more attractive than raising one's voice as a reaction to firms underperforming in the perspective of the investor (with regards

[32] https://www.oecd-ilibrary.org/sites/306482b9-en/index.html?itemId=/content/component/306482b9-en (25 October 2023).

[33] See most importantly the revised shareholder rights directive (2017/828), and, for instance, SWD(2014)127, COM(2012)740 (Commission Action Plan on European company law and corporate governance), COM(2011)164 (The EU Corporate Governance Framework Greenbook).

to economic development or other metrics).[34] That, in and of itself, is not viewed as a problem, since generally, there will be other, larger shareholders engaging with the firm.

As far as factors which have largely been considered by the legislator,[35] there are a number of typical economic conditions that (generally) have to be fulfilled for a shareholder to get involved and engage. These do not connect to Sweden in particular, but pertain rather to general economic and financial theory. These conditions have nevertheless indeed been considered by the Swedish legislator as such:[36]

1. The first condition for shareholder engagement can, in principle, be formulated as follows: in order for a shareholder to engage, a condition is that that the shareholding is so large that potential voting will matter and that the increase in value that the shareholder's engagement may result in compensates for the costs of the commitment. The necessary size of a shareholding varies in practical experience, but a holding in the range of 5–30 percent of the outstanding shares in the company will generally suffice, depending on the other ownership structure in the company.[37]

2. The second condition for shareholder engagement is connected to the size of a holding in relation to the shareholder's total investment portfolio. This connection was highlighted early on by Lowenstein who explained it with reference to CALPERS: "CALPERS, for example, owns about $250 million of GM stock, a tidy sum and one worth protecting" but "even large improvements at any one company will have only trivial consequences in a portfolio of over 1,000 companies. It's like hitting only singles, with no one on base ... ever".[38] Coffee also arrived at a similar conclusion early on: "many institutions – pension funds in particular – are so widely diversified, holding literally a thousand or more stocks, that it is simply beyond their realistic monitoring capacity to make any meaningful evaluation of the competence of the management at individual firms

---

[34] Hirschman, *Exit, Voice and Loyalty*, Harvard University Press 1970.

[35] This is reflected in the preparatory works to the Swedish Companies Act from the late 1980s and onwards, and was researched rather extensively before that as well, see Hedlund, Hägg, Hörnell, and Rydén, *Institutioner som aktieägare*, SNS Publishing 1985 (Swedish only).

[36] See most importantly the Commission on Corporate Ownership, SOU 1988:38.

[37] Originally addressed by Berle and Means, see also, for instance, Grossman and Hart, "Takeover bids, the free-rider problem, and the theory of the corporation", Bell Journal of Economics 1980, 42; Shleifer and Vishny, "Large Shareholders and Corporate Control", Journal of Political Economy 1986, 461; Shleifer and Vishny, "A survey of corporate governance", Journal of Finance 1997, 737; Noe, "Investor activism and financial market structure", Review of Finance Studies 2002, 289; Admati and Pfleiderer, "The 'Wall Street Walk' and Shareholder Activism: Exit as a Form of Voice", Review of Financial Studies 2009, 2445; Easterbrook, "The race for the Bottom in Corporate Governance", Virginia Law Review 2009, 685.

[38] Lowenstein, "The effect of index investment policies on corporate governance", *The University of Toledo Annual Colloquium on Corporate Law and Social Policy* 1991, 16.

or of the likely impact of proposals raised by other shareholders of those firms."[39] The economic condition is quite well understood.[40]

3. The third condition for shareholder engagement is that the shareholder has the necessary corporate governance and branch specific competence required to engage with a particular company, and that it has an organisation that allows for engagement. This might sound trivial, but is important to note seeing as many institutional shareholders are not built for engagement. Noe, for instance, notes that "Shareholders typically lack intimate knowledge of the firm's management or line(s) of business. Those investors who possess the general skills required for effective corporate monitoring must still expend resources gathering the firm-specific information required to monitor management. The costs of these investments in corporate governance are borne by the investor undertaking the monitoring. However, the benefits of increased vigilance accrue to all shareholders."[41] Isaksson and Çelik similarly note that "it is worth noting that 76 % of the asset owners and 56 % of the asset managers stated that they had five or less staff members devoted to ownership engagement with investee companies (IRRC and ISS, 2011). This number should be compared to the hundreds or perhaps thousands of companies that these institutions may hold in their portfolios and are expected to monitor."[42]

What is asked of Swedish shareholders in general is that they "vote in an initiated way and monitor the board in the companies in which they invest", with a specific focus on remunerations, related party transactions and other activities that are connected to tunnelling-risks, and "engage in dialogue with the board".[43] Much the same seems to be true for what the European legislator wants from European shareholders. With this in mind, large funds (European as well as American giants such as BlackRock, Vanguard and State Street) cannot – *on the aggregate* – be expected to engage meaningfully and in a qualitative way with specific firms.[44]

---

[39] Coffee, "Liquidity Versus Control: The Institutional Investor as Corporate Monitor", Columbia Law Review 1993, 1337–1338.

[40] See for instance Lowenstein, "The effect of index investment policies on corporate governance", *The University of Toledo Annual Colloquium on Corporate Law and Social Policy* 1991, p. 16; Coffee, "Liquidity Versus Control: The Institutional Investor as Corporate Monitoe", Columbia Law Review 1993, 1337–1338; Ryan and Schneider, "Institutional Investor Power and Heterogeneity, Implications for Agency and Stakeholder Theories", *Business & Society* 2002, 398.

[41] See Noe, "Investor activism and financial market structure", Review of Finance Studies 2002, 289.

[42] See Isaksson and Çelik, *Institutional Investors as Owners: Who Are They and What Do They Do?* OECD Corporate Governance Working Papers, no. 11, OECD Publishing 2013, 26.

[43] See Lidman, *Kontrollägande och uppköpsreglering: Likabehandling vid offentliga uppköpserbjudanden och effekterna i bolagsstyrningen*, Corporate Governance Forum 2020.

[44] See Krouse, Benoit, and Ginty, "Meet the New Corporate Power Brokers: Passive Investors", Wall Street Journal, 24.10.2016.

4. The fourth condition for shareholder engagement is to a large extent a consequence of the conditions already discussed: fulfilling these conditions and engaging is a costly activity, and the opportunity cost in comparison to completely passive ownership or an exit-based investment strategy can be especially high in a bull market. This problem was addressed directly by Hirschman ("the cost of devoting even a modicum of [the shareholders] time to correcting the faults of any one of the entities he is involved with is likely to exceed his estimate of the expected benefits for a large number of them"[45]), and the condition that there needs to be an economic incentive in place for shareholder engagement is of course uncontroversial today, as well as the fact that this, however, often poses a problem for shareholder engagement.[46]

5. The final condition for shareholder engagement that is often discussed in Sweden is the need for an effective market for corporate control where control blocks of shares can be bought and sold between parties in a transparent manner, where price formation is governed by market participants' supply and demand and is not affected by high transaction costs or other external factors, and where the target company's management cannot seriously prevent or complicate control transactions. Such a market is generally viewed as a precondition for condition 1 above to be fulfilled (stable block holdings), and this has also been substantially addressed in the law and economics research.[47]

So, when it comes to shareholder governance, it is recognised that not all shareholders are the same, and that if it is a political goal to ensure that shareholders do engage – particularly in the long-term and not just in high-profile cases –

[45] Se Hirschman, *Exit, Voice and Loyalty*, Harvard University Press 1970, 40.

[46] See for instance Grossman and Hart, "Takeover bids, the free-rider problem, and the theory of the corporation", Bell Journal of Economics 1980, 42; Shleifer and Vishny, "Large Shareholders and Corporate Control", Journal of Political Economy 1986, 461; Coffee, "Liquidity Versus Control: The Institutional Investor as Corporate Monitor", Columbia Law Review 1993, 1278; Shleifer and Vishny, "A survey of corporate governance", Journal of Finance 1997, 737; Gilson and Gordon, "Controlling Controlling Shareholders", University of Pennsylvania Law Review 2003, 785; Gilson, "Controlling shareholders and Corporate Governance: Complicating the Comparative Taxonomy", Harvard Law Review 2006, particularly p. 1652; Gilson and Schwartz, "Corporate Control and Credible Commitment", International Review of Law and Economics 2015, 119.

[47] See Pacces, *Featuring Control Power, Corporate Law and Economics Revisited*, RILE 2007; Bhide , "The hidden costs of stock market liquidity", Journal of Financial Economics 1993, 31; Aghion, Bolton, and Tirole, "Exit options in Corporate Finance: Liquidity versus Incentives", Review of Finance 2004, 237; Edmans, "Blockholders and Corporate Governance", *Annual Review of Financial Economics* 2014, 23; Bebchuk, Cohen, and Ferrell, "What Matters in Corporate Governance?" Review of Financial Studies 2009, 783; Javaras, "Equal opportunity in the sale of controlling shares: a reply to professor Andrews", *Chicago Law Review* 1964, 420; Winter, "State Law, Shareholder Protection, and the Theory of the Corporation", *Journal of Legal Studies* 1977, 251; Hansen, "The Mandatory Bid Rule: The Rise to Prominence of a Misconception", Scandinavian Studies in Law 2003, 173.

legislation needs to pave the way for these conditions to be fulfilled by as many shareholders as possible. It is also generally understood that when there are one or a couple of large and engaged shareholders in a company which bears a large part of the engagement cost, this can also become a catalyst for other investors with smaller shareholdings (such as pension funds) to coordinate and engage with the company (much the same pattern that can be observed around activist investors in other jurisdictions).[48] As I will describe below, this mindset is generally reflected in the regulatory approach to "sustainable ownership" initiatives, not the least those which stem from the EU initiatives in the area.

II. General aspect on the use of voting rights and engagement by institutional investors

According to Art. 3g in the updated shareholders rights directive 2017/828 (the SRD2), institutional investors are to have an engagement policy and the content of the policy is fairly detail-regulated. Art. 3g has been implemented in Swedish law in a number of acts regulating investment companies and institutional investors, and the changes reflect what is stated in the SRD2 Article.[49] The implementation ultimately, however, had little meaningful impact on shareholder engagement. The type of documentation required by Art. 3g was common long before the implementation in the SRD2, though they were then known as "ownership policies" (sw. 'ägarpolicy').[50] In addition, as touched upon already, many Swedish institutional investors (not only large owners) are fairly actively engaging with their portfolio companies. There is no definite answer to why this is the case, but it is at least a common conception that the large shareholders that do engage become catalysts for other, smaller shareholders to engage as well. In practice, the SRD2 thus accomplished little when it came to shareholder engagement, other than that we now see an emerging standardisation on how engagement policies look. This standardisation can be perceived as a good thing, but can equally easily be framed as a negative development since what we want from shareholders are not standardised behaviours, but adaptive and tailored engagement with, ideally, as many companies in the portfolio as possible. Though the effects of the change have not been studied, there does not seem to be any signs that this regulation has changed shareholder behaviour other than changes in the policy documents.

[48] Though the connection and antecedents are poorly understood, it is at least clear that Swedish institutional investors engage more than what can reasonably be expected of them. See Billing and Silberg, "Active and Responsible: A Cost-Efficient Model for Integrating Sustainability", in Paul G. Fisher (ed.), *Making the Financial System Sustainable*, Cambridge University Press 2020; and Skog, "A Remarkable Decade: The Awakening of Swedish Institutional Investors", Die Aktiengesellschaft 2005, 2–8.

[49] See for instance law 2004:46, 2010:2043, and 2013:561.

[50] See preparatory work DS 2018:15 p. 228–229.

Other than the rules following from the SRD2 and some detailed rules for specific types of funds, there are no rules on shareholder voting relevant in this context (either mandatory or of comply-or-explain nature). The Swedish Corporate Governance Code does not regulate shareholders, but companies. However, it does contain rules for facilitating shareholder engagement from the companies' side (such as on the nomination committee), and also a general description on the role of owners in corporate governance, which can be said to summarise the regulators' expectation of owners as well as best practice (p. 8).[51]

There is no Swedish stewardship code, nor is there an ongoing discussion for the need for one.

III. Shareholder cooperation

One issue in focus in this volume is shareholder cooperation, such as in nomination committees, and whether it is in conflict with the rules on 'acting in concert' and the mandatory bid rule in Art. 5 in the Takeover Bids Directive (2004/25/EC). A fear that has surfaced now and then, especially among large institutions, is that shareholder cooperative engagement on long-term issues such as board monitoring and elections, remunerations and material issues addressed at the general meeting, might be construed as 'acting in concert' in the meaning of Art. 2 of the Takeover Directive, and that this would thus trigger the mandatory bid rule.

The conflict between the purposes of the Takeover Directive and the wish for shareholders to engage in a sustainable way in the long-term is apparent, since the duration of a cooperation is one factor that is relevant when evaluating whether a cooperation falls within the 'acting in concert' definition under Swedish law.[52] While there can be no question that this is at least a *potential* problem, to date, there has not been one instance where institutional investors cooperating has actually been deemed to trigger the mandatory bid rule, but it is hard to say if this is due to the rule itself or investors adapting their cooperation to avoid the issue altogether. There have been discussions on changing the rule to ensure that long-term cooperation is not limited by the related part definition, but this has been deemed to be impossible given the design of the Takeover Bids Directive. Here, it would likely be welcome if ESMA and the Takeover Bids Network issued clarifications in its whitelist.[53]

---

[51] https://www.corporategovernanceboard.se/Userfiles/Koden/Dokument/Eng/SvenskKod Bolagsstyrn_justerad_ENG_211220.pdf (25 October 2023).

[52] See law 2006:541 on takeover bids, ch. 3 sec. 5 p. 4.

[53] See ESMAs Public statement: *Information on shareholder cooperation and acting in concert under the Takeover Bids Directive.*

IV. The experience of engaging shareholders in foreign jurisdictions, particularly outside of the EU

One important focus on the EU's sustainability as well as corporate governance agenda is to ensure that institutional investors domiciled outside the EU are covered by the same rules as those domiciled in the Member States (not least US and now UK companies). The motivation to create a level playing field with regards to shareholder engagement seem to be sound and serves as an important measure for ensuring the competitiveness of European companies and the European market. From a Member State perspective, one word of caution should be raised. As outlined in section II.–III., corporate governance models as well as the framework's impact on sustainable development are particularly tied to national patterns of ownership, institutions, and political economy.[54] With regards to the engagement by large foreign shareholders, the Swedish experience is that this is fairly rare but generally good when it does occur, however, there are also some lingering issues that cannot be taken lightly. For instance, there are some national governance structures that are integral in the Swedish corporate governance system and which are poorly understood by foreign investors and which involve standard practices that may cause harm. One is, for example, the unwillingness to engage in nomination committees, which is a key mechanism for engagement with non-controlling shareholders.[55] Another is how foreign investors will at times (according to their international policies or due to misunderstandings) vote against discharge from liability, which can send negative signals regarding the management of a company and also makes it harder to find long-term directors.[56]

V. Creditors roles in corporate governance and sustainability

Regarding creditors' roles in corporate governance and sustainability, first, it should be noted that equity funding is exceedingly important for Swedish busi-

[54] For more on this, see OECD, *flexibility and proportionality in corporate governance*, OECD Publishing 2018.

[55] See for instance Carlsson, "Swedish Corporate Governance and Value Creation: owners still in the driver's seat", *Corporate Governance: an International Review* 2007, 1038–1055.

[56] Discharge from liability is a special feature of Swedish company law and a mandatory matter at the annual general meeting of a Swedish company. Discharge from liability is, simply put, granted unless the majority at the AGM, or a minority representing at least 10 % of all shares in the company, votes against discharge (which means that a relatively small group can block a decision). If a board member or the CEO has been granted discharge from liability with respect to their management during a particular financial year, no claim may, as a main rule, be brought against that individual for damages to the company based upon acts or omissions during that financial year, subject to exceptions such as that the discharge does not cover damages not known at the time of the decision or if the event was not included in the financial reporting presented to the general meeting where it should have been.

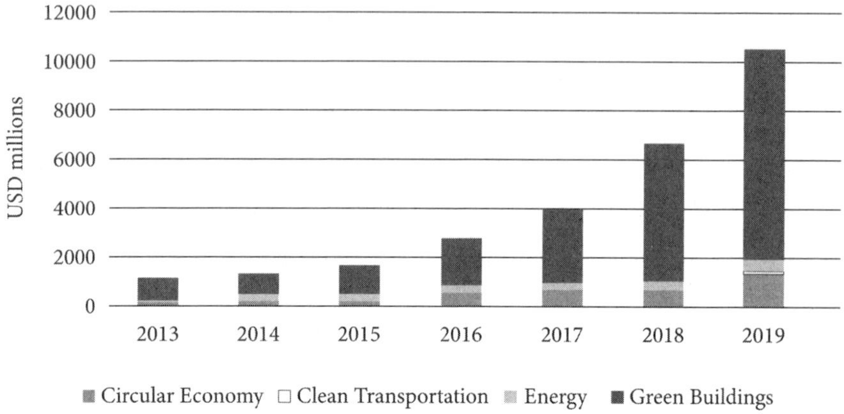

Accumulated green bond Issuances across corporate sectors in Sweden 2013–2019 (USD 2015).
Source: Torvanger, Maltais, and Marginea (2021), "Green Bonds in Sweden and Norway: What are the success factors?" *Journal of Cleaner Production* 324, p. 10.

nesses and overshadows other sources of capital such as corporate bonds.[57] Not only is the IPO-market active (as described above), but there is also an active market for new issuances for listed companies, with a little over 300 issuances in 2021.[58] The discussion on corporate governance and sustainability in this context is thus dominated by a focus on equity market aspects and issues, as well as shareholder governance. Bondholders will very rarely engage with a company outside of a restructuring or refinancing process, and almost never in general corporate governance matters.[59]

However, Swedish companies are increasingly using so-called green bonds as a source of financing, particularly for specific parts of their businesses, with Sweden being the 6th largest nation globally on labelled green bonds issuances.[60] Very high growth was recorded in the period between 2013 and 2019, especially in the real estate industry (see figure above). According to a study by Drage and Sundt, a few of the key drivers are that the issuing of green bonds makes it easier to access capital, easier to acquire a more diverse investor base and establishes an easier pathway to a bolstered reputation and credibility.[61] According to interviews carried out by Torvanger, Maltais, and Marginea, the Swedish

[57] See OECD (2022), *The Swedish Corporate Bond Market and Bondholder Rights*, OECD Capital Market Series.
[58] According to data provided by the Swedish stock-exchanges.
[59] Banks as creditors do however play a role, see OECD, The Swedish Corporate Bond Market and Bondholder Rights, OECD Capital Market Series 2022.
[60] Climate Bonds Initiative, *The Green Bond Market in the Nordics 2018*, https://www.climatebonds.net/files/reports/cbi-nordics-final-03b.pdf (25 October 2023).
[61] Drage and Sundt, *Green bonds in the Norwegian and Swedish Markets*, NTNU 2019.

public pension funds have "shown leadership and been frontrunners as active supporters of green bonds in Sweden", which is founded on a political mandate to emphasise sustainability when managing investments, together with other institutional investors such as the bank, SEB and the insurance fund, Folksam.[62]

Simply put, the growth of the green bond market in Sweden seems to be market driven, with researchers pointing towards the importance of business culture and institutional investors being focused on sustainability.[63] These institutions are to a large extent those that also dominate in the equity markets, and where there does not seem to be any particular conflicts between shareholders and creditors in the field.

VI. Dialogue between companies and shareholders and equal treatment of shareholders with regards to information

Another focus of this volume is one-on-one dialogues between anchor shareholders and management, wherein a problem particularly addressed is that desirable and useful exchanges of information between a company and its key owners collides with the *equal treatment interest* of non-involved (small) shareholders and the *principle of equal opportunities in equity markets*. This is a discussion that surfaces now and again in Sweden since these dialogues are not uncommon.[64]

First of all, it should be noted that the general understanding is that unequal treatment of shareholders with regards to information exchange is not prohibited by EU legislation. There is no general requirement for equal treatment of shareholders in European company law (though, of course, there are many specific requirements).[65] Furthermore, with regards to the specific issue on information, the EU-court has specifically stated that there is no requirement of equality of information stipulated by EU-law, and that this is instead regulated by Member States and their corporate governance frameworks accordingly.[66]

---

[62] Torvanger, Maltais, and Marginea, "Green Bonds in Sweden and Norwai: What are the success factors?" Journal of Cleaner Production 2021, 6.

[63] Torvanger, Maltais, and Marginea, "Green Bonds in Sweden and Norwai: What are the success factors?" Journal of Cleaner Production 2021, 8.

[64] For a general discussion on this topic under Swedish law (in Swedish), see Lidman, "Informationsmässig likabehandling enligt aktiebolagslagen", Svensk juristtidning 2021, 1–12. These types of investor soundings may be of particular relevance in a sustainability context, when considered actions might not be obviously aligned with shareholder interests.

[65] See for discussions on this Strampelli, "Knocking at the Boardroom Door: A Transatlantic overview of Director-Institutional Investor Engagement in Law and Practice", Virginia Law & Business Review 2018, 187; Mosca, "Director–Shareholder Dialogues Behind the Scenes: Searching for a Balance Between Freedom of Expression and Market Fairness", *ECFR* 2018, 805; Hopt, *The Dialogue between the Chairman of the Board and Investors, The Practice in the UK, the Netherlands and Germany and the Future of the German Corporate Governance Code Under the New Chairman*, ECGI Law Working Paper no. 365/2017; and Zetzsche, "§ 53a AktG als Informationsnorm?" Die Aktiengesellschaft 2019, 701.

[66] See paragraph 46 in ECJ judgment of 22.11.2005 – Case C384/02 (Grøngaard & Bang). See

As for Swedish law, the issue is not regulated separately, but by the general principles on equal treatment in the Swedish Companies Act. From them, it follows, that unequal treatment of shareholders is illegal if the handling gives an *unjust advantage to certain shareholders at a cost to the company or other shareholders.* The conclusion from this is that dialogues between the board or management and selected shareholders outside the general meeting are compatible with the principle of equal treatment, as long as they are carried out in the interest of the company and not in the interest of certain shareholders. The advantage that the shareholders selected for this dialogue get is also somewhat limited due to the specific regulation which gives shareholders the right to ask for information at the general meeting and, then, of course, there's the market abuse regime.[67] If a board thus wants to have a discussion with its controlling or most important shareholders (such as large institutions) on their view on sustainability issues, they are generally not limited by legislation from doing so.

E. Sustainable funding

I. On the conflict between portfolio strategies and sustainable investment

As has already been addressed above, there is an inherent conflict between (qualitative) shareholder engagement and the business model of many investors, which is an inherent consequence of the structure of the equity market. The market enables the spread of financial risk in a company among thousands or hundreds of thousands of investors as it allows investors to diversify their equity portfolios and take risk in accordance with their own risk preferences.[68] Risk can thus be,allocated to the investors who are most willing and typically best suited to bear it, while non-systemic risk can, to a large extent, be diversified away. However, diversification also creates financial disadvantages. One of the most debated disadvantages lies in the separation of ownership and control and the consequent agency problem.[69] Another is, as addressed above, that a well-diver-

also Hansen, "The Role of Shareholders in Public Companies in the Nordic Countries", *German and Nordic Perspectives on Company Law and Capital Markets Law* 2015, 104.

[67] Lidman, *Informationsmässig likabehandling enligt aktiebolagslagen*, Svensk juristtidning 2021, 14.

[68] See for instance Berk and DeMarzo, *Corporate Finance: Global Edition*, ed. 4, Pearson 2016, 369 ff.

[69] Gilson and Whitehead offers an eloquent presentation of the connection: "Public shareholders and agency costs are two sides of the same coin. If companies need residual risk capital, and if public investors who can diversify their shareholdings are the cheapest risk bearers, then we get agency costs. The capital provided by these cheap risk bearers necessarily is managed by someone else, whose interests are not perfectly aligned with those of investors." See Gilson and Whitehead, "Deconstructing Equity: Public Ownership, Agency costs and Complete Capital Markets", Columbia Law Review 2008, 231.

sified investor will, generally speaking, not have the economic incentives in place for engaging in the governance of its portfolio companies.

From a sustainability standpoint, one aspect of diversification is that it is highly beneficial from a sustainable economy view. That is, it allows comparatively low-risk saving in a high-return environment for savers (to a large part pensioneers) and lower costs of capital for companies and innovations. Another aspect, however, that is raised in this volume, is that it might stand in conflict with the "reorientation of portfolio management to ESG concerns". The Swedish perspective on the latter is, from a regulatory perspective, that the problem stems from mixing various societal functions. What is warranted is a certain *outcome* with regards to sustainable development. Here, state intervention via taxes, government spending, and prohibition on certain behaviours, materials and processes are viewed as the primary tools for solving sustainability issues, and another important tool is, as has been described above, a well-functioning equity market. For that to come true, there are several other factors that need to be realised. One factor deemed important is engaged and long-term shareholders. Another is that investing in the equity market is attractive to investors with different incentives, interests, and time horizons, both because investor diversity is important for an efficient market and for price discovery, but also seeing as it will give a broader range of companies access to funding.[70] If we want this to come true, however, all types of shareholders cannot be asked to behave in the same way given the conditions for shareholder engagement that have been presented above. Thus, it is recognised that some shareholders will play a direct and active role as owners, while others will have an inactive role by supplying capital and being a part of a deep and liquid equity market. Still others might not be viewed as contributing to corporate governance or sustainable development at all.

Due to this background, when rules on investment strategies of institutional investors were introduced in SRD2 (Art. 3h), the implementation took place without incident. SRD2's introduction, moreover, was not expected to affect investor behaviour, and no gold-plating occurred in Sweden.[71] It was advised that institutional investors who invest in stocks that are admitted to trading on a regulated market are now required to publish an account of how, with regard to these shares, the most important elements of their investment strategy cor-

[70] While perhaps being an intuitively obvious point, the literature on this topic is vast, see for instance Weinbaum, "Investor heterogeneity, asset pricing and volatility dynamics", Journal of Economic Dynamics and Control 2009, 1379–1397, Lim, Hooy, Chang, and Brooks, "Foreign investors and stock price efficiency: Thresholds, underlying channels and investor heterogeneity", The North American Journal of Economics and Finance 2016, 1–28; Heaton and Lucas, "The importance of investor heterogeneity and financial market imperfections for the behavior of asset prices", *Carnegie-Rochester Conference Series on Public Policy* 1995, 1–32. This is not a new view in Sweden, but rather topic that was discussed in the middle of the 1980, see Hedlund, Hägg, Hörnell, and Rydén, *Institutioner som aktieägare*, SNS-förlag 1985.

[71] See preparatory work DS 2018:15 p. 256 ff.

respond to the profile and the maturity of their commitments as well as how they contribute to the development of the assets in the medium to long-term. For insurance companies, this obligation only applies in relation to share investments that the insurance company itself has at its disposal.[72]

II. On the conflict between sustainability interests and client interests in portfolio management and long-term holdings

Another topic of this volume relates to the fact that companies are contractually obligated primarily to their clients as fiduciary asset managers when planning and executing investment strategies, and how this does not necessarily coincide with pursuing ESG interests in the relationship with individual portfolio companies. On the contrary, some ESG strategies are aimed at accepting economic disadvantages and are in conflict with return interests. The question is how this conflict is resolved under the national legal system. The Swedish approach here coincides with what has been discussed above on the legislative approach being "pro-market" in the sense of not directing market participant behaviours, but instead focusing on disclosure. A few examples will illustrate this.

When it comes to the Swedish public pension funds (AP-funds), the law regulating them states in ch. 4 section 1 that the fund assets shall be managed "in such a way that they come to the greatest possible benefit for the insurance for income-based pension".[73] With regards to sustainability, it is then added in ch. 4, section 1a that the funds are to manage the

> "fund assets in an exemplary manner through responsible investments and responsible ownership. In the administration, special emphasis shall be placed on *how sustainable development can be promoted without sacrificing the goal in section 1*".

It is thus left up to the funds to find a way to maximise pensions while at the same time taking sustainable development into consideration. This might seem like a lofty regulation, but as mentioned above, the public pension funds seem to be able to handle the obligation on the equity markets as well as the market for corporate bonds.[74]

When it comes to mutual funds and alternative investment funds[75], there is no material regulation focusing directly on sustainable investment. The rules on sustainable investments instead pertain to disclosure: references are made to Art. 6–9 in Regulation 2019/2088 on sustainability-related disclosures in the financial services sector and Art. 5–7 in Regulation 2020/852 on the establishment of a framework for facilitating sustainable investment, requiring the funds to be

[72] See preparatory work DS 2018:15 p. 256.
[73] See law 2000:192 on public pension funds.
[74] See section III.
[75] A collective investment fund not requiring authorisation under Directive 2009/65/EG.

transparent and for providing fund investors with information on their sustainability strategies and investments.[76] In addition to this, it can also be noted that the law on financial advice to consumers is silent when it comes to sustainability issues.[77]

III. Index funds

A category of investor that has received extra focus in the debate on long-term shareholdings is index funds, which by nature are passive investors. On the one hand, they are sometimes viewed in a positive light in this discussion, since they are, by definition, long-term shareholders due to the exit option in an individual firm being generally unavailable to them. On the other hand, these funds compete on very low costs, and based on the economic conditions for shareholder engagement outlined in section IV.1, these funds cannot be expected to engage in the governance of a particular company (other than in very high-profile cases). Given the generally positive view of investor heterogeneity in Sweden, this has not been discussed as a policy problem, and no specific regulation on index funds has been discussed or enacted in Sweden so far.

F. Product governance and sustainable trading

I. General rules on product governance

The label "Product Governance" originates from the Second EU Markets in Financial Instruments Directive (MiFID II), and is also regulated by the Delegated Directive 2017/593, and ESMA Guideline ESMA 35-43-60.[78] In national law, the directives have been adopted into the Securities Market Act (2007:528) and the Swedish Financial Supervisory Authority's (the FSA) regulation FFFS 2017:2. In addition, the FSA has announced that it will follow the ESMA Guideline without any reservations or divergences. Below, a short description is given of the relevant regulation in the Securities Market Act as well as the FSA regulation.

According to the Securities Market Act, a financial service provider that produces financial instruments for sale to clients shall establish, apply and review a process for the approval of each financial instrument and any significant change to existing instruments before they are marketed or distributed to clients

[76] See for mutual funds law 2004:46 ch. 4 sec. 15, paragraph three p. 2–3 and for alternative investment funds law 2013:561 ch. 10 sec. 1, paragraph 2 p. 2.

[77] Law 2003:862.

[78] The Commission has additionally issued another Delegated Directive in 2021 (2021/1269), amending Delegated Directive 2017/593, integrating sustainability factors into the product governance obligations in the first Delegated Directive.

(product approval). The product approval process shall specify an established target group of end customers for a financial instrument and ensure that all relevant risks for the target group are assessed and that the intended distribution strategy is compatible with the target group. The financial service provider shall also regularly review the financial instruments offered or marketed by the institution, taking into account any events that could significantly affect the potential risk for the identified target group for the purpose of assessing whether the product still meets the needs of the established target group and whether the intended distribution strategy is still appropriate accordingly.[79]

The FSA regulation FFFS 2017:2 is based on the Securities Market Act and can be said to complement the Act by virtue of the implementation of the Delegated Directive 2017/593. According to the regulation, a financial service provider shall, when producing a financial instrument, ensure that it complies with the requirements of applicable laws and regulation's management of conflicts of interest. In this context, the provider has to ensure that the design and characteristics of the financial instrument do not affect an end customer in a negative manner.[80] When producing a financial instrument, moreover, the provider shall also ensure that the financial instrument does not have a negative effect on the financial market or that it negatively effects the operations of the financial market, and that the instrument does not threaten the stability of the market.[81]

For each financial instrument, the financial service provider that produces it must specify a target group of end customers in sufficient detail and take into account the needs of the target end customers, their characteristics and their goals. The provider must also specify the customer groups that the financial instrument is not intended for and consider each customer group's needs, characteristics and goals. In this context, the provider must base its judgments on its knowledge about and experience of the financial instrument in question or similar financial instruments, as well as the financial markets.[82]

When assessing the end customer's needs, characteristics and goals, the financial service provider shall take into consideration whether the customer is a professional or not, the customer's risk tolerance, the ability to handle a loss, as well as their knowledge and experience and investment goals.[83] Furthermore, when producing a financial instrument, it shall also conduct an analysis of different scenarios for each financial instrument in order to evaluate whether a risk is present that the financial instruments yield a poor outcome for an end customer and what circumstances may lead to that scenario. The service provider shall, in that context, take into consideration whether there is an overall

[79] See Securities Market Act (2007:528) ch. 8 sec. 13.
[80] FSA regulation FFFS 2017:2, ch. 5 sec. 3.
[81] FSA regulation FFFS 2017:2, ch. 5 sec. 4.
[82] FSA regulation FFFS 2017:2, ch. 5 sec. 5.
[83] FSA regulation FFFS 2017:2, ch. 5 sec. 6.

negative development in the financial markets at hand, whether the firm or a third party suffers from financial difficulties, whether the financial instrument will not actually become commercially viable, whether the demand for the instrument is much higher than expected, and/or any other event that may have a negative impact on the financial instrument accordingly.[84] When determining the fee structure, the provider shall ensure that costs and fees are compatible with the needs, characteristics and goals of the intended customers, that the fees do not undermine the yield of the financial instruments, that the fee structure is transparent for the intended target group and that it is also generally suited for the intended customers.[85]

A financial service provider is also supposed to regularly review each financial instrument which it produces and in this context, take into account all events that can significantly affect the risk for a target group, and continuously examine whether the financial instrument is still compatible with the needs, characteristics and goals of the group. The provider must ensure that the financial instrument is distributed to the target group and that it is not distributed to others with needs, characteristics, and goals incompatible with the product.[86] Consideration is also to be taken to the complexity of the instrument, as well as its innovativeness.[87] Internal policies are to be established for the monitoring process, where it has to be plainly stated what factors may trigger additional monitoring.[88]

II. ESG in product governance

With regards to the formal review and approval procedure for the intended target groups described above, it can be noted that sustainable development is currently to be considered by financial service providers *if that is a part of the goal and needs of the intended target group*. After the implementation of the new Delegated Directive 2021/1269, this is still the case, with the addition that funds must now have an organisation which ensures that it can take sustainability factors and risks according to Art. 2.24 and 2.22 into account.[89]

Another ESG-related issue in relation to financial products is that past practice in fund management shows that above-average management fees are charged for managing "sustainable" portfolios in line with the ESG doctrine. As described in the previous section, under Swedish law, a financial service provider shall ensure that costs and fees are compatible with the *needs, characteristics and goals of the intended customers*, that the *fees do not undermine the yield of the financial in-*

---

[84] FSA regulation FFFS 2017:2, ch. 5 sec. 7.
[85] FSA regulation FFFS 2017:2, ch. 5 sec. 8.
[86] FSA regulation FFFS 2017:2, ch. 5 sec. 10.
[87] FSA regulation FFFS 2017:2, ch. 5 sec. 11.
[88] FSA regulation FFFS 2017:2, ch. 5 sec. 11–12.
[89] See FFFS 2022:14.

struments, that the *fee structure is transparent for the intended target group* and that it is also generally suited for the intended customers when determining fee structure. There are no specific instructions on how the customer's interest in returns vis-à-vis interest in sustainable investment is to be weighed in this part of the process.

III. Greenwashing

Financial firms may face different incentives for working with sustainability. For example, they may view climate change from a profitability perspective as a risk that needs to be managed or as an opportunity to be pursued. They may also see it as a way to enhance their brand and raise their public reputation, but without necessarily making any major changes to their operations (greenwashing).

Problems pertaining to greenwashing have been on the political agenda in Sweden for several years.[90] There is no specific Swedish regulation on greenwashing today, that is, other than the general rules that information on products and services may not be misleading, which of course applies to greenwashing, as well as the EU Regulation 2019/2088 on sustainability-related disclosures in the financial services sector (the disclosure regulation). At the end of 2022, a working group within the International Organization of Securities Commissions (IOSCO) published a recommendation on sustainability-related practices, policies, procedures and disclosures in asset management, aiming to decrease the risks of greenwashing.[91] The working group was headed by the director general of the FSA, *Erik Thédeen*, and a review of the occurrence of greenwashing in the financial sector is one of the officially prioritised areas for 2022 for the FSA, both with the IOSCO and disclosure regulations in mind.[92]

IV. ESG-quality labels

While transparency has been a key focus in the Swedish product governance framework, quality measures for ESG-compliant financial products have not been standardised. Though the Morningstar Sustainability Score is well-used, many financial institutions provide their own ESG-rating systems.

The difficulty of comparing products has been raised as an issue. Initiatives have not been taken by the FSA or the legislator in spite of this, but an important reason for the passivity can be explained by the anticipation leading up to the

---

[90] For instance, the Swedish FSA has published 19 communications relating to greenwashing in the last five years.

[91] Available at https://www.iosco.org/library/pubdocs/pdf/IOSCOPD688.pdf (25 October 2023).

[92] See Memorandum FI dnr 22–3235, available in English at: https://www.fi.se/contentassets/4259350a12fd4455b9afc6b2a16ac4e6/fi-prioriterade-omraden-2022-eng.pdf (25 October 2023).

adoption of the EU Sustainable Finance Disclosure Regulation (2019/2088) as well as the EU Taxonomy (2020/852). It is to be expected that these issues will also be raised by the FSA during 2022 or 2023, given that greenwashing and ESG-communication is one of the annual prioritised areas.[93]

G. Conclusion and a critical perspective

In this report, the Swedish ESG-regulation regarding listed companies were described, and a recurring theme is that the Swedish regulator has steered clear from a dirigiste approach. The regulatory measures taken have been aimed at removing obstacles to shareholder engagement, and to increasing the transparency and quality of disclosure. Judging by the growth and development of the Swedish equity market as well as the performance of Swedish companies and business in international sustainability and ESG-ratings, the system has worked well. Against this background, a few critical reflections on the development in the area within the EU can be presented as a concluding remark.

The underlying idea behind many (but of course not all) of the sustainable development initiatives in the equity markets area in the EU is based on the view that shareholders and equity markets force companies to act in the short-term. This is, based on the best current empirical understanding – and despite the narrative on "quarterly capitalism" with its elegant simplicity – simply not true.[94] In reality, and most definitively in the prevailing political view in Sweden, the equity market is a key driving force in the green transition by requiring company management to consider climate risks, seeing as both shareholders and investors are interested in companies' long-term results as being decisive for the present-day value of their shares and the future return on their investment. As discussed in section III, it has also been empirically shown that broad and deep public equity markets present investors with the ability to diversify firm-specific risks associated with technological innovation, and thus lower the overall societal cost of capital for research and development, which, in turn, results in new patents, products and processes that have a smaller carbon footprint .

One important reason why the EU should try to strengthen and grow its equity markets is that they may have a key role in the green transition and in solving the climate crisis. In that vein, the conclusion regarding how to design a coherent European legal framework in terms of sustainability-related financial law is, from a Swedish perspective, that it must allow for this type of "pro-market" approach.

---

[93] See Memorandum FI dnr 22–3235, available in English at: https://www.fi.se/contentassets/4259350a12fd4455b9afc6b2a16ac4e6/fi-prioriterade-omraden-2022-eng.pdf (25 October 2023).

[94] See Roe, *Missing the target: why stock-market short-termism is not the problem*, Oxford University Press 2022.

Interventions in investor incentive structures and obligations on how to act at a strategic level risk weakening the equity markets and ultimately contribute to the already declining use of equity markets as a means of financing in the EU[95] (which often is explained with over-regulation[96]). The strength of the market economy is that there is a genuine pluralism when it comes to the acquisition, assessment and use of information about individual companies and markets. At a time when the ability of the equity market to handle risk and to further innovation and sustainable growth might be what we need most of all, the stakes attached to introducing experimental and unfounded corporate governance standards are high. Indeed, poorly substantiated and system-changing rules that push everyone in similar directions can entail significant costs in lost time, systemically misallocated investments, as well as public trust if the direction is not the right one. Resources must therefore not only be dedicated to ensuring that the European legal framework around ESG is swiftly implemented, but also evidence based and well-crafted.

[95] See Oxera, Primary and secondary equity markets in the EU, available at: https://www.oxera.com/wp-content/uploads/2020/11/Oxera-study-Primary-and-Secondary-Markets-in-the-EU-Final-Report-EN-1.pdf (25 October 2023).

[96] See most recently the Assonime study *Corporate Governance in Italy: the implementation of the Italian Corporate Governance Code (year 2021)*, available at: https://www.assonime.it/en/publishingactivities/notes-and-insights/Pages/Notes-and-Studies-4.2022.aspx (25 October 2023).

Country Report Poland

Krzysztof Oplustil / Anne-Marie Weber

A. Introduction

Recent years have witnessed calls for unlocking private capital and unleashing a wave of sustainable finance that can support sustainability-driven policy efforts[1]. In the early days of what can be identified as the 'sustainable finance movement', Poland's approach to the looming metamorphosis of financial markets seemed quite promising. When the Polish government issued the first sovereign green bonds in the world in 2016[2] – despite the country's previous less than exemplary record regarding international and domestic climate policy[3] and its strong economic reliance on coal[4] – hopes were high regarding the potentially transfor-

[1] For a comprehensive account and review of the relevant literature see in particular: D. Busch, G. Ferrarini, and S. Grünewald (eds.), *Sustainable Finance in Europe. Corporate Governance, Financial Stability and Financial Markets*, EBI Studies in Banking and Capital Markets Law, Palgrave Macmillan 2021; S. Boubaker, D. Cumming and D. K. Nguyen, *Research Handbook of Finance and Sustainability*, Edward Elgar 2018; H. Liang and L. Renneboog, *Corporate Social Responsibility and Sustainable Finance: A Review of the Literature*, European Corporate Governance Institute – Finance Working Paper No. 701/2020, https://papers.ssrn.com/sol3/papers.cfm?abstract_id=3698631.

[2] A. Whiley, *Poland wins race to issue first green sovereign bond. A new era for Polish climate policy?* 15.12.2016, https://www.climatebonds.net/2016/12/poland-wins-race-issue-first-green-sovereign-bond-new-era-polish-climate-policy (24 October 2023); Ministry of Finance, *Sovereign Bonds in Poland*, October 2018, https://pubdocs.worldbank.org/en/893761541540770521/BS-5-R-Zima-Sovereign-Green-Bonds-in-Poland.pdf (24 October 2023).

[3] J. Skjærseth, "Implementing EU climate and energy policies in Poland: policy feedback and reform", *Environmental Politics*, 2018, 27:3, 498–518; K. Marcinkiewicz and J. Tosun, "Contesting climate change: mapping the political debate in Poland", *East European Politics*, 31:2, p. 187–207; D. Tilles, *Poland may seek to block EU climate package, says deputy PM*, 14.01.2022, https://notesfrompoland.com/2022/01/14/poland-may-seek-to-block-eu-climate-package-says-deputy-pm/ (24 October 2023); C. Turp-Balaz, *Fit for 55: Poland's stalling casts dark cloud over EU's climate goals*, 19.01.2022, https://emerging-europe.com/news/fit-for-55-polands-stalling-casts-dark-cloud-over-eus-climate-goals/ (24 October 2023); M. Martewicz, *Poland Threatens to Block EU Climate Talks Over Access to Funds*, https://www.bloomberg.com/news/articles/2021-10-20/poland-wants-deal-on-eu-funds-before-starting-climate-talks?leadSource=uverify%20wall (24 October 2023); J. Strupczewski and G. Baczyńska, *EU leaves Poland out of 2050 climate deal after standoff*, https://www.reuters.com/article/us-climate-change-eu-idUSKBN1YG01I (24 October 2023).

[4] The carbon intensity of the Polish economy is 172 % above the EU average, and second-highest among EU Member States. See data on coal consumption and production by country: https://www.worldometers.info/coal/poland-coal/#:~:text=Poland%20produces%20143%2C9

mational role which sustainable finance was poised to play. After all, as Poland generates 10.5 % of the EU's total greenhouse gas emissions and its carbon intensity ranks as the second highest in the Union[5], an internal policy effort for seizing upon the opportunities of sustainable finance for urgent infrastructural investments essential to the energy transformation could have been reasonably expected[6]. Disappointingly, however, the trailblazing sovereign green bond issuance of 2016 has proven to be the only remarkable episode of Poland's initiatives in the field of sustainable finance so far.

After years of silence and practicing a relatively passive attitude towards the EU's endeavours in mobilising capital for sustainable investments, nebulous strategic commitments regarding sustainable finance were first announced in the Capital Market Development Strategy ("CMDS"), which was prepared in 2019 by the Ministry of Finance in cooperation with the European Bank for Reconstruction and Development[7]. In late July 2022, the Ministry of Finance announced that in reference to declarations given in the CMDS, it is commencing work on a roadmap for the development of sustainable finance in Poland[8]. To this end, a working group composed of representatives from the public administration, financial market participants, Polish and international development institutions, and the UN Global Compact Network in Poland came together to establish the

---

96%2C029%20tons%20(short,ranking%209th%20in%20the%20world (24 October 2023); see also: European Parliamentary Research Service, *EU progress on climate action – How are the Member States doing? Climate action in Poland Latest state of play*, October 2021, https://www.europarl.europa.eu/RegData/etudes/BRIE/2021/698766/EPRS_BRI(2021)698766_EN.pdf (24 October 2023); H. Brauers and P.-Y. Oei, "The political economy of coal in Poland: Drivers and barriers for a shiftaway from fossil fuels", *Energy Policy*, 2020, 144, p. 1–12; W. Karpa and A. Grigonović, "(Not so) Stranded: The case of coal in Poland", *Energies*, 2021, 14, 8476; J. Cienski, *Breaking up is hard to do for Poland and coal*, https://www.politico.eu/article/poland-coal-energy-green-deal-eu/ (24 October 2023).

[5] European Parliamentary Research Service, *EU progress on climate action – How are the Member States doing? Climate action in Poland Latest state of play*, October 2021, https://www.europarl.europa.eu/RegData/etudes/BRIE/2021/698766/EPRS_BRI(2021)698766_EN.pdf (24 October 2023), p. 1.

[6] Under EU effort-sharing legislation, Poland was permitted to increase its emissions by 14 % compared with 2005 levels by 2020 and now needs to achieve a 7 % reduction by 2030. Poland reached a 12.2 % share of renewable energy sources in 2019 and aims to reach a renewables share of at least 23 % by 2030, by focusing on biomass, offshore wind, and biofuels. In 2019, Polish per capita emissions were at an average of 10.4 tonnes of carbon dioxide equivalent (CO2e), a figure that was above the EU average of 8.4 tonnes and the eighth highest in the EU-27. Between 2005 and 2019, Polish per capita emissions decreased by only 2.3 %, against an EU average reduction of 22 % over the same period.

[7] Ministry of Finance, *Capital Market Development Strategy*, Appendix to the Resolution No. 114 of the Council of Ministers of 1 October 2019, https://www.gov.pl/web/finanse/strategia-rozwoju-rynku-kapitalowego (24 October 2023), p. 60–62.

[8] Ministry of Finance, https://www.gov.pl/web/finanse/ruszaja-prace-nad-mapa-drogowa-dla-rozwoju-zrownowazonych-finansow-w-polsce#:~:text=Ministerstwo%20Finans%C3%B3w%20(MF)%20rozpoczyna%20prace,gospodarki%20w%20kierunku%20neutralno%C5%9Bci%20klimatycznej (24 October 2023).

"Platform for Sustainable Finance". In October 2023 a report on the realization of the CMDS ("CMDS Report") was published[9]. This document articulates the aspirations to transform the Polish financial market into a thriving hub for sustainable finance while elucidating the strategic and organizational endeavors dedicated to this vision[10]. Furthermore, it affirms the commitment to prepare a roadmap for the advancement of sustainable finance in Poland by the end of 2023 through the Platform for Sustainable Finance[11]. Nonetheless, the CMDS Report unmistakably illustrates that Poland's engagement in sustainable finance is currently at the planning stage rather than the execution phase.

In this country report, we aspire to examine the peculiarities of how sustainable finance works and is currently developing in Poland. Naturally, to a large extent, the legal framework for sustainable finance stems from EU legislation and subjects Poland to the same rules as other EU member states. Given that background, we refrain from a detailed analysis of the harmonised legal regime related to sustainable finance that applies across the EU. Instead, we aim to depict the idiosyncrasies in the administration and evolution of sustainable finance in Poland. To this end, we first deem it necessary to briefly describe the characteristics of the Polish financial market, which provide a practical explanation for the sustainable finance trend's peculiar absorption (sec. B). Subsequently, we examine these characteristics in the subject area of sustainable ownership and shareholder governance (sec. C), sustainable funding and portfolio governance (sec. D) as well as sustainable trading and product governance (sec. E).

B. The characteristics of the Polish financial market

The Polish financial market's post-war history dates back to the early '90s. The Warsaw Stock Exchange ("WSE") was founded in 1991 and was upgraded to 'developed market status' only fairly recently, in 2018. Although the WSE surely is a regional leader, from a global perspective, its capitalisation rather conveys lilliput status. Poland is the 21st economy in the world in terms of nominal GDP[12]. Yet, the WSE's market capitalisation is only the world's 35th and amounts only to c.a. 266 bn EUR[13] (e.g., around 8x smaller than Frankfurt Stock Exchange)[14]. What is more, the WSE market is shallow as its yearly turnover value only amounts to c.a.

[9] Ministry of Finance, https://www.gov.pl/web/finanse/rok-20238 (24 October 2023).

[10] CMDS Report, p. 73

[11] CMDS Report, p. 73

[12] As per year 2022, https://datacatalog.worldbank.org/search/dataset/0038130 (24 October 2023).

[13] As per 8 April 2022, source: https://www.gpw.pl/statystyki-gpw (24 October 2023).

[14] As per 8 April 2022, source: https://www.boerse-frankfurt.de/en/know-how/glossary/market-capitalisation (24 October 2023).

83 bn EUR. Moreover, the WSE is actually currently shrinking, as the number of listed companies has been decreasing constantly since 2016.

In terms of assets under management (AUM), Poland still remains far from the European lead, which is mainly attributable to the historically substantiated lack of private savings and the dominating role of the banking sector. That is, at the end of 2020, banks' assets accounted for 73 % of the financial system's assets in financing business[15]. Consequently, at the end of 2020, Poland's share in the European AUM amounted to 0.2 % (around EUR 61 bn)[16]. A glance at the value of assets in the financial market in relation to GDP shows a ratio more than four times lower than the average in the Eurozone[17]. Non-aggregated investments dominate, as only around 60 bn EUR of assets fall under institutional investor's management (about 50 x less than in Germany)[18]. Only around half of the share in turnovers of the Warsaw Stock Exchange that domestic investors generate can be attributed to institutional investors. Concentrated ownership structures prevail in most listed companies, and the state essentially controls strategic companies as such (see further sec. C. I.).

C. Sustainable Ownership / Shareholder Governance

I. The ownership structure of Polish listed companies – The role of the State Treasury and institutional investors

The corporate governance of listed companies in Poland is a typical example of an insider-controlled system in which concentrated ownership structures dominate. Institutional investors play a relatively small role, both as a source of financing and monitoring agents. In every listed company, at least one shareholder has more than 5 % of voting rights.[19] Almost 50 % of the listed companies have a shareholder who holds 50 % of the voting power, and another 40 % have a shareholder who holds more than 25 % of the voting power[20]. In almost 70 % of the companies, the most significant three shareholders hold more than 50 % of the voting power[21]. As of July 2014, the median voting power of the largest

---

[15] Narodowy Bank Polski, *Rozwój system finansowego w Polsce w 2020 r.*, https://nbp.pl/wp-content/uploads/2022/09/rozwoj2020.pdf (24 October 2023), p. 12.

[16] EFAMA, *Asset Management in Europe 2021*, https://www.efama.org/newsroom/news/asset-management-report-2021 (24 October 2023), p. 7.

[17] *Ibidem*, p. 7.

[18] *Ibidem*, p. 7.

[19] Own research based on public data available at: https://www.gpw.pl/ (24 October 2023).

[20] Own research based on public data available at: https://www.gpw.pl/ (24 October 2023).

[21] *OECD Corporate Governance Factbook 2021*, https://www.oecd.org/corporate/corporate-governance-factbook.htm (24 October 2023).

shareholder amounted to 38.2 %, and the average was 41.73 %[22]. Although more recent studies on the ownership structure of Polish listed companies do not exist, it can be reasonably assumed that these figures have not changed in recent years.

Controlling shareholders often directly influence management and stay "in touch" regarding ongoing activities. Furthermore, according to prevailing opinions and practice, they are to be treated as insiders within the meaning of art. 8 sec. 4 c) (and b)) MAR[23]. Consequently, the provision of inside information to such a shareholder is conducted within the "normal exercise of an employment, a profession or duties" and therefore falls within the exemption from unlawful disclosures as referred to in art. 10 MAR. The problematic issue of one-to-one dialogue between controlling shareholders and listed companies and the resulting tension regarding the principle of equal treatment intensifies the horizontal agency conflict inherently associated with insider-controlled corporate governance models. In addition, the new law of groups of companies which entered into force on October 13, 2022[24], strengthens the position of the parent company through the possibility of issuing binding instructions to the subsidiary and the right to access its information and documents directly.

In Poland, institutional investors – mainly investment and pension funds – hold minority stocks in listed companies. Hence, their bargaining power in influencing the company's operations is very limited. According to one empirical study, they "do not play a crucial role [in the corporate governance] and are unable to influence or supervise company operations."[25] As clearly pointed out,

[22] T. Regucki, *Mechanizmy zwiększające kontrolę (control enhancing mechanisms) w polskich spółkach akcyjnych. Analiza prawno-ekonomiczna*, Warszawa 2018, p. 12 et seq.; A. Radwan and T. Regucki, *The Possibilities for and Barriers to Sustainable Companies in Polish Company Law*, University of Oslo Faculty of Law Legal Studies Research Paper Series No. 2012–32, p. 10 (https://papers.ssrn.com/sol3/papers.cfm?abstract_id=2159217 (24 October 2023)); W. Patena, "Koncentracja własności i kontroli w spółkach notowanych na GPW w Warszawie" (Concentration of ownership and control in companies listed on the Warsaw Stock Exchange), in Zeszyty Naukowe Uniwersytetu Szczecińskiego; *Finanse, Rynki Finansowe, Ubezpieczenia*, 2008, No. 14, p. 325.

[23] Regulation (EU) No 596/2014 of the European Parliament and of the Council of 16 April 2014 on market abuse (market abuse regulation) and repealing Directive 2003/6/EC of the European Parliament and of the Council and Commission Directives 2003/124/EC, 2003/125/EC and 2004/72/EC (OJ L 173, 12.6.2014, p. 1).

[24] Provisions of Article 4 sec. 1 No. 5(1) and Articles 21(1)–21(16) of the Code of Commercial Companies, added by the Act of 9 February 2022, amending the Act – Code of Commercial Companies and certain other acts (Official Journal of 2022, position 807). Criticism of the proposed solutions and fear of the reaction of rating agencies led to the adoption of a provision according to which a listed company cannot be included in the formalised corporate group as a subsidiary in relation to which the parent company can exercise the abovementioned rights.

[25] D. Malinowska and J. Gad, "Institutional investors in the largest Polish capital companies – theory and practice", *Ad Alta: Journal of Interdisciplinary Research* (1804–7890), 2012, vol. 2, p. 23.

even if institutional investors decided to pursue certain goals jointly, they would not be in a position to affect the company's management.[26]

Another key characteristic feature of Polish corporate governance is the significant involvement of the State Treasury in the ownership structures of the largest listed companies. Out of the twenty highest-capitalised companies traded at the WSE, eight are controlled by the State Treasury[27]. In addition, four of the five most actively traded companies are state-controlled[28]. Many are post-transformation remnants of state-owned enterprises which were converted into companies and subjected to partial privatisation[29]. Thanks to the dispersion of the remaining shareholder structure and the provisions of the company's articles, the State Treasury maintains control powers, however often formally being a minority shareholder. In particular, it is common practice in these companies to cap shareholders' voting rights above the thresholds of 10 % or 20 %. Importantly, these caps do not apply to the State Treasury.

An example is the largest Polish listed company, a parent company of the fuel and energy corporate group, PKN Orlen S.A. Currently, after the takeover in 2022 of another state-controlled listed company, Lotos S.A., the State Treasury owns 35.66 % of the voting shares of PKN Orlen (before the takeover, it was 27.5 %), and is thus formally a minority shareholder. However, in practical terms, the State Treasury, as the largest blockholder, completely controls this company and consequently the whole group, since other blockholders, i.e., two pension funds, control respectively 6.99 % and 5.43 % of the voting shares whilst the rest of the share capital (51.92 %) is dispersed accordingly[30]. The State Treasury's control is guaranteed through the company's articles of association, which state that no shareholder, except for the State Treasury, may exercise more than 10 % of votes at the general meeting and provide for a qualified majority of 90 % of votes. Similar provisions are contained in the articles of association of other listed companies in which the State Treasury holds a minority stake.

In the Polish insider-controlled corporate governance model, controlling shareholders should be identified as the – potentially – most important catalysts for transposing sustainable development goals into corporate behaviour. In terms of the listed companies controlled by the State Treasury, shareholder governance is being used as a direct instrument of economic policy, in particular, in such areas as energy and mining. While the declarations of these companies follow international commitments regarding the net-zero goal (investments in renewable

[26] *Ibidem*, p. 23.

[27] Own research based on public data available at: https://www.gpw.pl/ (24 October 2023).

[28] Own research based on public data available at: https://www.gpw.pl/ (24 October 2023).

[29] See A.-M. Weber, "Privatization in Poland – goals, constraints and new approaches", in: *Sektor Publiczny – Racjonalizacja Gospodarowania* [The public sector – rationalising management], Białystok 2012, p. 223 et seq.

[30] See https://www.orlen.pl/en/about-the-company/company/bodies-and-structure/shareholders-structure (24 October 2023).

energy sources, decarbonisation, CO2 neutrality, etc.)[31], actual execution remains dependent on political will. Similarly, as regards listed companies controlled by other shareholders, both industry holding structures (domestic and foreign) and individual investors, sustainability efforts all remain primarily dependent upon the "willingness" of such controlling shareholders. The role of institutional investors is limited to initiating and supporting ESG objectives through the tools provided for in general company law and capital market law, such as minority rights or the right to information. Due to the insider-controlled ownership structures, the voting rights of institutional investors are not likely to have any definitive influence and are thus unable to "inject" sustainability-driven strategies as such.

The above illuminates the issue of incompatibility of the EU legislator's approach to introducing sustainability through shareholder governance with actual ownership structures and corporate governance models in certain member states. While the current legal state-of-play addresses certain obligations of institutional investors, controlling shareholders are a regulatory blind spots. It seems that the legislative efforts at the EU level assumed a dispersed market structure across member states and the existence of a corporate governance model in which the voice of institutional investors "matters". These assumptions do not hold in the case of Polish listed companies and, consequently, render the current efforts to push ESG through shareholder governance largely ineffective (see further sec. C.II.)[32].

II. Regulatory environment for institutional investors

The role of institutional investors as minority shareholders is determined by the provisions of the law in force in Poland. First, it is necessary to point out the statutory investment restrictions provided by investment funds in both EU and

[31] E.g., PKN Orlen's strategy includes a commitment to achieve the Group's long-term goal, i.e. total emissions neutrality in 2050. By 2030, the Company will reduce CO2 emissions by 20% from its current refining and petrochemical assets and by 33% per megawatt hour in the energy sector.

[32] See also general reflections on the challenges for institutional investor engagement: H.S. Birkmose, "European Challenges for Institutional Investor Engagement – Is Mandatory Disclosure the Way Forward", *European Company and Financial Law Review*, 2014, pp. 214–257; G. Stapledon, "Institutional Investors: What are their Responsibilities as Shareholders?" in: J. Parkinson et al. (eds.), *The Political Economy of the Company*, 2000, p. 225 et seq.; E. Micheler, "Facilitating Investor Engagement and Stewardship", *European Business Organization Law Review*, vol. 14, 2013, p. 29–56; C. Strenger and D.A. Zetzsche, "Corporate Governance, Cross-Border Voting and the (Draft) Principles of the European Securities Law Legislation – Enhancing Investor Engagement Through Standardisation", *Journal of Corporate Law Studies*, October 2013, pp. 503–552; H.S. Birkmose, "The transformation of passive institutional investors to active owners – mission impossible?" in: H.S. Birkmose et al. (eds.), *The European Financial Market in Transition*, 2011, p. 130 et seq.

Polish law. According to Article 56 UCITS Directive 2009/65/EC[33], an investment company or a management company acting in connection with all of the common funds which it manages and which fall within the scope of this Directive shall not acquire any shares with voting rights attached which would enable it to exercise significant influence over the management of an issuing body. This provision of EU law was implemented in Article 104 sec. 1 of the Act of 27 May 2004 on investment funds and management of alternative investment funds[34] ("Investment Fund Act"), which excludes the acquisition by an investment fund of securities giving more than 10 % of the total number of votes in any governing body of the issuer of these securities. Moreover, if securities purchased by open-end investment funds managed by the same fund management company[35] were to give more than 10 % of the total number of votes in the issuer's governing bodies, these funds could then exercise voting rights from securities yielding a total of 10 % of the total number of votes. In such a case, exercising voting rights from securities (e. g., shares) above this threshold is thus ineffective (Article 104 sec. 7 and 8 Investment Fund Act).

The aforementioned statutory provisions aim to protect the clients of investment funds through the mandatory diversification of investment risk and the avoidance of excessive concentration. Although no explicit regulation refers to the potential conflict, one should reasonably assume that based on the current legal framework the principle of risk diversification prevails over the implementation of ESG objectives. However, this does not preclude institutional investors from playing the role of active minority shareholders, acting either individually or in concert with other minority shareholders and encouraging the investee companies to pursue sustainability-driven strategies[36]. The stewardship code ("Code of Good Practices for Institutional Investors" *fosters such an active role* It is an act of industry self-regulation adopted on the private initiative of the Chamber of Fund and Asset Managers in 2006. It sets out the basic principles of commitment, the application of which is based on the self-defined "comply or explain" principle. Unfortunately, the code has not been updated since its adoption and does not contain provisions related specifically to ESG issues. Nonetheless, the following provisions of the code which support the activity and involvement of institutional investors in corporate governance are worth mentioning:

---

[33] Directive 2009/65/EC of the European Parliament and of the Council 13 July 2009 on the coordination of laws, regulations and administrative provisions relating to undertakings for collective investment in transferable securities (UCITS) (OJ L 302, 17.11.2009, p. 32).

[34] Act of 27 May 2004 on investment funds and management of alternative investment funds (Official Journal of 2022, position 1523.

[35] Pursuant to Polish law, an investment fund is a legal person separate from the fund management company, which is a joint stock company that manages the fund. One management company can manage multiple funds.

[36] For a comprehensive review of stewardship models around the globe, see: D. Katelouzou and D. W. Puchniak, *Global Shareholder Stewardship*, Cambridge 2022.

– An institutional investor should participate in all general meetings of companies in which, on his/her own behalf or on behalf of his/her clients, it holds a block of shares equal to or greater than 5 % of the votes. In the event of a lower capital commitment, an institutional investor should participate in the general meeting where important matters of the company are discussed, and failure to exercise voting rights could increase the risk of a significant reduction in the value of shares held (sec. 7.1. and 8.1. of the Code);

– In the interests of the company and its shareholders, institutional investors should have the right to exchange views and opinions about the company and the planned meeting, as well as agree on a common position on how to vote at the general meeting, provided that (1) making arrangements between institutional investors will not create any legal or economic obligation between the contracting investors and will not give rise to any obligation (apart from purely moral) to act in accordance with the agreed agreement, (2) possible arrangements will be made ad hoc, i. e., for the needs of one general meeting (sec. 10.1 and sec. 27.1 of the Code);

– Institutional investors can contact their representatives directly with representatives of the management board and supervisory board of a portfolio company, as well as raise worrisome issues in discussions or correspondence with representatives of these corporate bodies (sec. 29.1. of the Code).

The aforementioned provisions of stewardship code are also intended to mitigate the risk that results from the unclear statutory regulation of acting in concert for institutional investors who aim to implement a "voice strategy"[37] in their portfolio companies. The Polish legislator has implemented the relevant provisions of the European law concerning acting in concert (i. e., Article 10 lit a Takeover Bid Directive[38] and Article 2 sec. 1 lit d the Transparency Directive[39]) in a uniform manner, i. e., for the purpose of both the obligation to notify about the acquisition or disposal of major holdings and the obligation to submit a mandatory bid. As provided for in Polish law, these obligations also apply jointly to all entities that are bound by a written or oral agreement for directly or indirectly acquiring shares in a listed company, or for voting at the general meeting or for conducting a long-term (permanent) policy towards the listed company, even if only one of these entities has taken or intended to take the steps that would give rise to these

[37] On voice and exit as corporate governance tools see further: M. Becht, J. Franks, and H. Wagner, *Corporate Governance Through Voice and Exit*, ECGI Finance Working Paper N° 633/2019, November 2019.

[38] Directive 2004/25/EC of the European Parliament and of the Council of 21 April 2004 on takeover bids (Official Journal of the EU L 142/12).

[39] Directive 2004/109/EC of the European Parliament and of the Council of 15 December 2004 on the harmonisation of transparency requirements in relation to information about issuers whose securities are admitted to trading on a regulated market and amending Directive 2001/34/EC (Official Journal of the EU L 390/38).

obligations[40]. The aforementioned statutory provision, moreover, raises doubts about whether acting in concert also includes one-off arrangements between minority shareholders before or during a general meeting regarding concerted voting on specific items on the meeting agenda. According to the prevailing and accurate view of Polish legal commentators, this statutory provision covers only shareholder agreements that constitute the basis for the long-term, coordinated exercise of corporate influence by their participants over a company through concerted voting at several general meetings[41]. This opinion is also in line with the stewardship code mentioned above. As a result, agreed-upon voting of institutional investors on such ESG issues as organisational matters (e.g., focusing the remuneration policy on achieving ESG objectives, appointing a specialised committee within the board or a "sustainability board member" and tasking her to ESG issues) or the amendment of the company's articles of association for extending the company's purpose as defined by ESG objectives, should not be regarded as acting in concert therein triggering obligations under Polish capital market law.

III. Engagement policy of institutional investors in law and practice

Article 3g Directive 2007/36/EC[42] concerning the engagement policies of institutional investors and asset managers was implemented almost verbatim into Polish law, i.e., in the Investment Fund Act. Based on the "comply or explain" principle, Polish law requires a fund management company to develop and publish an engagement policy that describes how the involvement of shareholders of investee companies listed on the regulated market is taken into account in the fund's overall investment strategy. The engagement policy should describe the methods of: (1) monitoring investee companies, in particular, in terms of strategy, results and financial and non-financial risks, capital structure, social and environmental impact, and corporate governance; (2) dialogue with investee companies; (3) exercising voting rights and other rights related to the

---

[40] Article 87 sec. 1 No. 5 of the Act of 29 July 2005 on Public Offering, Conditions Governing the Introduction of Financial Instruments to Organized Trading, and Public Companies (Official Journal of 2021, position 1983 as amended).

[41] K. Oplustil and M. Sas, "Działanie w porozumieniu (acting in concert) a wykonywanie uprawnień korporacyjnych w spółkach publicznych" (Acting in concert and exercising corporate rights in listed companies), *Przegląd Prawa Handlowego*, Nr 5/2015, p. 14; M. Mataczyński in: T. Sójka (ed.), *Prawo rynku kapitałowego. Komentarz* (Capital market law. Commentary), Warszawa 2015, p. 482 et seq.

[42] Directive 2007/36/EC of the European Parliament and of the Council of 11 July 2007 on the exercise of certain rights of shareholders in listed companies (OJ L 184, 14.7.2007, p. 17). Articles 3g was added by the Directive 2018/828 (EU) of the European Parliament and of the Council of 17 May 2017 amending Directive 2007/36/EC as regards the encouragement of long-term shareholder engagement (OJ L 140, 6.6.2018, p. 5).

shares of investee companies; (3) cooperation with their other shareholders; (4) communication with other shareholders and members of the bodies of these companies; (5) managing actual and potential conflicts of interest in relation to the fund's involvement. In addition, the fund management company should produce and publish an engagement policy report on an annual basis, which includes, in particular, a general description of how that company votes at investee companies' meetings. If the fund management company decides not to develop or publish an engagement policy or an annual report on its implementation, it must issue an explanation of the reasons accordingly. All disclosures related to the engagement policy should be made on the fund management company's website (Articles 46d–46e Investment Fund Act).

As revealed by a review of the engagement policies published by some leading Polish fund management companies, they strive to participate in general meetings of portfolio companies only if the total share of all funds and portfolios managed by them amounts to more than 5% of votes. This corresponds to the provision of the stewardship code mentioned above. Asset managers declare participation in the general meeting of a portfolio company in which they hold less than 5% of votes only if, in their opinion, the agenda of the meeting covers important matters of the portfolio company, and failure to exercise voting rights could increase the risk of a significant reduction in the value of shares held[43]. Moreover, in their engagement policies, fund management companies emphasise that "responsible business conduct requires respecting the rights of all stakeholders, as well as taking into account non-financial aspects of this activity, including social and environmental impact", and adopting "this type of comprehensive prospects by the competent bodies of portfolio companies, contributes to long-term value growth and is in the interest of all shareholders and clients of the funds." Polish asset management firms generally declare that by choosing the method of voting at the general meetings of issuers being the subject of the investments, they will try to, inter alia, follow the rules relating to environmental issues, social responsibility, and corporate governance[44].

Some asset managers refer directly to the concept of ESG in their engagement policies, indicating that in the fundamental analysis of portfolio companies, they take into account ratings of the latter, including ESG ratings published by reputable rating agencies. If such a rating is unavailable, the analysis has to be based on other information used for the sustainability risk assessment, particularly where available, non-financial information is published by issuers[45]. In some relatively rare cases, the engagement policy defines the tasks of the ESG

[43] E. g., engagement policy or voting policy of funds managed by BNP Paribas TFI S.A.; Generali Investments TFI S.A.; PKO TFI S.A.; Nationale-Nederlanden TFI S.A.; Skarbiec TFi S.A.

[44] Nationale-Nederlanden TFI S.A.; BNP Paribas TFI S.A.

[45] E. g., Skarbiec TFi S.A., PKO TFI S.A.

committee operating within the organisational structure of the asset manager responsible for sustainable investments, and following the guidelines of the entire international group, including the Polish fund management company which is a part of it[46].

D. Sustainable Funding / Portfolio Governance

I. Disclosure obligations

The Polish regulatory landscape regarding sustainable funding and portfolio governance consists of two fundamental EU legal acts, i. e., the Regulation (EU) 2019/2088 of the European Parliament and of the Council of 27 November 2019 on sustainability-related disclosures in the financial services sector ("SFDR") and the SRD II.

Article 3h Directive 2007/36/EC, which pertains to the institutional investors' investment strategies, was implemented through the legal acts regulating the types of Polish entities that fall under the definition of an institutional investor. Pursuant to art. 142c sec. 1 of the Act on the organisation and administration of pension funds[47] ("Pension Fund Act"), pension funds are obliged to disclose how the main elements of their equity investment strategy are consistent with the profile and duration of their liabilities, in particular, long-term liabilities, and how they contribute to the medium to long-term performance of their assets. If a fund manager invests on behalf of the pension fund – whether on a discretionary client-by-client basis or through a collective investment undertaking – the pension fund must publicly disclose the terms of this arrangement (Art. 142c sec. 2 Pension Fund Act). The information must, furthermore, specifically include a description of (a) how the arrangement with the fund manager incentivises the asset manager to align its investment strategy and decisions with the profile and duration of the liabilities of the pension fund, and especially, long-term liabilities; (b) how that arrangement incentivises the fund manager to make investment decisions based on assessments of medium to long-term financial and non-financial performance of the investee company and to engage with investee companies on improving their performance in the medium to long-term; (c) how the method and time horizon of the evaluation of the fund manager's performance and the remuneration for asset management services are in line with the profile and duration of the liabilities of the pension fund, especially long-term liabilities, as well as how they take absolute long-term performance into account; (d) how the pension fund monitors portfolio turnover costs incurred by the fund manager

[46] E. g., Generali Investments TFI S. A.

[47] Act of 28 August 1997 on the Organization and Operation of Pension Funds (Official Journal of 2020, position 105 as amended).

and how it defines and monitors a targeted portfolio turnover or turnover range; (e) the duration of the arrangement with the fund manager (Art. 142c sec. 3 Pension Fund Act). If the required information is not provided, the pension fund must explain and justify the reasons accordingly (Art. 142c sec. 4 Pension Fund Act). Disclosure should be made free of charge via the pension fund's website and – in the event of significant change – be updated annually (Art. 142c sec. 5 Pension Fund Act). An analogous implementation of art. 3h Directive 2007/36/EC concerning insurance and reinsurance companies has been accomplished through the Art. 222b–222c Act on insurance and reinsurance activity[48].

The corresponding fund managers' transparency obligations towards the institutional investors as regulated in art. 3i Directive 2007/36/EC were transposed into Polish law through Art. 46f Investment Fund Act. According to Art. 46f sec. 1 Investment Fund Act, fund managers are supposed to inform institutional investors on an annual basis about how their investment strategy and its implementation comply with their arrangement with the institutional investor as well as how it contributes to the medium to long-term performance of the assets of the institutional investor. The information referred to should, in particular, include a description of (i) significant medium and long-term risk factors associated with investments; (ii) the structure of the portfolio, how the portfolio is managed, and the costs of such management; (iii) how the proxy advisor referred to in Article 4 § 1 item 16 of the Commercial Companies Code is used; (iv) any conflicts of interest that have arisen in connection with engagement activities, and how they have been resolved; (v) whether, and how, the company makes investment decisions based on an assessment of the medium and long-term performance of the company in whose shares – submitted for trading on a regulated market – investments have been made (Art. 46f sec. 1 Investment Fund Act).

As reflected above, the Polish lawmaker has pursued the SRD II's path of minimum harmonisation[49] and transposed the SRD II into Polish law in strict accordance with the directive's wording. The disclosure obligations regarding investment strategies derived from the SRD II framework are consequently only marginally tapping into the pool of ESG aspects. Sustainable portfolio governance is promoted only to the extent to which a disclosure obligation towards a restricted category of investors (i. e., institutional investors) can be presumed to be an effective tool for promoting the medium and long-term performance of assets. Meanwhile, the EU legislator claims (see recital 19 of SRD II) that such a medium to long-term approach will constitute a key enabler of responsible stewardship of assets. However, both the substance of this claim and the choice of

[48] Act of 11 September 2015 on insurance and reinsurance activity (Official Journal of 2021, position 1130 as amended).

[49] D. Katelouzou and K. Sergakis, "When Harmonization is not enough: Shareholder Stewardship in the European Union", *European Business Organization Law Review* (2021) 22, p. 220.

basing the regulatory approach on a disclosure regime remain highly debatable. A review of the Polish market practice regarding the discussed disclosure regime, moreover, reveals perfunctory compliance on the part of the respective parties. The box-checking style of drafting the required information can hardly serve any informational purpose, and it seems shortsighted to assume that such information is actually able to promote institutional investors' stewardship and steer them away from short-term strategies.

The highly contestable actual influence of the SRD II-based regulation on the integration of ESG aspects into portfolio management is addressed and supplemented by the SFDR regime. Importantly, due to the broad definition of a financial market participant in art. 2 sec. 1 SFDR, the scope of application of the latter is broader and therefore partially overlaps with the former. As recital 24 SFDR confirms, according to EU lawmakers the pre-SFDR disclosure requirements set out in EU law did not require the disclosure of all the information necessary for properly informing end investors about the sustainability-related impact of their investments in financial products with environmental or social characteristics or financial products which pursue sustainability objectives. Consequently, the directly applicable SFDR delivers a set of specific and standardised sustainability-related disclosure requirements and thus introduce ESG-aspects as a new important factor of portfolio governance across EU jurisdictions. The EU's legislator's primary intention was as a disclosure framework, which was supposed to construct different informational obligations applicable to various degrees of sustainability-related ambitions. In that vein, the SFDR distinguishes between the requirements for financial products which promote environmental or social characteristics and those for financial products which feature a positive impact on the environment and society as an objective. As a result, the SFDR has developed a strong "labelling function"[50] and is being used as a product classification system[51]. Based on the different scopes of disclosure obligations regulated in the respective provisions of the SFDR, funds are commonly divided into (i) "Art. 6 funds" which do not subject their investment strategies to sustainability ambitions but ought to satisfy the disclosure requirements of art. 6 SFDR, (ii) "Art. 8 funds" which promote, among other things, environmental or social characteristics, or a combination of those characteristics and (iii) "Art. 9 funds" who identify sustainable investment as their objective.

As empirical data on SFDR reporting reveals, the management of Article 8 and Article 9 funds (hereinafter "ESG funds") is very unevenly spread across the EU. At the end of Q1 2021, 75 % of Article 8 funds were managed in only three Eu-

[50] EFAMA, *Asset Management in Europe 2021*, https://www.efama.org/newsroom/news/asset-management-report-2021 (24 October 2023), p. 20.

[51] EUROSIF, *EU Sustainable Finance & SFDR: making the framework fit for purpose Eurosif Policy Recommendations for Article 8 & 9 product labels*, June 2022, https://www.eurosif.org/news/eurosif-report-2022/ (24 October 2023), p. 3.

ropean countries: France (36 %), Sweden (22 %), and the Netherlands (17 %)[52]. Polish financial market participants subject to SFDR reporting manage only a fraction of the 0.3 % of Article 8 funds[53]. The management of Article 9 funds is even more concentrated, with more than 80 % being managed in France and the Netherlands[54]. As of 31st March 2022, 31.5 % of funds available for sale in the EU were classified as either Article 8 funds (27.9 %) or Article 9 funds (3.6 %)[55]. In terms of assets, the two fund groups account for an even larger share at 45.6 % of assets[56]. Their monetary value amounts to EUR 4.18 trillion[57]. Polish financial market participants subject to SFDR reporting manage less than 0.3 % of Article 8 and Article 9 funds[58]. Data regarding the Polish market shows that the share of ESG funds in the overall value of AUM amounts to slightly more than 1 %[59]. Such a share is generated by 28 ESG funds operating on the Polish market[60].

The Polish Financial Supervision Authority has focused its dedicated sustainable finance website almost exclusively to clarifications on the application of the SFDR[61], including a detailed Q&A section[62]. This suggests the Authority's perception of the regulatory burden which the SFDR creates for its supervised entities.

II. Conflicting strategies

The SFDR regulatory framework was envisaged by the EU legislator as a tool for addressing the "catastrophic and unpredictable consequences of climate change, resource depletion and other sustainability-related issues" by the mobilisation of necessary capital through the financial services sector (see recital 8 SFDR).

---

[52] EFAMA, *Asset Management in Europe 2021*, https://www.efama.org/newsroom/news/asset-management-report-2021 (24 October 2023), p. 21.

[53] *Ibidem*, p. 21.

[54] *Ibidem*, p. 19.

[55] EUROSIF, *EU Sustainable Finance & SFDR: making the framework fit for purpose Eurosif Policy Recommendations for Article 8 & 9 product labels*, June 2022, https://www.eurosif.org/news/eurosif-report-2022/ (24 October 2023), p. 6.

[56] *Ibidem*, p. 6.

[57] *Ibidem*, p. 6.

[58] EFAMA, *Asset Management in Europe 2021*, https://www.efama.org/newsroom/news/asset-management-report-2021 (24 October 2023), p. 3.

[59] See https://www.analizy.pl/raporty/27784/aktywa-funduszy-inwestycyjnych-czerwiec-2021#:~:text=Dzi%C4%99ki%20nap%C5%82ywom%20i%20efektom%20zarz%C4%85dzania,udanym%20miesi%C4%85cem%20na%20rynkach%20kapita%C5%82owych (24 October 2023); https://www.analizy.pl/tylko-u-nas/27824/coraz-wiecej-funduszy-esg (24 October 2023)

[60] See https://www.analizy.pl/fundusze-inwestycyjne-otwarte/notowania?&jednPodst=1&isEsgPolicy=1&page=1&sortDir=asc&sortCol=nazwa&#fundOpenRatings (24 October 2023).

[61] KNF, *Finansowanie zrównoważonego rozwoju*, https://www.knf.gov.pl/dla_rynku/Finansowanie_zrownowazonego_rozwoju (24 October 2023).

[62] KNF, *Pytania i odpowiedzi (Q&A) – SFDR*, https://www.knf.gov.pl/dla_rynku/Finansowanie_zrownowazonego_rozwoju/Q&A (24 October 2023).

The financial market participants' and financial advisers' disclosure obligations regarding their approaches to the integration of sustainability risks and the consideration of adverse sustainability impacts were consequently intended to facilitate ESG-supportive investors' decisions to allocate their capital in a suitable manner. The abovementioned consequential labelling of ESG funds signals a new "style" in portfolio governance as such. In fact, alongside the integration of ESG criteria into portfolio governance of ESG funds, a novel principle of financial regulatory law came into being. However, this principle was hardly born in a regulatory vacuum. In the case of Poland, the "traditional" principles of quantitative risk diversification and qualitative risk diversification constitute pivotal axioms of portfolio governance and are strongly embedded in the financial regulatory framework. For ESG funds, the principle of sustainable portfolio governance is therefore going to coexist with these other principles of portfolio governance. In many instances, such concurrence may be of a harmonious nature; nonetheless, the incompatibility of portfolio management principles cannot be excluded.

Despite having paved the way for the emergence of the principle of sustainable portfolio governance, the EU legislator has not provided any roadmap as to how its clash with other principles should be dealt with. In particular, no regulatory guidance has been given as to what priority should be assigned to the respective form of portfolio governance. Hypothetically speaking, supervisory authorities could take action to clarify the anticipated handling of a case of clashing strategies. In Poland, the Financial Supervision Authority has not issued any recommendations or statements on the subject so far. In light of the discussed marginal market share of ESG funds in Poland, the market supervisor's passivity in addressing the raised issue is understandable.

In addition, the comparably underdeveloped state of sustainable portfolio governance in Poland may be responsible for igniting a conflicting relationship between ESG interests and client interests in portfolio governance. The traditional fund managers' contractual obligation to serve their clients' (investors') interests through maximising returns may not coincide with a sustainability-driven strategy toward the individual portfolio companies. The very nature of these strategies allows for and even insists on the acceptance of economic disadvantages for the sake of "the greater good". This collision has not been addressed by the Polish legislator so far, and neither has the Financial Supervision Authority issued any clarifying recommendations or statements. What's more, current market practice has not revealed any specific remedy for the emerging conflict in the contracts concluded between funds and their clients. As argued before, the fact that ESG strategies have not yet significantly materialised in the vast majority of funds' practices serves to explain why the potential conflict between ESG interests and client interests in portfolio governance has not been identified as problematic by either the Polish legislator, the supervision authority or market practice.

According to the above, in Poland, the practical significance of a collision between traditional, long-standing financial regulatory principles and the newly surfacing principles that accompany ESG-driven strategies of portfolio governance is currently very low. Since these ESG-driven strategies remain nascent and ESG funds constitute a minuscule market fraction, one should expect that portfolio governance in Poland has not yet undergone a sustainability revolution as such.

E. Sustainable Trading / Product Governance

I. The 'supply problem' of the new MIFID-ESG regime

As postulated in the Action Plan "Financing Sustainable Growth"[63] and the impact assessment underpinning subsequent legislative initiatives published in May 2018[64], the EU's legal framework currently calls for sustainability factors to be taken into account by investment firms as part of their duties towards clients and potential clients. The integration of sustainability aspects into the suitability assessment and product governance obligations under MIFID II was carried out through the adoption of Commission Delegated Regulation (EU) 2021/1253 of 21 April 2021 amending Delegated Regulation (EU) 2017/565 as regards the integration of sustainability factors, risks and preferences into certain organisational requirements and operating conditions for investment firms ("MIFID ESG Regulation") and (ii) Commission Delegated Directive (EU) 2021/1269 of 21 April 2021 amending Delegated Directive (EU) 2017/593 as regards the integration of sustainability factors into the product governance obligations ("MIFID ESG Directive"). Consequently, the EU's sustainability-promoting policy approach has clearly paved its way into the distributional aspects of securities trading. The previous MIFID II regime provided that when an investment firm offers investment advice or portfolio management services to a client, it is first required to obtain information on (among other things) the client's investment objectives (i.e. financial objectives) and the client's risk tolerances in order to be able to recommend suitable investments. Under the MiFID ESG Regulation, it will also be mandatory to obtain information and assess investment suitability on the basis of a third element, that is, the client's sustainability preferences. The MiFID ESG Regulation outlines three categories of sustainability preferences, and investors will be asked if they want their investment to have one or more of these features and, if so, how much of each. Based on these preferences relating to sustainability, distributors will then have to deliver their investment recommendations accordingly. Moreover, under the MIFID ESG Directive, investment

[63] COM(2018) 97 final.
[64] SWD(2018) 264 final.

firms that are in the scope of MIFID II product manufacturer obligations will need to consider the sustainability-related objectives of clients when identifying a target market for the financial product.

In the case of Poland, the application of the new ESG-driven distribution regime might prove to be troublesome for investment firms. As underlined before, sustainable portfolio governance is still in a nascent stage in Poland, and ESG funds constitute a marginal market share. Because of a weak "supply-side" in terms of products that could suit investors' sustainability preferences, investment firms might face the problem of not being able to issue suitable recommendations. In particular, matching financial products to what could be highly aspirational preferences could be quite a challenge. This raises the important question of whether in such a case, the investor could modify the sustainability preferences declared in their suitability assessment.

II. The role of the trading venue: WSE's ESG initiatives

1. Best Practices for Listed Companies 2021

Recently, the activity of the WSE and its governing bodies has been visible, encouraging companies listed on it to include ESG matters in their strategy and reporting. These activities are in line with the declared goal of the WSE which is "to play key role in promoting responsible investment and ESG integration across the Polish and Central & Eastern Europe capital markets."[65]

In March 2021, the Supervisory Board of the WSE approved the new version of the code of corporate governance for issuers of shares listed on the WSE Main Market, "The Best Practice for WSE Listed Companies 2021"[66]. Soft Rules of the code are subject to the comply-or-explain principle anchored in the Listing Rules of the WSE[67]. For the first time in the history of the code, which dates back to 2002, its authors (i.e. experts grouped in the WSE Corporate Governance Committee) decided to explicitly address ESG matters. The Code provides that listed companies should integrate ESG factors in their business strategy, including, in particular, environmental factors, such as measures and risks relating to climate change and sustainable development, and social and employee factors, including, among others, actions taken and planned to ensure equal treatment of women and men, decent working conditions, respect for employees' rights, dialogue with local communities, customer relations (point 1.3. of the Code). ESG information to be published on the company's website should, among other things:

---

[65] GPW/EBRD, *ESG Reporting Guidelines. Guide for issuers*, May 2021, p. 3.
[66] See: https://www.gpw.pl/dobre-praktyki2021 (24 October 2023).
[67] https://www.gpw.pl/regulacje-prawne (24 October 2023).

– explain how the decision-making processes of the company and other members of its corporate group integrate climate change, including the resulting risks,

– present the equal pay index for employees, defined as the percentage difference between the average monthly pay (including bonuses, awards and other benefits) of women and men in the last year, and present information about actions taken to eliminate any pay gaps, including a presentation of related risks and the time horizon of the equality target (point 1.3. of the Code).

Although the cited regulations constitute soft law, their practical impact should not be underestimated as a tool for encouraging management and supervisory boards of listed companies to operationalise the issue of sustainability. A listed company should adopt an internal framework for managing ESG issues at strategic and operational levels, as well as disclose relevant information to shareholders and other interested parties. The above-mentioned provisions of the corporate governance code can be regarded as the first important step toward recognising ESG as part of the board's managerial and monitoring mission. Consequently, it may lead to the conclusion that board members who completely ignore ESG issues in the overall business strategy and planning are ultimately violating their statutory obligations towards the company, including, in particular, their duty of care[68].

2. ESG Reporting Guidelines

Another sign of the WSE's ESG-related initiatives is the document titled "ESG Reporting Guidelines. Guide for issuers" of May 2021. It aims "to contribute to better, more consistent, comparable and reliable sustainability reporting in a way that meets local and global market needs." Importantly, the guidelines go beyond reporting and also provide detailed guidance on managing sustainability and embedding ESG in the corporate organisation and business model. On a macro-level, the guidelines are intended to strengthen the Polish capital markets and the business community from a global perspective as well as raise the investment attractiveness of the WSE-listed companies.

3. The WIG-ESG index

An eye-catching initiative that falls under the WSE's ESG initiatives is the WIG-ESG index. Following similar trends around the globe[69], as of 3 September

[68] See A. Weber-Elżanowska, "Sustainability vs. Corporate Purpose: Will transforming values shift the paradigm?" *Journal for International and European Law, Economics and Market Integrations*, Vol. 7 No. 2, 2020, p. 62 "[...] directors must consider sustainability issues in structuring their decisions and the resulting corporate conduct, as they will be subject to verification through the lens of a renewed set of values [...]."

[69] E. g., MSCI USA Extended ESG Focus Index, Nasdaq-100 ESG Index, S&P 500 ESG Index.

2019, the WSE publishes this sustainability-linked index. Although the precise architecture of ESG indices may vary, as a rule, an ESG index features companies that adopt ESG ambitions. Consequently, companies typically need to meet eligibility requirements to be included in an ESG index[70]. Alternatively, there may be certain (negative) criteria inscribed into the index's methodology that bar the inclusion of companies into an ESG index (also known as exclusionary screening)[71]. The signalling function of those indexes toward investors strongly relies on a semi-certifying effect that stems from the inclusion of a company into the index[72]. Such an inclusion in an ESG index is supposed to help ESG-sensitive investors to discern their desired investment options. ESG indices thus play a key role in transforming "raw" ESG disclosure information into "digestible" investment guidance[73]. Based on ESG indices, sustainability performance becomes actionable to investors[74]. In particular, ESG indices are increasingly serving as a basis for passive investment strategies that use derivative instruments tracking a particular index[75]. ESG indexes also play an important role in the companies themselves as they enable benchmarking of their performance to peers[76]. In addition, the general media (public) may, to some extent, assess a company's sustainability performance based on ESG indexing[77].

According to a very short summary of the WIG-ESG's characteristics published on the official website of the WSE's index provider 'GPW Benchmark', the WIG-ESG calculation is "based on the value of portfolio of companies recognized as socially responsible, i.e. those that comply with the principles of socially responsible business, in particular in the field of environmental, social, economic and corporate governance issues"[78]. This statement suggests that the index features companies whose operations and strategies align – to an unspecified extent – with a sustainability commitment. Only a thorough examination of the underlying documentation may enable any manner of understanding the index's methodology as such.

---

[70] M. Pagano, T. Yang, and G. Sinclair, "Understanding ESG Ratings and ESG Indexes" in: S. Boubaker, S. Cumming, and D. K. Nguyen (eds.), *Research Handbook of Finance and Sustainability*, Edward Elgar 2018, p. 342.

[71] *Ibidem*, p. 357.

[72] *Ibidem*, p. 342.

[73] R. Boffo and R. Patalano (2020), *ESG Investing: Practices, Progress and Challenges*, OECD Paris, https://www.oecd.org/finance/ESG-Investing-Practices-Progress-Challenges.pdf (24 October 2023), p. 21.

[74] M. Pagano, T. Yang, and G. Sinclair, "Understanding ESG Ratings and ESG Indexes" in: S. Boubaker, S. Cumming, and D. K. Nguyen (eds.), *Research Handbook of Finance and Sustainability*, Edward Elgar 2018, p. 339.

[75] *Ibidem*, p. 342.

[76] *Ibidem*, p. 342.

[77] *Ibidem*, p. 342.

[78] https://gpwbenchmark.pl/en-karta-indeksu?isin=PL9999998955 (24 October 2023).

The rules for the WIG-ESG's functioning have been included in the Rules of the GPW Indices Family, adopted by Resolution No. 59/2020 of the GPW Benchmark S. A. Management Board of 17 August 2020[79] ("Index Rules"). According to sec. 8.1.1. of the Index Rules, "The objective of the Index is to measure the value of a portfolio of the Listed Companies classified for the WIG20 and mWIG40 Indices, verified using an adjustment factor, i. e., assessment of the degree of compliance with the environmental, social, economic and corporate governance principles (ESG – Environmental, Social, Governance)". The classification rules are further clarified in sec. 8.2.1. of the Index Rules, which states that "WIG-ESG Index Participants are Companies listed on the GPW regulated market, which are the Participants in WIG20 and mWIG40, as at the end of January, April, July, and October of a given year". The weighting of individual Participants in the WIG-ESG Index portfolio is determined based on a ranking system described in Section 8.3. (sec. 8.2.2. Index Rules). An ESG ranking of the companies included in the WIG-ESG is developed based on the results of ESG analyses and data contained in ESG Risk Rating Reports developed by the independent research agency Sustainalytics B. V. with a registered seat in the Netherlands ("ESG Ranking"). The rules for creating ESG Risk Rating Reports are set by Sustainalytics B. V. and available on its website (sec. 8.3.1. Index Rules). According to sec. 8.3.3. of the Index Rules, the Companies included in the WIG-ESG can obtain a score from 0 to 100 points in the ESG Ranking, where the lower the score awarded, the better the company is viewed as complying with the environmental, social, and corporate governance principles. The ranking according to compliance with the corporate governance rules set out in the document "Best Practice for GPW Listed Companies 2021" ("Best Practice Ranking") is based on the information from the companies prepared under § 29(3) of the Warsaw Stock Exchange Rules and declarations on the application of corporate governance principles included in their annual reports (sec. 8.3.10 Index Rules). The ESG Ranking and the Best Practice Ranking allow determining a company's weighting in the WIG-ESG index portfolio according to the method described in sec. 8.4. of the Index Rules.

Against the backdrop of the aforementioned functions and commonalities of ESG indexes that are calculated and published around the world, and in light of the summary of the WIG-ESG purpose on the WSE's website, the index methodology described is perplexing. Most importantly, according to the above, the list of companies featured in the WIG-ESG is a mere copy-paste of the companies featured in the WIG-20 and WIG-40. This means that the list of companies included in the WIG-ESG is, in fact, derived based on the criterion of market capitalisation. In other words, the inclusion in the WIG-ESG is not linked to any

[79] See: https://gpwbenchmark.pl/pub/BENCHMARK/files/indeksy-gieldowe-regulacje/en/Rules_GPWIndices_1.04.22.pdf (24 October 2023).

sustainability-related criterion. Only secondarily to such ESG-detached selection does the ESG ranking bring a sustainability component into play. However, the sustainability assessment delivered by an external provider, as well as the vaguely sustainability-related Best Practice Ranking, are only deployed as a tool for assigning weights to specific companies within the index portfolio. In particular, no rules in place would allow the exclusion of a company featured in the WIG-ESG if such companies' sustainability performance was poor. Consequently, the above-cited summary of the index purpose from the WSE website is plainly misleading.

We can thus conclude that the overall operating principles of the WIG-ESG presented result in puzzling outcomes which seem to violate the essential functions of ESG indices. This is best explained when glancing at the companies featured in the index. For example, within the WIG-ESG, we can find the company, JSW S.A., which declares on its website: "The JSW Group is the largest producer of high-quality hard coking coal in the European Union and one of the leading producers of coke used for smelting steel"[80]. Another interesting example is the company ENEA S.A. which states that "Nearly 8 % of the energy produced in the country comes from our power plants, and Enea Production SA in Kozienice is the country's largest coal-based producer of electricity".[81] No detailed sustainability check needs to be performed to determine that such companies should not be featured in any ESG index. It follows then, that the WIG-ESG's underlying methodology is clearly in violation of an ESG index's intrinsic functions. Under the WIG-ESG's 'disguising effects', capital may be channelled towards companies whose operating activities are very far from positively impacting the aspired sustainability transformation. As a result, instead of being a helpful tool for investors in identifying sustainability-friendly investments, the WIG-ESG constitutes a powerful greenwashing instrument. As ESG indices are increasingly being utilised by ESG funds and ETFs in shaping their strategies, the WIG-ESG's greenwashing capacities could actually be spread out along the investment intermediation chain accordingly[82].

Moreover, in its current mode of functioning, the WIG-ESG is patently incompatible with the WSE's ESG strategy (see sec. E.II.) and its avowals regarding the support of Agenda 2030's Sustainable Development Goals[83]. In particular, the declaration of supporting the transition to a low-carbon economy by developing environmentally sustainable solutions in the WSE's portfolio of services

[80] https://www.jsw.pl/en/about-us/about-jsw (24 October 2023).

[81] https://www.enea.pl/en/history-group (24 October 2023).

[82] R. Boffo and R. Patalano (2020), *ESG Investing: Practices, Progress and Challenges*, OECD Paris, https://www.oecd.org/finance/ESG-Investing-Practices-Progress-Challenges.pdf (24 October 2023), p. 19.

[83] See: "Strategia ESG GK GPW 2025 na lata 2022 -2025", https://www.gpw.pl/pub/GPW/ESG/Startegia_ESG_Grupy_Kapitalowej_GPW.pdf (24 October 2023), p. 3.

and products[84] is being gravely undermined by the WIG-ESG. Furthermore, in terms of the heated academic debate regarding the performance of ESG versus conventional indices[85], caution is warranted, as the performance of the WIG-ESG cannot be used as a viable source of information as regards ESG indices, as it does not fulfil any basic requirements which would allow differentiation from conventional indices as such.

III. Green bonds

Poland pioneered sovereign green bond[86] issuances in the world in 2016[87]. Its proceeds financed and refinanced projects that promoted the transition to a low carbon economy and, in particular, contributed to Poland's progress in meeting its greenhouse gas emission (GHG) reduction targets. A pre-issue demand of EUR 1.5 billion (from 91 accounts) allowed Poland's Ministry of Finance to increase the size of the issue from a mooted EUR 500 to EUR 750 million, which ultimately confirms a high market demand.

What seemed to be a promising signal for both public (sovereign and communal) and private issues that could help Poland bridge the financing gap regarding the pressing infrastructural investments that would enable the progress of de-carbonization of the economy and the interconnected energy transition, has not, however, developed into a significant market for green bonds[88]. According to data for 2020, green bond issuances are dominated by countries in Western and Northern Europe[89]. The leaders are issuers registered in France, Germany, the Netherlands, and Sweden, accounting for over 70 % of the volume of all green issuances[90]. At the same time, the ten countries in which – in terms

---

[84] See: "Strategia ESG GK GPW 2025 na lata 2022 -2025", https://www.gpw.pl/pub/GPW/ESG/Startegia_ESG_Grupy_Kapitalowej_GPW.pdf (24 October 2023), p. 5.

[85] See a comprehensive review of the relevant literature by G. M. Caporale, L. Gil-Alana, A. Plastun, and I. Makarenko, *Persistence in ESG and conventional stock market indices, Journal of Economics and Finance* 2022, 1–16 (Open Access).

[86] On the topic of green bonds see in particular: M. Ferreira, "The New ESG Bond Markets" in: P. Câmara and F. Morais (eds.), *The Palgrave Handbook of ESG and Corporate Governance,* Palgrave Macmillan 2022, p. 149–166; S. K. Park, "Green Bonds and Beyond. Debt financing as a Sustainability Driver" in: B. Sjåfjell and Ch. M. Bruner (eds.), *Cambridge Handbook of Corporate Law, Corporate Governance and Sustainability*, Cambridge University Press, 2019, p. 596–610; S. K. Park, "Investors as Regulators: Green Bonds and the Governance Challenges of the Sustainable Finance Revolution", 54 Stanford Journal of International Law 2018, p. 1–47.

[87] A. Whiley, *Poland wins race to issue first green sovereign bond. A new era for Polish climate policy?* 15.12.2016, https://www.climatebonds.net/2016/12/poland-wins-race-issue-first-green-sovereign-bond-new-era-polish-climate-policy (24 October 2023).

[88] KPMG, *Perspektywy rozwoju rynku zielonych obligacji w Polsce*, December 2021, https://home.kpmg/pl/pl/home/insights/2021/12/raport-perspektywy-rozwoju-rynku-zielonych-obligacji-w-polsce.html (24 October 2023), p. 24.

[89] *Ibidem*, p. 24.

[90] *Ibidem*, p. 24.

of volume – the most green bonds issuances were recorded, account for about 90 % of the total volume of issuances[91]. Poland is not one of these ten countries.

As of December 2021, there is one issuer of green municipal bonds on the Polish market whose documentation and issuance processes are consistent with market standards – the City of Łódź. The bond is tasked with financing the construction of retention tanks and reconstructing the pavement of one of Lodz's streets. Other issues of "green" municipal bonds currently do not fully meet market-recognised standards. In total, at the end of 2021, ten issuers of green corporate bonds were active in Poland, including seven issuers from the non-financial sector and three financial institutions[92]. These issuances are pursued according to popular international seals and standards with no national initiative on the development of a national labelling system so far in sight.

The CMDS reminisces fondly about Poland's 2016 pioneering sovereign green bond issuance and identifies the analysis of the possibilities of further development of the green bond market as a separate action point[93]. In light of the sobering numbers on actual green bond issuances, the statements that in recent years, "the interest in green bonds has been strongly growing" and that the "Ministry of Finance observes the changes taking place in this market and actively supports its participants" seem inflated[94]. The declaration that the Ministry of Finance considers an issue of green bonds denominated in the Polish zloty, which would be "the next stage in the development of this market"[95] remains fuzzy and has not been translated into action so far. Similarly, the professed analysis of the possibilities for further development of the green bond market in Poland so far remains to be conducted.

[91] *Ibidem*, p. 24.
[92] *Ibidem*, p. 24.
[93] Ministry of Finance, *Capital Market Development Strategy, Appendix to the Resolution No. 114 of the Council of Ministers of 1 October 2019*, https://www.gov.pl/web/finanse/strategia-rozwoju-rynku-kapitalowego (24 October 2023), p. 61.
[94] *Ibidem*, p. 61.
[95] *Ibidem*, p. 61.

Country Report Hungary

Tekla Papp / János Dúl

A. Introduction

Sustainable finance should not be seen as a single compass, but as a set of building blocks that contribute to viewing an investment as green, with the ability to serve the interests of its members. Based on the Commission's communication, "sustainable finance" generally refers to the process of taking due account of environmental and social considerations in investment decision-making, leading to increased investments in longer-term and sustainable activities. More specifically, environmental considerations refer to climate change mitigation and adaptation, as well as the environment more broadly and related risks (e.g. natural disasters).[1]

Dealing with sustainable finance in Hungary involves a range of difficulties. It is at an early stage overall seeing as there is hardly any relevant Hungarian legal literature on the issue, Hungarian law firms do not have experience in the topic, and the detailed rules are sporadic and lacking an overall system.

The Hungarian National Bank (HNB) issued its Green Recommendation in April 2021. The measures proposed in it will increase the resilience of the banking sector to crises and ensure that banks appraise sustainability considerations accordingly. Domestic banks are not yet prepared to deal with sustainability risks, but the HNB's green recommendation will help them prepare for the new international and domestic regulatory changes expected in the green area, said Vice-President Csaba Kandrács at the HNB's online conference.[2] The managers of

[1] Communication from the Commission to the European Parliament, the European Council, the Council, the European Central Bank, the European Economic and Social Committee and the Committee of the Regions. Action Plan: Financing Sustainable Growth. Brussels, 8.3.2018. COM(2018) 97 final, 2; *Zetzsche/Anker-Sørensen*, European Business Organization Law Review 23 (2022), 50 ff; for a European Union outline overview, see: *Nyikos*, Fenntartható finanszírozás és fejlesztés. Stratégia és szabályozás: átállás a fenntartható finanszírozási modellekre, Budapest, 2022. https://mersz.hu/dokumentum/m949ffef__11 (05.09.2023); Green Finance Report. Status Report on the Sustainability of the Hungarian financial system, 81 ff, https://www.mnb.hu/letoltes/20210303-zold-penzugyi-jelentes-angol.pdf (05.09.2023); Sustainable Finance Roadmap 2022–2024, https://www.esma.europa.eu/sites/default/files/library/esma30-379-1051_sustainable_finance_roadmap.pdf (05.09.2023).

[2] https://www.portfolio.hu/bank/20211123/kiabrandito-jelentes-erkezett-a-bankokrol-mar-most-lemaradtak-a-klimavaltozas-elleni-harcban-512244# (05.09.2023).

the banks must have sufficient knowledge and responsibility in the field of green risks, and in addition to the transformation of corporate governance, the banks must have a separate organisational function subordinate to the management body. They should assess the risks through, among other things, sensitivity and scenario analysis and stress testing. In the first step of the document, the credit institution is expected to develop a self-evaluation survey and an action plan to be submitted to the central bank by September 2021.[3]

In order to adapt the thematic of the research group, we followed the main topics received earlier, which include the following: I. Sustainable Ownership and Shareholder Governance, II. Sustainable Funding and Portfolio Governance, III. Sustainable Trading and Product Governance. With respect to the aforementioned reasons, we shared the opinion of adjusting certain subtopics, having the strong belief they would be suitable for the Hungarian legal acts and practice in this way.

B. Sustainable Ownership and Shareholder Governance

I. Legal background of shareholder engagement

The regulation on the identification of shareholders by the company to facilitate the exercise of shareholder rights and direct communication between the company and the shareholder has remained unchanged in Act V of 2013 on Civil Code (hereinafter Hungarian Civil Code, HCC)[4]: the rules for shareholder quality certification[5] and ownership matching[6] have not changed. The implementing act [Act LXVII of 2019 on the encouragement of long-term shareholder engagement (hereinafter ELTSE)] establishes the company's right to identify its shareholders, with reference to the European Commission's Implementing Regulation[7] on the details, and shortly amended the Act CXXXVIII of 2007 on investment enterprises and commodity exchange service providers (hereinafter IECESP) and the Act CXX of 2001 on capital market (hereinafter CMA); these modifications are as follows:

---

[3] Ibid.

[4] We used the translation of Ministry of Justice of Hungary for terminus technicus, therefore in case of the Hungarian Civil Code we use the term "Section" instead of "Article" among others. https://njt.hu/jogszabaly/en/2013-5-00-00 (05.09.2023).

[5] Section 3:254 HCC.

[6] Section 3:248 HCC.

[7] Commission Implementing Regulation (EU) 2018/1212 of 3 September 2018 laying down minimum requirements implementing the provisions of Directive 2007/36/EC of the European Parliament and of the Council as regards shareholder identification, the transmission of information and the facilitation of the exercise of shareholders rights.

– the provision of data by the securities account manager to the public company limited by shares for providing shareholder identification to the public company limited by shares does not constitute a breach of securities secrecy;[8]

– the ownership matching shall be carried out without prejudice to the shareholder identification requirements provided for in a separate legal act for a public company limited by shares.[9]

ELTSE merely repeats the text of EU Directive 2017/828.[10]

Acts	*Personal scope*	*Substantive scope*
Act V of 2013 on Civil Code (HCC)	natural persons, legal persons, organisations lacking legal personality	Section 1:1 [Scope of the Act] This Act governs the property and personal relations of persons (...)
Act LXVII of 2019 on the encouragement of long-term shareholder engagement (ELTSE)	public companies limited by shares institutional investors, asset managers, shareholder representative advisors, companies, institutional investors, asset managers, shareholder representative advisors[11]	shareholder engagement – engagement policy, remuneration policy
Act CXXXVIII of 2007 on investment enterprises and commodity exchange service providers (IECESP)	a person or organisation established in Hungary; a branch of an enterprise established in Hungary; a branch of a foreign enterprise (established in an EEA State or in a third country)	investment service activities, services auxiliary to investment service activities, commodity exchange services, supervision of investment enterprises and commodity exchange service
Act CCXXXVII of 2013 on credit institutions and financial enterprises (CIFE)	credit institution, financial enterprise, supervision authority	financial services, auxiliary financial services and banking activities, voluntary institutional protection, and deposit insurance[12]

[8] Section 120 IECESP.

[9] Section 149 para. (1) CMA.

[10] Directive (EU) 2017/828 of the European Parliament and of the Council of 17 May 2017 amending Directive 2007/36/EC as regards the encouragement of long-term shareholder engagement.

[11] Art. 1 ELTSE.

[12] Art. 1(1) CIFE The provisions of this Act shall apply to:

(a) financial services, ancillary financial services and banking activities, voluntary institutional protection and deposit insurance carried out in the territory of Hungary, as defined in this Act,

b) the supervision of credit institutions and financial enterprises established abroad by credit institutions having their registered office in the territory of Hungary in respect of the activities

Acts	*Personal scope*	*Substantive scope*
Act CXX of 2001 on capital market (CMA)	Hungarian issuer; stock exchange, central securities depository; Investor Protection Fund; investment enterprise, financial institution, institutional investor[13]	placing of a security, public offering of a security, admission of a security; acquisition; supervisory activity of the Hungarian authority[14]

The personal scope and substantive scope of the relevant acts. Edited by János Dúl based on the acts.

As we can see in the Table, there are different approaches in the relevant legal acts concerning their personal scope and substantive scope, which makes them much harder to apply in this area. One must thus be very cautious regarding all the factors at play. The Hungarian legislation on sustainable finance has not been coherently incorporated into the legal system. For example, ELTSE is applicable to public companies limited by shares, institutional investors, and asset managers among others (Art. 1), however, CMA is applicable to Hungarian issuers, excluding the Hungarian State; a publicly traded company incorporated in Hungary or listed on a regulated market in Hungary; stock exchange, central securities depository, central counterparty established in Hungary (Art. 1–1/B). These persons are not all mutually exclusive in all cases. Apart from the statements of the HNB, there is no traceable practice, and the practice of HNB is fragmented and overly Central Bank-focused. Another problem is the relationship of all the acts mentioned: most of them are cogent, except for the Civil Code (see certain rules of legal persons and obligations), hence the deviation cannot be a solution for solving this incoherence; it is even very hard to decide what can be considered as a general act and what as a special act *(lex specialis derogat legi generali)*.[15] The legislator has not made use of the directive's mandate, which was given by the European Union as room for manoeuvre.

II. Engagement policy in service of shareholders and the voting right

The institutional investors and the asset managers are to elaborate an engagement policy, which is part of their investment strategy.[16] The institutional inves-

---

of financial services, ancillary financial services and banking representation as defined in this Act pursuant to point c),

c) the supervisory activities of the Hungarian authority as defined in this Act,

(e) the supervision under this Act of a person carrying out outsourced activities.

[13] Art. 1 CMA.

[14] See ibid.

[15] *Papp/Dúl,* "Sustainable finance: The relating actual Hungarian legislation in EU frame", Zbornik Radova Pravnog Fakulteta u Novom Sadu 4 (2022), 1145-1170.

[16] Section 9 (1) ELTSE.

tors and the asset managers shall disclose their engagement policy annually and publicly, including, among other things, a general description of their voting behaviour and an explanation of the most significant votes.[17] They shall publicly disclose how they have cast votes in the general meetings of companies in which they hold/own shares, excluding such votes on the subject matter in proportion to company ownership.[18] Institutional investors and asset managers shall develop an engagement policy that describes how to incorporate shareholder participation into their investment strategy; the engagement policy shall include – among other things – how they engage in a dialogue with the companies involved in the investment.[19] The proxy advisor shall disclose at least the following information on an annual basis in relation to the preparation of its research, advice and voting recommendations in order to provide adequate information to clients on the accuracy and reliability of its activities – among others – whether and to what extent it engages in a dialogue with the companies and stakeholders that are the subject of its research, advice or voting recommendations.[20]

The engagement policy shall contain the mode of exercising of voting rights or other rights connected to shares.[21] The reasoning of Article 9 mentions that the Directive uses the phrase "the relevant stakeholders of the investee companies" twice in the related section. The term "interested parties" has no equivalent in Hungarian law, but it can be clearly established based on international and EU case law that there are four main categories of interested parties: investors, employees (employees and their representative bodies), creditors and suppliers. However, the concept of "stakeholder" or "relevant stakeholder" cannot be defined in a taxonomy, since, in practice, companies have a specific group of subjects which are economically linked to them and are therefore directly or even indirectly involved in the company's activities. Hence, for example, in the case of a company that may also be a polluter, such a stakeholder could be the local community of residents. The institutional investor should, in the engagement policy of the company, describe the persons whose interests are significantly affected by the activities of the company and how it will communicate with them.

If the asset manager fulfils the engagement policy in the name of the institutional investor, including voting, then the institutional investor shall give the place of public disclosure related to voting information.[22]

If the institutional investor or the asset manager decides not to go through the aforementioned provisions fully or partly, then they are obliged to give an

[17] Section 10 (1) ELTSE.
[18] Section 10 (1) ELTSE.
[19] Section 9 (1), (2) b) ELTSE.
[20] Section 15 (1) f) ELTSE.
[21] Section 9 (2) c) ELTSE.
[22] Section 10 (3) ELTSE.

obvious explanation with arguments in reference to the publicly disclosed information on their website[23] (comply-or-explain).

The Hungarian Civil Code regulates the voting rights and the voting in a public company limited by shares. The shares shall grant voting rights in proportion to their nominal value. Furthermore, except for the cases specified in the HCC, provisions of the articles of association attaching extra rights to certain shares shall be null and void.[24] The shareholders shall not exercise their voting rights before they have provided their contributions in cash or in kind.[25] Members may exercise their rights by means of electronic communications instead of personal attendance at the meeting of the supreme body if the instrument of incorporation specifies the electronic communication equipment allowed to be used, as well as the condition and the mode of their use in a manner that ensures the identification of members and their mutual and unrestricted communication.[26] If the articles of association of a public company limited by shares allow for exercising voting rights by mail before the general meeting, the exercise of that right may only be made subject to the establishment of the identity of shareholders.[27] When adopting a resolution, no vote shall be cast by those:

a) who, by the resolution, would be exempted from an obligation or responsibility or would gain certain other kind of advantage to the detriment of the legal person;

b) with whom, according to the resolution, a contract would have to be concluded;

c) against whom, according to the resolution, legal action would have to be brought;

d) whose relative, being neither a member nor a founder of the legal person, has a vested interest in the resolution;

e) who have a relationship based on majority control with an organisation having a vested interest in the resolution;

f) who are personally interested in the resolution.[28]

The holders of voting preference shares may exercise multiple voting rights to the extent specified by the articles of association.[29] The volume of voting rights attached to a single share of a public company limited by shares shall not exceed ten times the voting rights corresponding to the nominal value of the share; any provision of the articles of association to the contrary shall be null and void.[30]

---

[23] Section 11 ELTSE.
[24] Section 3:260 (1) HCC.
[25] Section 3:260 (2) HCC.
[26] Section 3:111 (2) HCC.
[27] Section 3:273 (4) HCC.
[28] Section 3:19 (2) HCC.
[29] Section 3:232 (1) HCC.
[30] Section 3:232 (1) HCC.

In the case of voting preference shares with a veto right, general meetings shall adopt resolutions by a simple majority vote of holders of such shares attending and being in favour of the resolution at hand or, if there is only one voting preference share, resolutions shall only be adopted if supported by the holder of this share.[31]

The investment enterprise shall have a comprehensive, efficient, and sound corporate governance system in place which is commensurate with the nature, scale, and complexity of the risks inherent in the investment services, ancillary services and business model used and the internal control function, including as follows:

(1) its organisational structure is clearly set out in its internal rules;
(2) responsibilities and tasks are separated and clearly defined;
(3) conflicts of interest within the organisation are monitored, prevented and eliminated;
(4) effective procedures are in place to identify, measure, manage, monitor and report on emerging risks;
(5) internal control mechanisms, administrative and accounting procedures are applied in accordance with the law;
(6) the investment enterprise has a gender-neutral remuneration policy and practice that promotes its application in accordance with effective and efficient risk management;
(7) contribution is made to the smooth and efficient operation of the organisation, the maintenance of trust in the institution and the protection of the economic interests and social objectives of the owners and customers in relation to the institution.[32]

The supervision authority, the Hungarian National Bank, is convinced that it is essential for the operation of the listed and long-term successful companies – besides the responsible corporate governance by management – to have the active shareholder involvement/engagement in monitoring and controlling the operation of the company. We're specifically referring to the shareholder – even if in a small part in many instances, but – the owner of the listed company. Today, in addition to the proactive supervisory action, it has therefore become necessary to strengthen corporate ownership control. To that extent, the HNB encourages shareholders to continue monitor issuers' disclosures to the best of their ability, as well as exercise their ownership rights, participate in general meetings, ask questions, find out and exercise their voting rights!"[33]

[31] Section 3:232 (2) HCC.
[32] Section 17 (3) IECESP.
[33] *Barnóczki* (Director of Capital Market and Consumer Protection Enforcement of HNB): Fenntartható(bb)an működő tőzsdei cégeket! (Sustainable listed companies!), 3; https://www.mnb.hu/letoltes/19-07-23-barnoczki-peter-srd-hosszu.pdf (05.09.2023).

The HNB also examines the commitment of bond issuers to sustainable development, therein reducing the so-called "green washing" risk. In the near future, for example, this will be the so-called SBTi (Science Based Target) or similarly explicit emission reduction targets. Where the bonds do not meet the expectations from a green point of view in the future, for example, lies in the environmental impact of the projects below the company level, or where there is a lack of compliance with the green objectives in the issuer's general activities ("Green default"), in which case, the HNB may decide to sell the bonds.[34] In addition, the move by banks to cater to green clientele will also be encouraged by the Hungarian National Banks's green investment capital relief in Hungary. The Taxonomy Regulation is also an important part of domestic financial market incentives, such as the Green Recommendation issued by the HNB[35] or the Budapest Stock Exchange ESG[36] Reporting Guideline.[37]

III. The confirmation of shareholder voting in Hungary

The Implementing Regulation applies a four-step solution for the assurance and verification of the exercise of shareholder rights: identification of the shareholder, confirmation of the right to exercise the shareholder's rights at the general meeting, notification of participation in the general meeting and formalising the confirmation of the casting, recording and counting of the vote.[38] The implementing act (ELTSE) amended the Civil Code only with regard to the provability of the vote, but not in full and with respect to the same voting moment:

– at the request of a shareholder, the board of directors shall confirm to the shareholder, or a person designated by him that the shareholder's vote has been duly *recorded and counted* at the general meeting, unless the necessary information is available to the shareholder;[39]

---

[34] Fenntarthatóság és jegybanki politika – zöld szempontok az MNB monetáris politikai eszköztárában (Sustainability and central banking policy – green aspects of the HNB's monetary policy instrument), 22–23; https://www.mnb.hu/letoltes/zold-eszkoztar-strategia-publikacio-2021-hun-0706-2.pdf (05.09.2023).

[35] 5/2021. (IV. 15.) HNB Recommendation on climate and environmental risks and the integration of environmental sustainability considerations into the activities of credit institutions. Another useful webpage: https://www.mnb.hu/letoltes/zold-jogtar-0104-1.pdf (05.09.2023).

[36] ESG is the abbreviation for "(environmental social governance)".

[37] https://blog.kpmg.hu/2021/06/az-eu-taxonomiarendelet-hattere-es-varhato-jelentesi-kotelezettsegei/ (05.09.2023).

[38] 2018/1212/EU Regulation Section 4 and Schedule 3, Section 5 and Schedule 4, Section 6 and Schedule 5, Section 7 and Schedules 6, 7.

[39] Section 3:273 para. (5) HCC: participation in the general meeting.

– if a vote is taken at a conference general meeting by electronic means, it shall be ensured that the shareholder voting by electronic means receives an electronic confirmation of the *casting* of the vote.[40]

The Hungarian implementing act penalises the failure to confirm the vote (treated as a corporate obligation). In such a case, the shareholder may initiate a judicial review of the resolution passed by the general meeting (even if he or she has consented to the resolution).[41] We do not consider this legislation to be an adequate solution because

– the decision is not illegal here: it does not infringe any law or the memorandum of association;
– here the participation in the decision-making/voting and the vote were not confirmed. In this case, it is not a question of the shareholder not being able to exercise his/her voting rights, but of the fact that the public company limited by shares does not prove that the voting process per shareholder (voting/casting the vote, recording, counting, and confirming) has taken place in accordance with legal regulations. In view of this, and taking into account who is entitled to sue in the judicial review of decisions (a person who has not consented to the adoption of a decision by a vote),[42] and without breaking this clause, we consider it much more appropriate to initiate the judicial oversight proceedings of the court of registration. Judicial oversight proceedings are appropriate if [...] the firm does not comply with the legal provisions concerning its organisation and operation and the provisions of its memorandum of association during its operation.[43]

The Budapest Stock Exchange Corporate Governance Recommendations[44] do not contain any express recommendation or reference to the certificates, nor does the website of the respective Hungarian listed companies [*Magyar Olaj- és Gázipari Nyrt.* (MOL), *OTP Bank Nyrt., Richter Gedeon, Zwack Unicum,* and *Magyar Telekom*].[45]

[40] Section 3:281 para. (3) HCC: conduct of a conference general meeting.
[41] Section 7 para. (3) ELTSE.
[42] Section 3:34 HCC.
[43] Section 74 para. (1) Act V of 2006 on firm disclosure, firm court procedure and winding-up proceeding.
[44] *Neither at 1.2. The convening of a general meeting, 1.3. The holding of a general meeting, nor at 1.4. The other matters concerning the general meeting* https://www.bet.hu/Kibocsatok/Ajanlasok-kibocsatoknak/Felelos-tarsasagiranyitas (05.09.2023).
[45] https://molgroup.info/hu/befektetoi-kapcsolatok/kozgyules; https://www.otpbank.hu/static/portal/sw/file/220311_kgy_hird_027.pdf; https://www.gedeonrichter.com/hu-hu/befektetok/kozgyulesek; https://zwackunicum.hu/hu/befektetoknek/kozgyulesek/ https://www.telekom.hu/rolunk/befektetoknek/befektetoi_kozlemenyek/2022/marcius_10 (05.09.2023).

IV. Proxy advisors

The holders of shares belonging to the same series shall not be discriminated against in connection with the exercise of their shareholder rights.[46] The shareholders shall be entitled to attend, ask for information and make observations and proposals at the general meeting and, if in possession of shares with a voting right, cast their votes.[47] Shareholders shall not exercise their voting rights before they have provided their contributions in cash or in kind.[48]

The shareholders may exercise shareholder rights through representatives, however, neither the executive officers, the supervisory board members, nor the auditor may represent shareholders.[49]

A shareholder may appoint an agent to exercise his shareholder rights, who, after being registered in the shareholder register, shall act in his own name and for the benefit of the shareholder.[50]

Besides private law, we can pinpoint several rules in public law. The securities depository, the depositary, or the central securities depository (CSD) may, based on a written contract with the shareholder as the proxy advisor, exercise the shareholder's rights in his/her own name in favour of the shareholder in relation to the public company limited by shares.[51] The proxy advisor may exercise all the shareholder rights that the shareholder is entitled to exercise. A proxy advisor may exercise shareholder rights only based on shares registered in a securities account held by him/her or deposited with him/her.[52] A proxy advisor may exercise shareholder rights in relation to the company after being entered in the share register as a proxy holder. The entry must specify the number of shares by class of shares on which the rights are based.[53] The proxy advisor must indicate or declare that he/she is not acting as an owner but as shareholder proxy.[54] In matters not regulated by this Act, the provisions of HCC relating to contracts of agency shall apply to the contract between the shareholder and the proxy advisor and to the exercise of shareholder rights by the proxy advisor.[55]

One can mention various obstacles laid out in ELTSE: these are rules in connection with shareholder proxy advisor's transparency and legal status[56] and the

---

[46] Section 3:253 HCC: equality of shareholders.

[47] Section 3:257 HCC: right to attend the general meeting.

[48] Section 3:260 (2) HCC.

[49] Section 3:255 (1) HCC: shareholder representation.

[50] Section 3:256 HCC: shareholder's agent.

[51] Section 151 (1) CMA.

[52] Section 151 (2) CMA.

[53] Section 152 CMA.

[54] Section 153 (1) CMA.

[55] Section 155 (4) CMA. See also: *Auer*, in: Dúl/Lehoczki/Papp/Veress (eds.), Társasági jogi lexikon, 2019, 212.

[56] Section 14–15 ELTSE.

approval of related party transactions[57] (as same in the EU Directive 2017/828). The proxy advisors shall mark – but not disclose – the code of conduct applied by them and report on its application.[58] If the proxy advisors do not apply a code of conduct, they have to provide a clear and reasonable explanation for doing so.[59] If the proxy advisors depart from any recommendation of the code of conduct, they have to declare from which parts they depart. Furthermore, they have to explain the departure, indicating the measures adopted.[60] This information shall be disclosed free of charge on the websites of proxy advisors, and be updated annually.[61]

The proxy advisors have to make these pieces of information publicly available on their websites and free of charge for at least three years from the date of publication.[62]

V. Corporate Social Responsibility (CSR) and shareholder engagement[63]

In companies, "systems of relationships covered by multifactorial networks of interests"[64] appear, and several theoretical approaches have emerged to explore, understand, and explain them.

In addition to the two basic theoretical approaches,[65] an investor model favours the interests of its members (shareholder theory)[66] while a contractual model[67] factors in the interests of those who have an interest in the business relationship with the company (stakeholder theory).[68] Moreover, several theoretical approaches embedded in the amendment of Directive 2007/36/EC on the exercise of certain rights of shareholders in listed companies are specifically designed to encourage long-term shareholder participation.[69]

[57] Sections 14–15, 23–27 ELTSE.

[58] Section 14 (1) ELTSE.

[59] Section 14 (2) ELTSE.

[60] Section 14 (1) ELTSE.

[61] Section 14 (3) ELTSE.

[62] Section 15 (2) ELTSE.

[63] *Papp/Dúl*, "Sustainable finance: The relating actual Hungarian legislation in EU frame", Zbornik Radova Pravnog Fakulteta u Novom Sadu 4 (2022), 1145-1170.

[64] *Kisfaludi*, Társasági jogviták választottbíróság előtt, in: Papp (eds.), Acta Conventus de Iure Civili Tomus X., 2009, 119.

[65] *Bebchuk/Kastiel/Tallarita*, The Business Lawyer, 77 (2022), 1–29; *Fenwick et al.*, ESG as a Business Model for SMEs, ECGI Working Paper Series in Law, May 2022, 3–4. https://papers.ssrn.com/sol3/papers.cfm?abstract_id=4098644 (05.09.2023).

[66] *Friedman*, Capitalism and freedom, 1962.

[67] *Bodzási*, A hosszú távú részvényesi (befektetői) szerepvállalás ösztönzésére irányuló uniós törekvések, Fontes Iuris, 2 (2018), 32–33.

[68] *Freeman*, Strategic management: a stakeholder approach, 1984.

[69] Directive (EU) 2017/828 of the European Parliament and of the Council of 17 May 2017 amending Directive 2007/36/EC as regards the encouragement of long-term shareholder engagement.

Related to investor theory is agency theory, in which it describes the conflicts of interest in the relationship between the principal [member(s) of the company] and the agent (operative body of the company: executive officers, management) and identifies attitudes toward managerial decisions made for running the organisation (member's control, liability of the executive officer, preference for short-term benefits: profit maximisation versus day-to-day management requiring specialised knowledge tailored to growing company size).[70] The long-term benefits of the investor model – stewardship theory – focuses on the priorities arising from the alignment of management's responsible corporate asset management activities with organisational goals (confidence and mutual value building, managerial sense of duty and loyalty).[71]

Related to the contractual model is resource dependence theory, which measures the success of an organisation in terms of its ability to subordinate, coordinate and control its internal and external resources with respect to the overall corporate goal (the role of management qualifications and experience in shaping internal and external organisational environments).[72]

It seems the approach to the relationship systems within the company has become more nuanced and management-oriented accordingly.

In addition to the examination of the diverging, converging and conflicting interests of the companies that arise and are associated with the company, the interests of the company as an entity are also important. The theory and practice based on this is Corporate Social Responsibility (CSR),[73] on the basis of which a company also operates in accordance with ethical standards, meeting the requirements of responsible business and investment.[74] Under the umbrella of CSR,[75] there's[76] corporate governance (CG),[77] sustainable finance, the corporate governance that takes environmental and social aspects into account (ESG:

[70] *Derakshan/Turner/Mancini*, International Journal of Project Management, 37 (2019), 99–100; *Muth/Donaldson*, Scholarly Research and Theory Papers, 1 (1998), 5–6.: managerial control; *Talbot*, Legal Studies Research Paper, 22 (2010), 5.

[71] *Derakshan/Turner/Mancini*, 99–100; *Muth/Donaldson*, 6.: managerial empowerment.

[72] *Derakshan/Turner/Mancini*, 99–100; *Muth/Donaldson*, 6.: co-optation.

[73] *Pacces*, in: Busch/Ferrarini/Grünewald (eds.), Sustainable Finance in Europe, Corporate Governance: Financial Stability and Financial Markets, 2021, 151–174.

[74] *Ferrarini*, in: Busch/Ferrarini/Grünewald (eds.), Sustainable Finance in Europe, Corporate Governance: Financial Stability and Financial Markets, 2021, 99.

[75] *Fleischer*, European Company and Financial Law Review, 2 (2021), 166–167; *Knoll-Csete/Tóth*, Glossa Iuridica, Különszám (2021), 157; *Auer*, Corporate governance. A felelős társaságirányítás jelenkori dimenziói, 2017, 26–27. Ádám Angyal worked on the subject in Hungary as a monograph. See: *Angyal*, Vállalatok társadalmi felelőssége, felelős társaságirányítás. Corporate social responsibility, 2009, 270; *Ventura*, European Business Organization Law Review, 23 (2022), 603–632.

[76] Climate Change and Corporate Governance, 14 ff. https://doi.org/10.1787/272d85c3-en (05.09.2023).

[77] *Auer*, Corporate governance. A felelős társaságirányítás jelenkori dimenziói, 2017, 26.

environmental social governance,[78] RBC: responsible business conduct)[79] and the concept of a higher social purpose that provides social legitimacy and "increasing its value"[80] (CP: corporate purpose),[81] which are all interlinked. There is a need to include the public good / public interest CPs in the memorandum of association that also serve long-term corporate success, to vote (make decisions) based on company reports that also explain their implementation, and to establish dual-purpose companies (public benefit-oriented for-profit organisations: the Italian *società benefit*, the French *société à mission*, the American benefit corporation, the German *GmbH im Verantwortungseigentum*).[82]

CSR is now a global operation that functions in accordance with multi-level sustainability criteria, and includes tools for encouraging long-term shareholder engagement[83] by avoiding inadequate corporate governance and corporate performance resulting from short-term risk-taking.[84] The European Commission's Communication "Action Plan: European Company Law and Corporate Governance – A Modern Legal Framework for Greater Shareholder Involvement and Sustainable Companies",[85] which serves as a starting point for these goals, is rooted in the interpretations detailed in the introduction. Based on the Action Plan, the personal scope of Directive 2017/828/EU on the promotion of long-term shareholder engagement covers listed companies, institutional investors, and asset managers in EU Member States, as well as shareholder representation advisers.[86]

---

[78] *Fenwick et al.*, 7–12; https://elemzeskozpont.hu/esg-befektetesek-mit-jelent-milyen-hozama-lesz-mennyire-jo-az-esg, (05.09.2023); *Nyikos*, https://mersz.hu/dokumentum/m949ffef__12 (05.09.2023).

[79] *Puskás*, Közjogi Szemle, 1 (2021), 38–44.

[80] European Model Company Act, Chapter 1 General Provisions and Principles, Section 1.06 Purpose of Company (1), https://cesifin.it/wp-content/uploads/2018/09/EMCA.pdf (05.09.2023).

[81] *Ferrarini*, in: Busch/Ferrarini/Grünewald (eds.), Sustainable Finance in Europe, Corporate Governance: Financial Stability and Financial Markets, 2021, 100; *Fleischer*, European Company and Financial Law Review, 2 (2021), 161–189; *Mayer*, The Governance of Corporate Purpose, ECGI Working Paper Series in Law. Working Paper, 609 (2021), https://ecgi.global/sites/default/files/working_papers/documents/mayerfinal_1.pdf (05.09.2023).

[82] *Fleischer*, European Company and Financial Law Review, 2 (2021), 182–186; from other aspect: *Ferrarini*, in: Busch/Ferrarini/Grünewald (eds.), Sustainable Finance in Europe, Corporate Governance: Financial Stability and Financial Markets, 2021, 108–118.

[83] *Chiu*, Governing the purpose of investment management: how the 'stewardship' norm is being (re)developed in the UK and EU, ECGI Working Paper Series in Law, August/2021.

[84] 2017/828/EU Directive Preamble (2).

[85] 12 December 2012; COM/2012/0740 final; Document 52012DC0740.

[86] 2017/828/EU Directive Section 1 it. a).

VI. The remuneration policy and report of company directors in Hungary

The Hungarian implementing legislation[87] applies a consultative solution to the remuneration policy and reporting of directors. That is, shareholders could only express their views and in the event of a resolution of the general meeting rejecting the remuneration policy, but the payments must nevertheless be made to the company's directors on the grounds of the rejected remuneration policy. The consultative powers of the general meeting of public companies limited by shares are alien in company law, having German roots as such. First, this implementing act establishes this new type of competence held by the general meeting in Hungarian company law. In our view, with this regulation, the shareholders and the general meeting were given "likelihood" authority. That is, the Hungarian Civil Code regulates that in the event of a significant change in the remuneration policy – but, in any case, at least every four years – it shall be placed on the agenda of the general meeting.[88] The new competence of the supreme body of public company limited by shares spawns continuous dialogue and cooperation between the decision-making and the operating bodies in order for the company either to operate for legitimate and public interest purposes, or else results in the management becoming self-sufficient and the opinion of the general meeting on the remuneration policy not being validated.

The provisions of ELTSE on remuneration reporting shall apply regarding credit institutions and investment enterprises if the Hungarian National Bank – acting in its area of responsibility for the supervision of the financial intermediation system – complies with the prudential requirements for credit institutions and investment enterprises pursuant to Article 450 (1) (j) of Regulation (EU) No 575/2013 of the European Parliament and of the Council of 26 June 2013.[89]

The Budapest Stock Exchange Corporate Governance Recommendations exhibit a passive attitude on this issue, seemingly designed to defer decision-making; reference to some practical experiences on that note will be summarised a few years later.[90] The websites of the respective Hungarian listed companies show a somewhat mixed picture:

---

[87] Section 16 para. (5) ELTSE.

[88] Section 3:268 para. (2) HCC.

[89] Section 22 (2) ELTSE.

[90] 1.5. Remuneration – Repealed: During the 2020 review of the recommendations, the Corporate Governance Committee repealed the recommendations in Chapter 1.5 and Section 1.6.7 on remuneration and amended Sections 1.6.2, 1.6.9 and 2.2.2 points and No. 1. Annex accordingly, having regard to the fact that, from July 2019, the rules on remuneration are laid down in Article LXVII of 2019 on the encouraging of long-term shareholder engagement and the amendment of certain laws for the purpose of legal harmonisation settled these. However, the Committee intends to make explanatory and guidance recommendations to issuers in the future to supplement these legal provisions, but this will require the development of practices related to the new legal provisions. The new recommendations and proposals that will be adopted by the Corporate Governance Committee, which will replace the repealed points, will summarise

– MOL published its detailed remuneration policy,[91]
– *OTP, Zwack Unicum* and *Magyar Telekom* included less detailed remuneration guidelines on their websites,[92]
– *Richter Gedeon*'s remuneration policy is not published on the website; it can only be concluded that there is (based on the 2022 general meeting proposal).[93]

These companies did not make it easy to find their remuneration reports, because they can be accessed with a few searches and many clicks on their websites, at the end of the general meeting submissions.[94]

VII. Remuneration policy and the reorganisation under ESG aspects

The company establishes a remuneration policy for directors; the remuneration policy should contribute to the company's business strategy, long-term interests and sustainability and explain how it does so.[95]

The supervision obliges the investment enterprise to consider realistic requirements and resources, both in terms of time horizon and the maintenance of its own funds and liquid resources, whether liquidation or cessation of operations is necessary, considering the viability and sustainability of its business model and strategy throughout the whole exit process.[96]

SFDR[97] serves several purposes: sustainability risks by financial market participants and financial advisers' integration into their processes – taking into account adverse effects on sustainability in these processes – and increasing transparency regarding the sustainability characteristics of financial products. The HNB attaches great importance to SFDR, which prioritises sustainability

---

these practical experiences. https://www.bet.hu/Kibocsatok/Ajanlasok-kibocsatoknak/Felelos-tarsasagiranyitas (05.09.2023).

[91] https://molgroup.info/storage/documents/altalanos_dokumentumok/fobb_tarsasagiranyitasi_dokumentumok/mol_remuneration_policy_2020_hun.pdf (05.09.2023).

[92] https://docplayer.hu/30422536-Az-otp-bank-nyrt-javadalmazasi-iranyelvei.html; https://zwackunicum.hu/files/befektetoknek_vallalatiranyitasi-elvek__ertekelesi-es-javadalmazasi-iranyelvek_hu_1559567250/zwk20200625_or03h.pdf; https://www.telekom.hu/static-tr/sw/file/2020AGM-Javadalmazasi-Politika.pdf (05.09.2023).

[93] https://bet.hu/newkibdata/128693174/Igazgatosag%20eloterjesztese%20a%202022%20evi%20kozgyulesre.pdf (05.09.2023).

[94] https://molgroup.info/storage/documents/eves_rendes_kozgyules/agm_documents_2022_hu.pdf; https://www.otpbank.hu/static/portal/sw/file/220322_kozgy_eloterjesztesek_h.pdf; https://bet.hu/newkibdata/128693174/Igazgatosag%20eloterjesztese%20a%202022%20evi%20kozgyulesre.pdf; https://zwackunicum.hu/files/befektetoknek_tozsdei-bejelentesek_2021_javadalmazasi-nyilatkozat_hu_1622014405/zwk20210526or_02h.pdf; https://www.telekom.hu/static-tr/sw/file/2022AGM_eloterjesztesek_0321_boritoval.pdf (05.09.2023).

[95] Section 16 (1)–(2) ELTSE.

[96] Section 101 (9) IECESP.

[97] Regulation (EU) 2019/2088 of the European Parliament and of the Council of 27 November 2019 on sustainability-related disclosures in the financial services sector.

and consumer protection, also with regard to Monitoring Strategy, and specifically for the Green Programme. Prudent application of SFDR for financial risks related to sustainability raises the awareness of organisations and customers, thereby managing risks whilst expanding funding for sustainability and, in this context, for financial institutions through the expansion of the information to be collected by the HNB, with the activities of the HNB as a supervisory authority. The HNB's intention is to make green, sustainable investment and savings and expand the range of credit products and information on product offerings for investors be more informative, understandable, and reliable – for which SFDR is an extremely important structural step. Specifically in connection with Article 3, the HNB draws attention to the following:

– integrating sustainability risks into investment decision-making processes, and the inclusion of sustainability risks in investment and insurance boards is not a new requirement, as the SFDR only sets out the new related transparency obligations;

– for undertakings for collective investment in transferable securities, alternative investment fund managers and investment enterprises delegated Union legislation related to Article 3 is in the process of being issued, but they will also not contain detailed content elements with the requirements of Article 3. However, the HNB recommends that the minimum sustainability risks referring to Article 3 shall cover the following: the physical risks of climate change and the transition risk associated with climate change. In the opinion of the HNB, in the case of public investment funds, it is associated with the entry into force of the SFDR whether an amendment to the management rules is subject to authorisation, which, in turn, depends on whether the fund manager intends to amend the fund's investment policy or its risk profile in the context of the application of the Regulation.[98]

C. Certain aspects of Sustainable Funding and Portfolio Governance

The second aspect of the research group is focused on sustainable funding and portfolio governance. We have already pointed out the difficulties and barriers of sustainable finance in Hungary. There are several measures which are at an early stage, however, certain Hungarian acts and another regulation involving

[98] Executive circular of HNB 17 March 2021 2., 5., 7. https://www.mnb.hu/letoltes/129526-3-2021-sfdr-vezetoi-korlevel.pdf (05.09.2023). See also: Green Finance in Hungary, Consultation document by the Central Bank of Hungary, 4, https://www.mnb.hu/letoltes/green-finance-in-hungary-consultation-paper.pdf (05.09.2023).

pieces of soft law (executive circulars[99]) can be added to other topics (i.e. viewpoint "Generalities on the reorganisation of funding management under ESG aspects" to remuneration policy). To maintain the unity of this project, we were committed to doing this chapter in this form.

The institutional investors are enterprises with the same life cycle funds set up in the same year in the Central and Eastern European region, created with much smaller amounts compared to the whole. Only fund managers in the region – a negligible proportion – are considered experienced fund managers, as most of them have not yet started at least three new funds.[100] Companies in the transport and finance/insurance sectors made the highest unique investments, relatively speaking, and the smallest amounts were used to finance real estate companies in the region. For classical venture capital investments, the average individual value was usually only a third or a quarter of the total investments in the sector of the average value of the investments in the same sector.[101]

Institutional investors, furthermore, have to disclose how the key elements of their capital investment strategy are consistent, in particular, with the profile and duration of their long-term liabilities and how they contribute to the medium and long-term performance of their assets.[102] If the asset manager invests on behalf of the institutional investor – either based on portfolio management specified in the IECESP or through an investment fund manager performing investment fund management activities specified in the public company limited by shares – the institutional investor shall disclose the following:

1. how the agreement with the asset manager encourages the asset manager to tailor its investment strategy and decisions primarily to the profile and duration of its long-term liabilities;
2. how the agreement encourages the asset manager to make investment decisions based on assessments of the medium and long-term financial and non-financial performance of the investee companies, to play a role in the average performance of the investee companies, and to improve it in the long-term;
3. how the method used to assess the performance of the asset manager and the timing of the valuation and the remuneration of the asset management ser-

---

[99] The HNB, acting in its supervisory capacity, directly addresses the heads of supervised institutions in the management circulars issued. The purpose of an executive circular is to draw the attention of a specific group of managers to the need to comply with a specific rule. Compliance with the requirements set out in the circular is examined and assessed by the HNB. The addressees are the heads of the institutions supervised by the HNB, the heads of the organisations concerned by the subject matter. https://www.mnb.hu/felugyelet/szabalyozas/felugyeleti-szabalyozo-eszkozok/vezetoi-korlevelek (05.09.2023).

[100] *Karsai*, A kockázati tőke gazdaságfejlesztő hatása Kelet-Közép Európában, 8.

[101] Ibid. 18.

[102] Section 12 (1) ELTSE.

vices are consistent with the profile and duration of the institutional investor's long-term liabilities and take long-term absolute performance into account.[103]

The asset manager shall inform the institutional investor with whom it has entered into the agreement specified above as to how exactly its investment strategy and its implementation comply with the agreement, as well as the contribution of the institutional investor or the fund's assets and long-term performance, all on an annual basis;[104] the information shall also include a report covering significant medium to long-term investment risks, as well as whether and how the asset manager makes investment decisions based on an assessment of the medium and long-term, including non-financial, performance of the companies involved in the investment.[105]

D. Sustainable Trading and Product Governance

I. General aspects of product governance in the EU and in Hungary

The label "Product Governance" originates from Commission Delegated Directive (EU) 2017/593 supplements Directive 2014/65/EU of the European Parliament and of the Council (MiFID II). Among its core elements is the regulatory obligation for financial service providers to formally approve newly issued financial products and to continuously monitor product distribution, including distribution chains. The original aim of the regulation was to prevent "dangerous" financial products with excessively high-risk potential from coming into circulation in the first place. MiFID II added to this by further specifying, among other things, product governance obligations. This Directive clarifies that sustainability factors and sustainability related objectives should be taken into account in both the product oversight and governance process.[106]

Financial markets have focused on sustainable finance already for many years, without a legal and regulatory framework imposing such focus on them. The EU legislator has taken inspiration from current market practices and seeks to accelerate the move to "green finance" by elevating existing market principles and guidelines on legal requirements applicable to all throughout the European Union.[107]

---

[103] Section 12 (2) a)-c) ELTSE.

[104] Section 13 (1) ELTSE.

[105] Section 13 (2) a), e) ELTSE.

[106] See also: *Lamandini/Cerrato* (Fn. 66); *Lidman* (Fn. 73) 27.

[107] *Driessen*, in: Busch/Ferrarini/Grünewald (eds.), Sustainable Finance in Europe, Corporate Governance: Financial Stability and Financial Markets, 2021, 350. See also: *Colaert*, in: Busch/Ferrarini/Grünewald (eds.), Sustainable Finance in Europe, Corporate Governance: Financial Stability and Financial Markets, 2021, 462–468.

Compliance with the relevant EU rules can be found in IECESP, in the Decree[108] of the Ministry of National Economy on the product approval process to be applied by the investment enterprise, and in the Recommendation[109] of the Hungarian National Bank (HNB) in relation to product approval requirements governing the capital market.

The HNB expects that the provisions of the recommendation will be implemented by the company in accordance with the decree of the Ministry of National Economy, and the provisions of the recommendation of HNB shall be applied in an appropriate and proportionate manner in accordance with Section 2 and Section 6 (1),[110] taking into account the nature of the product, the investment service and the target market for the product. The HNB also expects that if the company is both a developer and a distributor of products, it will apply the provisions of the recommendation properly, so that the considerations concerning designers and distributors are taken into account accordingly.

II. Sustainable distribution regulation in the fund industry

1. Product approval process

An investment enterprise that develops financial instruments for sale to clients shall maintain, administer and review a process for approving individual financial instruments and approving significant adjustments to existing financial instruments ("product approval process") before placing a financial instrument on the market or distributing it to customers.[111] The product approval process establishes the identified end-user target market within each customer category of financial instruments and ensures that all relevant risks in that identified target market are assessed and that the planned marketing strategy is appropriate for the respective target market.[112] An investment enterprise that develops financial instruments has to make all information regarding the financial instrument and the product approval process available to any distributor, including also the identified target market for the financial instruments.[113]

For a financial instrument, the investment enterprise shall identify the potential target market in sufficient detail and identify the type or types of clients for which the financial instrument is compatible with its needs, characteristics and purposes. As part of this process, the investment enterprise shall identify the group or groups of clients whose needs, characteristics and objectives are incom-

[108] 16/2017. (VI. 30.) Decree of the Ministry of National Economy.
[109] 25/2018. (VII. 5.) Recommendation of the Hungarian National Bank.
[110] 16/2017. (VI. 30.) Decree of the Ministry of National Economy.
[111] Section 17/A (1) IECESP.
[112] Section 17/A (2) IECESP.
[113] Section 17/A (4) IECESP.

patible with the financial instrument.[114] An investment enterprise shall establish and maintain procedures and arrangements for deciding on the range of financial instruments and services it offers or recommends and the relevant target markets that ensure compliance with all applicable requirements, in particular, disclosure, suitability or adequacy assessment, incentives and requirements for the proper management of conflicts of interest.[115]

By publishing 25/2018. (VII. 5.) HNB Recommendation, the HNB ensures compliance with the European Securities and Markets Authority's (ESMA) Guidelines on MiFID II requirements for product governance (ESMA Guidelines), ESMA 35-43-620 of 5 February 2018.

The potential target market cannot be identified solely based on quantitative criteria, so the designer must also take due account of qualitative aspects accordingly. In particular, for mass-market services, process automation based on formulae or algorithm-based methods that process quantitative criteria for products and customers may be relevant. The HNB expects that the enterprise should not rely exclusively on quantitative criteria when identifying the target market, but should also balance them with qualitative criteria to a sufficient extent.[116] Identifying the potential target market – in sufficient detail – is a legal obligation.[117]

The identification of a potential target market by the developer involves the following categories for consideration:

(1) the type of customers that make up the target group of the product ("retail customer", "professional customer" or "eligible partner");

(2) knowledge and experience: the company provides information to potential customers on how to understand the product;

(3) financial situation, with particular emphasis on loss-bearing capacity;

(4) appropriateness of risk tolerance and product risk / return profile for the target market: (it is recommended to categorise and clearly characterise the basic attitude towards risk: "risk-seeking", "speculative", "balanced", "conservative");

(5) customer goals and needs: the company specifies the investment goals and objectives of the customers of the product group, designed to meet the needs of the client, including the broader financial goals of potential clients and the overall strategy they are pursuing in relation to the investment.[118]

The identification of a potential target market must be carried out in an appropriate and proportionate manner, taking into account the nature of the product. This means that when identifying the target market, product characteristics,

---

114 Section 5 (1) 16/2017. (VI. 30.) Decree of the Ministry of National Economy.
115 Section 8 (1) 16/2017. (VI. 30.) Decree of the Ministry of National Economy.
116 Point 3 25/2018. (VII. 5.) Recommendation of HNB.
117 Point 7 25/2018. (VII. 5.) Recommendation of HNB.
118 Point 8 25/2018. (VII. 5.) Recommendation of HNB.

including its complexity (including cost and fee structure), risk / reward profile or liquidity, and innovative nature are all important factors for consideration.[119]

2. Guidelines of the Hungarian National Bank

The aim of the HNB is to facilitate the transition of domestic credit institutions to sustainable operations and to facilitate opportunities in terms of climate change and environmental risks with relevant legislative changes; in this respect, this website www.zoldpenzugyek.hu was created (the "Knowledge Base" section provides practical help with examples, good practices and usable data, and a collection of methodological resources).[120] The HNB considers it important to highlight the potential business of these processes, which is why they also provide opportunities for credit institutions, which may include new or even innovative developments of financing solutions, for example, for the financing of local energy communities, or the development of dedicated green banking products, such as improving energy efficiency financing and a loan related to sustainability or ESG aspects (ESG linked loan or sustainability linked loan).[121] The HNB expects the credit institution to identify the effects of climate change and environmental damage, as well as risks at the level of key sectors, geographical areas, products and in the timeframe context of the services in which it carries out or intends to carry out its activities, given that some of these risks may materialise over a fairly long period of time.[122] The HNB also considers climate change and environmental risks to be included in the corporate governance requirements set out in Article 109 of Act CCXXXVII of 2013 on credit institutions and financial enterprises. Accordingly, the management body with governance powers must have sufficient knowledge and understanding of climate change and environmental risks to ensure that the level of risk assumed is consistent with the credit institution's risk appetite and strategy, internal rules and policies, and that the credit institution complies with applicable legal requirements and other obligations. For example, the HNB considers it good practice for the management body with governance powers to receive regular reports on climate change and environmental risks or to be regularly informed about them under a specific agenda item at its meetings.[123]

"The HNB also attempted to determine the preparedness and climate risk exposure of credit institutions with numerical data. The preparedness of financial institutions in four areas (corporate governance, risk management, and business model and strategy and readiness for disclosures) is based on the self-reporting of credit institutions, the results of which showed a strong dispersion in the

[119] Point 11 25/2018. (VII. 5.) Recommendation of HNB.
[120] Point I 5/2021. (IV. 15.) Recommendation of HNB.
[121] Page 4 5/2021. (IV. 15.) Recommendation of HNB.
[122] Point 3 5/2021. (IV. 15.) Recommendation of HNB.
[123] Point 11 5/2021. (IV. 15.) Recommendation of HNB.

examined areas, but overall low readiness can be detected. At the business model, strategy and disclosure categories, the banks – more than 75% – were significantly unprepared. This means that environmental sustainability considerations do not prevail in or with strategy-making, the disclosures are extremely incomplete or no information is available on the sustainability actions of the financial institution or the pollution data of the financed activities."[124]

III. Product governance and greenwashing

The management body of investment enterprise shall be responsible for the integrity of the accounting and financial reporting system, including ensuring financial and operational control and compliance with laws and standards, and for providing information, disclosure and communication.[125] The governing body with management power is responsible for implementing the strategies and regulations of the investment enterprise.[126]

The investment enterprise and the commodity exchange service provider shall comply with the provisions of the laws and regulations concerning its operation and activities as follows:

(1) the chairman and member of the board of directors and supervisory board of an investment enterprise and a commodity exchange service provider in the form of a company limited by shares,

(2) the chairman and member of the board of directors and supervisory board of the commodity exchange service provider operating in the form of a cooperative,

(3) an appointed manager and deputy manager of an investment enterprise and a commodity service provider in the form of a branch, excluding an investment enterprise and a commodity service provider established in another EEA State, or

(4) a manager of a commodity exchange service provider in the form of a limited liability company is responsible for ensuring that the material, technical, organisational, and personal conditions, rules and procedures necessary for the operation and performance of the activity are in place and applied.[127]

The HNB issues investors warnings in connection with ESG standards.[128] Data scarcity and data inconsistency are major obstacles to proper assessment of climate risks. A challenge for green finance products and brown assets is also the

---

[124] *Deák,* MNB Zöld Program, Polgári Szemle, 4–6 (2021), 107.

[125] Section 21/A (1) IECESP.

[126] Section 21/A (3) IECESP.

[127] Section 94 IECESP.

[128] See: https://www.mnb.hu/felugyelet/piacfelugyelet/befektetoi-figyelmeztetesek?gclid (05.09.2023).

availability of data on climate risks. On the other hand, it is likewise a challenge in terms of the time horizon involved, with current data covering timespans that are simply too short. In many cases, the role of the financial sector is thus still necessary for obtaining a thorough analysis of the risks associated with climate change.[129]

According to the HNB, it is important to avoid expanding any green funding on green transactions and products that have been officially set up but do not have an actual environmental benefit – this is the definition of the risk of greenwashing.[130]

There are several definitions for greenwashing, one of them is the following: "practice of promoting environmentally friendly programs to deflect attention from an organisation's environmentally unfriendly or less savoury activities".[131] A more appropriate definition is when greenwashing "intuitively refers to market practices, both intentional and unintentional, whereby the publicly disclosed sustainability profile of an issuer and the characteristics and / or objectives of a financial instrument or a financial product either by action or omission do not properly reflect the underlying sustainability risks and impacts associated to that issuer, financial instrument or financial product".[132]

The main benefit of external certification is to maintain the "cleanliness" of the green label and reduce the risk of greenwashing. At the same time, certification is a cost disadvantage on the green side of other financial products. This element, which can in fact be considered a barrier to entry, is therefore useful, on the one hand, and a market in children's shoes on the other, insofar as excessive a restrictive effect should thus be avoided. The HNB will therefore analyse in detail the extent to which it is appropriate to rely on external rating agencies in connection with green products.[133]

---

[129] Fenntarthatóság és jegybanki politika – Zöld szempontok az MNB monetáris politikai eszköztárában, 16. https://www.mnb.hu/letoltes/zold-eszkoztar-strategia-publikacio-2021-hun-0706-2.pdf (05.09.2023).

[130] https://www.mnb.hu/letoltes/zold-penzugyek-konzultacios-dokumentum-2.pdf, 4. (05.09.2023).

[131] *Vieira de Freitas Nettó et al.*, Environmental Sciences Europe, 32, 19 (2020), 1–12. https://doi.org/10.1186/s12302-020-0300-3 (05.09.2023).

[132] Sustainable Finance Roadmap 2022–2024, 8 ff, https://www.esma.europa.eu/sites/default/files/library/esma30-379-1051_sustainable_finance_roadmap.pdf (05.09.2023); *Papp/Dúl,* "Sustainable finance: The relating actual Hungarian legislation in EU frame", Zbornik Radova Pravnog Fakulteta u Novom Sadu 4 (2022), 1145-1170.

[133] https://www.mnb.hu/letoltes/zold-penzugyek-konzultacios-dokumentum-2.pdf, 27–28. (05.09.2023). See more in the Green Financial Product Search Concept of HNB (professional consultation document.) https://www.mnb.hu/letoltes/mnb-zold-penzugyi-termekkereso-szakmai-konzultacios-dokumentum-ifua-final.pdf (05.09.2023).

E. Conclusions

The HNB closed its Growth Bond Programme as part of its tightening cycle, raising the question of whether there will be any more corporate green bond issuance. The other question is what will happen to the bonds already issued, or more precisely, to the part of them that the central bank did not purchase.[134] In the latest greenwashing case, the Dutch competition authority has challenged Decathlon and H&M's commercial practices on sustainability. Similar investigations could increase in Hungary, as international and domestic authorities are showing increased interest in investigating various green claims.[135]

In 2021, the HNB announced the Green Mortgage Bond Purchase Program, the aim of which is to develop the domestic green mortgage bond market, which will contribute to the growth of green mortgage loans. In order to further encourage green home lending, the Green Home Program was launched as part of the Growth Loan Program, which provides low-interest green loans to households if the goal is to build and buy nearly zero energy homes.[136]

We hope that Hungary will continue the path of ESG, SF, CSR, RBC and CG after a promising start. If so, we have some suggestions for consideration.

In our opinion, the measures for encouraging long-term shareholder engagement are currently embodied in declarations in Hungary that are not easily accessible. There is still work to be done for Hungarian public companies limited by shares, but also in the light of the joint proposal for a directive of the European Parliament and of the Council on Corporate Sustainability Due Diligence.[137]

Furthermore, it is very important to underline that ESG-related labels should only be given to companies that are genuinely associated with sustainable finance. The legal provisions must also meet the requirements of legal certainty and trade safety.

The Hungarian theoretical and practical perspective to sustainable finance is still in its infancy in the sense that there is no comprehensive[138] approach in place in Hungary yet.

---

[134] *Kovács*, Heti Világgazdaság, 27.01.2022, 50–51.

[135] https://piacesprofit.hu/cikkek/klimablog/felhetnek-a-zoldremoso-vallalatok.html (05.09.2023).

[136] *Deák*, MNB Zöld Program, Polgári Szemle, 4–6 (2021), 111.

[137] COM(2022) 71 final 2022. 02. 23., *Papp/Dúl*, "Sustainable finance: The relating actual Hungarian legislation in EU frame", Zbornik Radova Pravnog Fakulteta u Novom Sadu 4 (2022), 1145-1170.

[138] *Lowry*, The Blurring Lines between Private and Public Ownership, ECGI – Finance Working Paper 844/2022. https://papers.ssrn.com/sol3/papers.cfm?abstract_id=4200794 (05.09.2023).

Country Report Slovakia*

Mária Patakyová / Ján Mazúr

A. Introduction

Slovak company law and financial markets law are determined both by EU membership and a rather poorly developed capital market, resulting from the small and open economy and post-socialist heritage. As a result, Slovak law tends to focus on what appear to be "more pressing issues", such as corporate and public finance transparency, financial consumer protection or market integrity, especially in relation to financial consumers. The same tendency applies to economic policies, which focus on economic growth, under the mantra of "catching up" with Western Europe.

Our task is to provide a critical assessment of the implementation of selected issues related to sustainability agenda within the Slovak financial market law and corporate law. We proceed as follows. First, we provide the context of Slovak corporate structures, data on the volumes and specifics of the Slovak financial market, from which we identify important limitations of the European approach at hand. The question of the relevancy of individual legislative elements arises due to low volumes in the Slovak market.

Second, we briefly present the status of the corporate and financial market sustainability research in Slovakia. Based on the previous research, we hypothesise that too much stress on formalism and formal adoption – typical of fringe topics in Slovakia – may in fact lead to increased administrative burden without actual (positive) impact on the sustainability agenda. Instead, it may lead to concentration on the market, which would be to detriment of competition and consumers. Finally, we present and examine the implementation of respective topics into the Slovak law: (i) sustainable ownership and shareholder governance; (ii) sustainable funding and portfolio governance; (iii) sustainable trading, sustainable distribution, and product governance.

Overall, we find that issues of sustainable finance are relatively underdeveloped in Slovakia. No national strategy deals with sustainable finance. Furthermore, the implementation of the EU rules is mechanical in nature, featuring no innovation. There is hardly any information in relation to sustainable finance

* This work was supported by the Slovak Research and Development Agency under the contract No. 16-0553 (project PIKAP).

among the financial markets umbrella organisations or reporting thereof. We have also not identified any relevant case law in relation to sustainable finance. These tendencies may be driven by sheer lack of volume and limited impact in a small market such as Slovakia.

B. Context: Slovak Corporate Structures

The limited development of the capital market in Slovakia can be evidenced by the economic and financial data. For instance, there are only a handful of companies listed on the Bratislava Stock Exchange (BSE): 31, although only 14 issuers recorded price quote in 2022, typically with extremely low volumes.[1] All of the listed companies have concentrated shareholdership with only negligible volumes of stocks floating on the market. Capitalisation of stocks on the stock exchange is thus minuscule – only €2 billion in total, while the annual trade volumes of equity instruments is less than €12 million, as evidenced by Table 1.[2] The stock market has in fact lost on capitalisation since 2018 (from its peak €4.84 billion in 2018). Only 2 of the top traded issuers are among the 100 highest earning companies in Slovakia.[3] Long-term trend shows that the volume of equity instruments is stagnant or falling.[4]

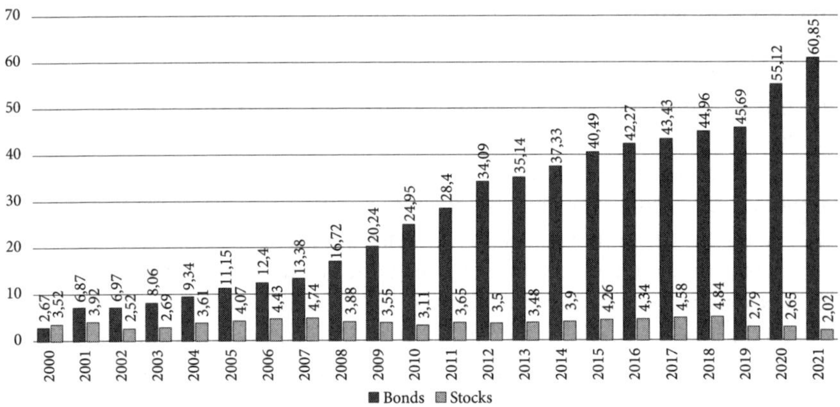

Figure 1: Capitalization of stocks and bonds traded on the Bratislava Stock Exchange 2000–2021 (in billions EUR)

[1] Bratislava Stock Exchange, *Annual Report 2021* (Bratislava Stock Exchange, 2022) 3–4, https://www.bsse.sk/bcpb/wp-content/uploads/2023/06/BSSE-Anual-Report-2022.pdf (25 October 2023).

[2] Bratislava Stock Exchange (fn. 1) 3–4. Data till end 2021.

[3] These were: Tatra banka a. s. (member of Raiffeisen group) and Allianz – Slovenská poisťovňa a. s. (member of Allianz group).

[4] Lojschová, 'Kapitálový Trh Na Slovensku', *Biatec* 24, no. 2 (2016): 14–17.

Source: Bratislava Stock Exchange, *Annual Report 2021* (2022), 6.

Slovak capital market originates in privatisation of state enterprises in 1990s, which, in turn, heavily influenced the almost negligible size of the Slovak regulated market. The regulated market never really worked as a source of primary capital for growth of companies, but rather as a liquidity source for shareholders who acquired titles from privatisation (i. e. the process of transferring ownership from state to private individuals or their proxies and institutional investors that took place in several waves in 1990s and early 2000s).

Rather than floating stocks of privatised companies on the stock market, a tendency arose toward concentrated ownership of these stocks (companies) in the hands of, first, local oligarchs and, later, more professional private equity groups. There have been only a handful of new issuers whose stocks are actively traded in modern history (post 2000), yet these are insignificant. This implies a dominance of foreign or private sources of finance for Slovak companies.

Relatively higher volumes are recorded for the debt market. The capitalisation of debt instruments on the BSE was around €60 billion (grew ninefold since 2001), while annual trade volume was €230 m by the end of 2021.[5] Yet 76.5 % of total debt issues were state bonds and treasuries.[6] The remainder is split primarily between the monetary financial institutions (12.76 %), non-monetary financial institutions (4.62 %) and non-financial corporations (6.14 %).

The inclination towards banking finance and debt finance can generally be assessed from the composition of assets of financial markets in Slovakia (2019) as illustrated by Table 2.

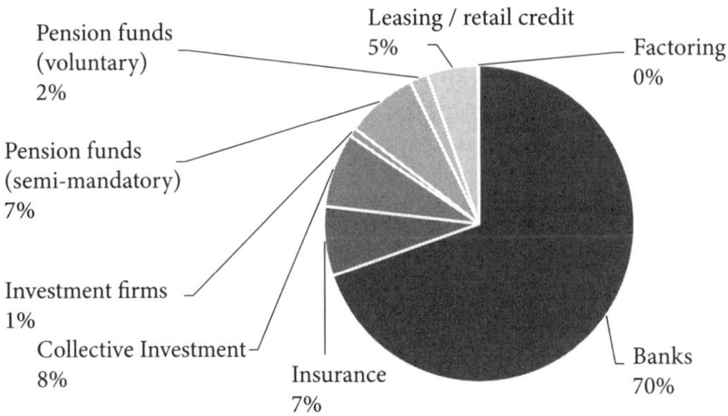

Figure 2: Composition of assets of financial markets
Source: National Bank of Slovakia, *Analýza slovenského finančného sektora* (2020), 17.

[5] Bratislava Stock Exchange (fn. 1) 3–4.
[6] National Bank of Slovakia, *Statistical Bulletin 4. Quarter 2021* (National Bank of Slovakia, 2022) 104, https://www.nbs.sk/_img/documents/_publikacie/bulletinmfs/2021/bulletinmfs_122021.pdf (25 October 2023).

Apart from banks, the assets of institutional investors are mostly run by managers of collective investment schemes (€12 billion of net assets, February 2022), IORPs (€3 billion of net assets, Dec 2021) and semi-mandatory pension funds (€11,6 billion, April 2022).[7]

The dominant legal form is by far the limited-liability company (LLC, Slovak: *spoločnosť s ručením obmedzeným*), representing almost 97 % of the registered companies (see Table 1). Meanwhile, joint-stock companies (JSC, Slovak: *akciová spoločnosť*) represent the second-most used form, yet there were only 5,392 by the end of 2021.[8] The vast majority of JSCs are a private type of company, which cannot issue publicly traded stocks.

Table 1: Statistics on Slovak company forms

Limited-liability company	96.7 %	242,056
Joint-stock companies	2.2 %	5,392
Other company forms (partnerships, simple joint-stock companies)	0.5 %	1,314
Cooperatives	0.6 %	1,444
TOTAL	100 %	250,206

Source: Statistical Office of the Slovak Republic, 2022.

The Slovak economy is open, dominated by large subsidiaries of multinational corporations, and has a few important partially state-owned enterprises – partially privatised companies and a host of small and medium enterprises. This applies to both the financial and non-financial sectors. The prevalence of subsidiaries of multinational corporations among large enterprises is clearly visible in the banking sector. In case of 26 domestic credit institutions, over 94 % of their subscribed capital originates abroad (most dominantly in Czech Republic (56 %), Luxembourg (11,7 %), Austria (10 %), Belgium (8 %)).[9]

We can draw a similar picture from the statistics of the constellation of groups of companies in Slovakia. From the 2019 data, more than three quarters of multinational groups were controlled from abroad; this dominance of foreign control is even more stark when it comes to large companies with 11 and more enterprises – 96 % of such groups are foreign-controlled (see Table 2).

[7] Various sources of respective umbrella organisations: Slovak Association of Managers of Collective Investment Schemes, https://www.ass.sk; Association of Managers of Semi-mandatory Pension Funds, https://www.adss.sk; Association of IORPs, https://www.adds.sk (25 October 2023).

[8] Statistical Office of the Slovak Republic, 2022.

[9] The majority of these banks are members of large groups, such as: Erste, Raiffeisen, Intesa SanPaolo, etc. See National Bank of Slovakia (fn. 6) 104. Note: Data till end 2021 / for 2021 (NBS).

Table 2: Groups of Companies in Slovakia

Multinational groups controlled domestically	2,681	22 %
Multinational groups controlled from abroad	9,470	78 %
Multinational groups total	12,151	72 %
Fully domestic groups	4,614	28 %
Groups total	16,765	100 %

Groups with 11+ enterprises

Multinational groups controlled domestically	91	4 %
Multinational groups controlled from abroad	2,256	96 %
Multinational groups total	2,347	96 %
Fully domestic groups	105	4 %
Groups total	2,452	100 %

Source: Statistical Office of the Slovak Republic, 2019.

These findings have certain implications for the applicability of the research objects on the market actors. Subsidiaries of foreign companies would not typically seek capital on domestic markets, as they would be part of the group financing structures.[10] Consequently, lower demand for capital limits the financing potential of regulated markets in Slovakia. Similarly, subsidiaries can refer to the reporting of their parent companies. As a result, there is limited regulatory potential in Slovak law. Both limitations lead us to hypothesise that the estimated approach to sustainable finance through capital markets would not work in the Slovak context.

C. State of Research in Corporate and Financial Market Sustainability in Slovakia

There is only a limited constitutional framework and constitutional court case law specifically dedicated to sustainability issues in Slovakia. Furthermore, Slovakia remains a laggard in the implementation of sustainability considerations within company law, investment law and financial markets law.

[10] In yet unpublished research, we looked into practices of the Slovak corporate bond market, which is dominated by domestic real estate developers. We found that during 2020, only one bond issuer issued bonds mentioning ESG criteria, and, while not committing to issue green bonds (according to the European Taxonomy), the issuer claimed to have ambitions to have a positive environmental impact.

Contemporary issues of company law or financial market law are driven mostly by the need to tackle long-suffered problems of the business environment, not necessarily the sustainability agenda. Hence, among the most prominent issues of the company and corporate law, we may include the illicit practices of tunnelling, use of strawmen (nominee structures to hide true beneficiaries), irregular bankruptcy methods, or chain-mergers of indebted companies. These issues have been a subject of multiple reforms in company law in the past 7 years.

Similarly, in the field of financial markets law, public procurement law or investment law or state-related matters, the focus was on transposition of the EU laws, typically in a restrictive and conservative manner. In the field of financial markets law, there has also been a lot of attention paid to the increase in consumer protections, especially in light of the financial scams and scandals of the mid-2000s. Still, the state has no explicit or structured approach to sustainability in its investment policy.[11] Furthermore, a lot of attention was paid to increasing the overall transparency of the business sector, especially when it comes to trade with the state.[12] The focus of policymakers on sustainability has thus been limited.

A relatively recent addition to the sustainability agenda in close connection with the company law is the Social Economy Act (2018), which creates a legal and economic framework for social economy, including various types of social enterprises and framework for investment and compensatory aid.[13]

The Slovak company law provides for standard institutes of duty of loyalty and duty of care. Directors are obliged "to exercise their powers with professional care and in accordance with the interests of the company and all of its shareholders" (§ 194(5) Commercial Code). This implies no priority to their own interests, but rather, the interests of only certain shareholders or the interests of

[11] Patakyová et al., *Specificities of Corporate Governance and Financial Regulation of Companies under the Challenges of Sustainability* (Bratislava: Univerzita Komenského v Bratislave, Právnická fakulta, 2018), 67, https://www.flaw.uniba.sk/fileadmin/praf/Pracoviska/Katedry/KOPHP/rozne/Specificities_of_Corporate_Governance_and_Financial_Regulation_of_Companies_under_the_Challenges_of_Sustainability.pdf (25 October 2023).

[12] Two prominent examples are the open register of public contracts and the register of ultimate beneficiaries of companies dealing with state. The law establishing the register of public contracts requires publication of all contracts of the public sector bodies and their metadata prior as a condition to the effectiveness of contracts (see Freedom of Information Act no. 211/2000 Col.). The register of ultimate beneficiaries of companies includes the ultimate beneficiaries of companies dealing with state, i. e. providing services or delivering goods to public sector entities or receiving any money from state. The legal framework requires rigorous due diligence on the part of the ultimate beneficiaries performed by attorneys, tax advisors and other similar professions in order to correctly assess the ultimate beneficiaries, regardless of who the shareholders are. Attorneys and other service providing professions may be held personally liable for any wrongful information.

[13] Patakyová et al. (fn. 11) 55. There were 531 registered social enterprises as of mid-September 2022. See: Register of Ministry of Labor, Social Affairs and Family, https://www.employment.gov.sk/sk/praca-zamestnanost/socialna-ekonomika/register-sp/ (25 October 2023).

third parties (stakeholders) over the company's interests. Directors with a strong sustainability preference may face liabilities for the breach of duty of loyalty (if they cause damages).[14]

Under § 176b(1) of the Commercial Code, "A shareholder may not exercise the rights of a shareholder to the detriment of rights and legitimate interests of other shareholders," and, furthermore (2): "A company must treat all shareholders equally on equal terms." This implies equal access to information and the duty of confidentiality.

CSR reporting is not widespread among V4 countries, including Slovakia; the understanding of CSR reporting is quite rudimentary.[15] More in-depth research into non-financial reporting is presented by Frank Bold.[16] The research reviews the practices of non-financial reporting as regulated by the Directive on non-financial directive within the Visegrad countries (Czechia, Hungary, Poland and Slovakia).[17] Under the Directive, only a very limited number of companies is subject to non-financial reporting obligations in Slovakia (the majority is in the financial sector).[18]

In fact, a large proportion of the obligated companies refer to group reporting executed by parent companies. The research found that non-financial reporting in the Visegrad countries generally lagged behind the EU and that especially Slovak and Hungarian companies lagged well behind the EU average in reporting on climate change and human rights issues. The reporting was generic and rudimentary; the disclosure with respect to specific policies, outcomes and risks was likewise overall vague.

Recently, there has been a marketing hype around sustainable financial products, yet the availability of truly sustainable products appears to be relatively low. There has been no real uptake of taxonomy. There is also no government

---

[14] Patakyová et al. (fn. 11) 51; Patakyová, Grambličková, and Duračinská, "The Legal Basis and Contextual Interpretation of the Duty of Care in the Slovak Republic: From a 'Gentlemanly Amateur' to a Professional Director?", *Acta Universitatis Carolinae. Iuridica LXVIII*, no. 3 (2022) 87–106.

[15] Przytuła et al., "Corporate Social Responsibility in Visegrad Countries (Poland, Czech Republic, Slovakia, Hungary) Overall Landscape", in: Długopolska-Mikonowicz, Przytuła, and Stehr (eds.), *CSR, Sustainability, Ethics & Governance* (Cham: Springer International Publishing, 2019), 327, 335, https://doi.org/10.1007/978-3-030-00440-8_20 (25 October 2023). See also: Marková and Lesníková, "Utilization of Corporate Sustainability Concept at Selected Enterprises in Slovakia", Procedia Economics and Finance 34 (2015) 630–37, https://doi.org/10.1016/S2212-5671(15)01678-0 (25 October 2023).

[16] Kwiatkowski, Vejvodová, and Gregor, *The State of Sustainability Reporting in the Visegrad Region* (Frank Bold, 2020), https://en.frankbold.org/sites/default/files/publikace/the_state_of_sustainability_reporting_in_the_visegrad_region.pdf (25 October 2023).

[17] See also https://en.frankbold.org/sites/default/files/publikace/analyza_1000_korporaci.pdf (25 October 2023).

[18] See § 2(14) and 20(9) of Accounting Act no. 431/2002 Col. (further as "Accounting Act").

policy on sustainable finance and no reports on sustainable finance have been recorded to date in Slovakia.

D. Legal Framework of Company Law and Financial Market Law

The legal framework of company law and the financial markets law in Slovakia is composed primarily of the following acts:

– Commercial Code (513/1991 Col.) includes company law, corporate governance and contractual law;[19]

– Securities Act (566/2001 Col.) includes regulation of securities, investment services and investment firms under MiFID2 ("securities dealers");[20]

– Banking Act (483/2001 Col.) includes regulation of banks and banking services;[21]

– Stock Exchange Act (429/2002 Col.) includes regulation of stock exchange;[22]

– Collective Investment Act (203/2011) includes regulation of fund managers and funds (including UCITSD, AIFMD);[23]

– Insurance Act (39/20015 Col.) includes regulation of insurance companies, life and non-life insurance;[24]

– Supplementary Pension Savings Act (650/2004 Col.) regulates institutions for the voluntary occupational retirement provision;[25]

– Retirement Pension Savings Act (43/2004 Col.) regulates institutions for the semi-mandatory occupational retirement provision.[26]

Company law falls under the purview of the Ministry of Justice, whereas financial market law falls under the Ministry of Finance. There is only one supervisory body with legislative power, the National Bank of Slovakia. The financial market actors include the following:[27]

---

[19] Obchodný zákonník č. 513/1991 Zb.

[20] Zákon č. 566/2001 Z. z. o cenných papieroch a investičných službách a o zmene a doplnení niektorých zákonov.

[21] Zákon č. 483/2001 Z. z. o bankách a o zmene a doplnení niektorých zákonov.

[22] Zákon č. 429/2002 Z. z. o burze cenných papierov.

[23] Zákon č. 203/2011 Z. z. o kolektívnom investovaní.

[24] Zákon č. 39/2015 Z. z. o poisťovníctve a o zmene a doplnení niektorých zákonov.

[25] Zákon č. 650/2004 Z. z. o doplnkovom dôchodkovom sporení a o zmene a doplnení niektorých zákonov.

[26] Zákon č. 43/2004 Z. z. o starobnom dôchodkovom sporení a o zmene a doplnení niektorých zákonov.

[27] Source: open register of supervised subjects of the National Bank of Slovakia (further as "NBS", data as of Oct 15 2022), excluding institutions providing services from other EU member states without establishing a branch.

Table 3: Financial market actors

Investment firms ("obchodník s cennými papiermi")	27 (23 domestic)
Banks providing investment services	15 (7 domestic)
UCITS fund managers ("správcovská spoločnosť")	15 (12 domestic)
Mutual funds ("podielový fond")	309 (71 domestic)
Registered fund managers	22 (22 domestic)
AIF managers ("správcovská spoločnosť")	11 (11 domestic)
AI funds ("alternatívny investičný fond")	306 (68 domestic)
IORPs ("dôchodkové správcovské spoločnosti", "doplnkové dôchodkové spoločnosti")	5 (DSS) + 4 (DDS)
IORP funds ("dôchodkové podielové fondy")	17 (DF) + 19 (DDF)
Insurance companies ("poisťovne")	10 domestically authorised + 17 branches

Source: open register of supervised subjects of the National Bank of Slovakia (further as "NBS", data as of Oct 15 2022), excluding institutions providing services from other EU member states without establishing a branch

In the following section, we analyse respective components of the sustainable finance framework, including sustainable ownership and shareholder governance, investment strategies and investment policies. Specifically, we review whether Slovak law includes any specific institutes or norms related to sustainable finance, especially when deviating from EU legislation. Slovak law is, incidentally, known for its gold-plating activity when transposing EU law,[28] and for that reason, we will undertake reviewing whether gold-plating takes place. We hypothesise that the Slovak law would stay rather true to the wording of the EU directives.

Such straightforward transposition would be driven by several factors. First, we may assume that the usefulness of any legislative invention would be rather low, and second, it would necessarily introduce additional administrative burden to a rather small number of financial institutions as such. Third, sustainable finance as a topic has so far appeared neither on the national legislative agenda nor in recent relevant national policy documents.[29]

---

[28] OECD, *Regulatory Policy in the Slovak Republic: Towards Future-Proof Regulation*, OECD Reviews of Regulatory Reform (OECD, 2020), https://doi.org/10.1787/ce95a880-en (25 October 2023) Chapter 8.

[29] Slovakia's Vision and Development Strategy 2030: A Long-term Strategy for Sustainable Development of the Slovak Republic – Slovakia 2030 (Ministry of Investments, Regional Development and Informatization of the Slovak Republic, 2020); National Reform Programme of the Slovak Republic 2022 (Ministry of Finance of the Slovak Republic, 2022); National Reform Programme of the Slovak Republic 2020 (Ministry of Finance of the Slovak Republic, 2020); Greener Slovakia: Strategy of the Environmental Policy of the Slovak Republic until 2030 (Ministry of

I. Sustainable Ownership, Shareholder Governance

In the context of sustainable ownership and shareholder governance, we examine the legislative framework of remuneration policies and engagement policies. We review existing legislation, especially the transposed EU legislation, and additional sources of law, such as corporate governance code.

II. Remuneration Policy (art. 9a–9b of Directive 2017/828)[30]

The remuneration policy set by the articles 9a and 9b of Directive 2017/828 is transposed without much creativity into § 201a–201e of the Commercial Code. The wording of the remuneration policy regulation is essentially true to the wording of the directive. As the remuneration policy concerns only companies whose stocks are admitted to trading on a regulated market situated or operating within the EU, there are only a handful of companies subject to this regulation in Slovakia.

The Slovak public joint-stock company has a typical two-tier structure with the management board and the supervisory board. The management board is elected either by the general meeting or the supervisory board, with the supervisory board always elected by the general meeting.[31]

The remuneration policy of the public joint-stock companies concerns both members of the management board and the supervisory board, but also persons "at the highest level of management of the company, if such a position exists in the company, and his/her deputy, if they are not members of the company's board of directors or supervisory board," implying C-level executives.[32]

The application of the remuneration policy is mandatory, while the Slovak transposition allows for the derogation under the art. 9a(4) of the Directive 2017/828. Companies are allowed to derogate from the remuneration policy temporarily in exceptional circumstances foreseen by the policy. Such deviation must, however, be in the interest of the sustainability of the company and its long-term objectives.[33]

Remuneration policy must be developed in line with the company's business strategy, its long-term objectives, the interest of sustainability, be clear and under-

---

Environment of the Slovak Republic, 2019); Climate Adaptation Strategy of the Slovak Republic (Update) (Ministry of Environment of the Slovak Republic, 2018).

[30] Directive (EU) 2017/828 of the European Parliament and of the Council of 17 May 2017 amending Directive 2007/36/EC as regards the encouragement of long-term shareholder engagement (Text with EEA relevance) (further as "Directive 2017/828").

[31] § 187(1), § 194(1) of the Commercial Code.

[32] § 201a(2) of the Commercial Code. See also: M. T. Patakyová, "Commentary to § 201a–201e of the Commercial Code", in Patakyová (ed.), *Commercial Code. Commentary*, 1. Issue, (Bratislava: C. H. Beck, 2022) 901–14.

[33] § 201a(3) of the Commercial Code.

standable and include measures for avoiding conflicts of interest.[34] The policy shall be valid for a maximum period of four years and must be made public on the company's webpage. The remuneration report duties are also in line with the wording of the directive.[35]

III. Engagement Policy (art. 3g of Directive 2017/828)

The primary transposition of the engagement policy is in the § 78 and 78a of the Securities Act. Individual institutional investors and asset managers are obligated to follow these policies based on their respective laws, including fund managers (§ 46(4) of the Collective Investment Act), Institutions for occupational retirement provision (§ 32c Supplementary Pension Savings Act) and insurance companies (§ 64a Insurance Act).

The term "institutional investor", moreover, covers *insurance companies* (poisťovne) and reinsurance companies (zaisťovne) under the Insurance Act (as based on the art. 2(3) and art. 13 of Solvency II) and *institutions for occupational retirement provision* falling within the scope of Directive (EU) 2016/2341, under the Supplementary Pension Savings Act (doplnkové dôchodkové spoločnosti, based on § 32c(1) of the act). Under the term "asset manager", Slovak law recognises *investment firms* (obchodníci s cennými papiermi) under the Securities Act and *management company* (správcovské spoločnosti) under the Collective Investment Act.

The transposition is true to the wording of the Directive 2017/828. As with other similar institutes, the engagement policy is new to Slovak investment law; prior to the transposition from the directive, there was no specific requirement for institutional investors or asset managers to develop or uphold their engagement policies. The current setup requires institutional investors and asset managers to develop, comply with and publish their engagement policies in relation to investee companies whose stocks are traded on the regulated market, or explain why they have chosen not to.[36] The scope of the policy is identical to the wording of art. 3g(1)(a) of the Directive 2017/828.

There are two main duties to provide information in relation to engagement policy. The first relates to the duty to publish the engagement policy on the institutional investors' or asset managers' websites free of charge.[37] Second, there is a duty to publicly disclose information on the implementation of the engagement policy; this information should specifically contain information on the most significant votes and the use of proxy advisors.[38]

---

[34] § 201b(1) of the Commercial Code.
[35] § 201e of the Commercial Code; M. T. Patakyová (fn. 32).
[36] § 78(2) of the Securities Act.
[37] § 78(1, 5) of the Securities Act.
[38] § 78(4, 5) of the Securities Act.

Respective laws requiring the implementation of the engagement policies by other financial institutions roughly follow the same logic. Under § 46(1) of the Collective Investment Act, a management company (UCITS) is obligated to adopt and comply with an appropriate strategy of engagement with the objective that the execution of rights attached to financial instruments goes exclusively to the benefit of the fund concerned. On the other hand, the law requires insurance or reinsurance undertakings and IORPs to align the main elements of their equity investment strategies with the profile and duration of their (funds') liabilities, in particular long-term liabilities, and examine how they contribute to the medium to long-term performance of their (funds') assets.[39] This also applies to situations where the insurance or reinsurance undertakings and IORPs entrust the performance of certain activities to asset managers.

Similarly limited in applicability is the Slovak Code of Corporate Governance (further as "CCG"), published by the Central European Corporate Governance Association in 2016. The CCG applies on listed companies, as based on § 34(2) of the Stock Exchange Act and § 20(6) of the Accounting Act. It sets forth principles of corporate governance, the treatment of shareholders and stakeholders, relationships with investors and disclosure and transparency principles. Sec. 1(D) of the CCG allows shareholders to mutually discuss issues related to their rights, excluding issues of market abuse, or instances contrary to the competition rules.

As based on Sec. 2(A) of the CCG, institutional investors should publish their corporate governance policies, strategies and procedures of exercising voting rights. Such documents should include explicit strategies of intervention in investee companies, methodology of evaluating effectiveness of these strategies, and voting records. In order to prevent information asymmetries and conflicts of interest, institutional investors and other investors are encouraged by the code to maintain ongoing dialogue. Institutional investors should also publish how they deal with "significant" conflicts of interest, which could have an impact on the exercise of ownership rights related to their investments.[40]

In connection with shareholders' cooperation, it is useful to remember that the Slovak Commercial Code provides for the prohibition of abuse of shareholders' rights.[41] This prohibition applies both to majority and minority shareholders and its violation may lead to action for damages.[42] Certain specific rights are assigned to a single or multiple shareholders whose nominal value of stocks is at least 5 % of the registered capital (minority shareholders).[43] These rights include most

[39] Compare § 64a(3) of the Insurance Act and § 32c(2) of the Supplementary Pension Savings Act.

[40] Sec. 2(C) of the CCG.

[41] § 176(1) of the Commercial Code.

[42] Patakyová and Gramblíčková, "Commentary to § 176a–183a of the Commercial Code", in Patakyová (ed.), *Commercial Code. Commentary*, 1. Issue, (Bratislava: C. H. Beck, 2022) 805.

[43] § 181 of the Commercial Code.

prominently the right to call for the convening of a general meeting. In addition, the board of directors is obliged to convene the general meeting to take place within 40 days from the day of receiving such a request.[44]

IV. Investment Strategy of Institutional Investors and Arrangements with Asset Managers (art. 3h of Directive 2017/828)

The requirement to publicly disclose investment strategies of institutional investors was transposed into § 32c of the Supplementary Pension Savings Act (IORP) and § 64a of the Insurance Act (insurance companies). There are no specific deviations from the wording of the directive. The law requires transparency of institutional investors, although, in case of IORPs, it does not specify any details as to how this disclosure should actually take place. It does, however, provide this detail for the insurance companies.[45] The obligations arise when an institutional investor makes contractual arrangements with an asset manager (e.g. under the Slovak law, these may be: MiFID investment firms (obchodník s cennými papiermi) and the UCITSD/AIFMD *management company* (správcovská spoločnosť) – providing an investment service of portfolio management[46].

Although in principle, management companies carry out the management of collective investment undertakings independently, they may entrust the conduct of certain activities or functions to other authorised financial institutions.[47]

V. Transparency of Asset Managers (art. 3i of Directive 2017/828)

The requirement for transparency of asset managers towards institutional investors (insurance companies and IORPs), as based on art. 3i of the Directive 2017/828, was transposed into § 78a of the Securities Act.[48] This requirement

[44] Minority shareholders furthermore hold other rights: (i) the right to request the general meeting to discuss certain matters (and the right to request that the board of directors places such matter on the agenda of the general meeting); (ii) the right to request the supervisory board to review exercise of the powers of the board of directors in specified matters; (iii) the right to request that the supervisory board asserts, on behalf of the company, claims for damages or other claims that the company has against the members of the board of directors; (iv) other rights to request that the company's bodies assert company's rights against shareholders, or members of the company's bodies. See § 182 of the Commercial Code. See also Patakyová and Gramblíčková, "Commentary to § 176a–183a of the Commercial Code", in Patakyová (ed.), *Commercial Code. Commentary*, 1. Issue, (Bratislava: C. H. Beck, 2022) 830–831.

[45] Compare § 32c of the Supplementary Pension Savings Act and § 64a(6) of the Insurance Act.

[46] As based on § 37 of the Supplementary Pension Savings Act (Entrusting the performance of activities related to the administration of supplementary pension funds) and § 185 of the Insurance Act (Entrusting of performance of activities).

[47] § 48(1), 57 and 57a of the Collective Investment Act.

[48] For *management companies* see also § 48(12) of the Collective Investment Act, which refers to the § 78a of the Securities Act.

arises when institutional investors concluded contracts entrusting the performance of specific activities to asset managers.[49] Transposition is true to the wording of the directive.

VI. ESG Considerations in Investment Policies: Asset Management Companies – Fund Managers in Slovakia

Upon review of the relevant laws, we find no specific rules governing ESG considerations, besides mandatory transpositions of the EU directives. Certain requirements are placed on the IORPs and management companies (under UCITS).

A management company shall consider risks to sustainability when complying with the organisational and governance requirements set forth by the law.[50] These requirements include establishment, implementation and maintenance of management and organisational structures, internal audit mechanisms or a system of internal reporting (incl. in relation to stakeholders). It is a duty of the management company's top management to integrate sustainability risks into the execution of all their duties, including setting up and supervising investment strategies and enforcing accountability for breaches of the investment policies.[51]

The management of collective investment undertakings must follow the best interest of unit-holders and must be conducted in the interest of market stability. The management company must act honestly and fairly, with professional care and prudence, and treat all investors fairly, as based on art. 22–23 of the Delegated directive 2010/43/EU of 1 July 2010 implementing Directive 2009/65/EC of the European Parliament and of the Council as regards organisational requirements, conflicts of interest, the conduct of business, risk management and the content of the agreement between a depositary and a management company.[52]

Acting in the best interests of unit-holders and in the management of funds features several crucial aspects. First, it means equal treatment of unit-holders, i. e. preventing the interests of one group of unit-holders from taking precedence over the interests of another group of unit-holders. Moreover, the management company should also prevent unfair practices which may reasonably be expected to affect market stability and to that end, adopt appropriate preventive measures and procedures accordingly. It also covers ensuring adequate, correct, and transparent models and systems for the valuation of the assets and liabilities and charging reasonable costs to the assets in the fund and to the unit-holders.[53]

---

[49] See fn. 38.
[50] § 32(7) of the Collective Investment Act.
[51] § 34(2) of the Collective Investment Act.
[52] § 48(2) of the Collective Investment Act.
[53] § 48(4) of the Collective Investment Act.

Acting with professional care in the administration of funds, moreover, likewise includes certain features, such as, prominently, ensuring a sufficient degree of case in the selection and continuous monitoring of the assets in the fund in the best interest of the unit-holders and in the interest of market stability.[54] It also represents a requirement for adequate knowledge and understanding of the funds' actual or perspective assets in line with the investment policies of respective funds. Finally, acting with professional care in the context of risk management compels the fund managers to consider the nature of the intended investment, prepare forecasts and carry out analyses for assessing the impact of investments on the funds' properties.

The National Bank of Slovakia has the right to lay down – by its own legislative power (*measure*, Slovak: *opatrenie*) – details on what constitutes acting in the best interests of unit-holders and what constitutes acting with professional care, including the manner in which the management company has to demonstrate such actions.[55] However, the NBS has not yet issued such a measure.

When acting with professional care in the best interest of the unit-holders, the law explicitly requires the management company to take sustainability risks into account.[56] Moreover, linking the Collective Investment Act with the Sustainable Finance Regulation 2019/2088, management companies take the main adverse impacts of investment decisions on the sustainability factors under the article 4 of the regulation into account. Moreover, such management companies factor in the main adverse impacts in complying with the requirements of acting with professional care in the best interest of the unit-holders and in the interest of market stability.[57]

In order to operationalise these duties, management companies are obliged to adopt and comply with an internal management act on the measures and procedures relating to professional diligence and ensuring that any investments are made in accordance with the investment policy and its objectives, the investment strategy and the risk limits of the fund concerned. Moreover, management companies are, at the request of the National bank of Slovakia, required to demonstrate the exercise of professional care. The management company has to prove such exercises, as otherwise it is deemed to have failed to exercise professional care.[58]

§ 59 of the Collective Investment Act requires the management companies to employ employees with the experience, knowledge, and competence necessary to comply with the duties assigned to them. § 99 of the Collective Investment Act further requires that this knowledge and competence explicitly refers to sus-

[54] § 48(4) of the Collective Investment Act.
[55] § 48(11) of the Collective Investment Act.
[56] § 48(13) of the Collective Investment Act.
[57] § 48(14) of the Collective Investment Act.
[58] § 48(6–7) of the Collective Investment Act.

tainability risk, besides traditional counterparty risk, market risk, operational risk, and liquidity risk.[59] Moreover, the risk management policy must take sustainability risks into account.[60] Such a policy must define procedures, tools and measures for enabling compliance with statutory obligations and the allocation of responsibilities related to risk management within the company itself. The performance of the risk management function is reported to the board of directors, senior management and the supervisory board.

In identifying the types of conflicts of interest whose existence may be detrimental to the interests of the fund, the management company shall consider those types of conflicts of interest that may arise as a result of the incorporation of sustainability risks into its procedures, systems and internal controls.[61]

VII. ESG Considerations in Investment Policies: IORPs in Slovakia

There are certain options for IORPs to include ESG considerations in investment decision-making due to the implementation of IORPs Dir. IORP may take into account environmental, social, organisational and governance factors in investment decisions relating to its assets.[62] In doing so, an IORP conducts its own risk assessment of new or emerging risks, including risks relating to climate change, resource use and the environment, social risks and risks arising from regulatory changes, where they would affect the composition of the assets in the funds it manages.[63]

Such an assessment would be commensurate with the size, internal organisation and the nature, scale and complexity of the activities of an IORP. The assessment must be carried out at least once every three years and when material changes to the IORP's risk profile take place. The assessment would include methods and procedures for identifying and assessing the risks to which the IORP may be exposed and which could affect its ability to meet its obligations to members or beneficiaries.

Risk management function must include, among other issues, reviewing and defining environmental, social and organisational and governance factors where an IORP takes such factors into account when making investment decisions in relation to its assets or the assets in the supplementary pension fund.[64] Similarly,

[59] A measure of the National bank of Slovakia further details risk management systems; see the Measure of the National Bank of Slovakia from 27 September 2011 on risks and risk management system, risk measurement and calculation of total and counterparty risk as amended by Measure No 7/2015. However, this measure omits the sustainability risk and has not been updated to include the risk so far.

[60] § 101(2) of the Collective Investment Act.

[61] § 43(5) of the Collective Investment Act.

[62] § 28(7) of the Supplementary Pension Savings Act.

[63] § 28(5)(e) of the Supplementary Pension Savings Act.

[64] § 29a (4)(g) of the Supplementary Pension Savings Act.

when making investment decisions concerning the assets in a supplementary pension fund, an IORP may consider environmental, social, organisational and governance factors, although any assets of the funds must be in accordance with the portfolio rules under § 53a of the Supplementary Pension Savings Act.

IORPs are required to review the focus and objectives of the investment strategy of respective funds and draw up an investment policy report for each fund it manages at least once every three years.[65] The investment policy report must contain, among other information, also the consideration of environmental, social, organisational and governance factors.

VIII. Sustainable Finance Disclosure Regulation in Slovakia[66]

So far there has been a limited amount of information regarding the proliferation of the SFDR in Slovakia. Although the NBS is charged with supervision of the adoption of the regulation, so far it has not published any data on sustainable finance. A minor development is represented by the first ESG equity pension fund established in 2021.[67] Based on the information published on selected financial institutions' webpages, we conclude that the ESG criteria are normally not considered (due to "low volume", "lack of information from market participants – investees").

---

[65] § 48a of the Supplementary Pension Savings Act.

[66] Regulation (EU) 2019/2088 of the European Parliament and of the Council of 27 November 2019 on sustainability-related disclosures in the financial services sector (Text with EEA relevance) (further as "SFDR").

[67] National Bank of Slovakia, Re*port on the activities of the Financial Market Supervision Unit* (National Bank of Slovakia, 2021), 39, https://www.nbs.sk/_img/documents/_dohlad/makropolitika/soc-udf_2021_web.pdf (25 October 2023).

Country Report Spain

David Pérez Millán / Eva Recamán Graña

A. General Aspects on the Use of Investors' Influence for ESG Purposes

When it comes to environmental, social, and corporate governance (ESG) factors, the role of certain shareholders, particularly, institutional investors and asset managers, provides a scenario with a novel sheen on the surface, but raises debates that are considered classic issues in this field.

To begin with, in order to achieve certain objectives that are generally agreed upon, instead of resorting to external regulation that directly imposes or prohibits certain behaviours on large corporations from the outside, rules are used that indirectly seek to influence the decision-making process within these organisations. Furthermore, at least as far as investors and shareholders in general are concerned, relying mainly on the effects of public disclosure and accountability would ultimately lead to the decisions sought.[1]

In any case, when it comes to the part that institutional investors and asset managers can play as shareholders of portfolio companies, this seems to be the philosophy of the EU legislation, as can be seen in recitals 15 and 16 of the Directive (EU) 2017/828 amending Directive 2007/36/EC as regards the encouragement of long-term shareholder engagement (SRD II). These ideas are behind the "complain or explain" approach of the rules on engagement policy (Art. 3g SRD II), whose wording is so generic and offers such diverse options that, in some cases, they seem more like standards of a Code of Conduct than legal regulation.[2] This was to be expected in any case, as the amendment of the Directive was inspired on this point by the UK Stewardship Code and consequently shares its strategy.[3]

Something similar can be said about the rules on disclosure by institutional investors of their investment strategy and their arrangements with asset managers (Art. 3h SRD II). Since their engagement policy depends on the previous selection of portfolio companies, it seems logical that there is a need for disclosing

---

[1] For the debates on the different alternatives for legislative policies on corporate power in general, cf. *Parkinson*, Corporate Power and Responsibility, 1993, esp. 2 et seq., 346 et seq., 374 et seq.

[2] *Sequeira*, Revista de Derecho de Sociedades 61 (2021), 1 (29) (online version).

[3] *Roncero*, in: Festschrift for Alonso Ledesma, 2018, 766; *Herrero Morant*, Revista de Derecho del Mercado de Valores 28 (2021), 1 (3) (online version).

their decision-process to the market in this respect. In the words of recital 16 of the Directive, this information is also thought to have a positive effect on investor awareness and to strengthen their accountability to stakeholders and even civil society, in the belief, as recital 19 makes clear, that a long-term approach enables responsible asset stewardship.

In this sense, it is evident nowadays that any ESG legislative policy that hopes to be in any way successful needs to massively engage in sustainable activities not only involving corporations, but also retail consumers. The most important rules in this regard are to be found in EU Regulation 2019/2018 on sustainability-related disclosures in the financial services sector (SFDR), with the aim of enabling end investors to make informed investment decisions considering ESG factors, as inferred especially from recitals 5, 9 and 10 of that regulation.

In order to evaluate the effectiveness of European measures, however, it is vital to know how they have been incorporated and are being interpreted by EU member states, as well as to analyse the possible barriers that they may be facing from both a legal and practical point of view, in this case, in Spain.

B. Sustainable Ownership or Shareholder Governance

I. Spanish Legal Framework and its Limits

The strategy behind EU regulations on shareholder engagement can be justified by the competences of the European institutions, but Spanish legislators – who had more powers in this respect – have not gone further for the time being. On the contrary, the relevant rules of the SRD II have been transposed almost literally into Spanish law. Consequently, the content of Art. 3g SRD II is reproduced in different provisions: i) Art. 79 bis Act 20/2015 (LOSSEAR) and 89 bis Royal Decree 1060/2015 (ROSSEAR), for life insurance and reinsurance companies; ii) Art. 69.8 Royal Decree 304/2004, for pension funds and their management companies (RPFP); iii) Art. 47 ter Act 35/2003 (LIIC), for collective investment schemes (IIC), in particular, addressed to their asset managers (SGIIC); iv) Art. 67 bis Act 22/2014 for venture capital funds, and other closed-ended collective IIC and their management companies (LCR), specifically aimed also at the asset managers (SGEIC); v) Art. 224 bis Securities Market Act (LMV), regarding firms that provide investment services and banks that manage portfolios.

Spanish lawmakers have confined themselves to incorporating the measures required by SRD II in these rules as a minimum. Hence, the comply or explain alternative is replicated in the same terms that can be found in the Directive, with the idea that the reputational effect would encourage engagement.[4] At very

[4] *Chamorro*, La Ley 97 (2022), 1 (19) (online version).

least, formal compliance is to be expected, if only due to the fact that it could be easier than justifying why it has not been complied with. However, effective compliance will be more difficult to achieve in the absence of any enforcement mechanisms and sanctions.[5]

Apart from that, it has not been considered necessary for developing and specifying the provisions on the conduct to be followed by institutional investors and asset managers. Yet there may be both legal and practical obstacles to coordination with other shareholders and dialogue with the companies. In addition, it is not clear which investors are specifically targeted by the rules on engagement policy, and whether they are suitable for the task at hand.

II. Investors Subject to Rules on Engagement Policy

As is well known, the notion of institutional investors according to Art. 2 (e) SRD II is very narrow, comprising exclusively undertakings carrying out activities of life insurance or reinsurance and institutions for occupational retirement provisions, probably because all of them are supposed to have a long-term investment strategy. This restriction of the Directives' subjective scope could, however, be compensated to some extent by the fact that asset managers are defined in a broad sense under Art. 2 (f).[6] In this regard, Spanish regulation has extended the rules on shareholder engagement to different kinds of asset managers and in that way, at least, indirectly, to other institutional investors.[7]

Notwithstanding this, the rules on engagement policy do not generally apply to investors domiciled outside the EU. Only in some cases is it conceivable that these rules could be extended to those seeking to operate in Spain (Art. 2.1, 15 quater and 15 quinquies LIIC). On that basis, the National Securities Market Commission (CNMV) could in theory refuse the relevant authorisation to investment funds or investment companies in Spain which do not comply with the EU engagement policy as incorporated into Spanish law. There is, however, no previous experience suggesting that this will be the case.

As far as hedge funds are concerned, even if they have been set up under Spanish law, it is doubtful whether they are subject to the rules on engagement policy. In Spain, it has not been necessary to establish a new form of fund management

[5] *Herrero Morant* (fn. 3), 1 (13). However, explicitly in favour of this strategy and the lack of sanctions, *Martínez-Echevarría*, in: Interés social y gobierno corporativo sostenible: deberes de los administradores y deberes de los accionistas, 2019, 10 et seq. (online version).

[6] Cf. *Roncero* (fn. 3), 762 et seq.; *Rodríguez Artigas*, in: Festschrift for Alonso Ledesma, 2018, 1275 et seq.; *Martínez-Echevarría*, in: Interés social y gobierno corporativo sostenible: deberes de los administradores y deberes de los accionistas, 2019, 4 et seq. (online version); *Valmaña*, in: Rodríguez Artigas et al (eds.), Sociedades cotizadas y transparencia en los mercados, I, 2019, 1369 and 1370; *Sequeira* (fn. 2), 1 (30) (online version).

[7] *Herrero Morant* (fn. 3), 1 (7).

company devoted exclusively to hedge funds. Instead, special requirements, including additional capital requirements, are imposed on companies seeking to manage hedge funds pursuant to Art. 73 Royal Decree 1082/2012 (RIIC) and Circular 1/2006 CNMV. Nevertheless, the rules on prospectuses and periodic reporting are the same as those applicable to conventional IIC, and in general, the rules on financial funds apply to hedge funds unless provided otherwise (Art. 33 ter LIIC and Art. 73.1 RIIC).

As a result, at least in theory, it could be understood that hedge funds would also be subject to the rules on engagement policy. The real issue is whether these are investors who can play a significant role in ESG in practice. While the problem of institutional investors is their general lack of interest in monitoring management of the companies in which they invest, the problem of hedge funds is that their strategy is usually aimed at maximising returns at the risk of a short-term approach.[8] Strategies, however, may be different depending on the fund, and short-termism is not exclusively attributable to hedge funds.[9] Moreover, hedge funds may also pragmatically choose to promote sustainable policies to obtain higher profits.[10] In fact, as will be seen below, precisely those which seem to be most active in ESG issues concerning Spanish listed companies are, for whatever reason, interestingly, hedge funds.

III. Legal Obstacles to Shareholder Cooperation

In any case, it seems clear that in order to develop any engagement policy regarding the exercise of shareholder rights in their portfolio companies, institutional investors of all kinds will have to coordinate with each other and major shareholders. In this regard, that cooperation could theoretically encounter an obstacle in the Spanish regulations on mandatory takeover bids.[11] Nevertheless, the risk of shareholders being considered to be acting in concert for these reasons appears to be very low in practice.

Unlike Art. 5, paragraph 1, of the European Takeover Directive, Spanish law does not require the acquisition of securities to trigger the duty to make a public offer. According to Art. 128 b) LMV and Art. 3 Royal Decree 1066/2007 of 27 July (RD OPAs), a takeover bid shall be made by the person who obtains control of a listed company, whether or not they obtain such control by the acquisition of securities or by means of shareholders' agreements or by acting in concert with other holders of securities (Art. 131 LMV; Art. 4 and 5 RD OPAs).

[8] *León*, in: Festschrift for Rodríguez Artigas and Esteban Velasco, I, 2018, 156.

[9] *Roncero*, in: Festschrift for Alonso Ledesma, 2018, 752 and 758.

[10] *Noval*, Revista de Derecho de Sociedades 64 (2022), 1 (6).

[11] *Roncero* (fn. 3), 771 and 772, considering that this is the main legal obstacle, and it should be a necessary reform to prevent takeover regulations from impending cooperation between institutional investors.

Hence, it is true that acting in concert to influence the company policy by shareholders who jointly hold 30 % of voting rights could theoretically trigger the duty to make a bid irrespective of the objectives pursued by such a policy. However, to that effect, the coordination between shareholders should involve a substantial and stable change in the control structure of the offeree company, while shareholders acting in concert should intend to acquire the control of the company in this way.[12] Moreover, it has recently been argued that if shareholders do not acquire shares jointly, only a formal shareholders' agreement would legally force them to make an offer as such.[13]

On top of that, any change in control for those reasons seems very unlikely due to the concentrated ownership structure of Spanish listed companies, and the fact is that in the more than fifteen years that these regulations have been in force, there has not been a single case of a mandatory takeover bid due to acting in concert, as it were. It would be more than surprising if the first one was for cooperation between institutional investors on ESG policies.

The real problem is whether the engagement of institutional investors is possible due to other legal restrictions. In this regard, Spanish law does not distinguish according to the type of fund or the branch which a portfolio company belongs to for the purposes of limiting the possible engagement in the management of the company. However, depending on the nature of the issuer and the collective investment scheme, limitations may be introduced on the maximum percentage that the investment may represent in the outstanding securities of the same issuer, and in no case may such a holding enable institutional investors to exercise significant influence over the company (Art. 30.2 LIIC and Art. 51.2 RIIC).

Those provisions restrict the direct influence on the company because of the maximum percentages of shareholdings in the company's capital that it imposes. These limits could certainly be seen as an obstacle to the engagement policy. In this sense, it is indeed paradoxical to call for the activation and involvement of institutional investors on the one hand, and to restrict it on the other.[14] Nevertheless, these boundaries do not necessarily prevent coordination between shareholders and the exercise of certain membership rights, as will be seen, and other ways of influence in the decision-making of the portfolio companies that are available.

---

[12] *Pérez Millán*, in: Juste/Recalde (eds.), Derecho de OPAs, 2010, 135 et seq., with further references.

[13] *García de Enterría*, Revista de Derecho del Mercado de Valores 31 (2022), 1 (18 et seq.), although this is still a minority opinion.

[14] *Córcoles*, Asesores de voto (proxy advisors) y el ejercicio del derecho de voto en las sociedades cotizadas, 2014, 54.

IV. Legal Obstacles to Dialogue with the Directors

Just as important as influence through the exercise of membership rights can be influence exercised through informal channels. In this regard, calls for greater engagement of institutional investors via dialogue with the directors are not new, nor are the legal barriers they can sometimes encounter. To date, a satisfactory solution so far remains elusive.

At least since the Olivencia Report 1998, an official recommendation called for greater involvement of institutional investors in corporate governance of listed companies (9.4).[15] In the same vein, principle 4 of the Good Governance Code of Listed Companies 2020 (CBGSC) foresees that listed companies should maintain a publicly disclosed policy for communication and contacts with shareholders, institutional investors, and proxy advisors.[16] However, no specific measures have been adopted in Spanish law to further encourage such dialogue; national rules simply replicate the provisions of Art. 3g SRD II, and one of the reasons may be precisely that it is not clear how to reconcile this kind of communication with certain directors' duties.

In principle, the flow of information from the administrators only to certain shareholders could go against several duties of the directors in Spain. That is, in addition to the duty of equal treatment for shareholders (Art. 97 and 514 Companies Act) and the duty of confidentiality (Art. 228 c) Companies Act), there is the duty to refrain from communicating inside information based on (Art. 227.1 Companies Act and 14 c) Regulation (EU) 596/2014, of 16 April, on Market Abuse [MAR]).[17] In this sense, similarly to recital 19 MAR, principle 4 and recommendation 4 CBGSC consider it possible to reconcile the prohibition on unlawful disclosure of inside information and the principle of equal treatment of the shareholders with a communication policy about business and market developments between directors and investors. Nevertheless, there is no further indication of what the content of such a policy should be so as not to become unlawful.

However, some opinions may be useful in this context.[18] In general, it has been said that representative directors can inform the shareholders who appointed them since, compared to the rest, these shareholders are not in identical conditions or the same position as regards information, stakes, holding, or voting rights under Art. 97 and 514 Companies Act. In this sense, this kind of sharehold-

---

[15] The Report is available at https://www.cnmv.es/DocPortal/Publicaciones/CodigoGov/govsocot.pdf (25 October 2023).

[16] The Code is available at https://www.cnmv.es/DocPortal/Publicaciones/CodigoGov/CBG_2020.pdf (25 October 2023).

[17] In particular, on the risk of such a dialogue being considered inside trading, cf. *Valmaña* (fn. 6), 837.

[18] *Paz-Ares*, in: Festschrift for Rodríguez Artigas and Esteban Velasco, II, 2018, 96 et seq. and 135 et seq.

ers are to be considered blockholders that would play a different role in corporate governance monitoring the directors and mediating the interests of different groups of shareholders. For blockholders to fulfil these functions, managers must provide them with the necessary information. In the same vein, communication to blockholders would not represent unlawful disclosure of inside information by the directors because the disclosure would be made in the normal exercise of their duties in the terms of the exception foreseen in Art. 10.1 MAR.

The provisions with origins in the SRD II would reinforce this vision. This applies, in particular, when it is stated that institutional investors and asset managers have to describe how they monitor investee companies on relevant matters in their engagement policy. It would be contradictory if the same legislator who demands dialogue between investors and administrators on the one hand were to punish it on the other.[19]

V. Chances of Effective Engagement in Practice

As indicated above, Spanish capital markets are characterised by ownership concentration. Most Spanish listed companies are controlled by a majority shareholder, often part of a group of companies, or by a group of significant shareholders acting in concert. Avoiding the investment in companies dominated by main or anchor shareholders seems unrealistic.

In general terms, the common view is that the prevalence of the concentrated ownership structure in Spanish listed companies serves to work against the engagement of institutional investors and hedge funds. However, there are some rules in the Spanish Companies Act empowering shareholders that might increase the monitoring of majority shareholders. In particular, it has been argued that the Art. 161 Companies Act – allowing legally binding instructions and authorisations to the directors by the shareholders at the general meeting – will give activist shareholders bargaining power vis-à-vis controlling shareholders to find more effective ways of cooperation.[20]

In this sense, certain minority rights, even if exercised in a coordinated manner, could be important for the involvement of institutional investors and asset managers in the decision-making process of the investee companies. In particular, this entails the right to include new items on the agenda of the general meeting. It follows then, that, perhaps, for listed companies, this percentage should be 3% following what it is foreseen in Art. 495.1.a) and 519 Companies Act[21] when concerning significant shareholders or blockholders, despite the fact

[19] In favour of a revision of the principle of equal treatment due to the new duties imposed to institutional investors, *Viera*, in: Rodríguez Artigas et al (eds.), Sociedades cotizadas y transparencia en los mercados, I, 2019, 1475.

[20] *Saez Lacave*, InDret 2002, 1 (62 et seq.).

[21] Cf. *Chamorro* (fn. 4), 1 (4).

that reference is usually made to holders of at least 5 % of the share capital[22] in accordance with Spanish corporate law.

In any case, the possible intervention of these shareholders is not limited to the exercise of their rights at the general meeting, but includes "voice" in a broad sense, from the appointment of directors to communications with the company and its directors by other means, and also the "threat" to use their rights, claim liability from the directors, or exit the company altogether.[23]

The real problem seems to be if ESG factors are better taken into account by shareholders voting or threatening to vote at the meeting. In Spanish practice, the question has been raised in relation to the say-on-climate votes sponsored by the management of some companies. The findings that can be drawn from this experience are, however, inconclusive.

As already noted, contrary to what might have been expected, the most active investors in Spain as far as ESG issues are concerned have been precisely some hedge funds, most notably The Children's Investment Fund (TCI), founded and controlled by British billionaire, Chris Hohn. The TCI has organised a worldwide campaign in favour of say-on-climate votes, i.e., resolutions passed at the general meeting on climate action plans or strategies that have affected important Spanish listed companies.

Largely due to the pressure by this sort of investor, the directors of three IBEX 35 companies (Aena, Ferrovial e Iberdrola) made a proposal in 2021 that climate issues be subjected to a vote at their general meetings in all cases where a majority support level of over 90 % of the share capital is present. Yet some dissenting shareholders believed that the company's climate action strategy should be the responsibility of the board of directors and feared that voting on climate action plans could lead to inadequate climate strategies. Despite this background, it was expected that, in 2022, more companies would opt to include proposals in this area, in particular, an advisory vote on emissions reduction reports and the approval of the climate change strategy.[24] In the end, the numbers have been, however, rather modest and reluctance is only growing in that respect, which, unfortunately, paints an uncertain picture for the future.

VI. Nature and Initiative of the Proposals

In order to evaluate say-on-climate votes in Spain, the first thing to note is that all votes taken to date have been purely consultative, i.e., the resolutions passed at the general meeting on these matters were not binding for directors. It there-

---

[22] *Edmans*, ECGI 385 (2013), 1 (4) for the United States. For Spanish companies in general, *Paz-Ares* (fn. 18), 22.

[23] Cf. *Lacave* (fn. 20), 1 (18).

[24] *Georgeson/Cuatrecasas*, Corporate Governance and Institutional Investors, 2022, 14 and 42.

fore seems that this kind of voting is intended, in reality, not to seek the opinion of the shareholders, but rather to simply provide them with information and, at most, provide the possibility for supervising or controlling the decisions of the directors.[25]

In this respect, it should be kept in mind that climate-related shareholder proposals have mainly been submitted by shareholders in the USA, whereas in Europe, proposals by directors predominate. In fact, the Spanish market was a global pioneer in this regard, as is evidenced by Aena's hosting of the first-ever vote on a directors' climate-related proposal. Moreover, the proposals put forward by the directors are normally approved by the majority of the shareholders, while shareholder proposals do not usually have much support[26]. Some of them are even withdrawn before the annual meeting, typically after a settlement with the company, and they are nonetheless seen as successful cases by their proponents.[27]

However, it should also be noted that some of the proposals by the directors are the result of pressure from certain shareholders and, in particular, from institutional investors. Without going any further, Aena's directors were greatly influenced by the pressure personally exerted by Chris Hohn, who, in 2019 and 2020, sent letters to Ferrovial's and Aena's executive directors, as well as to Teresa Ribera, the Spanish Minister for Ecological Transition and Demographic Challenge, seeing as the state owns 51 % of Aena's shares through ENAIRE, the public corporate entity responsible for the air navigation management in Spain. It should nevertheless be pointed out that until February 2022, when he resigned, Mr Hohn – representing TCI Advisory Services, the manager of his fund – held a seat on the board of directors of Aena.

Some of these climate-related proposals were even accompanied by amendments to the Art. of association to reinforce the directors' commitment to consulting shareholders on the company's environmental policy, as in the case of Aena and Ferrovial. On the contrary, Iberdrola, which approved its Climate Action Policy at the 2022 annual general meeting, amended its bylaws to give the board the power to update that policy accordingly.

In any case, shareholder support for plans or reports on climate policy or strategy has been falling and opposition is even increasing, as it were. For example, while the votes held in 2021 exceeded 90 % support in all the cases, on 6 May 2022, at Repsol's annual general meeting, the consultative vote on the Company's Climate Strategy was approved by a majority in favour (83 % of the share capital), but with a significant vote against (14 %), including BlackRock.

---

[25] Cf. *Ellice*, Should Shareholders have their "Say on Climate"?, 2021, 1 (55).
[26] Cf. ISS Corporate Solutions, The Rise of Say on Climate Proposals, 2022, 2 et seq.
[27] *Tallarita*, Hastings Law Journal, 73 (2022), 1697 (1727).

VII. Opposing views

Some of the reasons that may explain the loss of support for climate action plans or reports in Spain are related to the criticisms that have been directed at them, especially when they are presented to the shareholders by the directors. The reservations, however, are indeed along the same lines as the doubts expressed in general about say-on-climate votes.

Among the critical voices in Spain are those of some proxy advisors. Glass Lewis, for example, is known to have expressed doubts and reservations about say-on-climate votes. In its policy guidelines for 2022, they stated that sufficient information is often not available to shareholders and the board may be abdicating this responsibility.[28] Consequently, on the occasion of Aena's General Meeting on 31 March 2022, they recommended that shareholders abstain and refrain from voting in favour of this item, because, in their opinion, the company did not provide sufficient information, and supporting it would relieve the directors of their responsibility for the plan.[29]

From a legal point of view, however, the resolution of the meeting would not exonerate the directors from liability, as it is generally clearly expressed in Art. 236.2 Companies Act, especially when the resolution is not binding, and the decision remains with the directors. Paradoxically, if the vote were not merely consultative and the directors received binding instructions at the general meeting, it would be more questionable whether they would continue to be liable at least vis-à-vis the shareholders.[30]

In any case, the real concern seems to be that this kind of director-sponsored plan can serve as a distraction for shareholders by contributing to greenwashing.[31] Along these lines, there is criticism that the company's plans are not regularly submitted to the general meeting for scrutiny. In this sense, TCI's original campaign called for annual voting on the company's plans so that investors could evaluate its climate strategy over time.

In Spain, it is precisely only at Aena and Ferrovial that votes specifically on climate reports are scheduled to take place annually. in Gestamp Automoción, too, the sustainability strategy was approved in 2021 (over 99 % in favour) and the board was to present the degree of progress of the group's ESG objectives for approval annually and on a consultative basis. However, there was no vote on the matter at the annual general meeting of 11 May 2022. At Iberdrola, only the Climate Action Policy was voted on and approved (almost 100 % in favour) in

[28] Glass Lewis 2022 Policy Guidelines ESG Initiatives, 7 and 27. Cf. also Glass Lewis Policy Guidelines ESG Initiatives, 30.

[29] More details in La Información, 16.3.2022.

[30] Cf. in general *Gandía*, La renuncia a la acción social de responsabilidad, 2017, 220 et seq.; *Recalde*, Anales de la Academia Matritense del Notariado 59 (2019), 625 (669 et seq.).

[31] Cf. *Eccles*, Forbes, 5.1.2021; *Sommer/Tufford*, Say on Climate: Investor Distraction or Climate Action?, 15.2.2022.

2021, but there was no vote on that policy in 2022, because, as seen above, the updating of the plan is the responsibility of the board according to the bylaws.

Another recurrent criticism is that the emission reduction targets are unclear or not verified, for which verification or approval by the Science-Based Target initiative (SBTi) is often requested.

Sometimes the objection that the information is not homogeneous also arises, and in this respect, it is argued that the recommendations of the Task Force on Climate-related Financial Disclosures (TCFD) should be followed.[32] Obviously, this demand should be compatible with compliance with the rules introduced by Directive (EU) 2022/2464 of the European Parliament and of the Council of 14 December 2022 amending Regulation (EU) 537/2014, Directive 2004/109/EC, Directive 2006/43/EC and Directive 2013/34/EU, as regards corporate sustainability reporting. Companies subject to the Directive will have to report according to European Sustainability Reporting Standards (ESRS), which, in principle, are considered to be aligned with the TCFD's recommendations (recital 30), and should therefore not impose an unnecessary burden on companies (recital 43).

Finally, there are objections to the content of these plans because of reasons of opposition. On the one hand, some of the climate plans presented by the administrators have been accused of lacking ambition. On the other hand, and conversely, they are considered to be going too far. BlackRock's change of heart is striking in this respect. Whereas in 2020 Larry Flink declared climate risk to be an investment risk, in May 2022, BlackRock considered some climate-related shareholder proposals to be more prescriptive or constraining and announced that they would sometimes vote against them.[33] This has been the case with some climate plans submitted by directors in Spain, such as Repsol's. Everything suggests, however, that, apart from the possible weaknesses of the plan, the war in Ukraine and the subsequent energy crisis also had something to do with it.

This review of the Spanish corporate practice in relation to say-on-climate votes indicates that the engagement of institutional investors and asset managers on ESG issues poses problems even when they relate to relatively well-defined objectives, such as the reduction of greenhouse gas emissions. It can be agreed that the investment according to ESG factors is nothing more than investment taking into account factors, among other things, that refer to the long-term value of the company. It is, furthermore, also legitimate to have different views on the company's intangibles and the factors that bring value to the company over that timespan.[34] This is precisely, however, why it is misguided to ultimately rely on investors in large corporations as an effective instrument for developing concrete and urgent legislative policy measures.

---

[32] Cf. ISS Corporate Solutions, The Rise of Say on Climate Proposals, 2022, 7 et seq.

[33] BlackRock, 2022 climate-related shareholder proposals more prescriptive than 2021.

[34] *Endmans*, ECGI 847 (2022), 1 (esp. 21 et seq.).

C. Sustainable Funding or Portfolio Governance

I. Outline of the Spanish Rules on Funding Management under ESG Aspects

Besides the legal or factual obstacles that it can encounter, moreover, the development of an engagement and dialogue policy by portfolio managers obviously depends on their investment strategy. Consequently, a second area of the regulation on sustainable finance is the one that targets, on the one hand, how sustainability guides the investment decisions of asset managers integrating ESG factors in the selection of the portfolio companies and, on the other hand, disclosure of that process to the market and potential clients.[35]

In this regard, Art. 3h SRD II on disclosure of the investment strategy of institutional investors and their arrangements with asset managers, has also been almost literally translated into Spanish law by virtue of various provisions: i) Art. 79 ter LOSSEAR, and 89 ter ROSSEAR, for life insurance and reinsurance companies; ii) Art. 16.9 Royal Decree 1/2002 (LPFP) and Art. 69 bis RPFP, for employment pension funds and their management companies; iii) Art. 47 quarter Act 35/2003 (LIIC), for asset managers investing on behalf of insurance companies or employment pension funds; iv) Art. 67 ter LCR, also for asset managers acting on behalf of insurance companies or employment pension funds. Nevertheless, the most important rule in terms of ESG aspects is to be found directly in Art. 3 SFDR.

In this regard, the integration of sustainability risks in the investment decision-making process or investment advice should be compatible with other principles of the financial regulatory law. In this sense, the principles of quantitative and qualitative risk diversification are to be found in several Spanish rules: Art. 23 and 30 LIIC; Art. 50–52, 90, and 104 RIIC; Art. 16 LPFP; Art. 69.2 and 72 RPFP; Art. 16 LCR. None of these rules have been amended in recent years to consider ESG selection criteria, which leads one to believe that Spanish legislators consider them to be compatible with ESG-orientated investment, however limited they may be in terms of effectiveness.

For example, investment funds in general should limit the concentration of risk in a way that ensures sufficient diversification (Art. 23.b) LIIC). In order to comply with this principle of risk diversification, as a general rule, investment in assets and financial instruments of the same issuer, or of entities of the same group, may not exceed 5 %, respectively, of the assets of the fund. The 5 % limit is extended to 10 % provided that the total investments of the fund in securities – in which it exceeds 5 % – do not exceed 40 % of its funds. Depending on the nature of the institution, the participant, and the assets involved in the investment, a higher limit may be established by regulation, as well as by additional risk di-

[35] Cf. *Krishnan*, in: Caldana/Levaldur (eds.), EFPA ESG Handbook, 2022, 208 et seq.

versification percentages (Art. 30.2 LIIC and Art. 50.2 RIIC). However, it has been noted that such percentages should not be misleading, as the power of institutional investors may be greater than their shareholding due to the dispersed ownership structure or possible alliances between them or with shareholders.[36]

As indicated above, private equity funds, venture capital funds, and, even, to some extent, hedge funds, are subject in Spain to rules similar to those applicable to mutual or more traditional funds. In particular, Art. 67 ter LCR extends the rules on investment strategy foreseen in Art. 3h SRD II to private equity funds and venture capital funds, and the rules on financial funds apply to hedge funds unless provided otherwise according to Art. 33 ter LIIC and Art. 73.1 RIIC.

Similar to what happens with their engagement policy, it therefore seems that the lack of suitability of alternative investment funds at developing an effective investment strategy in ESG terms has more to do with their business model than with the rules to which they are subject. These rules, in Spanish law, moreover, do not, in any case impose active involvement in the company's decision-making, but only the publication of that policy, if there is one at all.[37]

II. ESG Suitability and Investment Strategy

The development of an ESG-compliant investment strategy by portfolio managers is conditioned by their business model and structural details. Considering this economic reality to be a necessary premise for any analysis willing to effectively serve any future policymaking, the different nature of some particular investment vehicles should be briefly examined to review its suitability for enhancing the integration of ESG factors in their portfolio companies.

In this sense, as far as active mutual funds are concerned, their structure and business model relies on the management of a complex range of assets and designing of investment strategies. Contrary to what usually happens with passively managed funds, their portfolio is often more concentrated, allowing for a deeper analysis of the ESG compliance of their investee companies.[38] Consequently, at least in theory, the influence capacity of these funds is, due to its structure, higher, as a result.[39]

From a market perspective, international studies show an increasing flow of assets into ESG investment funds, as well as a correlation between the performance of funds with a higher rating ESG portfolio composition compared to their

---

[36] *García/Martínez*, in: Festschrift for Sequeira, 2022, 833.

[37] *Roncero* (fn. 3), 766; *Valmaña* (fn. 6), 1372.

[38] Cf. *Shawky/Smith,* The Financial Review 40 (2005) 481 (482 et seq.).

[39] *Mitaine*, in: Caldana/Levaldur (eds.), EFPA ESG Handbook, 2022, 210 et seq. However, not as much as hedge funds, making active mutual funds less suited for engagement in comparison with the first and more prone to suffering from the *free rider effect*, *Lund*, Standford Law Review, 2019, 687 (718).

peers (although the biases of certain parameters of the analysis have likewise been pointed out).[40]

In the Spanish context, no evidence has been found to that effect. That is, no specific literature specifically addresses assessing the impact that these active fund management strategies have had on the implementation of ESG policies in portfolio companies. That said, investment funds with active strategies are, as above-mentioned, precisely the ideal vehicles for promoting such policies – both through engagement and exit policies, or even exclusion of certain companies or sectors from the portfolio design.

For their part, passively managed investment vehicles (exchange traded funds or index traded funds, collectively "index funds")[41] follow the investment strategy of replicating the performance of a given index or market benchmark.[42] This type of fund began to be marketed in Spain in 2006. For all intents and purposes, they are legal investment funds. As such, index funds are regulated by LIIC and RIIC.

As a result of its passive investment strategy, these funds are necessarily connected over the long-term to the companies that constitute their portfolio.[43] However, there is uncertainty as to the extent to which they could or even should be required to have an engagement policy.[44] The peculiar nature of these funds requires analysing their aptness for the promotion of ESG standards also from the perspective of their portfolio design, as it were.

The mainstream opinion, moreover, is that passive funds are likely to be weakly motivated voters.[45] Regarding ESG engagement, it has been pointed out that requiring the inclusion of index funds in the ownership governance system – therein demanding of them specific research and analysis – could undermine their competitive advantage, i. e., their lower costs and fees.[46] Even more, it has been argued that it is doubtful whether index funds are actually allowed to be traded on the basis of information, as they offer their customers not the potential opportunity to beat the designated benchmark, but, instead, a market rate of return based on substantial diversification.[47]

Moreover, when it comes to disinvesting, the constraints of this type of fund limit its capacity to influence through an exit strategy. The mere fact of offering

---

[40] *Tan*, in: Caldana/Levaldur (eds.), EFPA ESG Handbook, 2022, 188 et seq.

[41] Challenging the idea of identifying "passive investment" with "passive management", *Robertson*, Yale Journal on Regulation, 2019, 795 (807).

[42] On their functioning, e. g., *Robertson* (fn. 42), 795 (808 et seq.).

[43] For an overview of the nature and functioning of these funds from the Spanish perspective, *Alda/García/Marco*, Boletín Económico de ICE 3069 (2015), 35 (36 et seq.).

[44] *Fisch*, in: Katelouzou/Puchniak (eds.), Global Shareholder Stewardship, 2022, 454 (461 et seq.).

[45] I.a., *Lund* (fn. 40), 687, (717 et seq.). However, cfr. *Robertson* (fn. 42), 795 (798).

[46] *Lund* (fn. 40), 687, (717 et seq.); *Fisch* (fn. 45), 454 (461).

[47] *Fisch* (fn. 45), 454 (461).

investment strategies which, in principle, track indexes (hence producing, by nature, a sort of rational apathy from the stewardship perspective), however, does not, per se, prevent the development of active strategies which are not necessarily less cost-efficient, therein complementing passive investment strategies by implementing small active ones[48]. Passive investment funds have, furthermore, increased their governance engagement, especially in areas that they identify as affecting a large number of their portfolio companies, in which they are trying to implement the best practices of industry leaders.[49] The same will presumably start happening with, for example, climate risks.

However, from the perspective not of ownership governance but of portfolio governance, nothing would prevent – at least hypothetically – a preselection of the composition of the fund in line with the implementation of ESG, influencing the possible assets invested prior to their investment even through exclusion mechanisms,[50] a sort of "sustainable sample optimization".

As concerns synthetic traded funds, they are composed of financial instruments (derivatives, swaps, etc.) that, in principle, do not provide them with voting rights. As a result, they do not appear to be structurally efficient vehicles for promoting ESG factors from an ownership governance perspective. It is likewise far from evident how it would be possible to design a portfolio based on a sustainable sample.[51]

Regarding alternative investment funds, the legislation that has been implemented by the European Union in recent years has also led to the need for their transformation and internal reorganisation (as of the other market participants).[52] As seen above, hedge funds are subject in Spain to rules like those applicable to mutual funds (Art. 73.1 RIIC). On the other side, Art. 67 ter LCR extends the rules on investment strategy foreseen in SRD II to private equity funds and venture capital funds.

It therefore appears that the suitability of alternative investment funds for enhancing sustainable funding and portfolio governance also depends more on their business model than on the rules to which they are subject.[53]

---

[48] This is, for example, the case of the ETFs Research Enhanced Index Equity (REI) ESG, *Camarero/Pascual,* Aestimatio, The IEB International Journal of Finance, 14 (2017), 26 (29 et seq.); *Alda/García/Marco* (fn. 44), 35 (37).

[49] *Fisch* (fn. 45), 454 (462).

[50] *Mitaine* (fn. 40), 210.

[51] Without the sustainable perspective, this idea can be found in a both appealing and sophisticated fashion in *Robertson* (fn. 42), 795 (804).

[52] *Plana Paluzie,* Revista Española de Capital Riesgo, 1 (2021), 37 (62). On the impact of the integration of sustainability risks in alternative investment funds, *Tapia,* Revista de Derecho Bancario y Bursátil, 164 (2022), 435 (435 et seq.).

[53] On the possibility of activist hedge funds acting as "ESG Arbitrageurs", see *Christie,* UC Davis Law Review, 2021, 875 (922 et seq.).

Finally, notwithstanding the limitations that institutional investors have to act as stewards, pension funds are considered to be a suited vehicle for incorporating not only the economic but also the sustainability preferences of their beneficiaries. In the words of the High-Level Expert Group on Sustainable Finance, "pension funds' long-term liabilities make them ideal providers of sustainable finance".[54] In fact, there is data showing that pension funds in Spain are one of the main institutional investors in ESG products.[55]

With specific regard to the Spanish regulatory context, Art. 16.1 LPFP was amended through Royal Decree 3/2020 to transpose the Directive (EU) 2016/2341 and, only for employment pension funds, the Directive (EU) 2017/828. Now, in a similar vein as the latter, a "comprehensive statement of the principles of its investment policy" is to be elaborated (Art. 16.8 LPFP).[56]

In the case of employment pension funds, it must be specified whether socially responsible investment criteria (ethical, social, environmental and governance) affecting the various assets of the fund are actually considered in investment decisions (Art. 16.8 III LPFP). A "long-term investment strategy statement" must also be drawn up and sufficiently disclosed (Art. 16.9 LPFP, regulation developed in Art. 69 bis RPFP).[57]

For the case of publicly promoted pension funds approved by Act 12/2022, a special control committee shall be set up, being required, inter alia, to evaluate the fund's policy on engagement and voting at general meetings and the fund's sustainable investment policy on a quarterly basis. It must also approve the annual publication of information on sustainability policy, engagement, and the exercise of shareholder political rights [Art. 58.1 g) LPFP].

III. ESG Interests and Client Interests in Portfolio Management

Apart from the possible conflicting relationship between ESG-compliant and prudential portfolio strategies, the integration or consideration by fund managers of ESG or sustainability strategies when deciding the composition of their portfolio may, in theory, at least, clash with the interests of their clients in search of the highest return on their investment.[58]

Under Spanish law, it is not regulated how exactly the possible conflict arising between fund companies or asset managers pursuing ESG goals and their

---

[54] Final Report 2018 by the High-Level Expert Group on Sustainable Finance Secretariat provided by the European Commission, 74.

[55] Spainsif Report, La inversión sostenible en España, 2022, 69.

[56] On the transposition of these instruments, *Palá Laguna*, Transposición reglamentaria de la Directiva sobre implicación a largo plazo en cotizadas en materia de fondos de pensiones de empleo, 2022, 1 et seq.

[57] *Herrero Morant* (fn. 3), 1 (16 et seq.).

[58] For instance, regarding pension funds, Art. 69.1 and 7 I LPFP. On the possibility of the conflict ESG preferences *v* return, *Fisch* (fn. 45), 454 (465 et seq.).

clients has to be mediated, apart from the usual rules that demand managing or investing in the exclusive benefit or interest of the client or final beneficiary. In particular, neither the general rule on the interest of the customer (that is to be found in Art. 208 LMV), nor the references to the concept of the "best interest of the clients" in other provisions (e.g., Art. 61 Royal Decree 217/2008) consider the sustainability perspective, so far.

Similarly, the CNMV does not seem to have an interpretation of the consumer interest from a specific sustainability perspective. The CNMV document on consultations on the implementation of MiFID II refers to the concept of "best interests of the client", but without going, for the moment, into the perspective of sustainability either.[59]

Nevertheless, it seems that if the information on the ESG investment policy of the fund is properly available to the final client before investing, such a conflict would not transpire as long as the investment strategy advertised and duly disclosed in the precontractual information is actually complied with.[60]

Something similar can be sustained regarding whether there is any legal limitation to the shareholder activism of fund managers. Under Spanish Law, there are apparently no other specific limitations to the stewardship strategy of the fund, apart from it being consistent with the existing regulation and the information disclosed to the public, in particular, specifically to the final beneficiary. In addition to the prospectus, the fund discloses its sustainability objectives as an annex to the prospectus (cf. Art. 23 RIIC).[61] In turn, asset managers are required to disclose their engagement policy – both as shareholders as well as managers of third parties' assets (cf. Art. 47 ter LIIC). All this together allows the properly targeted client to make an appropriate assessment accordingly.

Furthermore, in line with MiFID II, investment firms designing financial instruments to be marketed to clients must implement an approval process for each instrument to identify a market of end clients to whom the instrument will be addressed, with the aim of ensuring that the characteristics of the products are the most appropriate for each type of client identified. In this way, the goal of investor protection is reinforced, since questions relating to the suitability of the financial instrument for the specific customer at whom it is aimed are present not only at the time of marketing, but from the very conception and design of the instrument itself (Art. 71 Royal Decree 217/2008). If this procedure is followed, it should not reach the point where the conflict we are discussing exists.

---

[59] CNMV, Questions and answers on the implementation of the MiFID II Directive (last updated 14.12.2020). However, this perspective is already present in practice. For example, cf. Sustainable and Responsible Investment Policy of Santander Asset Management Group, March 2022.

[60] *Fisch* (fn. 45), 454 (466).

[61] E.g., Sustainabilty Annex of Abanca Renta Fija Transición Climática 360, FI., last updated on the CNMV online portal in January 2023.

Interestingly, where a conflict may arise is between asset owners and asset managers. It has been identified as a possible risk that certain institutional investors (e.g., investment funds) may be interested in engagement policies that require, for example, long-term investments, while asset managers could have an interest in policies that generate short-term returns. Including asset managers in the SRD II is a way of also tackling this issue.[62]

D. Sustainable Trading or Product Governance

I. Overview of the Spanish Legal Framework

The main Spanish rules on product planning and distribution of investment shares are to be found in Art. 208 ter LMV and Art. 30 sexies and 76 et seq. of the Royal Decree 217/2008 modified by the Royal Decree 1464/2018, transposing Art. 10 Del Directive 2017/593.

In accordance with European requirements, the Spanish regulation provides a regime whereby investment firms that design financial instruments for marketing must implement an approval process by the board of directors of the investment firm itself for each instrument produced, and in that approval process, identify the market of end clients to whom the instrument will be addressed. The aim is to ensure that the characteristics of the product are the most appropriate for each type of client detected, including the distribution channels of the financial instruments concerned in the analysis.

It follows then, that financial service providers producing financial instruments shall ensure that such instruments are designed to meet the needs of a defined target market of end clients within the relevant client category. They shall also make sure that the distribution strategy for financial instruments is compatible with the defined target market and shall take reasonable steps to guarantee that the instrument is distributed in the defined target market (Art. 208 ter.1 LMV).

In addition to that, they must assess the compatibility of those instruments with the needs of the clients to whom they provide investment services, taking also the defined target market of the end clients into account. The financial service providers must also ensure that the instruments are offered or marketed only when it is in the client's interest to do so (Art. 208 ter.2 LMV).

Moreover, investment service providers must identify customer groups whose needs, characteristics and objectives are not compatible with the product or service (Art. 74.2 *in fine* Royal Decree 2017/2008). Where the distributor does not have the necessary information for assessing one or more aspects of the target market, it is particularly relevant that it takes the target audience and the distribution strategy provided by the producer of the financial instrument into ac-

[62] *Herrero Morant* (fn. 3), 1 (7).

count. In such a case, and provided that it is a service other than advice or discretionary portfolio management, it shall warn the client that the investment firm cannot guarantee the client's compatibility with the product. For particularly complex or high-risk products as well as in situations where significant conflicts of interest could arise, the institution shall consider the non-inclusion of such a product in the product offering for its client base or a group of clients (Art. 75.3 Royal Decree 2017/2008) before the provision of the investment service as such.

In this manner, investor protection is reinforced, since issues relating to the suitability of the financial instrument for the specific customer at whom it is aimed are no longer present only at the time of marketing, but also from the very conception and design of the instrument itself.

Furthermore, the CNMV may specify the procedures and factors to be considered in determining the target market for financial instruments, as well as the processes and systems that institutions must implement to reasonably ensure that products are distributed to the identified target market (Art. 208 ter.3 LMV).[63]

Failure to comply even occasionally with the obligations on the design and distribution of products provided for in Art. 208 ter is considered a "very serious infringement" of internal organisational measures and prudential requirements (Art. 283.12 LMV). When the noncompliance is "merely occasional or isolated", it is already considered a "serious infringement" (Art. 296 TRLMV) as such.

II. ESG Implications on Formal Product Release and Monitoring of the Distribution of Fund Units

Under Spanish Law, the regulation on product surveillance and monitoring by investment firms producing and distributing financial instruments is found under Art. 66 ff. Royal Decree 2017/2008, which complements and develops the general legal framework presented above.

As of this moment, no alteration has been identified on the standards on target market determination connected to ESG integration. As regards the integration of sustainability factors into the product governance obligations, neither Delegated Directive (EU) 2021/1269 nor Delegated Directive (EU) 2017/593 has been transposed. However, certain reports point toward interpreting the modification in the sense of having to consider sustainability in defining the target market and its distribution strategy, as well as the circumstances of the customer, including their sustainability preferences, in order to verify that they are part of the product's target market.[64]

---

[63] Cf. also Art. 220 sexies 1 LMV, on the competence of the natural persons providing such advice.

[64] For example, FinReg360, Los criterios ASG se incorporan a la evaluación de la idoneidad, la gestión de inversiones y los procedimientos de las entidades, 02.09.2021.

Nevertheless, regarding the impact of the recent European regulations on the market of fund units – especially in connection to the information of sustainability risks and principal adverse impacts – the CNMV has published several documents trying to clarify the practical implementation of the Regulation (FAQ documents,[65] documents on disclosure of sustainability risks and PAIS templates, on updating the prospectus,[66] etc.).

Finally, the upcoming ESG-oriented production and distribution may also require attention to be paid to ESG specific expense-related issues as, for instance, whether the investment on certain products could generate specific management costs, resulting in higher fees or, even, in charging the final client with an overpriced fee.

In principle, according to Art. 5.11 RIIC, the only expenses that can be charged to the funds are those (i) included in the prospectus (ii) that correspond to services effectively rendered to the fund, (iii) that are essential for the normal development of the activity, and (iv) which do not represent an additional cost with respect to the remuneration charged by the fund manager or the depositary in their respective fees.

Yet, the CNMV states that the costs of sustainability analysis relating to investment decision-making and the selection of securities may be charged, provided that they are disclosed in the prospectus and are original thinking with significant conclusions that are not obvious or in the public domain, since under these requirements, they could be considered to be assimilable to the costs of financial analysis. Other types of sustainability-related expenses, however, such as ESG risk integration, expenses arising from updating prospectuses and periodic reports, or expenses generated by the consideration of principal adverse impacts, should not be charged to the fund, since they correspond to functions assumed by the fund manager and are already remunerated in the corresponding fee. Among the expenses that cannot be charged would also be those derived from the drafting of the contract of the sustainability index.[67]

III. Product Intervention and Prohibitions ("Brownlisting")

Art. 20 et seq. of the Royal Decree-Law 21/2017 on urgent measures for the adaptation of Spanish law to European Union Regulations on the securities mar-

[65] Cf. CNMV Preguntas y Respuestas sobre la Normativa de Sostenibilidad Aplicable a los Productos Financieros: Reglamento 2019/2088 (SFDR) y Reglamento 2020/852 (Taxonomía) (last updated 19.07.2022).

[66] Reglamento (UE) 2019/2088: simplificado procedimiento de actualización fondos de inversión, 18.02.2021.

[67] CNMV Preguntas y Respuestas sobre la Normativa de Sostenibilidad Aplicable a los Productos Financieros: Reglamento 2019/2088 (SFDR) y Reglamento 2020/852 (Taxonomía) (last updated 19.07.2022), question 6 bis (13).

ket (transposition an adaptation to the MiFID package) establishes the current rules on suspension and exclusion from trading of financial instruments by the governing bodies of regulated markets and by the CNMV.

Specifically, Art. 21.1 provides that the CNMV may decide to suspend trading in financial instruments admitted to regulated markets subject to its supervision when there are special circumstances that may disrupt the normal course of transactions of those financial instruments or that make such a measure advisable in the interests of investor protection. In particular, one of the circumstances that allows the exclusion includes the issuer's failure to comply with its obligations, especially with regard to the submission and publication of information (Art. 21.1 c) Royal Decree-Law 21/2017).

However, to date, Spanish regulation does not have any special rules on product intervention or prohibition regarding non-sustainable fund units, neither does there appear to be any kind of "brownlisting" strategy in place. Hence, in the current state of the regulation, it seems that the possibilities for control of the distribution of a given "brown" product could only be articulated through control of the advertising and precontractual information that the offeror provides on the product, specifically regarding information on the sustainability of the financial product, and especially, regarding the main adverse sustainability risks and adverse impacts on sustainability factors, i. e. their "substantial contribution" and "significant harm" to the environmental objectives.

IV. Boosting Sustainability through Investment Advice

Reorienting capital flows towards a more sustainable economy is, *expressis verbis*, one of the main goals of the Financing Sustainable Growth Action Plan.[68] It remains unclear, however, whether that goal is to be pursued to the extent of allowing the investment adviser to "steer" the client's investment decision in the direction of sustainable products, even at the expense of or in the knowledge of the lower profitability of that product.

In Spain, there is no particular concrete information from the CNMV regarding practices or investment advice aiming to steer the purchase resolutions of private investors towards financial products that qualify as sustainable, or, at least, no concern has been expressed accordingly. However, it could be inferred from the communications and reports published by the Supervisory Authority that this "investor targeting or steering" – insofar as it is at the core of EU policy –

[68] Communication from the Commission to the European Parliament, the European Council, the Council, the European Central Bank, the European Economic and Social Committee and the Committee of the Regions, Brussels, 8.3.2018 COM(2018) 97 final.

is desired and therefore does not generate conflict[69] if the client is properly consulted about its profile and informed about the product.[70]

Moreover, studies support that "the incentives to invest in these sustainable products do not always correspond to a better expected return on investment, which shows that in many cases investors are willing to receive lower returns in exchange for investing in more sustainable companies".[71] One issue to rethink in that respect, perhaps, would be how to define "optimal return" on the light of sustainable investments. Given the purpose of the policy of tackling the climate emergency and pursuing ESG needs, perhaps even performing above-market value could be inadequate if the portfolio composition does not match the client's climate-friendly preferences accordingly.

Connecting the prior matter with the issue of liability claims from private investors derived from "steering" the client into sustainable investments with suboptimal profits (this "steering" understood as inaccurate advice regarding ESG information), not much has been said in Spain.

In principle, the issue should therefore be solved as a typical prospect liability case (Art. 38 TRLMV).

Be it as it may, so far, we have no knowledge of case law claiming damages based on a breach of the expectations of obtaining higher returns when investing in sustainable products. The limited existing literature doubts that an investor could, in practice, gather the evidentiary material necessary for the success of such an action ("an investor would have a hard time proving that he suffered a financial loss").[72]

From another perspective, another possibility is contemplated:

> "Once the possibility of claiming financial losses has been discarded, an investor could argue that there were non-pecuniary motives for investing in a sustainable product. Finding out that the investment was not sustainable might have then caused him mental distress, suffering and inconvenience as the investment not only had an objective value but also a subjective one. The problem is that obtaining an award for moral damages is usually more cumbersome than being awarded pecuniary losses".[73]

---

[69] *Gómez/Guyón,* CNMV Boletín Trimestral III (2021), 1 (10 et seq., esp. text to note 10).

[70] On the use (and limitations) of the pre-contractual obligations as the main mechanisms to redirect capital flows towards sustainable investments, *Cerrato*, Revista de Derecho del Sistema Financiero 4 (2022), 297 (307 et seq.).

[71] *Alessi/Ossola/Panzica,* Journal of Financial Stability, 2021, 1 (2): "This means that investors accept a lower remuneration for their investments, ceteris paribus, insofar as these investments are linked to greener and more transparent firms. We interpret this as evidence of climate risk being viewed as significant, with the market seeing value in investing in greener assets as a hedging strategy towards worse environmental outcomes."

[72] *Fanego*, Revista de Derecho del Mercado de Valores 27 (2020), 1 (10) (online version).

[73] *Fanego* (fn. 73), 1 (10).

In the end, preliminary conclusions from authors who have hypothetically considered these two possibilities point out the unlikely success of such a claim.[74]

V. Product Governance and Greenwashing

For its part, the CNMV has expressed its concern regarding possible abuses arising from the perverse incentives that may appear in a market that increasingly demands sustainable investments, which could lead to "dressing up" information to appear "greener" than it really is.[75] Consequently, the Supervisory Authority has provided Guidelines regarding the minimum information to be contained in the prospectus of collective investment schemes (IIC) promoting environmental or social features or aiming at sustainable investments (Art. 8 or 9 SFDR, respectively), and considerations on the principal adverse impacts (PAIs) and their material impact on investments.[76]

In particular, a financial product qualifying as Art. 8 SFDR (which "promotes, among other characteristics, environmental or social characteristics, or a combination of those characteristics, provided that the companies in which the investments are made follow good governance practices") may include ESG elements in its name only if the minimum percentage of investments indicated in the prospectus for achieving the environmental or social characteristics it promotes exceeds 50 %, provided that the remaining investments do not alter the achievement of such environmental or social characteristics.

In the case of financial products under Art. 9 SFDR – which have "sustainable investment as its objective and an index has been designated as a reference benchmark" – the answer of the CNMV is based on the European Commission Decision of 6 July 2021 regarding the questions submitted by the European Supervisory Authorities on 7 January 2021. This Decision provided that, in this case, it should be invested in underlying assets qualifying as "sustainable investments" as defined in Art. 2(17) of the SFDR, although "sustainable investments" may include investments for certain specific purposes such as hedging or liquidity as long as they are in line with the sustainable investment objective. As a result, the CNMV considers that financial products according to Art. 9 SFDR may include ESG elements in their names since, with the exceptions of liquidity and hedging in the terms indicated, all their investments must be sustainable.

Regarding the use of ESG elements in commercial communications in general – outside the scope of their name – only financial products falling within Art. 8

[74] *Fanego* (fn. 73), 1 (10).

[75] CMNV, La necesidad de seguir avanzando en las finanzas sostenibles, statement of the Vicepresident, Ms. Montserrat Martínez, 30.11.2021.

[76] CNMV Preguntas y Respuestas sobre la Normativa de Sostenibilidad Aplicable a los Productos Financieros: Reglamento 2019/2088 (SFDR) y Reglamento 2020/852 (Taxonomía) (last updated 19.07.2022).

or 9 SFDR may include such terms, provided that the content of the advertising message is aligned with the information in the prospectus.[77]

As of June 2022, the assets of investment funds registered as Art. 8 or 9 SFDR reached 71,430 million euros, representing 24.1 % of the total. Of these, investment funds promoting environmental and social characteristics (Art. 8) accumulated 68,548.6 million euros (23.1 % of total investment funds) and 3,054 million euros (1.0 % of the total) funds with a sustainable investment objective (Art. 9).[78]

Finally, regarding the precise topic of ESG labelling, the Spanish supervisor has issued certain guidelines in relation to the information that companies generally "release" to the market, calling for (i) more quantitative information, not just qualitative information; (ii) comparable information; (iii) complete information; (iv) reliable information; and finally (v) understandable information.[79]

However, it has been pointed out that the lack of harmonised remedies against the misuse of ESG labelling to date – combined with the burden of proof of the client in the event of a dispute – could perversely incentivise the "green" labelling financial products as a result.[80]

---

[77] CNMV, La CNMV publica criterios para la aplicación de la nueva normativa europea en materia ambiental, social y de gobernanza (ASG) en los servicios financieros, press statement, 01.06.2021.

[78] Asociación de instituciones de inversión colectiva y fondos de pensiones, Fondos de inversión nacionales ESG, 30.06.2022.

[79] CMNV, Supervisión del desempeño no financiero, statement of the Vicepresident, Ms. Montserrat Martínez, 20.10.2021.

[80] *Cerrato* (fn. 71), 297 (312 et seq.). It also should not be forgotten that the Regulation (EC) 66/2010 of 25 November 2009 is more than a decade old.

Country Report Netherlands*

Christoph Van der Elst

A. Introduction

Sustainable growth and development have been on the agenda of various fora of Dutch society for a long time. When the OECD started developing its thirty green growth indicators, the Netherlands was the first country to apply these OECD indicators, with demonstratable development on twenty points.[1] The Netherlands has provided thorough reporting on progress on indicators such as water use intensity, energy efficiency, etc. since the late 1980s.[2]

More recently, awareness of the importance of sustainable growth is soaring everywhere in Dutch society. Notably, a new proposal by the legislature for a law on undertaking internationally responsible and sustainable pursuits was launched in March 2021 requiring companies' awareness that their activities can have an adverse effect on the environment or human rights. The law likewise calls for reasonable measures preventing and/or limiting these effects and even halting the activities if these effects could not reasonably be restricted.[3] In a broader perspective, the Dutch legislator enacted the Law on Climate in 2019, that stipulates the following in article 2:

"a framework for the developments of policy aimed at irreversibly and step-by-step reduction greenhouse gas emissions in the Netherlands, to a level that will be 95 % lower in 2050 than in 1990, in order to prevent global warming and limiting the change of the climate. To achieve this target for 2050, our Ministers responsible for climate change and emissions aim to achieve a 49 % reduction in greenhouse gas emissions by 2030 and a fully CO_2-neutral electricity production by 2050."

A climate plan was consequently developed providing the policy which would achieve these reduction goals.[4] The plan requires the government to develop

* This chapter keeps track of the developments in the Netherlands up to November 2022.

[1] OECD, Towards Green Growth: Monitoring Process, Paris, OECD Publishing, 2011, 17.

[2] Statistics Netherlands, Green Growth in the Netherlands, The Hague, CBS, 2011, 52 p.

[3] Wet verantwoord en duurzaam internationaal ondernemen, Kamerstukken II 2020/21, 35761, https://www.tweedekamer.nl/kamerstukken/wetsvoorstellen/detail?id=2021Z04465&dossier=35761#wetgevingsproces (17 September 2023).

[4] Ministry of Economic Affairs and Climate, Klimaatplan 2021–2030, April 2020, 60 p., https://open.overheid.nl/repository/ronl-c66c8a00-ac14-4797-a8ea-973a98c5bee0/1/pdf/Klimaatplan%202021-2030.pdf (17 September 2023).

measures across all levels of Dutch society. In addition, the Dutch judiciary is using its powers to emphasise the role of the government as well as companies in taking appropriate action in the fight against climate change. Next to the famous Shell case[5], in the Urgenda case, the Dutch Supreme Court confirmed the court of appeal's decision in 2019 that the state is obligated to reduce the greenhouse gas emissions by the end of 2020 by at least 25 % compared to the emissions in 1990, based on the fact that the emissions provide a real and immediate risk to people's lives or welfare and the Dutch state is aware of this risk, thus being in breach with the provisions of the European Convention on the Protection of Human Rights and Fundamental Freedoms.[6]

The focus of this contribution is on several European regulatory developments in sustainable finance and its transposition and implementation in the Netherlands. The second section discusses the embedding of sustainability issues into Dutch corporate governance framework. The stakeholder approach has long since been adopted into Dutch company law, however, recently, pressure from various stakeholders that sustainability requirements likewise be included in the execution of the duties of the board of directors is increasing. The third section addresses the sustainability requirements of the financial entities. Section four addresses the state of the art of the (disclosures of the) financial products sustainability specifications. The AFM-studies show that significant progress has been made at adequately informing the financial end-investor, while also at assessing the quality of information (and the sustainable financial investment process) which could be improved. The finding was, however, that not all end-investors can fully and sufficiently fulfil the information disclosure requirement. Section five provides a brief conclusion.

B. Sustainability in the Dutch Corporate Governance Scene

I. The Dutch Corporate Governance Model

Book 2 of the Dutch Civil Code (DCC) provides the statutory legal framework for companies, their boards and their shareholders. The DCC distinguishes between two types of companies divided by shares: public limited liability companies (naamloze vennootschappen or NV) and private limited liability companies (besloten vennootschappen met beperkte aansprakelijkheid or BV). Since the beginning of the 70s, the private limited liability company has become very successful. While there are many differences between the two forms (open

[5] See Section II.2.

[6] Supreme Court, 20 December 2019, ECLI:NL:HR:2019:2007, an English version of the Court's decision can be found here: https://www.urgenda.nl/wp-content/uploads/ENG-Dutch-Supreme-Court-Urgenda-v-Netherlands-20-12-2019.pdf (17 September 2023).

versus closed, capital requirement differences, etc.), as both involve familiarity with the notion of capital, shares and shareholders, the one versus two-tier board structure and the division of powers between board and shareholders are actually very similar.

Larger Dutch companies typically have a two-tier board structure with a management board (in Dutch: *Raad van Bestuur*) and a supervisory board (in Dutch: *Raad van Commissarissen*). Following the 1949 Dutch Supreme Court's decision in *Doetinchemse IJzergieterij*[7], and the following enactment of Articles 2:129 and 2:239 DCC, the management board controls and oversees the management of the company and the company's overall strategy. Pursuant to articles 2:140 and 2:250 DCC, the supervisory board is responsible for exercising supervision over the management and policy of the management board and over the general course of the business of the company and its enterprise.[8] In the two-tier board system, the supervisory board is appointed by the general meeting of shareholders (AGM) pursuant to articles 2:142 jo 2:144 DCC[9], and has the legal duty to appoint and to remove members of the management board under the *structuurregime*, according to article 2:162 DCC.[10] The AGM has the right to remove the directors that are appointed by the AGM at any time and without reason, in accordance with article 2:134(1) DCC.[11]

Nevertheless, in the famous *Forumbank* case (Supreme Court 21 January 1955, *NJ* 1959, 43), the Supreme Court decided that the AGM is not empowered to give instructions to the board of directors,[12] nor is the general meeting allowed to exceed the limitation of its powers.[13] The Supreme Court specified the division

[7] Supreme Court 1 April 1949, Nederlands Juristenblad, 1949, 465.

[8] *de Brauw*, Strategiebepaling bij beursvennootschappen, activistische aandeelhouders en bescherming in het Nederlandse stakeholdermodel, Ondernemingsrecht. 2022, 141–155.

[9] In addition, the employees' council has the binding right to nominate one-third of the members of the supervisory board (article 2:158(6) DCC).

[10] And, since the Board and Governance Act, ex article 2:164a DCC for the one-tier board system.

[11] However, one may note that all resolutions must be in accordance with a standard of reasonableness and fairness following article 2:15(1) DCC.

[12] The articles of association can provide a right of instruction of a body of the corporation regarding the general policy, which is to be pursued in matters defined in the articles of association (article 129 (4)/239 (4) DCC). For the public limited liability companies, only general instructions can be issued.

[13] Until 2013, the two-tier board structure was mandatory for NVs that classify as a 'large' company under the so-called Dutch *structuurregime* (*see* article 2:153(2) DCC). With the introduction of the Dutch Board and Governance Act (Staatsblad 2011, 265) which went into effect on 1 January 2013, Dutch companies may determine in their articles of association whether they follow a one-tier or a two-tier board structure. Nonetheless, many large Dutch listed companies still use the two-tier board structure.

of powers in the ABN-AMRO case (and similarly in the ASMI[14] and Boskalis/Fugro[15] case) as follows:

(i) Determining the strategy of the company and its related enterprise is in principle, a matter for the board of directors, (ii) the supervisory board monitors this board matter and (iii) the general meeting of shareholders can provide its opinion related to the determination of the strategy through the use of law and articles of association mechanisms.

In general, the latter means that the board of a company is accountable for its policy to the general meeting of shareholders. The board is, however, not obliged to involve the general meeting of shareholders in advance of its decision-making process for those acts for which the board of directors is authorised, unless the law or the articles of associations provide otherwise.[16] With the addition of 'in principle' in the *ABN AMRO*-ruling, the Supreme Court left some room for uncertainty.[17] Resolving this uncertainty, the Dutch Parliament considered the power to determine the policy and the strategy pivotal for the board of directors and incorporated this rule in article 129 (1) DCC in 2021, but only for stock exchange listed companies. It remains a subject of debate why exactly the Dutch Parliament codified this power for the listed companies only.[18]

The (management and supervisory) board of both company types must take the interest of the company and its affiliated enterprise into account, including the interests of all stakeholders and shareholders (art. 2:129 (5)/2:239 (5) DCC). Directors of companies are responsible for the proper performance of their tasks, including the general conduct of the affairs of the company and the general financial policy (art. 2:9 DCC). In addition, the company and all corporate incumbents involved in its organisation must behave towards each other in accordance with what is required by standards of reasonableness and fairness (art. 2:8 DCC). In the *Cancun* case, the Supreme Courts addressed the matter as follows:

"In the performance of their duties, the directors must, partially based on the provisions of art. 2:8 Civil Code, exercise due care regarding the interests of all those involved in the company and its business. This duty of care may entail that when serving those interests, the interests of all those involved in the company and its business are not unnecessarily or disproportionally harmed."[19]

In addition to statutory corporate law, Dutch listed companies must also consider the 2016 Dutch Corporate Governance Code (DCGC 2016). While the Code

---

[14] Supreme Court 9 July 2010, Nederlands Juristenblad, 2010/544.

[15] Supreme Court 20 April 2018, Rechtspraak van de Week, 2018/532.

[16] Supreme Court 13 July 2007, Jurisprudentie Ondernemingsrecht, 2007/178, note *Nieuwe Weme.*

[17] *Assink*, Kanttekeningen bij Boskalis/Fugro, Maandblad voor Ondernemingsrecht, 2018, 183–197.

[18] *Van Olffen*, Wetsvoorstel wettelijke bedenktijd beursvennootschappen, Ondernemingsrecht, 2020, 50–58.

[19] Supreme Court 4 April 2014, Nederlands Juristenblad, 2014/286, note *van Schilfgaarde.*

does not impose binding obligations, it nevertheless postulates a mandatory comply-or-explain regime in accordance with European rules. The DCGC 2016 embodies 'long-term value creation' as its very first key principle. 'Long-term value creation' requires management board members and supervisory board members:[20]

"to act in a sustainable manner by focusing on long-term value creation in the performance of their work. Long-term sustainability is the key consideration when determining strategy and making decisions, and stakeholder interests are taken into careful consideration [...]."

In addition, Principle 1.1.1, section vi, mentions that when developing the company's strategy, attention should also be paid to: "any other aspects relevant to the company and its affiliated enterprise, such as the environment, social and employee-related matters, the chain within which the enterprise operates, respect for human rights, and fighting corruption and bribery"[21]. The code is being revised and the 2022 draft code refers explicitly to an ESG strategy in its proposed principle 1.1.1:

"The management board should develop a view on long-term value creation by the company and its affiliated enterprise and should formulate a strategy in line with this. This should include an ESG strategy (the Environmental, Social & Governance aspects of running a business), for which the management board should formulate specific objectives."

The final 2022 Code is expected to be published soon.

II. Sustainability and the Board of Directors

The Dutch model tasks the board of directors with setting the strategy and protecting the company against so-called short-term shareholder activism, but it also requires firm commitment to various stakeholder interests. For example, employees play a significant indirect role in the election of members of the supervisory board of large companies submitted to the "structuurregime". The employees' council is informed of the candidates for a supervisory board membership and the council recommends 1/3 of the members of this board.[22]

As for the requirements of corporate sustainability, which the board is also supposed to take care of, the recent Shell court case is very influential and illustrative. The District Court of The Hague asserted that according to Dutch tort law, companies must comply with the Paris climate goals vis-à-vis Dutch citizens.[23] In its dictum, it stated:

"[we] order[...] Royal Dutch Shell, both directly and via the companies and legal entities it commonly includes in its consolidated annual accounts and with which it jointly forms

[20] The Code can be found here: https://www.mccg.nl/english (17 September 2023).
[21] Part of which is also developed in anti-money laundry (AML) regulations.
[22] Article 2:158 DCC.
[23] Court The Hague, 26 May 2021, ECLI:NL:RBDHA:2021:5339 (English translation).

the Shell group, to limit or cause to be limited the aggregate annual volume of all CO2 emissions into the atmosphere (Scope 1, 2 and 3) due to the business operations and sold energy-carrying products of the Shell group to such an extent that this volume will have reduced by at least net 45 % at end 2030, relative to 2019 levels."

The court clarifies the different emission scopes as well as the distribution of scope emissions of Royal Dutch Shell (RDS) as follows:

"2.5.4. RDS reports on greenhouse gas emissions on the basis of the World Resources Institute Greenhouse Gas Protocol (GHG Protocol). The GHG Protocol categorizes greenhouse gas emissions in Scope 1, 2 and 3:
- Scope 1: direct emissions from sources that are owned or controlled in full or in part by the organization;
- Scope 2: indirect emissions from third-party sources from which the organization has purchased or acquired electricity, steam, or heating for its operations;
- Scope 3: all other indirect emissions resulting from activities of the organization, but occurring from greenhouse gas sources owned or controlled by third parties, such as other organizations or consumers, including emissions from the use of third-party purchased crude oil and gas.

2.5.5. RDS' reporting method and Shell's information on greenhouse gas emissions are available, inter alia, in their annual reports, Sustainability Reports, the Carbon Disclosure Project (CDP) – an international not-for-profit charity that runs the global disclosure system for investors, companies, cities, states and regions – and on the website of the Shell group. In 2018, RDS reported that 85 % of the Shell group emissions were Scope 3 emissions."

The case is pending in the court of appeal, and it is currently unclear how the court of appeal will decide. Notwithstanding the appeal, the case is currently being intensively discussed, criticised as well as praised in the Netherlands.[24] It requires the board of directors (in this case of the parent company) to consider these principles in the development of the strategy of the company's general sustainability issues.[25] Recent research shows that current sustainability goals of companies differ significantly, and planetary boundaries are not yet part of most corporate policies.[26]

Furthermore, a large group of corporate law scholars proposes introducing into Dutch law an explicit provision of responsibility of the board of directors to

[24] See for an overview *Xi*, De klimaatzaak tegen Shell, Deventer, Kluwer, 2022, 75 p.; *Spier*, SDGs: tussen droom en daad: een processie van Echternach, Tijdschrift voor vennootschapsrecht, rechtspersonenrecht en ondernemingsbestuur, 2021, nr. 6, 176–187.

[25] *van Calker* and *Steenkamp*, Het Shell-vonnis en bange bestuurders, Ondernemingsrecht, 2022/31; *Kastelein*, Klimaatzaak tegen Royal Dutch Shell dwingt ook kapitaalverstrekkers tot een actieve(re) rol bij verduurzamingstransitie, Tijdschrift voor Financieel Recht, 2021, nr. 7, 225–228; *Hoekstra*, RDS-Milieudefensie; de op-maat naar stakeholder litigation op het gebied van duurzaamheid, Tijdschrift voor Financieel Recht, 2021, nr. 8/9, 294–303.

[26] *van Aartsen*, *Olaerts* and *Bauer*, De verankering van duurzaamheid in Nederlandse beursgenoteerde ondernemingen, Ondernemingsrecht, 2022, 555–567.

act as a responsible company.[27] The logic behind the proposal is that the company is a responsible corporate citizen and the board of directors should incorporate this responsibility. To that effect, the group suggested amending the current legal behavioural guideline of the board of directors in article 2:129 (5) Dutch Civil Code, which states that: "the Directors shall, in the performance of their duties, direct their attention to the interests of the corporation and of its enterprise". The experts suggest adding to the guideline that "the directors must make sure that the company is participating in our society as a responsible company". The supervisory board must monitor whether the board of directors is adequately carrying out this duty. This responsibility covers a healthy environment and climate but covers also topics such as remuneration ratios, diversity, tax responsibilities, etc. The corporate lawyers clarify that the responsible company takes "responsibility towards its employees and is responsible for the consequences of its actions in the communities in which it operates and for the consequences of its actions for the environment and the climate. The goal of long-term profitable continuity must be embedded in this broad responsibility." The experts believe that a stronger commitment on the part of the board of directors of companies is preferable to an alternative distribution of powers in companies, especially for increasing the powers of the shareholders.[28]

III. Sustainable ownership and governance

The shareholders' position, role and involvement in the Dutch corporate governance scene resemble a pendulum. With the introduction of the structure regime in the 1970s in the Netherlands, an important part of the powers of the general meeting of shareholders shifted to the supervisory board who elected the board of directors and elected its own members and, in addition: "it elevated the supervisory and management boards to a legal position that made them immune to shareholder criticism".[29] Since the 1990s, there has been a shift towards a broader and intensified involvement of shareholders in the governance of Dutch companies. The general meeting of shareholders must approve the decisions of the board of directors, which serves to significantly change the identity and characteristics of the company, for example, in actions such as the acquisition and disposal of interests in other companies that constitute at least one-third of the amount of assets.[30] The general meeting must also approve the remuneration

[27] *Winter* e.a., Naar een zorgplicht voor bestuurders en commissarissen tot verantwoordelijke deelname aan het maatschappelijk verkeer, Ondernemingsrecht, 2020, 471–474.

[28] *Winter* e.a., Naar een algemene zorgplicht voor bestuurders en commissarissen, Ondernemingsrecht, 2021, 31–39.

[29] *Calkoen*, The One-Tier Board in the Changing and Converging World of Corporate Governance, Deventer, Kluwer, 2012, 322.

[30] Art. 2:107a Dutch Civil Code.

policy of the board of directors[31]. Furthermore, the Dutch legislator increased reporting requirements and corporate governance standards that the (supervisory) boards must comply with. Next, each shareholder holding 1 % or more of the capital may add an item to the agenda of the meeting.[32] In the first decade of the new millennium, active shareholders – especially several hedge funds – pursued significant reforms of listed Dutch companies, which should, according to these shareholders, increase shareholder value despite claims from the board of directors that such a reform would be contrary to the interests of the company.[33] It raised concerns that the balance of power shifted too far towards the shareholder community. Consequently, in more recent years, several shareholder-oriented legal changes were scaled back, including, for example, the right to put items on the agenda of the general meeting for which the threshold for shareholding increased to 3 % from the former 1 %.[34] What's more, the courts were holding back some of the requests by the shareholders, as in the famous *Akzo Nobel* case.[35]

This recent development of more and less shareholder rights must also be positioned in the evolution of shareholder ownership of Dutch companies, shareholder voting, and shareholder engagement. It should be noted that Dutch listed companies have, on average, a more dispersed ownership structure than other Western European countries such as France, Germany, and Belgium. According to a study by Lafarre, the free float of Dutch large and midcap companies is more than 80 % and only a few have less than 50 % of the shares widely dispersed.[36] In less than 20 % of the Dutch companies, the largest shareholders hold more than 50 % of the equity. In the three other mentioned Western European countries, the number of companies with a controlling shareholder stands at around 40 %.[37]

Many institutional investors are keen to vote at general meetings of the investees, executing their fiduciary duties vis-à-vis their beneficiaries. The increase in the institutional investors' shareholder base by many Dutch companies resulted in an increase of the average attendance on the part of shareholders in the general

[31] Art. 2:135 Dutch Civil Code.

[32] Old art 2:114a Dutch Civil Code.

[33] *Van der Elst, De Jong* and *Raaijmakers*, Een overzicht van juridische en economische dimensies van de kwetsbaarheid van Nederlandse beursvennootschappen, SER Onderzoeksrapport, 2007, 129 p.

[34] Art. 2:114a Dutch Civil Code.

[35] See for a short overview of this case, *Lafarre*, Shareholder Voting and Engagement in the Netherlands: The Dutch Institutional Approach, in *Kaur, Xi, Van der Elst* and *Lafarre* (eds.), Shareholder Engagement and Voting, Cambridge, Cambridge University Press, 2022, 405–406.

[36] *Lafarre*, Shareholder Voting and Engagement in the Netherlands: The Dutch Institutional Approach, in *Kaur, Xi, Van der Elst* and *Lafarre* (eds.), Shareholder Engagement and Voting, Cambridge, Cambridge University Press, 2022, 411.

[37] OECD, Corporate Governance Factbook 2021, Paris, OECD, 25.

meetings of Dutch companies to more than 75 %, which represents an increase of more than double the percentage in 2005.[38]

There is currently a discussion in the Netherlands regarding the voting item "say on climate". Some scholars are making a plea to have this topic tabled as a recurring voting item, similar to the vote for the financial report. With the sustainability report, the company is accountable for its sustainable behaviour. The director of Eumedion, representing the interests of over fifty large institutional investors in the field of corporate governance and sustainability, made a plea for a binding vote on the sustainability report.[39] Upholding arguments by many companies, Eumedion asserted that one single vote on the sustainability strategy would not be appropriate. They therefore anticipate that the sustainability report – in accordance with the upcoming Corporate Sustainability Reporting Directive – shall be submitted for a vote.[40] De Jongh argues for an advisory vote on the issue: it is the board of directors that is responsible for setting the strategy, including the sustainability strategy.[41] Others reject any (additional) power for the shareholders in this respect, largely arguing that the task of setting the sustainability goals of the company falls under the purview of the board of directors. At best, shareholders can request any of the ESG-criteria as an item for discussion at the general meeting.[42] A few companies effectively tabled sustainability as a discussion item for the general meeting, either initiated by the board[43] or the shareholders.[44] Meanwhile, Royal Dutch Shell, despite having its headquarters in London, organises an annual vote on a sustainability-related item (The Shell Energy Transition Strategy). In addition, since 2016, a group of shareholders has added the voting item of setting and publishing targets consistent with the goals of the Paris Climate Agreement and begun publishing targets that are consistent with the goal of the Paris Climate Agreement. The voting item gradually received more yes votes over the years, with up to 30 % of the votes in 2021, while the management voting item on the Transition Strategy received a large majority of the votes. In addition, it also became common practice for the auditors of Dutch

---

[38] Eumedion noticed that in companies with a shareholder base that consists of many retail investors, attendance is much lower (Eumedion, Evaluation of the 2022 AGM Season, 4, https://www.eumedion.nl/clientdata/215/media/clientimages/Evaluation-AGM-season-2022-def.pdf?v=221025104107; 17 September 2023).

[39] *Abma*, De duurzaamheid van de algemene vergadering, working paper, juli 2022, 13 p.

[40] *Abma*, Evaluation of the 2022 AGM season, working paper, 2022, 12, https://www.eumedion.nl/publicaties.html (17 September 2023).

[41] *de Jongh*, Say on Climate: Over negatieve externe effecten en verdeling van bevoegdheden, Ondernemingsrecht 2021, 696–703.

[42] *van Olffen* and *Breukink*, Say on what's next, Ondernemingsrecht, 2022, 110–115.

[43] Like at ING.

[44] Like at LyondellBasell in 2021. In this case, the shareholders asked to table the climate change commitment of the company and an annual advisory vote on its climate strategy. The board rejected any kind of vote.

companies to review the climate-related disclosures and risks, although most are silent in their opinion.[45]

Notwithstanding this discussion, the current practice is that during the general meeting of Dutch companies, sustainability is only indirectly discussed. In their annual report, companies must provide information on sustainability and these reports of the (supervisory) board are an item of discussion accordingly. The current reporting practices of climate-related risks are heterogeneous and only a small minority is compliant with the Task Force on Climate-Related Financial Disclosures (TFCD).[46] Furthermore, it has become more and more common for ESG-criteria to be used for setting the (variable) pay of the top executives. Both the remuneration policy and the remuneration report are (recurring) voting items.

Meanwhile, in November 2022, the Dutch Authority for the Financial Markets (AFM) issued recommendations for the future reporting practices of large stock exchange listed companies.[47] The AFM expects companies' non-financial statements to be coherent and complete related to environment, people, and corruption. The supervisor will assess how companies present their net-zero objectives and scope-3 disclosures. Companies must explain in concrete terms, specifically how they intend to achieve their net-zero or CO2-neutral objectives and the contributions of measures taken, including uncertainties in effectiveness and feasibility. The AFM also explicitly supports ESMA's priorities in non-financial reporting, including transition plans and disclosures on taxonomy eligibility.[48] The AFM already refers to the implementation of the proposed Corporate Sustainability Reporting Directive (CSRD), which will require all large companies to publish regular reports on their environmental and social impact activities.[49]

Another important difference of the Dutch ownership structure of listed companies when compared with other Western European countries is the international diversification of the shareholder base. According to one study, ap-

---

[45] *Abma*, Evaluation of the 2022 AGM season, working paper, 2022, 12–15, https://www.eumedion.nl/publicaties.html (17 September 2023).

[46] *Abma*, Evaluation of the 2020 AGM season, working paper, 2020, 18–19, https://www.eumedion.nl/publicaties.html (17 September 2023).

[47] *AFM*, Waar moeten beurgenoteerde ondernemingen op letten bij hun verslaggeving over 2022, 7 November 2022, https://www.afm.nl/nl-nl/sector/actueel/2022/november/aandachtspunten-verslaggeving-2022 (24 October 2023).

[48] *ESMA, European enforcers focus on Russia's invasion of Ukraine, economic outlook and climate related disclosures, 28 October 2022,* https://www.esma.europa.eu/press-news/esma-news/european-enforcers-focus-russia%E2%80%99s-invasion-ukraine-economic-outlook-and-climate *(ESMA, European common enforcement priorities for 2022 annual financial reports, 28 October 2022, 12 p.) (17 September 2023).*

[49] Proposal for a Directive of the European Parliament and of the Council amending Directive 2013/34/EU, Directive 2004/109/EC, Directive 2006/43/EC and Regulation (EU) No 537/2014, as regards corporate sustainability reporting, https://www.consilium.europa.eu/media/57644/st10835-xx22.pdf (17 September 2023).

proximately 87 % of all shares of the largest companies are owned by foreign institutional investors and 6 % by Dutch institutional investors.[50]

Like most other Member States countries, the Netherlands has transposed the Shareholder Rights Directive II almost word for word. Observing article 5:87c of the Dutch Financial Supervision Act, it sounds like the institutional investor and asset manager must have an engagement policy that describes how they monitor their investees on relevant matters, including strategy, financial and non-financial performance and risk, capital structure, *social and environmental impact* and corporate governance, how they conduct dialogue with investee companies, how they exercise the voting rights and other rights attached to shares, how they cooperate with other shareholders, and how they communicate with relevant stakeholders of the investee companies and manage actual and potential conflicts of interests in relation to their engagement. The investor or manager must disclose on a per annum basis how they have executed their policy which, at add: a minimum, should include how they voted at the general meeting of shareholders, their voting behaviour, an explanation of the most important votes, and how they made use of the services of proxy advisors.

Taken all together, these developments, including an increase in the institutional investors' ownership and the requirement for institutional investors of developing engagement policies and disclosing engagement reports that should include the monitoring of the ESG-criteria, should serve to positively affect the sustainability requests of investors. Research shows that investors are increasingly conscious of embedding sustainability issues in their investees[51], but engagement efforts are directed towards a (small) sample of Dutch companies and not all engagement efforts of (institutional) investors are related to ESG issues. Two studies illustrate these findings.

APB ranks as one of the largest pension funds in the world, it is the fifth largest pension fund in the world[52]. As a beneficiary of APB, moreover, I am also most familiar with the engagement of this fund. APB discloses in its corporate governance framework[53] that its investment policy considers four basic corporate governance principles that the investees must adhere to: long term value

[50] The remainder of the shares being held by other types of investors. *Abma*, *van Kleef*, *Lemers* and *Olaerts*, De algemene vergadering van Nederlandse beursvennootschappen, Deventer, Wolters Kluwer, 2017, 8.

[51] A recent study shows that at general meetings of Dutch companies more shareholder questions are sustainability-related (*Lafarre* and *Van der Elst*, Corporate Sustainability and Shareholder Activism in the Netherlands, in Cambridge Handbook of Corporate Law, Corporate Governance and Sustainability, *Sjåfjell* and *Bruner* (eds.), CUP, 2019, 260–275).

[52] Thinking Ahead Institute, Global Top 300 Pension Funds, 2021, 42, https://www.thinkingaheadinstitute.org/content/uploads/2021/09/PI-300-2021.pdf (17 September 2023). ABP manages around €500 billion.

[53] https://www.abp.nl/content/dam/abp/nl/documents/corporate-governance-raamwerk220422-2.pdf (24 October 2023).

creation, board responsibility, sustainability and transparency. The corporate governance framework of ABP includes the voting policy of the fund, which also entails its approach to climate-related topics which are being voted on at the general meeting of shareholders of the investees. Management proposals of climate transition plans are supported only if all of the following conditions are met. The plan contains a net-zero ambition (scope 1,2 and 3); it contains medium- and long-term climate goals; it is in line with the 1.5° Celsius limit or the sector-specific criteria from the International Energy Agency Net Zero Emissions Scenario; it also includes all major business units and is measurable and realistic and it does not include investments in new fossil capacity. To that extent, climate-related shareholder proposals are supported unless the company has a climate approach which it has disclosed and meets the same criteria which APB uses for assessing the climate transition plans. The proposal, furthermore, contains no illegal micro-management behaviour nor does it set expectations that may be harmful for the company and/or its shareholders or is counterproductive in addressing climate change by the company.

In its stewardship policy, ABP further develops how it votes, monitors, engages and cooperates. Like other major Dutch asset owners[54], the transparency of the fund is very high, but it illustrates the difficulties in combining and balancing all the goals as prescribed in the European SRD II: risks, returns, costs and sustainability. This approach of combining all these goals resulted in the following statement:

"ABP developed highly sophisticated inclusion policies, where the investment universe is based on a proprietary methodology and by categories of frontrunners and laggards. When investing in laggards, action must be taken to improve the sustainability performance. The engagement is one of the core elements of the inclusion policy. We strive to invest only in companies that either sufficiently perform on the identified sustainability indicators, or in companies where we expect them to make progress in these areas. ABP expects the portfolio companies to gradually change over time in line with our policy of inclusion. The inclusion policy requires investment teams actively consider the relevant ecological, social and governance factors, in addition to considerations in terms of return, risk and costs. [...] Since it is the responsibility of the portfolio manager to invest in line with these requirements, (s)he has a full understanding of the entities in which to invest and be responsible for the engagement process. In this way, responsible and sustainable investing is fully embedded in the way we invest and, in our culture, as well as in this of our asset managers."[55]

According to its report of mid-2022, APB invested in more than 3000 listed companies[56] in over fifty countries. 30 % are US companies and over 10 % are

[54] See for example PGGM, the asset manager of PFZW, the second largest Dutch pension fund at https://www.pggm.nl/onze-diensten/actief-aandeelhouderschap/ (17 September 2023).

[55] ABP, Stewardship Beleid, 2022, 5.

[56] Listed shares and convertible bonds (but only if the investment exceeds the threshold of EUR 500,000) which represents 99.9 % of all stakes.

Japanese and Chinese companies.[57] In 2021, ABP engaged with 16.3 % of the companies. The following Table illustrates the frequency of the engagement topics. While all but the last one can be qualified as ESG-topics, no sustainability topic was discussed in more than 10 % of the companies.

Frequencies of engagement of the pension fund ABP with its investees.

Topic discussed	*number of companies*
environment	7.5 %
labour conditions	2.3 %
human rights	2.2 %
ethics	3.5 %
corporate governance	6.4 %
sustainable finance	2.2 %
other	4.6 %

Note: engagement can include more than one issue. *Source:* our own calculations based on ABP *Engagement met bedrijven* and *beursgenoteerde beleggingen* (ABP.nl).

In a study on earnings calls and general meetings of 40 companies and interviews with 16 asset managers, analysts, pension fund managers and investor relation managers of large Dutch companies, The Dutch Authority for the Financial Markets (AFM) noticed that non-financial information is only of limited use, is discussed primarily in one-on-one meetings and does not play a very decisive role in investment decision-making. Sustainability-related topics have been addressed by analysts in 10 % of the companies and appeared as an issue in the presentations of less than 60 % of the companies.[58]

C. Sustainable Financial Institutions in the Netherlands

In the last decades, not only have the legislative and regulatory corporate governance, risk management requirements and sustainability obligations of stock exchange listed companies all experienced dramatic change, but many other types of entities – not the least financial institutions – must now incorporate strengthened governance and risk management standards into their setup. For banks, insurance companies and pension funds, the most important government requirements can be found in article 88 et seq. of the CRD IV[59], article 41

[57] ABP, Beursgenoteerde beleggingen van ABP, 2022, 28 p.

[58] AFM, Verkenning naar het gebruik van niet-financiële informatie door institutionele beleggers en analisten, 16 February 2021, 25 p.

[59] Sub-section 3 Governance of directive 2013/36/EU of the European Parliament and of the Council of 26 June 2013 on access to the activity of credit institutions and the prudential

et seq. of Solvency II[60] and art. 20 et seq. of IORP II[61]. These institutions also feature specific risk management and investment policy requirements which are transposed into the Dutch law on financial supervision and monitored by De Nederlandse Bank.[62] The European Commission works on the modernisation of these legal frameworks, originally and largely developed in the aftermath of the financial crisis and aiming at a reduction of the risk of financial collapse, in pursuit of contributing to long-term sustainable finance of the economy and managing climate risk with a long-term climate risk scenario analysis.[63]

For Undertakings for Collective Investments (UCIT) and alternative investment funds, governance-related requirements are more broadly defined. For example, the UCITS-Directive states the following: "the persons who effectively conduct the business of a management company are of sufficiently good repute and are sufficiently experienced".[64] Commission Directive 2010/43 provides further guidance, such as the requirement of employing personnel with skills, knowledge, and expertise necessary for the responsibilities of the management company. The Directive also adds organisational requirements, risk management requirements, etc. for the management company of an UCIT.[65] According to article 9, the management company must ensure that the investment policy of the UCIT is adequately implemented and that the risk management policies and arrangements are adequately approved and reviewed among other requirements. Note that next to the sustainability requirements to be found in the SFDR, the

---

supervision of credit institutions and investment firms, amending Directive 2002/87/EC and repealing Directives 2006/48/EC and 2006/49/EC, OJ L nr. 176, 27 June 2013.

[60] Section 2 System of governance of directive 2009/138/EC of the European Parliament and of the Council of 25 November 2009 on the taking-up and pursuit of the business of Insurance and Reinsurance (Solvency II), OJ L nr. 335, 17 December 2009.

[61] Chapter 1 System of Governance of Directive (EU) 2016/2341 of the European Parliament and of the Council of 14 December 2016 on the activities and supervision of institutions for occupational retirement provision (IORPs), OJ L nr. 354, 23 December 2016.

[62] *Nuijten*, *Vermeulen* and *van der Eerden*, Alleen samen krijgen we de klimaatverandering onder controle? Over handhaving van duurzaamheidsverplichtingen voor financiële ondernemingen, Tijdschrift voor Financieel Recht, 2021, nr. 8/9, 314–323; *Beekhoven van den Boezem* and *Vleeschhouwer*, De rol van De Nederlandse Bank als centrale bank en prudentieel toezichthouder bij de green recovery, Tijdschrift voor Financieel Recht, 2020, nr. 10, 487–492.

[63] See for example European Commission, on the review of the EU prudential framework for insurers and reinsurers in the context of the EU's post pandemic recovery, 22 September 2021, COM (2021) 580 final. See also *Schoute*, Via duurzame financiering naar een circulaire economie: de rol die banken kunnen spelen, Onderneming en Financiering, 2022, nr. 2, 62–81.

[64] Article 7 of Directive 2009/65/EC of the European Parliament and of the Council of 13 July 2009 on the coordination of laws, regulations and administrative provisions relating to undertakings for collective investment in transferable securities (UCITS), OJ L. nr. 302 17 November 2009.

[65] Commission Directive 2010/43/EU of 1 July 2010 implementing Directive 2009/65/EC of the European Parliament and of the Council as regards organisational requirements, conflicts of interest, conduct of business, risk management and content of the agreement between a depositary and a management company, OJ L nr. 176, 10 July 2010.

Commission delegated Directive (EU) 2021/1270 added several sustainability requirements to this list of governance requirements, including the retention of "the necessary resources and expertise for the effective integration of sustainability risks", the integration of "sustainability risks in the management of UCITS, taking into account the nature, scale and complexity of the business of the investment companies" and as an additional layer of responsibility for its senior management: "the responsibility for the integration of sustainability risks"[66]. The directive has been transposed in almost identical words in the Decree on the Supervision of the Conduct of Financial Undertakings Wft, which reads that: "investment companies integrate sustainability risks in the management of UCITS, taking into account the nature, scale and complexity of the business of the investment companies"[67].

At the same time, the UCITS-Directive prescribes in detail in which financial instruments it can invest as well as in what quantities.[68] These investment policy guidelines have been recently further elaborated on in a new European regulation (EU) 2019/2033.[69] According to Article 52 of the Regulation, investment firms must disclose detailed information regarding the use of their voting rights:

> "(a) the proportion of voting rights attached to the shares held directly or indirectly by the investment firm, broken down by Member State and sector; (b) a complete description of voting behaviour in the general meetings of companies the shares of which are held [...], an explanation of the votes, and the ratio of proposals put forward by the administrative or management body of the company which the investment firm has approved; and (c) an explanation of the use of proxy advisor firms; (d) the voting guidelines regarding the companies the shares of which are held [...]".

This information will, among other things, provide insights into how the investment firm executes its engagement policy, and also given the state of sustainable affairs of the investees, clarify how the investment firm responds to the sustainability efforts of these investees. The European Commission has developed a

---

[66] Article 1 of Commission Delegative Directive (EU) 2021/1270 of 21 April 2021 amending Directive 2010/43/EU as regards the sustainability risks and sustainability factors to be taken into account for Undertakings for Collective Investment in Transferable Securities (UCITS), OJ L nr. 277, 2 August 2021.

[67] Article 30a Besluit Gedragstoezicht financiële ondernemingen Wft. This decree transposed the other requirements of the Commission delegated Directive (EU) 2021/1270 in a similar way, such as for the requirement to take sustainability risks in the decision-making procedures, reporting lines, internal control mechanisms, internal reporting and communication into account. These and the other requirements raise several implementation UCITS issues: what is to be considered as an adequate level of "taking into account"? Furthermore, what is the nature, scale and complexity of a UCIT pursuing what level of integration of which type of sustainability risk? etc.

[68] See article 49 et seq. of Directive 2009/65/EC.

[69] Regulation (EU) 2019/2033 of the European Parliament and of the Council of 27 November 2019 on the prudential requirements of investment firms and amending Regulations (EU) No 1093/2010, (EU) No 575/2013, (EU) No 600/2014 and (EU) No 806/2014, OJ L nr. 314, 5 December 2019.

disclosure framework that will allow beneficiaries and third parties to compare the (sustainability of) the voting and engagement behaviour in the Commission Delegated Regulation (EU) 2022/1159 of 11 March 2022 supplementing Regulation (EU) 2019/2033 of the European Parliament and of the Council with regard to regulatory technical standards for public disclosure of the investment policy by investment firms.[70] Article 53 European regulation (EU) 2019/2033 further strengthens the transparency of the investment firms and lowers the risks of greenwashing by requiring the disclosure of "information on environmental, social and governance risks, including physical risks and transition risks". The instrument of European Regulations makes the requirements directly applicable in the Netherlands and all other European member states.

Sustainability is not to be seen as a "sidekick" of governance or risk management practices. Rather, it is viewed as a main goal toward which the financial industry must take major steps:

> "Sustainable finance refers to the process of taking environmental, social and governance (ESG) considerations into account when making investment decisions in the financial sector, leading to more long-term investments in sustainable economic activities and projects. [...] To this end, the Commission has since 2018 been developing a comprehensive policy agenda on sustainable finance".[71]

In this way, the European Commission presented its sustainable finance ambitions. The current result of the Commission's commitment is a complex and detailed system requiring massive changes in the investment policies, reporting schemes, remuneration practices, and product portfolios of (large) companies, and even more so for all financial institutions. Since the publication of the European Commission's Sustainable Finance Action Plan in 2018, numerous directives and (delegated) regulations have been issued, requiring significant human capital in financial institutions for the purpose of developing compliant sustainable frameworks. The abundance of European legislation also resulted in very modest additional national steps of governments and regulators of member states, limiting their interventions in the transposition of the European Directives accompanied by letters containing supervisory bodies' expectations of financial market participants.[72]

---

[70] OJ L. nr. 179, 6 July 2022.

[71] European Commission, Overview of sustainable finance, https://finance.ec.europa.eu/sustainable-finance/overview-sustainable-finance_en (17 September 2023).

[72] See for example the letters of the *AFM* of 3 July 2020 "Informatie over nieuwe wet- en regelgeving op het gebied van duurzaamheid" and of 16 December 2020 "Nieuwe regels over de publicatie van duurzaamheidinformatie" (https://www.afm.nl/~/profmedia/files/nieuws/2020/juli/sectorbrief-duurzaamheid.pdf?sc_lang=en&hash=2E4C812C52E4A0772B18D1ACF6AB2F61 and https://www.afm.nl/~/profmedia/files/doelgroepen/pensioenuitvoerders/sectorbrief-duurzaamheidsinformatie-pensioen.pdf?sc_lang=en&hash=D3E6A97EC46010C05F2CA987F86C073E) (24 October 2023).

In particular, Regulation (EU) 2019/2088 of the European Parliament and of the Council of 27 November 2019 on sustainability-related disclosures in the financial services sector (SFDR) which entered into force on 21 March 2021, is affecting investment policies of financial market participants. Dutch financial institutions must ensure that they have developed a policy on the integration of sustainability risks in their investment decision-making process, investment advice or insurance advice.[73] Dutch financial institutions must consider principal adverse impacts of investment decisions on sustainability factors[74], show how their remuneration policies are consistent with the integration of sustainability risks[75] and disclose the manner in which sustainability risks are integrated into their investment decisions[76]. Sustainability risks are broadly defined as "environmental, social or governance event or condition, that, if it occurs, could cause an actual or a potential material negative impact on the value of the investment".[77] All these demands must be disclosed in precontractual information, information on their website and information in periodic reports. The Dutch Authority for the Financial Markets confirmed that all the financial market participants will comply with these sustainability-related disclosure requirements.

The AFM explicitly refers to an ESMA supervisory briefing which serves as a guidance document for the financial market participants.[78] In the first phase, AFM expected the financial market participants to comply "in general" with SFDR. However, in the meantime, the AFM further elaborated on several uncertainties, such as the clarification as to *when* the parent company must publish a principal adverse impact statement, and that the statement must address the adverse effects on sustainability factors of the parent only. In addition, the ESMA supervisory briefing clarifies that in case of individual portfolio management, the investment firm must comply with the transparency requirements of the portfolio (in accordance with article 10 of the SFDR) which can be done by referring to model portfolios (if those are being used) for meeting the obligations of confidentiality. When managers are submitted to the registration system (and hence do not provide in a prospectus), they can elect the document providing the required precontractual information. The AFM further refers the financial institutions to the clarifications of the European Commission as well as to the

[73] Art. 3 Regulation (EU) 2019/2088 of the European Parliament and of the Council of 27 November 2019 on sustainability-related disclosures in the financial services sector, OJ L. nr. 317, 9 December 2019.

[74] And if they do "a statement on due diligence policies with respect to those impacts" and if they do not "clear reasons for why they do not do so" (Art. 4 (1) Regulation (EU) 2019/2088).

[75] Art. 5(1) Regulation (EU) 2019/2088.

[76] Art. 6(1) Regulation (EU) 2019/2088.

[77] Art. 2 (22) Regulation (EU) 2019/2088.

[78] See https://www.afm.nl/nl-nl/sector/themas/duurzaamheid/sfdr/verwachting (24 October 2023).

clarifications of the European Banking Authority, both involved in the development of answers to these and other questions.

Accordingly, the European Commission elaborated on specific disclosure regimes (technical standards) in April 2022 for disclosing sustainability-related information under the Sustainable Finance Disclosures Regulation (SFDR).[79] The Commission announced that the Delegated Regulation:

> "specifies the exact content, methodology and presentation of the information to be disclosed, thereby improving its quality and comparability. Under these rules, financial market participants will provide detailed information about how they tackle and reduce any possible negative impacts that their investments may have on the environment and society in general."

The Delegated Regulation predominantly provides product-related disclosure guidelines[80] but also contains sustainability-related governance reporting guidelines. These are as follows: the description of the principal adverse impacts of investment decisions on sustainability factors, the description of policies for identifying and prioritising principal adverse impacts of investment decisions on sustainability factors, and a summary of the engagement policy. The reporting guidelines further specify the different (sub)indicators and the adverse impact of investment decisions on sustainability factors. The indicators are related to climate and other aspects of the environment, such as the carbon footprint and water emissions, and those related to social and employee, human rights, anti-corruption and anti-bribery matters, like the gender pay gap and the share of investments in companies that violated the UN Global Compact principles or OECD guidelines for multinational enterprises or investments in weapon manufacturers. It also defines the indicators, for example, such as the unadjusted gender pay gap which is defined as the difference between average gross hourly earnings of male paid employees and of female paid employees as a percentage of average gross hourly earnings of male paid employees. It remains to be seen if a financial market participant holds stakes of different sizes in many investees, as well as how the (un)weighted(?) (binary) average pay gap appropriately signals sustainability.

[79] Commission Delegated Regulation (EU) 2022/1288 of 6 April 2022 supplementing Regulation (EU) 2019/2088 of the European Parliament and of the Council with regard to regulatory technical standards specifying the details of the content and presentation of the information in relation to the principle of 'do no significant harm', specifying the content, methodologies and presentation of information in relation to sustainability indicators and adverse sustainability impacts, and the content and presentation of the information in relation to the promotion of environmental or social characteristics and sustainable investment objectives in pre-contractual documents, on websites and in periodic reports, OJ L nr. 196 of 25 July 2022.

[80] See section D.

D. Sustainability and Financial Products

Recent European legislation not only affects the sustainability behaviour of financial institutions but also, and even more so (the development and disclosure of information of), the financial products (which are being marketed). According to article 6 (1) of Regulation (EU) 2019/2088 Dutch financial institutions, like all European institutions, must include in their precontractual disclosures "the manner in which sustainability risks are integrated in their investment decisions" as well as "the results of the assessment of the likely impacts of sustainability risks on the returns of the financial products they make available". A financial product is broadly defined as: "a portfolio, alternative investment fund, an insurance-based investment product, a pension product, a pension scheme, an undertaking for collective investments in transferable securities or a pan-European personal pension product"[81]. For some of these products, this requirement is not new. Pursuant to the IORP II Directive (EU) 2016/2341, pension funds have, already for some years now, had to consider environmental, social and governance risks relating to their investment portfolio in their risk-management system.[82]

More precisely, the SFDR, in combination with the Taxonomy Regulation[83] and their many delegated regulations and directives[84], ultimately enhance transparency and comparability of the sustainability levels of the products which financial institutions offer.[85] The product level disclosures are designed to give the financial consumers better insight into the sustainability and principal adverse impacts of financial products and funds. In addition to the aforementioned mandatory information that always has to be provided in accordance with article 6, there are two other types of funds and products offering "enhanced" sustainability – article 8 ("light green") and article 9 ("dark green") funds and products.

---

[81] Art. 2 (12) Regulation (EU) 2019/2088.

[82] See art. 18 (3) g Besluit financieel toetsingskader pensioenfondsen (implementatie IORP II).

[83] Regulation (EU) 2020/852 of the European Parliament and of the Council of 18 June 2020 on the establishment of a framework to facilitate sustainable investment, and amending Regulation (EU) 2019/2088, OJ L 198, 22.06.2020.

[84] See for an overview of the regulatory framework: https://finance.ec.europa.eu/regulation-and-supervision/implementing-and-delegated-acts/taxonomy-regulation (17 September 2023) and for an overview *Blom* and *Dickhoff*, EU geeft kleur aan duurzaamheid en de rol van de financiële sector, Tijdschrift voor financieel Recht, 2021, nr. 8/9, 257–263.

[85] Many commentators have discussed this European legal framework. See for example: *de Galan* and *Pijls*, Het civiel effect van de Taxonomie- en Transparantieverordening, Tijdschrift voor vennootschapsrecht, rechtspersonenrecht en ondernemingsbestuur, 2022, 3–14; *Kuijpers* and *de Klerk*, Hoe duurzaam belegd is de impact van "SFDR", Ondernemingsrecht, 2021, 809–820; *Blom* and *Dickhoff*, EU geeft kleur aan duurzaamheid en de rol van de financiële sector, Tijdschrift voor Financieel Recht, 2021, nr. 8/9, p. 257–263; *Siemers*, Informatieverschaffing over duurzaamheid door beleggingsinstellingen, Tijdschrift voor Financieel Recht, 2021, nr. 1/2, p. 16–28; *Buijink*, *Hazelzet* and *Mreijen*, Duurzaam financieren in het licht van vrijwillige initiatieven en Europese regelgeving, Tijdschrift voor Financieel Recht, 2020, nr. 10, 473–378.

An article 8 product promotes, *inter alia* (a combination of), environmental and social characteristics conditioned on the good governance practices of the investees, while article 9 products must have sustainable investment as an objective. Both article 8 and 9 products require additional disclosures accordingly.[86] In addition, the financial market participant must report on the taxonomy alignment of the products' content. The disclosure must be made in precontractual documentation, periodic reporting, and the website of the financial market participation. In the meantime, an abundant number of regulatory guidelines and requirements (mostly regulatory technical standards) have been issued, benchmarking the financial products, due diligence policies, monitoring requirements, the use of data sources, etc. Especially for "light green" and "dark green" products, these plentiful prerequisites should prevent *greenwashing* – deceptively using information and marketing that a product is more environmentally (and/or socially or more broadly sustainably) friendly than it is actually the case.

For most issues related to financial products, the Dutch AFM refers to the developments and guidelines developed and issued by the European regulators. Similarly to ESMA, the AFM considers it important for financial market participants to check the name of the product when it refers to sustainability.[87] How the name is supposed to be cross-checked can be found in ESMA's supervisory briefing of 31 May 2022.[88]

In its report from September 2021 – addressing the reporting practices of financial market participants, and in particular of investment funds –, the AFM acknowledged that all managers of these funds with sustainable characteristics or objectives had included information about these issues in their prospectuses of March 2021. Nevertheless, the AFM also noted that there is room for improving the quality of the information and questioned the sustainability classifications of many investment funds. The way in which the sustainability risks were integrated in the investment policy is of too general a nature and often not fund-specific as such. Furthermore, the estimation of the likely effects of the sustainability risks on returns is missing altogether. *Light green* as well as *deep green* funds provide too little specific information and give too limited insights and explanations of the objectives and how these are pursued through the investment policy. Based on the information, the supervisory authority raised questions about the sustainability classifications of the funds, especially those aiming for sustainable investments. It found that the funds appear to be more broadly oriented, and

[86] For a detailed analysis see *Boogaard*, Classificatie van financiële producten op grond van artikel 8 en 9 SFDR, Tijdschrift voor Financieel Recht, 2022, nr. 1, 13–21.

[87] See https://www.afm.nl/nl-nl/sector/themas/duurzaamheid/sfdr/verwachting (24 October 2023).

[88] ESMA, Supervisory Briefing – Sustainability risks and disclosures in the area of investment management, 31 May 2022, 16 p.

that the investment portfolio often does not focus exclusively on sustainable investments.[89]

In November 2022, the AFM repeated the study and also investigated the compliance of the pension fund industry as well as of banks, insurance companies and investment companies with the SFDR requirements.[90] The AFM observed that the sustainability disclosures of investment funds made significant progress and that several funds with sustainable objectives were revamped in funds to promote sustainable characteristics. In addition, almost all funds with an environmental objective and the funds that promote environmental characteristics publish the mandatory precontractual information under the taxonomy regulation, but there is nevertheless room still for further improvement. The same goes for the other financial market participants. The current policies of investment funds provide a global understanding, but concrete information about the process is missing and only partially explains how the sustainability risks are integrated. In addition, information on how the integration of sustainability risks in the remuneration policy gets accomplished is also too general.

At the same time, the statement of pension providers is incomplete vis-à-vis the accountability of the most important adverse effects of their investment decisions on sustainability factors. A significant majority of the pension beneficiaries (93 %) have a scheme that promotes sustainability. However, pension providers have an obligation to explain these sustainability characteristics and how they meet these characteristics. This description, however, is too often completely lacking altogether.

The information on the websites of banks, insurance companies and investment companies, moreover, is often difficult to understand, vague and repetitive. It is unclear how the companies include sustainability risks in the investment process and what steps are being taken for managing sustainability risks. The remuneration policy does not show how the sustainability risks are included nor how it encourages mitigating sustainability risks. Precontractual information for products must show how sustainability risks are integrated in the investment decisions and what the likely effects of sustainability risks are on the return of the financial products, but this information was often lacking. There is also

[89] AFM, Implementatie SFDR – Onderzoek naar implementatie van SFDR vereisten door beheerders van Nederlandse beleggingsinstellingen, September 2021, 14 p.

[90] AFM, SFDR in de praktijk: blijvende aandacht nodig – Onderzoek naar de naleving van de SFDR en Taxonomieverordening door beheerders van Nederlandse beleggingsinstellingen en icbe's, November 2022, 15 p.; AFM, SFDR in de praktijk: blijvende aandacht nodig – Eerste onderzoek naar naleving van SFDR-en Taxonomievereisten door pensioenfondsen en PPI's, November 2022, 20 p.; AFM, SFDR in de praktijk: blijvende aandacht nodig – Eerste onderzoek naar SFDR- en Taxonomievereisten onder banken, beleggingsondernemingen en verzekeraars, November 2022, 21 p.

little information on the taxonomy, and the information on the environmental objectives underlying the investments is likewise scarce.

At the same time, varying consumer sustainability preferences must also be considered. Investment firms must check the sustainability preferences of the retail clients. The minimum sustainability threshold of the clients must be considered for identifying the needs of the financial consumer.[91] Related to the sustainable investment products, the Dutch supervisor also performed consumer testing of the financial product disclosures of environmentally sustainable investments in precontractual and periodic disclosures in April 2021.[92] The questionnaire was based on "standardized information of investors that simply promote environmental characteristics or products that have a specific objective of investing in environmental activities". The document provided information from a fictitious investment fund. Only 34 % of the respondents correctly indicated that the product has a sustainable investment objective and 37 % ticked the box of "I do not understand the schematic". Overall, 43 % disagreed with the statement that they understand the information in the disclosure, whilst 60 % did not find the precontractual information useful for making a financial decision, deeming it either too detailed, vague or confusing, with difficult language and terms. Half of the respondents acknowledged that they did not understand the distinction between sustainable investments that are taxonomy-aligned and sustainable investments that are not. These results are disappointing, particularly given the particular qualifications of the respondents elected: highly educated, older, financially literate, and more likely to invest. Hence, when these respondents fail to understand, a representative sample of the Dutch population would (more than likely) likewise fail to understand. According to the AFM, retail investors should be aware that there are significant differences in the underlying interpretation of sustainability within the range of sustainable investment funds.[93]

E. Conclusion

The European green deal of 2018 did not start an evolution towards a sustainable society, but, instead, can be considered a revolution of sorts in many areas of society. The European Commission plans to meet the zero emission target by 2050 and decouple economic growth from exploitation of resources. In this context, not only emitters are envisaged, but instead, the whole financial indus-

[91] *Lafarre* and *Verhoef*, European Regulation of Sustainable Finance and Investor Sustainability Duties: Measuring is Knowing?, Banking and Finance Law Review, in press.

[92] AFM, Consumer testing on financial product disclosures for environmentally sustainable investments in precontractual and periodic disclosures under the Taxonomy Regulation, April 2021, 39 p.

[93] AFM, De retailmarkt voor duurzaam fondsbeleggen, April 2022, 13 p.

try must get actively involved in order to steer the overall economy towards a sustainable world. Since the deal's launch five years ago, the European financial landscape has changed dramatically and looks completely different compared to a decade ago. Companies must pro-actively develop new technologies and production methods designed to bring us closer to a sustainable world. More and more, investors are paying attention to the sustainability policies of companies and shareholder activism is being (partly) redirected toward sustainability issues. Currently, investors are under pressure to transform and move towards more sustainable investments and financial consumers. Despite having plenty of options in the financial product market, they are being nudged towards greener products. It does not come as a surprise, however, that all parties, investors, investees, and financial institutions are still struggling to meet the standards of the new regulatory environment. In that vein, there is still a long, steep way to go, but a promising start has already been made.

Country Report Romania

Emőd Veress

A. Introductory remarks

In Romania, “sustainable finance” is currently perceived mainly as a policy tool consisting of several elements. In a narrower sense, this includes the financing of projects that meet certain requirements – energy efficiency, pollution reduction, prevention and control, sustainable management of natural resources, appropriate use of agricultural land, environmentally friendly transport – e.g. development of railway infrastructure, green buildings, etc. In a broader sense, any business project should demonstrate elements that require consideration of ESG (environmental, social and governance) logic in the context of its financing decisions. But how do these ideas translate into reality? In the current economic context – if only to a limited extent, yet even at the level of legal norms – Romania has tried to loyally follow every move the EU has made in this field, as we will see.

In this setting, a general question can also be raised concerning the role and purpose of law (or regulation in general, e.g. the choice between soft law instruments, i.e. guidelines and binding rules) in directing capital flows towards sustainable investments. Beyond the obvious incentives, harder measures can turn out to be counterproductive by ultimately reducing competitiveness and diverting capital flows to other markets. In effect, strong regulatory measures represent direct government intervention in the market, which, however noble the cause, carries significant risks. These risks must also be addressed in the design of sustainable finance. Interestingly, a phrase like “what happens when the transition to sustainable economy intensifies?” contains the same wording used by Soviet-style dictatorships during the socialist transformation of East Central Europe’s economies.[1] The linguistic similarity shows that, in the case of

[1] In Soviet Marxist terminology, the concepts of “transition” and “intensification” were often employed in the context of economic and social changes. For instance, during the Soviet era, the transition to communism was described as a process that required intensification of efforts, particularly in terms of labor mobilization and economic planning. The Soviet approach to economic planning involved grandiose projects and the mobilization of the populace, often articulated through slogans and policies that highlighted the intensification of efforts to achieve these transitions. This language mirrored the utopian goals of creating a new society through planned, intensive efforts, which were integral to Soviet ideological rhetoric and phraseology. This is why at a first look this terminology suggests an authoritative and centralized approach characteristic to command economies.

sustainable finance, we are thus dealing with a form of planned economy, albeit a mitigated one compared to the historical precedents in East Central Europe. The similarity does not end there. Strict regulatory measures tend to create a new specific form of planned economy – in our case also in the name of a greater good, in a region where historical experience has already shown that centralism means rigidity, inelasticity and loss of competitiveness. These statements are not to be misconstrued, however, as, the environmental problems are very real, but the available solutions are nevertheless far from perfect.

The focus should be on investment culture and policy, as legislation can play an important but limited role in this major policy objective. There is also a risk that these policies will concentrate green investment in the EU, further shifting environmentally destructive activities to less developed regions. It is also a politically and legally feasible policy to link ESG objectives to EU funding of large projects, such as infrastructure development in Central and Eastern Europe. However, in the current context of energy access and the war in Ukraine, the construction of new coal-fired power plants may be planned in some countries, and so on. The complexity is doubled by the controversial attitude towards nuclear energy, etc. To put it very simply: does it pay to be green? For example, is a green project worth financing from a bank's point of view? Or can the bank opt for safer business? Is it worthwhile for pension funds and insurance companies to invest in green projects? These are economic questions and go well beyond the scope of this analysis. The question here is to what extent legislation as a tool can create an investment market that reconciles existing investment policies with ESG requirements. If a green investment is risky in terms of its effectiveness, this signals an uncertain future. These are not easy questions to answer in practice, especially by legal means.

As the topic is inordinately broad, even if we consider sustainability in its narrower sense of environmental goals and do not open up the topic to its broader sense – which includes not only the idea of circular economy but also many social issues – I decided to focus on the Romanian legislation in force. This also raises a very important question: is a company, as a legal instrument, suitable to become the multi-attribute optimiser required by the theory of sustainable finance?

B. Sustainable finance as a policy objective and tool

We use the term "finance" in the sense of allocating capital or savings to productive uses, and "sustainable" in the sense of choosing investments that at very least do not exacerbate environmental crises. This is a practically and at least relatively new concept, as "sustainability" traditionally meant sustained growth over time or the ability to pay sustainable dividends, i. e. on an annual basis, etc. This meaning thus fails to cover ESG.

For example, the Romanian Act No. 24/2017 on issuers of financial instruments and market operations[2] uses the term sustainable twice, but it only refers to the sustainability of the issuer, i. e. the sustainability and long-term interests of the issuer in the context of the remuneration policy of the chief executives. We can see that this is the traditional use.[3]

A first major difficulty with sustainable finance is that its goals are at the macro-political level. One important question to that effect is whether it should address the whole economy in this sense, or just selected sectors that are actually responsible for the largest environmental impacts, such as energy or infrastructure? There is also the question of scale. If we focus on small and medium-sized green projects, will they – apart from the obviously positive local effect, such as reducing air pollution, but strictly at the local level – have a real macro effect?

We face these dilemmas when analysing sustainable finance issues, even at a geographically limited, national level. What is certain is that sustainable ownership, sustainable financing and sustainable trading are limited by several factors in Romania. However, the attitude is absolutely favourable. I quote the statement of the Vice President of the Financial Supervisory Authority, Gabriel Grădinescu on this issue:

> "Romania has supported the European Union. Since 2019, as the member state holding the Presidency of the Council of the European Union, we have contributed to the adoption of EU Regulations 2088 and 2089 concerning the ESG impact on the capital market. [...] Certainly, the ESG area is innovative enough to be attractive also to those market participants who will build the best expertise. We, as the competent national authority, will be there to support them".[4]

---

[2] Legea nr. 24/2017 privind emitenţii de instrumente financiare şi operaţiuni de piaţă.

[3] Art. 106 allows issuers to derogate temporarily from the remuneration policy in exceptional circumstances, provided that the policy contains procedural clauses under which the derogation may be applied and specifies the elements of the policy from which the derogation may be made. Such exceptional circumstances shall only relate to situations where the deviation from the remuneration policy is necessary for serving the long-term interests and sustainability of the issuer as a whole or to ensure its viability. Issuers shall submit the remuneration policy for a vote at the ordinary general meeting of shareholders on the occasion of any material change and in any case, at least every four years. The remuneration policy shall contribute to the issuer's business strategy, sustainability and long-term interests and shall include an explanation of how it does so. The policy should be clear and easy to understand , describing the different elements of fixed and variable remuneration, including any bonuses and other benefits in any form that may be granted to senior executives and disclose the relative proportions of these elements accordingly. The remuneration policy should explain how the remuneration and conditions of employment of the issuer's employees have been taken into account in determining the remuneration policy.

[4] https://asfromania.ro/ro/a/2211/mesajul-domnului-gabriel-gr%C4%83dinescu,-vicepre%C8%99edinte-asf,-transmis-%C3%AEn-cadrul-summitului-de-educa%C8%9Bie-financiar%C4%83-%E2%80%9Dinvesti%C8%9Bii-personale-%C3%AEn-pia%C8%9Ba-de-capital%E2%80%9D (18 September 2023).

I will analyse the Romanian legislation on sustainable finance, skipping the analysis of the relevant EU legislation, which has already been addressed, although the Romanian legislation is indeed (strictly) based on EU law.

1 December 2022 marked the 140th anniversary of the official opening of the stock exchange in Romania. However, this development has not been without its interruptions. During the First World War, the stock exchange did not function, and after 1948, it did not exist for many decades due to the Soviet-style dictatorship, in which only state-owned companies functioned.[5] It was re-established in 1995.

The Romanian capital market was promoted from Frontier Market to Secondary Emerging Market by FTSE Russell in September 2020 (which is a development, because it is perceived that investment funds got a green light for investing with this ranking improvement). The market capitalisation of domestic listed companies is small, currently USD 21.51 billion, 56th in the world according to the World Bank, 90 times smaller than Germany, for example, or 7 times smaller than Poland. It is growing but still small with annual transactions in 2020 at 3.77 billion euros, and in 2021, with a record sum of 4 billion euros. In contrast to the negative effects of COVID and the war in Ukraine, this trend continued in 2022.

C. Sustainable finance in Romanian legislation

I. General aspects

The principal legal instrument in the field, Act No. 297/2004 on the capital market[6], does not contain ESG-related requirements. Hence, practically and currently speaking, it is neutral from an ESG point of view.

Romanian Act No. 24/2017 on Issuers of Financial Instruments and Market Operations, as amended in 2020[7], is based on EU law (Directive 2017/828[8], and in application of Regulation 2019/2088[9]), and contains important Romanian regulations in force on sustainability. The first thing to mention is that the term "sustainability" from Regulation 2019/2088 has been translated into the Ro-

[5] *Veress*, Nationalization, Collectivization, Reprivatization, and Privatization in East Central Europe: Arguments for a General Theory in: Pál Sáry (ed.), Lectures on East Central European Legal History, CEA Publishing, Miskolc, 2022, p. 246.

[6] Legea nr. 297/2004 privind piaţa de capital.

[7] Legea nr. 158/2020.

[8] Directive (EU) 2017/828 of the European Parliament and of the Council of 17 May 2017 amending Directive 2007/36/EC as regards the encouragement of long-term shareholder engagement.

[9] Regulation (EU) 2019/2088 of the European Parliament and of the Council of 27 November 2019 on sustainability-related disclosures in the financial services sector.

manian context in the official text of the regulation as "durabilitate", i.e. "durability", which does not seem to be the most fortunate choice, considering that the word sustainability also exists in Romanian. What is timeless and durable may not automatically be sustainable, and the normative content behind these words and their meaning, does not overlap. Obviously, they may be partially identical in meaning, but are by no means completely the same, and therefore other linguistic versions should be consulted when interpreting the Romanian text of the regulation. Moreover, the French text of the regulation also uses the term "durabilité", which may have been the inspiration for the Romanian translators. It is equally uncertain whether the French and Romanian meanings attached to the same word (durabilité, durabilitate) are completely identical. In my opinion – and with the proviso that my criticism does not apply to the French text, which I am not competent to judge – it would have been more appropriate to use the term "sustainability" in the Romanian text. Moreover, this terminological situation created uncertainty in the national legislation, which began to use the terms "durabil" and "sustenabil" simultaneously, thus disrupting the terminological unity.

It is also worth noting that Act No. 158/2020 – the first to introduce sustainability financing rules into Romanian legislation – was initiated by the government, and in the explanatory memorandum of the law, under the heading "environmental impact", it laconically and incongruously states: "not applicable" ("nu este cazul")[10].

Returning to the text of the Romanian Act No. 24/2017 on issuers of financial instruments and market operations when defining persons acting in concert, this law states that this category also includes the persons who have entered into an agreement (generally a shareholders' agreement) to vote in the same way on a particular resolution of the general meeting of shareholders[11] for the purpose of approving or rejecting, among others, the company's environmental policy or any other matter related to social responsibility or compliance with recognised standards or codes of conduct.[12] It should be noted that this provision does not serve the purpose of sustainable finance, but merely defines the persons acting in concert.

According to the same Act No. 24/2017[13], institutional investors and asset managers have to develop and publish an engagement policy describing how they integrate shareholder engagement into their investment strategies. The said policy is to describe, among other things, how institutional investors and asset managers monitor relevant aspects of the issuers in which they have invested,

[10] The situation is the same for Act No. 239/2022, analysed below.

[11] With the exception of the resolution on the appointment of the management/supervisory board.

[12] Art. 2 (2).

[13] Art. 101. There is a simplified transposition of Directive 2017/828.

including strategy, financial and non-financial performance and risks, capital structure, social and environmental impact and corporate governance. Institutional investors and asset managers can opt out of this requirement if they disclose a clear and reasoned justification for the decision not to comply with one or more of the requirements (the law contains a comply-or-explain rule). This tool has some impact on financial sustainability, but in practice, it is primarily an obligation to comply, not necessarily to make investments based on ESG factors. The effectiveness of such a legal tool seems limited, especially as it is a mechanical transposition of an EU directive without organic roots or development in the local legal culture. It can become natural or even organic, but this requires a cultural shift, and therefore a long time, and this change also depends on several factors.

Where an asset manager invests on behalf of an institutional investor – either under a discretionary mandate or through a collective investment undertaking – the institutional investor is to disclose the following information about its agreement with the asset manager: how that agreement incentivises the asset manager to make investment decisions based on an assessment of the medium and long-term financial and non-financial performance of the issuer in which the investment is made.[14]

Act No. 126/2018 on Markets in Financial Instruments[15] does not include ESG-related requirements (unless we include here, in a very broad sense, the policy of increasing the number of underrepresented gender in the board of directors or supervisory board).

The Code of the Bucharest Stock Exchange and the Corporate Governance Code of the Bucharest Stock Exchange are also neutral from an ESG point of view. (This does not mean that the Bucharest Stock Exchange does not actively promote sustainable investments; it has indeed initiated such programmes).

II. Transposition of Directive 2014/95/EU amending Directive 2013/34/EU as regards disclosure of non-financial and diversity information by certain large undertakings and groups

The Non-Financial Reporting Directive (NFRD) 2014/95/EU has been transposed into Romanian legislation by three norms of the Financial Supervisory Authority:

(a) Norm No 39/2015 for the approval of the accounting rules in accordance with International Financial Reporting Standards, applicable to entities authorised, regulated and supervised by the Financial Supervisory Authority in the

[14] Art. 102.

[15] Legea nr. 126/2018 privind pieţele de instrumente financiare.

financial instruments and investments sector and to the Investor Compensation Fund;[16]

(b) Norm No. 1/2017 for the amendment and completion of the Accounting Regulations for the individual and consolidated financial statements of entities engaged in insurance and/or reinsurance activities, approved by Norm No. 41/2015 of the Financial Supervisory Authority;[17]

(c) Norm No. 2/2017 amending and supplementing the Financial Supervisory Authority's Norm No. 14/2015 on accounting regulations in accordance with the European Directives applicable to private pension schemes.[18]

Norm no. 1/2017 requires insurance and/or reinsurance undertakings which, as of the date on the balance sheet, exceed the criterion of having an average of 500 employees during the financial year. The undertakings likewise have to include a non-financial statement in the directors' report containing, to the extent necessary for an understanding of the development, the performance and position of the company and the impact of its business, as well as information on environmental, social and human resources issues, respect for human rights and the fight against corruption and bribery, including:

(a) a brief description of the company's business model;

(b) a description of the company's policies on these issues, including the due diligence procedures applied; and

(c) the results of the above policies;

(d) the principal risks related to these matters arising from the company's operations, including, where relevant and appropriate, its business relationships, products or services that could have a negative impact on these areas, and how the company manages these risks;

(e) non-financial key performance indicators relevant to the specific business of the enterprise.

If the company does not apply policies in respect of one or more of the above, the non-financial statement must provide a clear and reasoned explanation of that choice accordingly. The non-financial statement shall also include, where

---

[16] Norma nr. 39/2015 pentru aprobarea Reglementărilor contabile conforme cu Standardele internaţionale de raportare financiară, aplicabile entităţilor autorizate, reglementate şi supravegheate de Autoritatea de Supraveghere Financiară din Sectorul instrumentelor şi investiţiilor financiare, precum şi Fondului de Compensare a Investitorilor.

[17] Norma nr. 1/2017 pentru modificarea şi completarea Reglementărilor contabile privind situaţiile financiare anuale individuale şi situaţiile financiare anuale consolidate ale entităţilor care desfăşoară activitate de asigurare şi/sau reasigurare, aprobate prin Norma Autorităţii de Supraveghere Financiară nr. 41/2015.

[18] Norma nr. 2/2017 pentru modificarea şi completarea Normei Autorităţii de Supraveghere Financiară nr. 14/2015 privind reglementările contabile conforme cu directivele europene aplicabile sistemului de pensii private.

appropriate, additional references to and explanations of amounts reported in the financial statements.

Similarly, Norm No. 2/2017 establishes that public interest entities which, as of the date of the balance sheet, exceed the criterion of having an average of 500 employees during the financial year, shall include a non-financial statement in the directors' report. To the extent necessary for an understanding of the development, performance and position of the entity and the impact of its activities, this non-financial statement reporting must contain basic information on environmental, social and human resources issues, respect for human rights and the fight against corruption and bribery, including:

(a) a brief description of the entity's business model
(b) a description of the policies adopted by the enterprise with respect to these issues, including the due diligence procedures applied; and
(c) the results of those policies;
(d) the principal risks related to those matters arising from the entity's operations, including, where relevant and appropriate, its business relationships, products or services that could adversely affect those areas, and how the entity manages those risks;
(e) non-financial key performance indicators relevant to the entity's specific business.

If an entity does not adopt a policy on one or more of the matters referred to, the non-financial statement should provide a clear and reasoned explanation for that decision.

In relation to environmental issues, the non-financial statement shall include details of the current and foreseeable environmental and, where relevant, health and safety impacts of the company's operations, renewable and non-renewable energy use, greenhouse gas emissions, water use and air pollution. With respect to social and human resources issues, the information provided in the non-financial statement may relate to measures taken to ensure gender equality, implementation of the core International Labour Organisation conventions, working conditions, social dialogue, respect for workers' rights to information and consultation, respect for trade union rights, health and safety at work, dialogue with local communities and/or measures taken to ensure the protection and development of these communities. With respect to human rights and the fight against corruption and bribery, the non-financial statement may include information on the prevention of human rights abuses and/or the tools put in place for fighting corruption and bribery.

The non-financial statement also includes the impact of the company's activities on climate change and the use of the goods and services it produces, as well as its commitments to sustainable development, tackling food waste, fighting discrimination and promoting diversity. The information required by the norm is not exhaustive.

III. Application of the Disclosure Regulation 2019/2088

Regulation (EU) 2019/2088 of the European Parliament and of the Council of 27 November 2019 on sustainability-related disclosures in the financial services sector is also directly applicable in Romania.

Romanian legislation provides for a whole system of sanctions in case of violation of the disclosure regime. Act No. 158/2020 introduced these rules in the Emergency Ordinance No. 32/2012 on undertakings for collective investment in transferable securities and investment management companies. The following, moreover, constitute an offence and shall be sanctioned by the Financial Supervisory Authority accordingly: infringement by an investment management company or a self-managed investment company of the provisions of Articles 3–13 on sustainability risks, transparency of sustainable investments and promotion of environmental and social features of financial products from Regulation (EU) 2019/2088 and of the regulations adopted in implementation thereof, or of the provisions of Articles 5–7 on transparency of sustainable investments and financial products promoting environmental features in precontractual information and periodic reports from Regulation (EU) 2020/852. This is an offence that gives rise to administrative liability. The sanctions range from a warning or a fine from 5,000 lei to 22,098,000 lei[19] for natural persons; a warning or a fine from 10,000 lei to 22,098,000 lei or 10 % of the total turnover achieved in the financial year preceding the sanction, depending on the gravity of the offence committed, for legal persons. The Romanian Financial Supervisory Authority therefore has wide discretionary power in this regard.

The Romanian Financial Supervisory Authority may also call for the application of complementary sanctions to legal entities and/or natural persons subject to Emergency Ordinance No. 32/2012. The complementary sanctions are as follows: suspension of one's licence, withdrawal of the licence and for a period of between 90 days and 5 years, prohibition of the right to hold a position, perform an activity or provide a service for which a licence is required in accordance with the provisions of the Emergency Ordinance. The Romanian Financial Supervisory Authority, moreover, has to immediately publish on its website any measure or sanction imposed due to non-compliance, against which there is no further appeal before the Financial Supervisory Authority nor after the person on whom the sanction or measure has been imposed has been informed of the decision accordingly. The publication is to include, at minimum, the information on the nature and type of the breach and the identity of the persons responsible. This

[19] 4,491,203 EUR in the moment of conclusion of the present chapter.

obligation does not apply in the case of a decision by the Financial Supervisory Authority for carrying random inspections on these infringements. Depending on the nature and seriousness of the violation, the Financial Supervisory Authority may apply administrative measures in case of violations, such as 1) a public statement specifying the person responsible for the violation and the nature of the violation of legal provisions; 2) a decision requiring the person responsible for the violation to cease the respective conduct and refrain from repeating it; 3) other warning measures and/or with the purpose of preventing or remedying situations of noncompliance with legal provisions.

The main sanctions (fines) may be applied cumulatively with one or more complementary sanctions. Administrative measures may be applied separately or together with the main or supplementary sanctions provided for in this emergency ordinance. However, by way of derogation from the general rules on administrative liability,[20] where two or more offences are found to have been committed, the penalty provided for the most serious offence shall be imposed.

If the publication of the identity of legal persons or personal data of natural persons is considered excessive by the Romanian Financial Supervisory Authority – following a case-by-case assessment of the proportionality of the publication of such information, or if the publication jeopardises the stability of financial markets or an ongoing investigation – the Romanian Financial Supervisory Authority may adopt one or more of the following measures:

(a) postpone publication of the individual act imposing the sanction or measure until the reasons for non-publication no longer apply;

(b) publish the individual act imposing the sanction or measure without indicating the identity of the legal persons or the personal data of the natural persons, provided that such publication ensures effective protection of the personal data concerned;

(c) non-publication of the individual act imposing a sanction or measure where the other options provided for by law are considered insufficient for ensuring that the stability of financial markets is not jeopardized and for ensuring the proportionality of the publication of such decisions in cases where the measures are considered minor.

In the case of a decision to publish the sanction or measure without indicating the identity of legal persons or the personal data of natural persons, the Financial Supervisory Authority may postpone the publication of the relevant data for a reasonable period of time if it is anticipated that the reasons for such publication will cease to apply during that period of time.

---

[20] Art. 10 (2) of Government Ordinance No. 2/2001.

IV. Transposition of Directive 2021/1269 regarding the integration of sustainability factors into the product governance obligations

Directive 2021/1269[21] was transposed into Romanian legislation by Regulation No 12/9/2022 amending and supplementing the Regulation of the Financial Supervisory Authority and the National Bank of Romania No 10/4/2018 on the protection of financial instruments and funds belonging to clients, product governance obligations and rules applicable to the granting or receiving of fees, commissions or other types of pecuniary or non-pecuniary benefits.[22]

Current legislation requires investment firms to identify, in sufficient detail, the potential target market for each financial instrument and to specify the type(s) of client with whose needs, characteristics and objectives, including any sustainability objectives, the financial instrument is compatible. These firms shall identify the client group(s) with whose needs, characteristics and objectives the financial instrument is not compatible unless the financial instrument takes sustainability factors into account. For its part, the investment firm has to, moreover, determine whether a financial instrument is compatible with the identified needs, characteristics and objectives of the target market by considering, among other things:

(a) whether the risk/return profile of the financial instrument is appropriate for the target market;

(b) whether the design of the financial instrument is driven by features that benefit the client and not by a business model whose profitability is based on poor client outcomes; and

(c) whether the sustainability factors of the financial instrument are in any way appropriate for the target market.

The sustainability factors of the financial instrument must be presented in a transparent manner and provide distributors with the relevant information to take proper account of any sustainability objectives of the client or potential client. The financial investment services firm is supposed to periodically review the financial instruments produced, taking into account any event that could significantly affect the potential risk for the respective target market. These firms shall also consider whether the financial instrument continues to meet the needs, characteristics and objectives of the target market, including any sustainability objectives of the target market, and whether it is distributed to the target

[21] Commission Delegated Directive (EU) 2021/1269 of 21 April 2021 amending Delegated Directive (EU) 2017/593 as regards the integration of sustainability factors into the product governance obligations.

[22] Regulament nr. 10/4 din 2018 privind protejarea instrumentelor financiare şi a fondurilor care aparţin clienţilor, obligaţiile de guvernanţă a produsului şi normele aplicabile la acordarea sau primirea de onorarii, comisioane sau alte tipuri de beneficii pecuniare sau nepecuniare. See art. 2, 28, 30, 31, 32, 35 and 38 of the Regulation No. 10/4/2018.

market or reaches clients with whose needs, characteristics and objectives it is incompatible.

The financial investment services firm must likewise have appropriate product governance arrangements in place to ensure that the products and services it intends to offer or recommend are compatible with the needs, characteristics and objectives of the given target market, including its sustainability objectives, and that the intended distribution strategy is consistent with the target market. The investment firm must, moreover, properly identify and assess the circumstances and needs of the clients on whom it intends to focus to ensure that their interests are not compromised by commercial or financial pressures.

As part of this process, the financial investment services firm shall identify client groups with whose needs, characteristics and objectives the product or service is not compatible unless the financial instruments take sustainability factors into account.

The financial investment services firm is also supposed to regularly review the investment products it offers or recommends and the services it provides, taking into account any events that could significantly affect the potential risk for the target market. In carrying out this process, the financial investment services firm has to, at minimum, consider whether the product or service continues to meet the needs, characteristics and objectives of the identified target market, including any sustainability objectives, and whether the intended distribution strategy continues to be appropriate.

V. Transposition of Directive 2021/1270

Directive 2021/1270[23] was transposed into the Romanian legislation by the means of Act No. 239/2022, therein amending and supplementing Government Emergency Ordinance No. 32/2012 on undertakings for collective investment in transferable securities and investment management companies and amending and supplementing Act No. 297/2004 on the capital market.[24]

Again, the amendment was envisaged in the Emergency Ordinance No. 32/2012 on undertakings for collective investment in transferable securities and investment management companies. Currently, the investment management company must establish, implement and maintain appropriate policies and procedures to identify any sustainability risks, taking into account the adverse impact on sustainability in its business. In complying with this requirement, the investment

[23] Commission Delegated Directive (EU) 2021/1270 of 21 April 2021 amending Directive 2010/43/EU as regards the sustainability risks and sustainability factors to be taken into account for Undertakings for Collective Investment in Transferable Securities (UCITS).

[24] Strangely enough, despite the title of this law, it contains no changes to the Act No. 297/2004 on the capital market.

management company has to take the nature, scale and complexity of its business and the nature and range of services and activities into account.

Investment management companies have to ensure that they integrate sustainability risks into the management of collective investment undertakings and also ensure that they have the resources and expertise to integrate sustainability risks effectively.

The investment management company shall ensure that, when internal functions are delegated, the directors/managers and the members of the executive/supervisory board are responsible for ensuring that the investment management company complies with its legal obligations, including ensuring that the directors/managers are responsible for integrating sustainability risks into the investment management activities of the respective company.

When identifying the types of conflicts of interest, the investment management company has to take the interests of a collective investment undertaking into account that result from the integration of sustainability risks. When the investment management company identifies the types of conflicts of interest – the existence of which may be detrimental to the interests of a collective investment undertaking in transferable securities –, it shall include those types of conflicts of interest that may arise as a result of the integration of sustainability risks into its processes and systems and its internal controls. Such conflicts of interest include those arising from the remuneration or personal dealings of relevant staff, those that could lead to environmental misinformation, misselling or misrepresentation of investment strategies, and conflicts of interest between different collective investment undertakings managed by the same management company.

The investment management company is also, furthermore, obliged to take sustainability risks into account throughout its entire period of operation. Where the investment management company considers the material adverse effects of investment decisions on sustainability factors, it is to take those material adverse effects into account in complying with the due diligence requirements and the rules of conduct on the prevention and management of conflicts of interest.

Investment management companies should, moreover, establish, implement and maintain an adequate and documented risk management policy that identifies the risks to which the collective investment undertakings they manage may be exposed.

An adequate and documented risk management policy involves identifying the risks to which the collective investment undertakings in transferable securities which it manages are or may be exposed. The policy shall also include the procedures necessary for enabling the investment management company to assess the exposure to risk for each collective investment undertaking in transferable securities which it manages, including sustainability risks.

D. The use of soft law tools in Romania

The Romanian Financial Supervisory Authority issued a set of "Recommendations on a prudent approach to climate risk".[25] The Financial Supervisory Authority has made recommendations for addressing sustainability risks as factors that may exacerbate other types of risks; for reviewing strategy with reference to short, medium and long-term business plans and activity programmes to include sustainability risks; for reviewing risk policies to include sustainability risks; for implementing a climate governance policy; for integrating sustainability risks into the organisation's internal processes and policies, depending on the nature, size and complexity of the business and the nature and range of services and activities provided by the organisation; and for ensuring transparency and public communication on how sustainability factors are addressed.

In addition, in order to make the set of recommendations more effective, the Romanian Financial Supervisory Authority has informally obliged the entities to which the recommendation is addressed to inform the Financial Supervisory Authority of the steps they have taken to implement these recommendations by filling in a form to that effect. The Financial Supervisory Authority will publish centralised and anonymous material on how the recommendation has been implemented accordingly.

The personal scope of the recommendations is wide, spanning from insurance companies, insurance intermediaries, pension fund managers, investment fund managers, investment firms, issuers, to financial advisers.

The Financial Supervisory Authority would like to emphasise that these recommendations are a first step in the field of regulation and supervision of sustainable finance activities. The aim is to be "up to date". Depending on how the issue of green finance evolves on the European or national agenda, there is the possibility of revising the current regulations or even adopting secondary legislation if necessary in the current context.

In some ways, the recommendations reflect concerns that the structural transformation of the economy towards a higher value-added and climate-sustainable economy also represents a significant challenge for the Romanian economy and financial sector, with both opportunities and costs that may be significant in the long-term. In the context of the transition to a green economy, the pace of which should be as uniform as possible across Europe in order to avoid negative spillover that could structurally unbalance economies as a result.

---

[25] https://www.asfromania.ro/uploads/articole/attachments/619627dfe59a1282090234.pdf (18 September 2023).

E. Conclusions

The policy of making finance more sustainable is fully justified, but I am not sure that the dilemmas raised at a very general level have been addressed in depth by the legislation.

We are pursuing macroeconomic objectives, and ESG-oriented product governance in formation raises the question of the relationship between investment risk and sustainability. There is a lack of precise reconciliation and the question can be raised whether potentially risky or underperforming but green financial products will be the key factors in solving Europe's pressing environmental problems. The legislative approach is certainly experimental.

The main driver of the whole process for Romania is the European Union. Romania is moving in synchrony with the European Union in the field of legislative harmonisation.

The language and method used in EU directives on sustainable finance is often policy-driven, and the Romanian legislator's approach of translating and transposing directives into national law is not in itself sufficient for bringing about targeted changes. The directives could have been transposed into a more creative, active and locally adapted way, turning policy into effective national law. The formal adoption of European law thus needs time in order to have a deep and organic effect.

The Financial Supervision Authority is also trying to drive the process at the policy level, and the Bucharest Stock Exchange is a partner in this process. There is yet no relevant case law, and academic analysis of the issue in Romania has so far been carried out almost exclusively by economists. Of course, the economic approach is perfectly legitimate, but it does not exclude or replace the analysis of the legal problems that arise. And there are undoubtedly legal problems. To what extent can investments be managed on the basis of different – even conflicting – principles (economic efficiency versus sustainability) using the legal instruments available to date? The basic problem can be seen in a global and European context, and undoubtedly also revolves around economic and competitiveness issues, and raises questions about the direction, strength and effectiveness of legal intervention, the measurability of results and, ultimately, the sufficiency and limits of legal instruments in a given context for achieving the desired results. There is thus a long way to go from formal alignment to real public policy success.

Sustainable Finance in the EU – A Legal Comparison

Jens Ekkenga / Karl Björn Erlemann

A. The Implementation of EU Legislation

In recent years, sustainable finance has emerged as one of the main priorities for the European Union as part of the European Green Deal for a more environmentally and socially responsible financial sector. The EU has introduced a comprehensive legislative framework with the goal of integrating duties that improve sustainability into the financial sector.

However, while the EU has established this far reaching legal framework, the reactions across its member states are diverse and the implementation of the EU legislation presents them with a complex challenge. Naturally, each member state faces unique challenges, be they legal, economic, or cultural. These factors influence first the adoption and subsequently the interpretation of EU legislation. The variations in Member States' approaches to transposition can significantly impact the effectiveness and coherence of green initiatives across the EU. Therefore, the goal of this legal comparison is to provide a comparative analysis of the challenges concerning the implementation of EU legislation on sustainable finance across the member states participating in this study. Similarities, differences, and challenges encountered in the transposition and enforcement of these rules shall be examined to shed light on the factors that shape the effectiveness and harmonization of the recent measures in the European financial sector.

Through a comparative lens[1], this comparison aims to identify the challenges for the implementation of EU legislation on sustainable finance among the member states. By understanding the divergences and convergences in the member states' approaches, we aim to provide insights for policymakers, regulators, and stakeholders on how to strengthen and harmonize sustainable finance practices across the EU.

We examine selected member states that had already implemented national legislation on sustainable finance before the recent EU initiatives, highlighting their specific measures and frameworks. These countries had demonstrated an early recognition of the importance of sustainable finance and had taken proactive steps to integrate sustainability considerations into their financial systems. However, it is important to note that the focus and extent of their sustainable

[1] See *Reimer*, Juristische Methodenlehre, 2nd ed. 2020, p. 192 et seq.

finance measures varied considerably. The analysis showcases the diverse approaches taken by member states and highlights the various instruments they employed to promote sustainable finance practices within their respective jurisdictions. We explore the drivers and motivations behind the early adoption of sustainable finance measures in these member states. Factors that could have influenced their decisions include strong political commitment to sustainability, public awareness of and demand for responsible investments, a robust financial sector that recognizes the risks and opportunities associated with sustainability, and the presence of influential stakeholders advocating for sustainable finance. These drivers – or the lack thereof in other member states – may also give a hint regarding the relevance of these issues and the acceptance of the implemented measures in these member states, which are both crucial for such a legal framework to be effective.

These member states with existing legislation on sustainable finance played a significant role in shaping EU legislation in this area as their influence during the design of the concrete measures was likely the biggest. Nonetheless, their influence can have both positive and negative effects on member states that did not have comprehensive sustainable finance measures in place prior to the introduction of EU initiatives:

On the positive side, member states with pre-existing legislation served as valuable sources of knowledge and expertise for other countries. They were able to share their experiences, lessons learned, and best practices in implementing sustainable finance measures. This knowledge transfer may have accelerated the development and implementation of sustainable finance frameworks in member states that were still lagging behind. Additionally, their influence on EU legislation helped establish comprehensive regulatory frameworks and standards at the EU level. This regulatory guidance provided clearer direction to member states without pre-existing legislation, assisting them in developing and implementing effective sustainable finance measures aligned with common standards.

However, the influence of member states with pre-existing legislation may also have been less benevolent. Member states without such legislation may face hurdles in adapting to ambitious requirements set out by EU legislation influenced by more advanced states. They need to invest additional resources, build capacity, and develop new regulatory structures to align with the standards established by the EU legislation. Furthermore, the influence of member states with pre-existing legislation may not fully align with the priorities and specific circumstances of other member states. EU legislation shaped by these states may not adequately address the unique challenges and characteristics of individual countries, potentially requiring further adjustments at the national level. In some cases, member states with pre-existing legislation may even have gained a competitive advantage in developing sustainable finance practices and attracting sustainable investments. This advantage could create disparities in market competitiveness between countries with advanced frameworks and those without. Therefore, member states without pre-existing legislation may face challenges in catching up and attracting sustainable investments for their own financial market.

B. The Conditions in the Member States status ante

The introduction of EU directives and regulations often builds upon existing national contexts and legal frameworks within the leading member states. The case of MiFID II[2] and SRD II[3] was no different. However, it is necessary to delve into the conditions prevailing in the member states before the introduction of the relevant EU legislation to comprehend the varying levels of preparedness for aligning the national legal system with EU requirements and thus the effort and political will needed to implement or transpose them.

Regarding MiFID II and SRD II, parts of their contents had already been in force in some member states, either years before the EU planned to introduce them or shortly before they came into force. In particular, to a large extent the contents of MiFID II had been in force in France prior to the introduction of the directive:[4] The former French rules concerning product planning and the distribution of investment funds were identical to the corresponding rules in MiFID II. This was not the case for the other countries participating in this study. Therefore, it is clear that some of the contents of MiFID II were largely inspired by French legislation. While the EU can obviously profit from the experience of one member state regarding a certain legal solution, negative impacts may also be associated with the approach of copying such legislation. Especially, smaller member states are at a structural disadvantage[5] and the transposition of national legislation into European legislation jeopardizes the democratic and federalist nature of the EU. This problem becomes even more severe if EU legislation is not appropriately customized to fit the needs of all member states as far as possible. Regarding MiFID II: The French corporate environment may differ significantly from others, and a one-size-fits-all approach may not adequately address the complexities of varying shareholder dynamics across member states. Whether

[2] Directive 2014/65/EU of the European Parliament and of the Council of 15 May 2014 on markets in financial instruments and amending Directive 2002/92/EC and Directive 2011/61/EU (recast), OJ L 173, 12.6.2014, p. 349.

[3] Directive (EU) 2017/828 of the European Parliament and of the Council of 17 May 2017 amending Directive 2007/36/EC as regards the encouragement of long-term shareholder engagement, OJ L 132, 20.5.2017, p. 1.

[4] See Country Report France, D. I.

[5] See *Panke*, Small States in the European Union: Structural Disadvantages in EU Policy-Making and Counter-strategies, Journal of European Public Policy 09/2010, pp. 799–817.

this weak point of MiFID II also causes factual problems in other member states will be addressed later.

Regarding SRD II, Denmark and the Netherlands opted for an approach that involved the incorporation of major elements of SRD II into their Stewardship Code (Denmark) or Corporate Governance Code (the Netherlands). This took place in 2016, shortly before the directive took effect. The integration of SRD II principles into these codes can be viewed as a way to signal intent and demonstrate responsiveness to evolving European governance standards. This method may also have provided a framework for institutions to adhere to SRD II's principles while acknowledging the specificities of their financial ecosystems, therefore practically extending the time for the addressees to implement the upcoming EU standards and to include the new standards into their practices more effectively.

But such symbolic premature implementation of EU policies – while common[6] – is not always the reason for which countries introduced legislation before mandated to do so by the EU. France had already implemented rules on the duty to vote in 2003 – far before the introduction of EU directives like SRD II. This hints at a proactive stance on corporate governance, particularly with regard to shareholder engagement. However, one has to consider the broader context as well, such as France's position in the European capital markets. One key reason for France's early adoption of the duty to vote and the aforementioned contents of MiFID II is the size and significance of its capital market, especially after the merger of the Paris regulated market with the stock exchanges of Amsterdam, Lisbon and Brussels in September 2000. France is home to a considerable financial ecosystem, including the biggest European stock exchange with a market capitalization of 4.58 trillion USD and almost 800 listings.[7] In such an environment, ensuring active shareholder participation and responsible corporate governance becomes paramount. By instituting voting duties early on, France aimed to assert control over its domestic capital market dynamics, potentially safeguarding against governance issues that might arise due to a lack of shareholder involvement.

France's substantial presence in the European financial landscape gives it a significant voice in EU policy discussions, particularly those related to corporate governance and shareholder rights. This influence seems to be both beneficial and disconcerting. On the one hand, France's proactive stance on the duty to vote demonstrates a commitment to enhancing shareholder engagement and corporate governance. This commitment aligns with broader EU goals of increasing

[6] E.g., the newly adopted German Supply Chain Due Diligence Act ("Lieferkettensorgfaltspflichtengesetz") was adopted in 2021 during the discussion about the EU's pending Corporate Sustainability Due Diligence Directive.

[7] See https://sseinitiative.org/stock-exchange/euronext-paris/ (8 October 2023).

transparency, accountability, and investor protection. France's pre-existing legislation may well serve as an example for other member states, encouraging them to adopt similar measures promoting responsible shareholder behavior.

On the other hand, the substantial influence wielded by France can potentially lead to a situation where its pre-existing policies disproportionately shape EU directives and regulations. This dynamic could well raise questions about whether EU policies are truly reflective of the diverse needs and contexts of all member states. It opens the door to concerns of policy capture, where a single member state's policies drive the agenda due to its economic or regulatory dominance, effectively protecting its position due to its competitive advantage.[8] Additionally, the influence exerted by France's pre-existing legislation could inadvertently create a competitive advantage for French companies within the European market. These companies might already be accustomed to complying with the new EU requirements, giving them a head start which could potentially disadvantage companies from member states without such legislation, creating an uneven playing field and undermining the goal of harmonizing standards across the EU.

Hence, pre-existing legislation and its impact on EU policymaking could potentially lead to an unlevel playing field. However, one would fall short if one were to look only at legislative developments and not at actual business practice, as can be demonstrated by one specific example: In Sweden, the engagement policy became legally binding only with the transposition of SRD II, but was already practiced as a business standard. Sweden's approach underscores the significance of organic, industry-driven engagement practices that have been adopted without a corresponding legal obligation. Therefore, the argument regarding the development of an unlevel playing field between countries with and without pre-existing legislation cannot be answered with the avoidance of transposition of effective national legislation on the EU level. However, it also underscores the need for flexibility in regulatory approaches that recognize the diverse ways effective governance can be achieved. While concerns about unlevel playing fields are valid, making use of alternatives to rigid transposition can lead to innovative solutions that balance harmonization while respecting regional distinctions.

---

[8] Analogous to concerns of protectionism at the higher level between the EU and Non-EU States: *Bertram*, The trade-sustainability nexus: the evolution of the European Commission's trade and sustainable development discourse from 1993 to 2022, in: Journal of European Public Policy, published online on 04 August 2023, https://doi.org/10.1080/13501763.2023.2238207, p. 17 et seq.

C. Issues Regarding the Implementation in the Member States

I. Wording Differences

The translation of legal terms and concepts is a critical aspect of implementing EU legislation across member states. However, differences in translation can introduce challenges and potential issues, as evidenced by the use of "durability" in lieu of "sustainability" in the French ("durabilité")[9] and Romanian ("durabilitate")[10] version of the SFDR. Language carries subtle nuances and cultural connotations, and the translation of legal terms is no exception. While the term "durability" in the local language may capture elements of sustainability, it may lack the comprehensive scope and precise meaning conveyed by "sustainability" in the original text.

The difference between "durability" and "sustainability" lies in the underlying concepts and connotations. While both terms relate to the longevity or long-term viability of a system, they differ in their broader implications: Durability typically refers to the ability of a system or product to withstand wear, decay, or damage over time. It emphasizes the resilience, robustness, and long-lasting nature of a particular entity. Durability primarily focuses on the physical aspects of an object's lifespan, often associated with material goods or infrastructure.

On the other hand, sustainability encompasses a broader and more comprehensive concept. It refers to the capacity of a system to endure and thrive over time while considering the social, environmental, and economic dimensions. Sustainability involves meeting present needs without compromising the ability of future generations to meet their own needs. It encompasses responsible resource management, social equity, environmental preservation, and economic viability. This divergence in wording can lead to varying interpretations and understanding of the regulations' intent, potentially undermining harmonization and consistency across member states.

Thus, translating "sustainability" as "durability" may result in a narrower focus on the physical durability or resilience of a product or system. This narrower scope may neglect the broader environmental considerations related to resource efficiency, pollution prevention, and climate change mitigation that are encompassed by the concept of sustainability. Furthermore, sustainability also encompasses social and governance aspects. The term "durability" may not adequately convey the importance of social equity, human rights, labor standards, and corporate governance practices that are integral to the concept of sustain-

[9] It should, however, be noted that the French word "durabilité" – despite the etymological roots of the word and the existence of the word "soutenabilité" – seems to be used and understood as "sustainability" in most cases and is the word of choice when "sustainability" is meant.

[10] Conversely to French, sustainability in the Romanian language seems to be usually translated as "sustenabilitate", the adjective "sustenabil" is already in use as a legal term.

ability. The translated version may mislead the addressees to overlook the need to integrate these critical social and governance dimensions into financial decision-making processes and disclosures as intended by the SFDR.

The problems resulting from this divergence may not unfold themselves in the application in front of the court as the relevant terms even in the light of different translations have to be interpreted consistently in the entire EU and thus should not influence their legal meaning. However, problems may still arise in the practical application that negatively influence the effectiveness and the acceptance of the contents of the SFDR across the member states. In the following, we examine two major flaws of the diverging translations in greater detail.

1. Inconsistent Application

The use of varying terms in different language versions of the SFDR may result in inconsistent interpretations and implementation by the addressees in different member states. Each translation carries its own nuanced meaning, raising different expectations and thus potentially leading to varying interpretations and practices. This is particularly problematic since the application of the SFDR will be supervised by national authorities and not by a centralized European agency, as it is the case for the majority of EU law.[11] Guidelines or recommendations by national authorities are the most prominent points of contact for the addressees of the SFDR. Therefore, inconsistent translations can create challenges for investor understanding and compliance. Investors rely on clear and consistent information to assess the sustainability performance of financial products.[12] Varying interpretations of the SFDR based on different translations can lead to confusion and misinterpretation among investors, hindering their ability to make informed decisions. Inconsistent application of the SFDR across member states may also result in uneven compliance requirements, potentially affecting market participants' ability to meet the regulatory obligations. Consequently, the societal acceptance of the ever-growing legal framework around ESG may shrink even further as the expectations beforehand do not match the factual obligations of the SFDR afterwards.

Furthermore, inconsistencies due to translation discrepancies can hinder harmonization efforts and impede the development of a unified sustainable finance market within the EU. The lack of consistent interpretation and application may result in differences in reporting standards and disclosure practices outside of the courts. This can affect the competitiveness and comparability of sustainable finance activities across jurisdictions, thus potentially impeding the development of a harmonized and integrated sustainable finance market within the EU.

---

[11] *Oppermann/Classen/Nettesheim*, Europarecht: ein Studienbuch, 9th ed. 2021, § 12 mn. 1.

[12] See *Mufarrige*, Simple rules for a complex regulatory world: the case of financial regulation, in: European Journal of Law and Economics Issue 2/3 2021, p. 288.

2. Cross-Border Context

Inconsistent application can pose challenges for cross-border activities and investments in sustainable finance. Investors seeking sustainable finance opportunities rely on clear and consistent information to make informed decisions. Divergent translations of sustainability-related terms may confuse investors and hinder their ability to compare investment products across different member states. This lack of consistency may erode investor confidence in the transparency and reliability of sustainable finance disclosures, impacting cross-border investment flows. Differences in interpretation and implementation may create legal uncertainties, impede cross-border information flows, and hinder the free movement of capital within the EU. This can limit the potential for cross-border investment opportunities and collaboration, constraining the growth and development of a unified sustainable finance market.

This issue becomes specifically virulent since the market for financial products of some member states is comparatively small and underdeveloped, leaving investors no choice but to turn to financial products on markets of other member states. Inconsistent translations can undermine investor protection and market integrity. Investors may face challenges in assessing the environmental, social, and governance factors of financial products, potentially leading to misaligned investment decisions. This lack of clarity can also raise concerns about greenwashing, where financial products are marketed as sustainable despite not meeting the intended criteria.

3. Possible Reasons for Diverging Translations

National legal systems may have existing sustainability frameworks, policies, or regulations with established terms. While translators may opt for terms that align with the existing national legal framework, like France, thereby maintaining continuity and consistency within the legal language, it is also possible that translators consciously choose a different term in their native language to differentiate between a national and a European interpretation of practically the same word, like possibly Romania, where the words "durabil" and "sustenabil" are now used simultaneously. The EU aims for a holistic and integrated approach to sustainability, encompassing environmental, social, and economic dimensions. However, member states might have specific policy priorities that they wish to highlight, leading to the selection of alternative terms. Again, it should be noted that the diverging translations do not affect the underlying legal meaning under an interpretation in line with EU law and that the beforementioned issues can be resolved using one of the other translations.

II. Manner of Transposition

The transposition of EU directives into national law is a crucial step in harmonizing legislation across member states. A notable achievement lies in the fact that all member states associated with this project have successfully transposed the SRD II and the MiFID II into their national legal frameworks. This accomplishment might suggest that member states are committed to align with EU standards and promote a unified approach to corporate governance and financial markets regulation. To what extent discretionary powers were used regarding the transposition of the directives, however, did not emerge from the country reports.

The transposition ensures that key principles and obligations outlined in directives are integrated into domestic law, facilitating cross-border operations and enhancing investor protection. It also emphasizes the importance of tailoring directives to national contexts to ensure their effective implementation and mitigate potential negative consequences. Consequently, the mere replication of the directive's text may result in regulatory frameworks that do not adequately address local nuances. However, such direct copy-pasting of directives into national law, without adapting them to national specificities, is the approach Spain and Hungary chose regarding the implementation of the SRD II.[13] The decision of Spain and Hungary to merely copy-paste the SRD II into their national law could be attributed to various factors. One potential reason might be the desire to swiftly implement the directive's provisions without significant modifications. This approach can save time and resources when legislating, particularly if the countries' legal frameworks are already aligned with the general principles of the directive. Economic considerations can also influence this choice. If Spain and Hungary viewed the SRD II primarily as beneficial for their markets without the necessity for major adjustments, they might have opted for direct transposition to avoid potential disruptions or complications associated with altering existing laws. This approach might have been seen as a pragmatic way to comply with their duty to implement directives.

From a more pessimistic perspective, the direct copy-pasting of the SRD II could indicate missing support for the directive's incentives. While it is important to avoid making definitive conclusions based solely on the transposition method, this approach could suggest a range of underlying dynamics that deserve consideration. Firstly, the decision to copy-paste the directive might indicate that the member state does not perceive the SRD II's incentives as a priority within their specific national context. This could be due to other pressing regulatory matters, economic challenges, or different emphases in their corporate governance agenda. Furthermore, if the directive's incentives clashed with existing practices or preferences in the member state, a direct copy-pasting approach

[13] See Country Report Spain, II. 1., and Country Report Hungary, I. 1., respectively.

could indicate a resistance to altering established norms. This might reflect concerns about disruption to the status quo or perceived challenges in implementing the directive's provisions.

To conclude, while direct copy-pasting does not necessarily indicate missing support, it does offer insights into the member state's approach, priorities, and level of alignment with the directive's incentives. A more comprehensive and individual assessment involving the political climate at the time of the transposition would provide a clearer picture of the member state's stance towards the directive and its underlying objectives.

D. Strategical Issues for Member States

The EU's commitment to promoting sustainable finance is a laudable endeavor, emphasizing the importance of ESG-considerations in the world of investment and corporate governance. However, as can be seen above, the path to achieving sustainable finance goals is not a one-size-fits-all journey. Member states of varying sizes and capital market structures face unique challenges in implementing and adhering to EU sustainable finance legislation. Apart from the issues regarding the implementation of EU legislation, some country reports have shown concerns regarding the strategy that underlies this EU legislation.

One notable challenge arises in smaller member states, where capital markets are comparatively diminutive. In these contexts, the availability of sustainable financial products, such as SFDR Article 8 and 9 funds, may be limited.[14] This constraint not only hampers the diversity of investment opportunities but also poses difficulties for institutional investors in providing comprehensive options to their customers. With a restricted array of sustainable instruments, institutional investors may find it challenging to construct well-rounded portfolios that align with the investor's ESG preferences. This limitation underscores the need for tailored approaches to sustainable finance in smaller member states, where the availability of ESG-compliant options remains limited.

At a more granular level, the very organizational structure of stock corporations within the member states poses a significant challenge to the effectiveness of the EU's regulatory measures. This challenge becomes particularly evident in the context of the SRD II, which aims to bolster the rights of shareholders across the EU. The issue arises since the measures of this directive clash with the competencies of the supervisory board in those member states where stock corporations follow a dualistic board structure.[15] As the supervisory body is tasked with monitoring compliance and representing the shareholders, the direct

[14] See Country Report Poland, E. I.
[15] See Country Report Germany, B. I.

strengthening of shareholder rights may overlap with competencies that were transferred to the supervisory board.

Moreover, the concentration of ownership within each stock corporation varies significantly. In member states characterized by high free float in their stock corporations, where ownership is dispersed among numerous shareholders, the traditional approach to shareholder engagement, as promoted by EU legislation, may face inefficiencies. Achieving consensus among a multitude of shareholders with differing interests can be complex, potentially hindering meaningful ESG advocacy. In these contexts, an alternative approach involving more significant obligations for the board of directors to integrate ESG matters into corporate strategies may be preferable.[16] Such an approach can streamline decision-making processes and ensure that sustainability is embedded in the core of corporate governance.

After a closer look into the diverse circumstances the member states find themselves in, it will become evident that flexibility and adaptability are essential elements for effective sustainable finance legislation.

I. Structures of the Capital Markets in the Member States

The European Union boasts a diverse landscape of capital markets, each varying in size and depth. However, a notable challenge arises from the fact that capital markets in certain member states are relatively small compared to the counterparts in France and Germany. This discrepancy has implications not only for investors but also for portfolio companies seated in those states.

The essence of this challenge lies in the availability of funds that adhere to the SFDR. In larger and more developed capital markets, investors have relatively easy access to a broad spectrum of SFDR Article 8 and Article 9 funds. This accessibility enables them to construct investment portfolios that align with their specific ESG strategies. However, in smaller capital markets, the availability of such funds is often limited. As a result, investors in these smaller markets may find it challenging to build diversified portfolios that cater to their ESG preferences. This challenge also extends to portfolio companies seated in these states. When investors are unable to access a sufficient number of SFDR Article 8 and Article 9 funds, portfolio companies may face difficulties in fulfilling their investors' ESG-driven investment preferences. Data sourced by the European Fund and Asset Management Association (EFAMA) and Morningstar supports these structural disadvantages.[17]

---

[16] See Country Report Netherlands, B. II.

[17] EFAMA Market Insights "The SFDR Fund Market – State of Play", Issue 12, June 2023.

Table 1: Domestic market shares of Article 8 and 9 funds per domicile (in % of total assets of UCITS and AIFs at end of Q4 2022)

Jurisdiction	*Article 8 funds in %*	*Article 9 funds in %*
Austria	n.s.*	n.s.
Czech Republic	n.s.	n.s.
Denmark	40.3	2.5
France**	50.3	3.4
Germany	15.8	0.2
Hungary	2.3	n.s.
Ireland	36.1	0.9
Italy	26.1	2.0
Netherlands	n.s.	n.s.
Poland	0.8	0.1
Romania	n.s.	n.s.
Slovak Republic	5.1	n.s.
Spain	31.1	0.8
Sweden	95.6	3.8

* n.s. = not selected; ** Excluding securisation funds.

As can be seen in Table 1, the share of Article 8 and 9 funds of the total UCITS and AIF assets differs immensely among the member states. Sweden, France, Denmark, Ireland and Spain stand out with a share of Article 8 funds of over 30 %, Sweden even with a staggering amount of 95.6 %. On the other side of the spectrum, Germany, Hungary, Poland and the Slovak Republic can be seen with shares of less than 20 %. While Germany may be able to compensate potential issues arising with the relatively low share of 15.8 % of Article 8 funds with the absolute size of its capital market, the same cannot be said about the markets in Hungary and Poland with shares of far below 5 %. This scarcity of ESG-focused investment options has multifaceted implications that extend beyond mere statistics. For investors in these countries, the restricted availability of Article 8 funds significantly limits their capacity to construct portfolios aligned with their ESG-preferences. The limited access to ESG-focused funds places investors in Poland and Hungary at a competitive disadvantage compared to their peers in countries with more extensive allocations to Article 8 funds.

This disadvantage has ripple effects on portfolio companies situated in these nations. These companies may encounter challenges in attracting investors who prioritize ESG considerations when making investment decisions. As the global market increasingly emphasizes ESG performance, portfolio companies must align their strategies with these principles to remain competitive and access international capital. The global context is pivotal in understanding the repercussions of such limited access to Article 8 funds. Sustainability and responsible investing have become central tenets of the global financial landscape. Consequently, investors and portfolio companies operating in countries with meager allocations to ESG-focused funds risk falling behind in this transformative movement. This development may also pose a risk to the significance of the capital market in these countries as investors may opt for in this regard more developed markets in other member states.

II. Organizational Structure of Stock Corporations in the EU

However, not only the structure of the capital markets may hamper the effectiveness of the EU's measures on sustainable finance. As the SRD II's approach is based on shareholder governance, which is a common tool in countries with monistic board structures in their companies, countries with a dualistic board structure may have to solve conflicts due to this approach. The purpose of the dualistic approach is to mitigate the inefficiencies of direct shareholder governance. Therefore, the effect of the SRD II's approach – especially in those countries with dualistic corporate governance – in terms of strategic decision making in favor of ESG-factors by the shareholders themselves comes down to the fact that it does not directly influence the management board but is only conveyed by the appointed members of the supervisory board. Furthermore, this representation in the supervisory board may even be somewhat reduced to allow for employee representation, depending on the size of the company.

Table 2: Overview of board structures of public companies[18]

Monist	*Choice*	*Dualist*
Ireland	Czech Republic	Austria
Spain	Denmark	Germany
Sweden	France	Poland
	Hungary	Slovak Republic
	Italy	
	Netherlands	
	Romania	

As can be seen in Table 2, the member states mainly concerned with this issue are Austria, Germany, Poland and the Slovak Republic. However, it cannot be

[18] See *Gelter/Siems*, Letting Companies Choose between Board Models: An Empirical Analysis of Country Variations, in: ECGI Working Paper Series in Law, 573/2021, p. 147.

concluded from this that the other member states will not be confronted with this issue, especially those that leave the option of which corporate governance model to use at their companies' disposal. Apart from this, it should, conversely, also be noted that every member state has access to the Societas Europaea (SE) and thus access to a company type that allows a monistic board structure even in the countries with a dualistic system.

III. Shareholder Structures in the Member States

Another decisive structural condition regarding the effectiveness of the EU legislation, specifically SRD II's measures concerning the informational duties about portfolio companies' exercise of voting rights, is the ratio of free float in the companies of each member state. In high free float markets, ownership of shares in a company is widely dispersed among a large number of shareholders.

This dispersion can range from institutional investors to the public sector or individuals and while it can contribute to market liquidity and diversity, it presents challenges for coordinated shareholder action which is required for strategic development since it prerequisites that no single shareholder or group of shareholders holds a significant controlling interest in the company. Achieving consensus and coordination among diverse shareholders in high free float markets is a complex task. Shareholders in these markets often have varied interests, investment horizons, and priorities. These differing perspectives can make it challenging to rally a collective voice for ESG advocacy, as shareholders may have conflicting views not only on the importance of sustainability but also the specific ESG issues that should be prioritized.

Generally, it can be argued that in countries with a low share of free float in their listed companies, stronger rights for shareholders might be the better option for legislators to promote sustainable finance, as coordination and decision-making processes are more likely to be successful in companies with few anchor shareholders as these shareholders are able to react more effectively. Conversely, in countries with a high share of free float in their listed companies, it might be more effective to directly address the board of directors in terms of their corporate duties to nudge their entrepreneurial strategies towards more sustainable approaches.

However, it should also be noted that not only the sheer ownership concentration is a relevant factor for deciding on the appropriate measures but also the percentage of institutional investors inside the free float since the institutional investors are the addressees of the SRD II's rules on the engagement policy. Therefore, the strategy of shareholder engagement as a measure of promoting sustainable finance practices should be particularly effective in countries with a high ownership concentration as well as a high share of institutional investors. Or to put it differently: A high share of institutional investors among the shareholders cannot necessarily forward the will of their customers to the board of directors if the ownership concentration of the company in question is relatively low, meaning the amount of free float is relatively high.

Table 3: Market and ownership characteristics[19]

Jurisdiction	*Ownership Concentration in %*	*Institutional Investors in %*
Austria	68	23
Czech Republic*	89	20
Denmark	41	36
France	60	27
Germany	59	30
Hungary	62	32
Ireland	23	49
Italy	69	29
Netherlands	35	40
Poland	68	35
Romania**	n.s.	n.s.
Slovak Republic*	100	0
Spain	50	25
Sweden	22	38

* The number of listed companies in the Czech Republic and the Slovak Republic is very low, therefore their data is not necessarily representative for the actual corporate structures of their companies.
** As Romania is not a member of the OECD, no data was collected in the OECD report regarding Romania.

Unfavorably for the legislators, the optimal conditions have not been found among the participating countries of this project, according to data from the OECD in Table 3. The ownership concentration file in this table shows the percentage of listed companies where the three largest shareholders hold the majority (> 50 %) of shares while the file for institutional investors shows the average percentage of shares that are hold by institutional investors. As can be seen above, countries with a high share of institutional investors like Ireland or the Netherlands have a significantly lower ownership concentration and vice versa. Reason for this is likely to be the fact that it is common practice for institutional investors to build up portfolios where the percentage of shares in a single

[19] OECD Corporate Governance Factbook 2021, p. 28 et. seq.; OECD Capital Market Series dataset, FactSet, Thomson Reuters, Bloomberg; see *De La Cruz/Medina/Tang*, Owners of the World's Listed Companies, 2019 for details.

company does not exceed single digit numbers for reasons of diversification and risk aversion, resulting in a high share of institutional investors in a country with a generally low level of ownership concentration.

While such generalized data among the whole spectrum of listed companies should be handled carefully as the concrete circumstances of a single company may not be accurately represented in this dataset, one conclusion may be drawn from this data: The use of shareholder engagement policies as a tool for ESG-advocacy is not necessarily the most effective tool legislators could have opted for.

E. Conclusion

First of all, it is to be noted that the relevant EU legislation entered into force successfully. However, the mere adoption of new legislation alone is not sufficient to reach the goal of promoting sustainable investment and corporate governance. If anything, the effectiveness of a policy is dependent on its successful implementation and enforcement.[20]

Translation discrepancies, like in the French and Romanian translations of the SFDR, pose challenges to the harmonized implementation and understanding of EU regulations, at least on the level of practice in the member states, even if the underlying meaning should be the same all over the EU. Therefore, while the interpretation of the translated terms has to conform to EU law, divergent terminologies jeopardize the main point of EU legislation, that is consistency and cross-border coherence in its practical application. Regarding the scope of transposition, it is hard to draw any conclusions from the approaches that Hungary and Spain chose. One conclusion, however, could be that the mere copy-pasting of a directive into national law is unlikely to enhance the effectiveness of the directives from the perspective of cross-border coherence, as it indicates that a more comprehensive transposition was not necessarily the top priority. Other than these points of criticism, no irregularities arose in terms of the implementation of the EU legislation on sustainable finance.

From a conceptual standpoint, this cannot be said about the policies implemented by the legislation. The size and depth of capital markets within the EU present varying levels of accessibility to SFDR Article 8 and Article 9 funds. The challenge of limited availability has implications not only for investors but also for portfolio companies seeking to meet the evolving ESG preferences of their investors. Expanding sustainable finance options in smaller capital markets is therefore vital to ensure that all investors and companies have the opportunity to engage with sustainable and responsible investment practices on an equal

[20] *van Zeben*, The European Green Deal: The future of a polycentric Europe?, in: European Law Journal, Issue 5/6 2020, p. 301.

footing. Despite having access to the SE, member states with a dualistic corporate governance system will likely not be positively affected by the engagement policies of the SRD II. Regarding the shareholder structures in the participating member states, the efficiency of the engagement policies may even be put in question for all member states.

The EU's strides in sustainable finance legislation serve as an example for other regions and countries worldwide. The global financial community is increasingly recognizing the significance of ESG considerations, not only for responsible investing but also for long-term economic stability and corporate resilience. As seen above, the EU's legislation on sustainable finance has posed various issues for the member states. We look forward to the continued development and implementation of legislation, which is able to effectively contribute to a more sustainable and equitable future.

List of Authors

Birkmose, Hanne, Professor of Company Law and Corporate Governance, University of Southern Denmark

Clarke, Blanaid, McCann FitzGerald Chair in Corporate Law, Trinity College Dublin

Conac, Pierre-Henri, Professor of Financial Markets Law, University of Luxembourg

Dúl, János, Assistant Professor, Ludovika University of Public Service, Budapest

Eichlerová, Kateřina, Associate Professor of Corporate Law, Charles University Prague

Ekkenga, Jens, Professor of Civil Law, Corporate and Commercial Law, Comparative Law, Justus-Liebig-University Giessen

Erlemann, Karl Björn, Research Assistant, Justus-Liebig-University Giessen

Fidler, Philipp, Associate Professor of Corporate Law, Vienna University of Economics and Business

Lamandini, Marco, Professor of Business Law, University of Bologna

Lidman, Erik, Associate Professor of Company Law, Universities of Gothenburg and Stockholm

Mazúr, Ján, Assistant Professor, Comenius University Bratislava

Mezzanotte, Félix E., Assistant Professor of Financial Services Law, Trinity College Dublin

Oplustil, Krzysztof, Professor of Company Law and Public Business Law, Jagiellonian University Kraków

Papp, Tekla, Professor of Private Law, Ludovika University of Public Service, Budapest

Patakyová, Mária, Professor of Commercial Law, Comenius University Bratislava

Pérez Millán, David, Associate Professor of Commercial Law, Complutense University of Madrid

Recamán Graña, Eva, Assistant Professor of Commercial Law, Complutense University of Madrid

Sørensen, Karsten Engsig, Professor of Company Law, Competition Law, EU Law, Aarhus University

van der Elst, Christoph, Professor of Business and Economics, Tilburg and Ghent Universities

Veress, Emőd, Professor of Civil and Business Law, University of Miskolc and Sapientia Hungarian University of Transylvania

Weber, Anne-Marie, Assistant Professor of Law, University of Warsaw

Winner, Martin, Professor of Business Law, Vienna University of Economics and Business

Jus Internationale et Europaeum

edited by
Thilo Marauhn and Christian Walter

The impact of international and European law on national legal systems is increasing constantly. This development presents an immense challenge, since what is involved is no longer the mere enforcement of international and European legal standards, but also the incorporation of the necessary adjustments into the national legal systems. Apart from the practical difficulties often involved, theories have yet to be developed for this procedure, something still very much at the beginning in public law, which continues to have an ambivalent attitude to international and European law. The goal pursued by the *Jus Internationale et Europaeum* series is to make a contribution to the theoretical and dogmatic penetration of public law by internationalization and Europeanization and to offer solutions for the practical problems resulting from this. This series accepts habilitations, outstanding dissertations and comparable monographs which deal with legal issues at the interface between national public law and international law or with subjects pertaining to genuine international or European law. A special focus is on works which bridge the gap between fundamental questions and the practical application of the law.

ISSN: 1861-1893
Suggested citation: JusIntEu

All available volumes can be found at *www.mohrsiebeck.com/jusinteu*

Mohr Siebeck
www.mohrsiebeck.com